"We had everything..."

To the Berkely family
(with apologies that I was
given a misspelling of the
name!)

Chris Rowley

"we had everything..."

Recollections of a Kent Village
Leigh 1900-2000

CHRIS ROWLEY

Chris Rowley

Chris Rowley was born in Manchester in 1938. He read English at Cambridge and then went into television, working in a wide variety of roles within ITV, including current affairs and documentary programmes, before going to the Independent Broadcasting Authority. He has also worked on various Channel 5 and radio projects, including being Chairman of the local radio station in West Kent.

He is concerned with a number of art prizes and a major international broadcasting charity. He is married with two daughters and the family haved lived in the village of Leigh for over forty years. He has been concerned with various local projects including the Village Design Statement and the Parish Plan and he is currently Chairman of the Leigh & District Historical Society. He writes regularly on local history and in addition, he organises a jazz band and is a distance runner.

©2000 Christopher Rowley

A catalogue entry for this title is available from the British Library

ISBN 0–9539340–0–4

First published in 2000
Second edition including index published in 2005
by Christopher Rowley
Oak Cottage, The Green, Leigh, Tonbridge, Kent TN11 8QL

Text design: Amanda Hawkes
Cover design: Juliet Rowley Inside cover map: Anna Rowley
Cover photograph: Leigh Cricket Club v South Nutfield. First published in *The Times*.
Printed and bound in Great Britain by Biddles Ltd, Kings Lynn

Dedication

This book is dedicated to all the people who have talked with me, with my thanks for their kindness and my delight in all they have told me.

"Without memories there are no images and, without images,
the existence of man, of a generation, of a people cannot be
collected, recognized or communicated".
PABLO QUINTANA

Contents

Contents

Life in Leigh in 1900

an Introduction by Chris Rowley

In 1900, "Britain ruled the world" and if that were not quite true, it was what the children in the Leigh School were taught. Billy Hayter, who died in 1984, remembered very clearly the celebrations in the village "when we had beaten the Boers". At a time when one in five of the world's population was in the British Empire, Leigh children were taught – and continued to be taught for the next forty five years – that they should be proud of our Empire. Children were staying at the school until they were fourteen – an innovation – and football was just becoming popular in Leigh and the Tonbridge area. In these respects, Leigh in 1900 was like most other English villages at the end of the Victorian era.

The school in 1904 when Mr Boby was the Headmaster.

Yet in 1900 "Leigh was fifty years ahead of its time". Alfred Houghton says so and the feeling is echoed by many people who know and remember the village from family stories. Again, it may not be completely accurate but because Samuel Morley, who virtually owned the village, was a committed

Christian – as well as an exceedingly rich one – the village did have amenities that most other villages did not have. He gave the village a sewage system and gas, light and water, headquartered in the gloriously ornate set of waterwork buildings, even if the sewage pipes were laid well before running water was installed. Harry Lucas's grandfather had to go round each Saturday at the turn of the century with water on the back of a cart and pour it down all the manholes to make sure the sewage reached the sewage works. Samuel Morley had already commissioned George Devey to build his new home, Hall Place but also to build much of the present centre of the village – in all, around half the houses. He also wished to cater for the soul of the village. A chapel had been erected for his fellow Non-Conformists in 1905, and my cottage, Oak Cottage, had earlier been converted into a Christian Reading Room. He provided for many villagers in other ways too. Gifts of coal and meat – later changed to a more varied fare – were given out at Christmas to all the estate workers and help was given to those with troubles. Samuel Morley and then his son, the first Lord Hollenden, and then in turn his grandson, Geoffrey, the second Lord

Park House, designed by George Devey and for fifty years the home of Doctor Frank Fraser and the main surgery in the village for most of that time.

Hollenden owned most of the houses in the village – including the ones lived in by some of the richer inhabitants like Doctor Fraser. The village was dominated by the Morley family (or the Hope-Morleys as they became in 1923), not only in 1900 when the picture of the village in this book starts but right through the first half of the century. Many families still speak of the care they had to adopt when dealing with the Estate and the people who ran it. The Estate was a philanthropic landlord but, in some ways, it was omnipresent. The Estate also owned most of the shops, many of the farms around the village and the Village Green itself; and the Estate had to be consulted on any changes, including any at the School. By the time that Samuel Morley's son had become

Lord Hollenden and a churchwarden, even the choice of hymns needed care in case it displeased his Lordship. The family or the Estate were involved directly or indirectly in almost all aspects of the village. The Estate records show that, even in 1950, the Estate still owned about a hundred houses and was the biggest employer locally; and, up until the early 1960's, when many of the houses were being sold, Geoffrey, Lord Hollenden, was President of the Cricket Club and the Produce Association, was still consulted about the school and was dominant in church matters (as well as owning the main village allotments, as the family trust still does).

In the period around 1900, there were between one and two dozen gardeners at Hall Place and well over a dozen servants in the house; three or four keepers plus a 'boy' or two; about five stablemen; two or three builders; two in the Engineering Department headed by Mr Sales about whom we hear from his grandson; and nearly a dozen estate workers. Even if you worked on a farm – and that was what a good number of young men wanted – you were probably employed by the Estate, although the Hope-Morleys never had the Turnip Townsend or Lord Egremont keenness to be at the forefront of agricultural progress. The second Lord, Geoffrey, was much more interested in shooting than farming and if there were conflicts between his farmers and his gamekeepers, the gamekeeper was likely to be favoured, as both Dick Selling and Donald Hallett – the current game-keeper – point out. Each of the three Morleys/Hope-Morleys from the 1870s, when Hall Place had been built, until 1977 when Samuel's grandson died, had been a central part of village life. Each were generally respected or actually liked, according to their different personalities and different eras, by the great majority of people in the village.

So in 1900, Leigh was ahead of its time in an Empire on which the sun never set and was seemingly dominated by the Estate and the family at Hall Place. Yet the village also had a life that was separate from Hall Place; the every day things for a poor family had to be coped with or enjoyed and the individual worlds of school children, teachers, doctors, shopkeepers, mothers and fathers, publicans, went on. This book is not about the changing role of the Hollenden family in the village, although that is part of the story. Many of the contributors to the book have talked for five to ten hours about their lives in the village from the First World War and in the 1920's and 1930's without more than a passing mention of the Hollendens. Even when the family are mentioned, it is for small personal things – "We used to collect pails of chestnuts for sixpence which Lady Hollenden would feed to her deer". "The two girls (the Hollenden daughters) used to come and sing with us". "We used to get cheaper rates for the village hall if we caught Lord Hollenden after church." "I used to have to touch my forelock when I went past Lord Hollenden – and I didn't think much of it".

Lawrence Biddle's scholarly book sets the scene on the village at the turn of the century. Leigh had around one thousand four hundred people in the parish. The Iron Room had been built and the Alms Houses on the Green had just been finished. (The Parish Council still has forty one documents about the building of the Alms Houses). In 1900, the row over the spelling of Leigh had quietened down. Leigh had just joined the local soccer league – and lost 12-0 to Tonbridge.

Leigh soccer team, 1905 – who were now winning matches.

Reports of another match mentioned the good attendance of ladies with brightly coloured sunshades – 'it is encouraging to see ladies have learnt to take a lively interest in the game', said the local paper. The Leigh Church Bell Tower was dedicated by Lord de Lisle in 1905 and the Vicar, the Rev. Hugh Collum, who served the village for thirty years, had his imposing new vicarage. The Green had a dusty track round it but it was in much better condition than fifty years earlier and my home and others nearby had rights to graze geese on the long grass which covered all except the main cricket pitch – an unmown state that persisted until after the Second World War. Indeed, the first phone call we received in 1964 on our newly installed phone was from Fred Wibley, the Parish Clerk, who puzzled us by asking if we still had the rights for grazing on our deeds. (Sadly, the deeds had been destroyed in the offices of Biddle & Co during the war and we were not quite clear what was being asked). In 1900 the three pubs thrived – each named after the main sources of employment – the Bat & Ball, the Fleur de Lys (part of the Hope-Morley coat of arms) and the Brickmakers, although brickmaking in the village was nearly finished, as Dick Wood points out.

There were a good number of village families who had been around fifty years earlier but there were always newcomers – not just middle class people but working class families who came from other parts of West Kent. Most of the old established village families with whom I have talked, say that their grandparents were born outside Leigh.

The book is not meant to be a history in the style of Lawrence Biddle's work. Indeed, Lawrence had doubts about whether all the facts I was being given would be wholly accurate. I always replied that what was interesting was the overall picture of a community that these reminiscences built up.

Standing under the oak tree outside my house, Bernard and Russ Thompsett, who were born in the village over sixty years ago, said recently what a good number of people have told me about the first half of the century – "we had everything in those days". This book is the story of Leigh, seen through the eyes of a wide variety of people whose memories and the memories of their parents and grandparents stretch back over the hundred years. I think it does give a graphic picture of a community that has been, in general, a happy and worthwhile place in which to live.

The Green from the Church tower.

The Fautly Sisters

Kathleen Johnson and Dorothy Fautly

I *first started taking notes from the Fautly sisters, Dorothy and Kath in 1995. The problem – a thoroughly enjoyable one – was that they often talked in an overlapping way, adding a half sentence or phrase to the other's story. It was difficult to write down who exactly said what. So what follows summarizes what they both told me. Sadly, Kath died two years ago but even in hospital she was still telling me new things about the village (and I have included them).*

THE FAMILY

The Fautly family have lived in Leigh since the turn of the last century. Dorothy is still in the house in which she was born, 5 Garden Cottages and Kath lived a few doors away. None of the grandparents were born in the village but their parents' first home after their marriage was in Leigh and the children, including Kath and Dorothy, were brought up in the village.

Their father's father, 'Grandfather Fautly', (James Edward) came from the Wittersham – Tenterden area. He lived in Leigh to over a hundred and the

sisters remember him and their father walking across the Green together on Fridays to collect their pensions. "It was ten shillings a week. Grandfather didn't have a tooth in his head but he ate everything. He didn't have glasses either and he read right through the newspapers everyday – I reckon he had second sight!" says Dorothy.

Dorothy and Kath Fautly's grandfather and father on Powder Mill Lane on the former's 100th birthday.

The Fautly grandparents had lived at the cottage on Tipps Cross Corner, the junction of Egg Pie Lane and Philpotts Lane, at the end of the nineteenth century and, later, for many years they lived in half of Green Ways Cottage in Powder Mill Lane, when Mr Fautly was working at Great Barnetts farm. After Grandfather finished working on the farm, he and his wife moved to the Round Houses which used to be on the old coach road to Chiddingstone Castle from Penshurst. For the last fourteen years of his life, after his wife's death, Grandfather Fautly lived with the family. In his youth, before he came to the village, Grandfather Fautly had dug graves: he got two shillings and sixpence. When his wife, Granny Fautly, died in the 1930's "the funeral cost about £12 and he complained about the cost". "When it came to his own funeral, the weather was so wet that the grave kept filling with water. Lots of people had died and he couldn't be put into his coffin till the day of the burial".

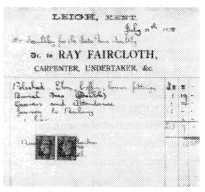

Roy Faircloth's bill for the coffin and funeral of Granny Fautly in 1938.

THE FAUTLY FAMILY

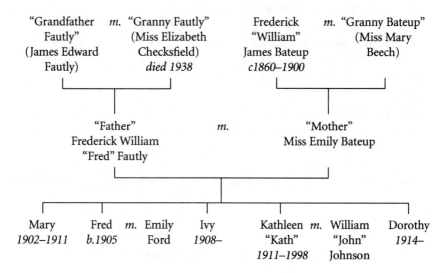

His wife, 'Granny Fautly', had been born in London "but when she was young she lived in one of the three cottages on the Green below the Church, between South View and Porcupine House. They were pulled down before the First World War".

Kath and Dorothy's mother was Emily Bateup whose family came from Horsmonden. Emily's father was Frederick William James Bateup "but he was known as William; he died just before our parents got married. Mother, who was the oldest child, had to be given away by an uncle". Her mother – "we called her Granny Bateup"and some of her family had a boarding house over a furniture shop off the High Street in Hastings and the Fautly family used to go to visit them. Both sisters remember Granny Bateup saying 'What do you call this? Skin and scutters? – it's meant to be custard'. Kath and Dorothy were there when the Prince of Wales came to open something in the town. The family did not approve of the Prince. "Our brother, Fred, spat out of the window at him". The Bateups had seventeen children even though Mr Bateup died when he was about forty. In spite of all the children, Granny Bateup always looked very fit. "I remember her saying that she had worked in the fields when she was young".

Kath and Dorothy's father, Fred, (Frederick William) was brought up with his parents at Tipps Cross. "In 1901, he got engaged. A 'keeper' was the name used in those days for an engagement ring. On the wedding day, Mother had walked from Pannets in Tonbridge where she was in service. They made two bouquets from flowers in Granny's garden, one for the bride and the other for the bridesmaid. My mother was allowed to choose the one she thought was the prettiest. Then they both walked from Tipps Cross to Hildenborough Church, had the ceremony and walked back to Tipps Cross and then back again to their new home in Leigh.

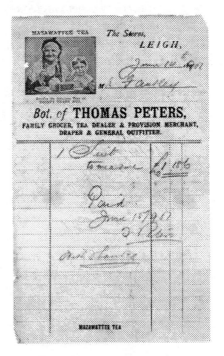

1901 bill from Thomas Peters – the village shop – for Frederick Fautly's wedding suit, which cost £1-18-6d.

That was all they did – no honeymoon or holiday". Dorothy Fautly still has two specially painted saucers given to her mother as a wedding present by her employers in Tonbridge. Although Emily's sister had died – in Great Barnetts kitchen – a fortnight before the wedding was due, the couple felt that they had to go ahead with the wedding because they had a house, 2 Forge Square, which was available and would not be kept for them if the wedding was postponed.

THE CHILDREN

The Fautly parents had five children. "Dr Fraser brought all of us into the world – he was Scottish". Mary, the oldest, was born in 1902 in No. 2 Forge Square but died, much loved by all the family, aged 9 of diphtheria. The illness could have started when Fred fell into a pond in Hildenborough and caught the disease which was then caught by both Mary and Kath. Mary's coffin was made by Fred Faircloth – who was both the wheelwright and coffin maker. Mrs Faircloth lined the inside of the coffin with white velvet which was provided by the local fire brigade with which the Fautlys' were closely involved. The grave was lined with flowers. Mary is buried in Hildenborough churchyard together with their father's sister and aunt – "the three generations together. And each Good Friday when we were children, the whole family would go up towards Meopham Bank and collect wild primroses to put on Mary's grave".

Fred was born in 1905, also in Forge Square, and lived in the village all his life. "He was short and jolly". He left the village school when he was fourteen to work in the butchers "but he had already been working at the slaughter house – killing – every Monday afternoon". He, too, lived in Garden Cottages and married a village girl, Emily Ford. Ivy was born in 1908: she now lives in Chippenham. Kathleen – but known as Kath to everyone in the village – was born in 1911. By this time the family had moved to Hildenborough, in Church Road, opposite the Library. Kath used to say to her mother 'you have given me the longest name and I am the only one who can't spell'. We all had three initials and all of us had nicknames as children. Mine was 'Sammy' – I can't remember why but it was". Dorothy Eveline May was born in 1914 – in the house where she still lives, 5 Garden Cottages – "I was the baby of the family".

The family had moved to No. 5 Garden Cottages soon after it was built in 1913/14. There had been one tenant in it for six months before them. Dorothy has lived there ever since. "Garden Cottages were built by the Kent Cottage

Company. Mr Hedges – the Liberal MP who lived at Kennards – and another gentleman put up the money. It was to help the village. But I think maybe they ran out of money". "The Cottages are still owned by the same firm, Tonbridge Properties. The agent is now Mr Banks: it used to be Mr Lawson". "There was a gas street light in the middle. It used to go off at ten o'clock. And at Christmas, the Salvation Army came and played under it – we loved it."

FATHER

"Father had various trades but mainly he worked as a coalman based at Penshurst Station. He was never out of a job. During the period before the First World War, he worked at Meopham Bank where they bred thorough-bred horses and later, after he was married, at Peters, the village shop at Orchard House. But the shop went broke. Father was a Volunteer during the First World War – a sort of Home Guard – with turned-up wide brimmed hats like Australians. There was a practice shooting range down Bird Cage Walk where they would spend quite a few Sunday afternoons and he worked at Great Barnetts during the war. He worked with the horses at Moorden Farm and then was a groom/gardener with the two Miss Heaths at the Woods, around 1908. They lived in the upstairs of the little cottage at the back and father always said it was damp. The horses were downstairs. Then he worked at Chilling House (which was called The Limes in those days) before becoming a coalman. Over the years he looked after a number of horses in the village, including the coal carthorses. One of the horses belonged to Mr Field, the baker in Lower Green – it was the worst-tempered horse in the village. He used to do everything for the horses. He curry combed and he trimmed them. And he used to make special pills for them – I don't know what was in them – they were like cigars. On one occasion the vet had said there was no hope for a particular horse and Father was called. He treated the horse and it got better. The owner said he would only ever let Father look after his horse after that".

The job as a coalman was not always easy. Mr Fautly used to say that for some reason dogs always seemed to bite coalmen. He told the story of refusing to deliver coal to one of the other coalmen's home where there was a dog. They told the coalman to deliver his own coal and he got bitten by his own dog. Inspite of occassional problems, Father enjoyed the job. Sometimes he would be given apples or walnuts when he did his rounds. Kath remembers him bringing home the walnuts which he would crack in his hands. "Even if there were only a few, they were carefully shared round amongst all the family". When Mr Fautly's boss died, he was buried with the coal lorry as the hearse. "Father drove the lorry".

As an unpaid job, their Father was also an enthusiastic volunteer fireman from 1902 until the Second World War. His son and daughter, Fred and Kath, joined too during the Second World War and Dorothy was a fire watcher. The children were aware of the dangers of being a fireman. Dorothy remembers going past a place where she was told by her father that one of his friends had died getting a cat down from a tree. "One of his jobs was to drive the horse drawn fire engine but he had to catch the horse first – not always easy. It was in the field where Barnetts Road is now". There were photographs taken of the fire crews in Leigh, including one during the Second World War with Mrs Pankhurst, who lived at The Chestnuts on the Green until she died in the mid-1980's, and one with their first lorry outside the Tonbridge Fire Station by Tonbridge Castle. The fire crew did numerous exercises and had competitions. Mr Fautly won medals which Kath has given to Christopher, her son. Mr Russell of South View was the leader of the team for a good number of years in the 1930's. Later, Bernard Pankhurst took over. In December 1940, what was probably Leigh's most famous fire occurred. There was a fault in the electrical wiring at Hall Place – at first it was thought to be a German incendiary bomb – which caused a major disaster. Later, there was some puzzlement in the village that the fire brigade had used the lily pond rather than the lake and did not put 'a basket' on the intake to stop the mud and plants being sucked up.

MOTHER

Their mother, Emily, was in service before she was married. After her marriage, their mother took in sewing and washing to help with the house-keeping money. (Laundry Cottage, by Bid Bridge, on the way to the station, was indeed a laundry but only for Hall Place washing.)

"Mother was a keen reader. She taught herself everything. If she didn't know the meaning of a word, she'd look it up in the dictionary. She was very good at spelling". As well as looking after the family, she also helped in the village. When she was first married and living in Forge Square, she used to run a soup kitchen in the Iron Room for the children. "It was all free. The children took their own basins. The butcher gave all the bones and mother boiled them up in the copper in the Iron Room. The next day she'd skim off the fat and add the vegetables". Ironically, in view of her husband's love and expertize with horses, "mother was always terrified of horses."

Dorothy Fautly nursed her father at No. 5 for eight and a half years before he died. Eventually, he had to move downstairs and slept on a bed in the sitting room. "You got no help from the State in those days – it was often the youngest daughters who were expected to look after the elderly parents". He died after being in the East Grinstead hospital for a week. "Our doctor said that I saved the hospitals a lot of money over the years – and I jolly well did".

THE FIRST WORLD WAR

The First World War greatly affected the people in the village. "Just look at the list of names on the village War Memorial. But our family were lucky". All three of Granny Bateup's sons went to war but all came back home safely. They had been on a farm. The oldest volunteered and was put in charge of looking after the horses. "He knew all about that. The officer said 'got any more brothers?' and he said 'yes, two'. So all three ended up together.

For young children like the Misses Fautlys, the most memorable thing about the First World War was the fact that the large village hall became a VAD hospital and that injured and recovering soldiers were in the village. Their mother helped the VADs, scrubbing out the main halls. Dorothy has a letter thanking her mother. The kitchen in the Large Hall was the surgery and what is now the Legion Hall was the dining room for soldiers. The Small Hall was for recreation. The soldiers had specially reserved pews in the Church and concerts were put on for them. "But if you were a young child, you did not realize that things were different in wartime – you had not seen anything else".

The inside of the VAD recouperation hospital in the Large Village Hall during the 1914-1918 war.

Children used to help by collecting conkers for the army mules which were in The Coach House by the Iron Room. The sisters also remember something called 'honey sugar' which came from Canada but "I never saw it again after the war ended".

However, although the Armistice was a big event for the village, for the Fautly family it had particularly vivid memories. "In early November 1918, father had been in bed with bad pneumonia and mother had not taken off her clothes for ten days to look after him. All us children were down with 'flu and all the washing was out in the garden. That was the day that the Armistice was declared".

Both sisters remember that, right through the 1920s and 1930s, celebrating Armistice Day continued to be important, with men taking off their hats as they passed the Cenotaph in Whitehall. There was a War Memorial in the middle of Tonbridge High Street opposite the station but it was moved to the Garden of Remembrance in Bradford Street near the police station.

SCHOOL DAYS

Dorothy and Kath followed the other children in the family and went to the village school, Kath from 1915-1926 and Dorothy from 1917-1928. "It was a wonderful time". Both Kath and Dorothy remember Dorothy's first day at school on her third birthday. It was on 9 March 1917 and the weather was perfect. Kath was asked by brother Fred whether she was taking Dorothy to see her grandmother and she said "no, I'm taking her to school". "You went to school in the mornings only till you were five. The older children sat on the staged end of the main classroom, the younger ones down on the floor level".

They also both remember Fred and Ivy getting medals for good attendance but are more proud of the ones that they won themselves. Kath remembered a first prize for making bread, even though it was the first time she had ever done it. Dorothy still has the certificate that she was awarded for an essay on the British Empire. "They didn't give the essays back which is sad because I would have loved to have seen what I said".

Kath remembered that she often had to walk up the High Street to The Firs before school to collect washing which her mother then did at home. But walking was a common part of most schoolchildren's lives. Children would walk to school every day. They remember, too, when floods would prevent children from places like Killicks Bank and the Powder Mills getting to school.

Infants class at Leigh School in 1920. The teacher is Miss Strong and Dorothy Fautly is second from the right in the front row.

There are several headmasters and teachers that they particularly remember. Mr Boby was the Head during three reigns and for part of the time the sisters were there. When he retired in 1919, well after the normal retirement age because of the War, he was given three special gold sovereigns, one for each of the monarchs, at a special ceremony by the School's Governors, Mr Baker – the newsagent, Mr Sturgess – an estate agent and Billy Goodwin – the farmer at Pauls Hill Farm. Mr Boby had a housekeeper who rode a tricycle. There was a teacher called Miss Hayhoe who played the piano each morning as the children marched into the school, always "The British Grenadiers". The boys had their entrance and the girls had their own. Mr Boby was replaced by Mr Nethercott who had been wounded in the War. "He had new ideas and introduced woodwork and gardening for the boys. The garden was up The Green Lane on the right".

After Mr Nethercott, there was Mr Gibbons who the sisters remember as having an awful temper. He would fling things around not only at school but at home too. "We thought he was more keen on the boys than the girls. We never got cooking lessons. And the school concerts seemed to stop too".

The infants teacher, Miss Strong, "was lovely" says Dorothy. She was tall and thin and came from Ashford everyday. Because of the difficult journey, it was not certain that she would arrive on time at 9 o'clock so one of the older girls, Nellie Ingram, was appointed to be in charge. Nellie was wonderful and the girls used to learn the main stories of the Old Testament with her. Kath remembered them all for the rest of her life.

Each summer there was dancing on the Green with all the children in their white costumes. The school's annual play was held in the Big Village Hall which in those days had a stage and curtains plus footlights made of what looked like halved, large tin cans. Dorothy particularly remembers the dancing and the plays with plea-sure. "And on Empire Day, we would all march past the flag post and salute the flag".

Kath Fautly dressed up as a Dutch girl and Dorothy Fautly as a gipsy for the school concert in the early 1920s.

Boys and girls dancing on the Green in about 1919. Dorothy Fautly is shading her eyes on the right.

"There wasn't a school uniform but girls would wear their own straw hats in summer, which had a badge with 'LCS' on it". "That stood for Leigh Church School". "In the winter the girls wore felt hats or hand knitted ones". "The boys all had caps with LCS on them". "Everyone wore black boots". However, on Sunday the children had brown boots which the girls wore with white embroidered dresses – "very beautiful, with careful starching and needing careful ironing".

Kath remembered that there were two cardboard ladders put up on the schoolroom wall, one marked 'soldiers' and one 'sailors'; and the children were encouraged to build up a tower of pennies against them (which they assume were given to the First World War soldiers' and sailors' charities).

There were nine classes. Between three and four years old, there were two infant classes. Five year olds were in Class 1 and so on up to Class 6, who were ten years old. There was an exam at age eleven and a few of the children went to Judd or the County School as the Tonbridge Girls Grammar was then known. However, most stayed at the village school till they were thirteen and then left to start work. The girls mostly went into service; the boys on to farms or to Hall Place or one of the local shops, or alternatively one of the local industries – the bat and ball factories in Hildenborough (Mount Pleasant) or, more often, Chiddingstone Causeway, or with builders or at the Powder Mills.

The lessons that both sisters remember best were when they made things – needlework, knitting, raffia work, including making table mats. "We even persuaded our father to make some table mats".

Most of the children who lived in the village went home for lunch at 1.30 pm. Those who lived further away brought sandwiches. The younger children went home at 3.30 pm and the older ones at 3.45 pm.

The girls were inclined to play together; skipping, spinning tops, marbles and hoops all had their season.

RELIGION

The Church and the Chapel played a big part in the lives of villagers. The Fautly family were Church of England – first at Hildenborough Church, then in Leigh. Both as children and then when they were in service, Kath and Dorothy knew that they would have to go to Church every Sunday. Dorothy Fautly remembers "One day, when I was about 12, I disgraced myself. I was sick in the Church. I went all black. Just like that. I was kept away from school for a week". She also particularly remembers when she was confirmed in the early 1930's. It was snowing as they went to the service. "I had made my own confirmation dress. It was white with a white veil".

After the First World War, there was a Church Shop in what is now the Old School House which sold things that parishioners had made. Mrs Ingram, who lived at Oak Cottage on the Green, was one of the great contributors of jams and marmalade. Indeed, "everyone got a bit bored with her winning the Produce Show prizes every year". The Old School House could also be hired for special occasions. "And at one time, Roger Dadswell had his hairdresser shop there".

Both sisters remember all the vicars – with their very different ways. "The Rev. O.F. (Octavius because he had been the eighth child) Walton was vicar till about 1920 and then moved to another parish, before moving back to Leigh when he retired. He had sons who went to the Bluecoats School and four daughters."

He was followed by Rev. Weston for a few years. Dorothy jokingly says she did not like him as a child because he did not give her a prize she was due to receive because she was away ill on prizegiving day. He died after being in Leigh for only a few years – very painfully, with cancer of the spine.

The Rev. Leofric Sealy – "he was known as Lee Lee"– then became vicar for a long period from the mid 1930's until after the Second World War, arriving as a young unmarried man. "All the young girls went to Church at that time". He proposed to a well known lady who still lives in the village but she turned him down. "Later he married a singer – a classical singer". He officiated at Kath's wedding in 1943. The Reverend Eyre Walker was after Mr Sealy. He was single but he had a father, a mother and a sister who lived with him. Dorothy says, "I didn't like him. I'd had tonsillitis and I hadn't been to Church. Mr Walker saw me and thought I'd been naughty and he wouldn't give me my prize – my mother had to buy me something instead". John Bounds, the next vicar, was the first one to live in the newly built vicarage.

The Chapel was also very lively for many years. The Fautly children, all of whom loved singing, sometimes went to sing hymns at the Chapel but some Church people complained and it was stopped – even though Kath said "there should not be rows between Churches if you're really Christian".

The Wells family were very big in the Chapel affairs. Kath remembers that while the Church gave the Harvest Festival gifts direct to the needy, the Chapel had a sale and gave money to good causes. She recalls Mr Wells shouting out at the end of a sale "Who'll give me something for this last bunch of carrots?"

KATH

Kath left school at fourteen. Neither she nor Dorothy found it difficult to get a job. Her first job was to look after three children of the Headmaster, Mr Gibbons, who lived in the School House. Once, someone dared her to take the children along the railway line and over the Lower Green railway bridge. "And I did. When I think now how far it would have been to fall ....". Then she went to live in Great Barnetts with the retired vicar, Octavius Walton and his family. The wife, Mrs Walton, wrote books, including 'Christy's Old Organ', 'Angel's Christmas' and 'Christmas Angels'. "They were quite famous in their day". The Waltons had four daughters, Ivy, Myrtle (who died young), Daisey and Olive. They were all older than Kath. Daisy, a wartime VAD, had met and later married Mr Cecil after he was wounded in the war and had been sent to Leigh to recover. "When he and Daisy first met, Mr Cecil could not even talk". After they married, the young Mr and Mrs Cecil came to live at Great Barnetts, so there were normally five people plus the two maids to be looked after and cooked for by Kath. "The maids slept in the attic and it was rather strange because there was only one staircase in those days and, to reach the attic, you had to go through the master bedroom. We all had to be home by nine o'clock in the evening". Mr Walton was a great photographer and gardener. He had a robin which used to sit on his spade when he dug the garden.

In the early Thirties, Kath worked for a short time for the family at The White House on the Green and then in the mid-Thirties in Philpotts House. "When I worked for Mrs Stevens, I met Dr Barnado's widow. She was ninety and as upright as a die. She looked very prim and proper and we were told she never wore anything but black after the Doctor died. But even though I met her, I've always been against the Barnados Homes. I knew one of the Barnados children who lived happily with a family until she was twelve. Then Barnados came and took her back again. Later in the 1930s, I went to The Limes to work for the Reverend Sealy's brother and his family. It was Mr and Mrs Sealy who changed the name of their house to Chilling House. Mrs Sealy had a picture of Chilling-something so I suppose it had some sort of family connection for her. Sadly, Mrs Sealy died young giving birth to their first baby. She is buried in the Churchyard in a grave by itself with a cross on it. Mr Sealy said later he wished he had buried his wife in her wedding dress". At one time Kath was promoted to be the nurse to a little girl. "She was only one year old. Of course, I didn't get paid the extra I should have got for being a nurse. She's a doctor now. When she was grown up, she asked me if she was kind when she was little and I said 'yes, you were – always'. I was married from Chilling House in 1943."

In 1934 Kath had met William Johnson, although he was always called John after an uncle who had died. The family lived in Tunbridge Wells. John's father was a brickmaker and bricklayer. He built Chestnuts on the Green – and he used to walk to work along the Straight Mile. As Kath said, "You didn't think anything of walking that much every day. You did it all the time. That and cycling. I always think of Chestnuts as my house. John worked on the bookstall at Tonbridge Station after he left school. He was very keen on the Territorial Army and once in Tonbridge High Street in his uniform a young boy shouted 'Joined the Terries to get a Sunday suit then?'. Then, when he was 19, he joined the regular army, he was in for twelve years and served in India, Palestine and Egypt. He had a great time. 'Port Said was the best Christmas I ever had', he said once."

Then in 1943, after knowing each other for nine years, John and Kath were married in Leigh Church. They had their reception in the Old School House. "There were four Freds at my wedding; my grandfather, my great uncle, my father and my brother." After the war, Mr Johnson was a postman.

Chilling House, as it is called now, formerly 'The Limes' in the High Street.

The Johnsons had four children, Christopher, Karina, Olive and June, all of whom were brought up in the village. "We couldn't think of what to call the first one but we were talking about names in the park. We thought Christopher was very unusual. But there were lots of others after then".

DOROTHY

Dorothy also went into service when she left school, working first for Miss Hicks at The Cottage, Garden Cottages. "I still had to wear a uniform, even there you know. Later I worked for the Bickersteth family at Pauls Hill House which was much grander. They had a cook, a chauffeur/butler, a nanny, a house parlour maid, a nursery maid and a governess. Mr Bickersteth worked in London and was always inclined to be late for the train. From the house he could see the train leaving Tonbridge station and he would then rush up to Hildenborough station in the car. Mrs Bickersteth, who was a cripple, used to organize the big Conservative Dance at Christmas."

The longest Dorothy was away from the village was a year during the Second World War when she went to work in Hildenborough with a really horrid family. They were friends of both P.G. Wodehouse and the Cazalets. The husband who was a writer – "I never knew what he wrote" – virtually never said a word to her in the whole year. The wife used to make cutting remarks. Once she said to Dorothy "You don't need to iron your clothes: you haven't got a man". Dorothy's brother, Fred, offered to have it out with them but Dorothy left – even if it meant she did not have a reference. She then went to work with Doctor and Mrs Herman in Tonbridge "who were lovely".

For twenty five years from 1963 to 1988 Dorothy looked after the very nice Miss Arnold "she was Miss Gladice – it really was spelt like that" who lived at Cranmore on the London Road in Hildenborough with her sister Elene. Elene was the Headmistress of Tonbridge Girls Grammar School. Dorothy has a beautiful silk umbrella which she was given by Miss Arnold. "They used to be given a lot of presents and if they didn't need them, they were put away in a room. I think the umbrella came from there". But much more important to Dorothy was another present. "Miss Arnold used to do china painting and I have a set of china that Miss Arnold made specially to celebrate when we had been together for 20 years. It has flowers on it and the main serving plate has both our initials put together."

Then when they had been together for twenty five years and Dorothy was approaching seventy five, "we decided that I should call it a day". So Dorothy retired in 1988 when she was 74 years old. A short time later Miss Arnold died. "I did not get invited to her funeral. I thought that was very sad".

IN SERVICE

Most of the larger homes in the village had at least two full-time servants – Park House (Doctor Fraser's family), South View (Mr Russell), The Vicarage, Chilling House, Kennards, Great Barnetts and so on.

A normal day for the servants meant starting work at seven o'clock or earlier, preparing early morning tea, getting the stove ready – sometimes it was an oil stove but normally coal – and in winter getting the other fires going and preparing porridge for breakfast.

Then it was a long day with the work finished when the lady of the house said it was finished. "Every alternate Sunday you had off – with the other servant doing the work. If there was only one servant in the house, then you were expected to get everything prepared before you went off and to do all the clearing up from Sunday when you started on the Monday. At one house where Dorothy worked, the lady was very catty. And I had to scrub the floor on Sundays. If you wanted to have an evening off, you had to ask permission specially."

If you were in service, you were expected to buy or make your own uniforms. Dorothy remembers that once when she started a new job, her very nice new employer gave her a dress but this was very unusual. "You didn't get given uniforms – not usually. If you did get one it was for a birthday or Christmas but you didn't think so much of it then", says Kath. There were morning uniforms and afternoon uniforms. The morning uniform was normally blue and white with a white apron and cap. The afternoon uniform was a different colour but still with the white apron and cap. You would have to wear full uniform even when you were the only servant and the home was tiny. However, it became more difficult in the Second World War because of clothing coupons. "Uniforms went out of fashion after that."

FOOD AND COOKING

Dorothy and Kath both remember how much most people they worked for ate but it was normal in those days. There was a large cooked breakfast at 8.00 am; lunch on the dot at 1.00 pm; a full tea – always at 4.30 pm; and dinner at 7.30 pm. Surprisingly, Kath and Dorothy do not remember people as being very fat – although large sometimes – even if by the 1930's their employers mostly had cars and were not taking that much physical exercise.

Grandfather Fautly looks at a Conservative election pamphlet in front of the kitchener in the Garden Cottage house.

The main cooking was usually done on the 'kitchener' – the coal burning range with its built-in oven. It also heated the hot water. However, there was gas at both Garden Cottages and at houses like Great Barnetts which meant a gas ring could be used as well. Gas cookers came later.

A typical day's food at a house like Great Barnetts would consist of porridge and toast for breakfast – always with home-made marmalade. 100lbs a year was made just at Great Barnetts and, if it was not there, Daisy, the daughter, would joke "there'll be another mark on the scullery beam". There was usually bacon, produced locally, on Wednesdays and Sundays. Lunch was really the biggest meal of the day – always with meat and two veg plus a sweet which might be rice pudding, apple tart or even French pancakes. The Waltons did not like steamed puddings. Sunday lunch always meant a huge roast – usually beef.

Tea would be bread and butter with jam – and marmalade for Miss Daisy. Mrs Walton insisted that the bread and butter was served on a special silver tray.

Supper would be something like scrambled eggs on toast or mushrooms in a creamy sauce on toast – the mushrooms often picked in the field behind Great Barnetts. Wednesdays often meant steak and kidney pie.

If people were a bit poorly, they were given beef tea which was made by cutting up shin of beef from the butcher. This was put in a big stone jamjar in a saucepan of water which was boiled for hours.

Washing clothes was done in the big copper – which had a fire under it and a small chimney on the side of the house. "They would boil up several Christmas puddings at once in it too".

There was running water in nearly all the homes in Leigh by the mid 1920's, although quite a few houses had pumps in the scullery from earlier times. Unusually, Garden Cottages had a flushing W.C. from the time that they were built – although gas and electricity were not installed until later. However, quite a few houses in the village had earth closets up until after the Second World War.

And if being in service had some compensations, employers were not always thoughtful. Dorothy was told she was no longer needed the day after her father died – "which I didn't think was very nice".

THE VILLAGE

On the Green, the grass for cricket and football was kept short but the grass at the Alms House end was left long, cut only once a year, right until after the Second World War. There was a clear footpath across the Green from the corner below the War Memorial to No. 4 Barden Cottages. "We didn't approve of the idea a few years ago of a playground on the Green. The Green has always been for anyone to walk across. Our father was very cross when the cricket club put a chain around the cricket pitch. He used to walk straight across it to show that anyone had the right to go anywhere on the Green".

The old, green painted, corrugated iron cricket pavilion "was given to the Cricket Club by Mr Goodwin in about 1902. He lived at Paul's Hill Farm and he owned quite a number of houses in the village including Barden Cottages on the Green."

The Iron Room was often used for village functions as well as by the school, and just past it was the village slaughter house – where the public toilets are now – demolished in the late 1960's.

In the mid-1920s Daisy Milliner – known to most people many years later as 'Aunt Dais', lived in half of Old Chimneys with her mother and daughter, Evelyn. The Fautly's remember Evelyn as a child – mainly looked after by her grandmother because Daisy worked in London. Evelyn had to remember addresses for letters she was carrying, so that the Post Master could write them on because her grandmother couldn't write. "Evelyn was a pretty, golden curled little thing. She would be going along, repeating the address to herself so that she didn't forget it".

There used to be ponds on the Green. As well as a small one beside Oak Cottage on the Old Chimney's side – which was filled in in the 1930's – there was a bigger one by the end of Green Lane which the Fautly's particularly remember. They used to be told that all the ponds in the village were because iron ore had been extracted years ago. They also remember the big ditch round the Moat Farm site but they do not remember it having any water in it as it does now that it has been excavated.

SHOPS

"There was one shop on the Green, the Post Office, but it was really only the front room of Mrs Izzard's house. The butcher was at Southdown House, next to the Bat & Ball. Mr Hammond was the butcher who took Fred Fautly on just after the First World War. Later, the shop was taken on by the Maupass family – who are still in the trade today in Tonbridge." The next butcher was Mr Whitehead who took Fred on. Mr Whitehead was about the same age as Fred, "but Fred knew much more about the work". During the Second World War, the village used to collect their lemons up and store them in the butcher's refrigerator – mainly to help people with rheumatism – particularly Mr Wells himself who suffered from it very badly later in life. Mr Wells later took over the butchers when it moved to the Green well after the Second World War.

The front part of Orchard House had a general store, taking up the whole of what became, for twenty years from 1978, Anthony Woodburn's The Clock Shop and the hairdressers. After Mr Peters, the Lindridge family bought it and, later in 1935, it became 'Adin Coates', run by the son of Adin, Spenser, and his wife Margaret. Adin Coates originally sold clothes like the other Coates drapers shops in Edenbridge, Rye and Tenterden but gradually moved into being more a high quality grocer. "When we were young, we used to get cream walnut sweets from Peters and go and eat them sitting on the gate down by Ensfield Cottages. The gate used to go right across the road when the animals were grazing. It was only a little road then with hardly any cars."

The General Store – under Mr Lindridge c1925.

Further up the High Street where Johnsons is now, there was a second general stores. In the twenties, it was owned by Mr and Mrs Sherman, then the Bakers. "She was short and he was thin. Fred used to mimic her. And if you didn't buy something proper, she wouldn't take your farthings".

Then there were the shops and tradesmen down the Halt Road, "which was what we called Lower Green then. The Old Bakery had the shop in the front and the bakehouse at the back with a huge wooden table in it. Originally the baker was Elsie Friend, then Mr Belton, then Mr Lakeland. There were others after the War but I remember when the baker used to call round to every house, every day."

Mr Lewis Brooker used to mend shoes in the wooden shed which now sells antiques at The Brickmakers and at the bottom end of Lower Green by the ramp up to the station was "a bicycle shop which also used to recharge radio batteries which we had to take down and collect as children". It became a printers workshop in the fifties and sixties owned by Mr Vic Loft. Opposite the bike shop there was a fish and chip shop for some time: "it was sort of in the hedge".

The village had its own dairy behind the cricket pavilion and the milkman, Arthur Sadler, was "one of the characters. He came round to all houses twice a day with a little cart and a big milk churn with beautifully polished bits of brass on it. When he wasn't doing the milk, he did the sewers. He died down at the sewage farm. He was one of the Leigh firemen too, so he got buried as a fireman".

"Then there was the wheelwright and coffin maker, Mr Faircloth, whose workshop was down the Lane beside the Village Halls, where Wheelwrights Cottage is now."

THE PARK AND FARMS

"The deer at Hall Place were beautiful. We used to go and look at them when we were children. Apparently, they were not allowed more than ninety-nine or you had to have a licence. So they used to kill off a few each year. We had venison once or twice in the war but mostly it went to London. Lord Hollenden had his shoots but Lady Hollenden wouldn't come down for them. She hated killing things."

"There were more and smaller farms in the 1920's and 1930's than there are now". Home Farm was managed for Lord Hollenden by Mr Wylie, a Scotsman. Great Barnetts Farm and Little Barnetts Farm were owned by two of the Faircloths. The sisters used to go hop-picking when they were children. "We loved it. The school term went on until August. Then the Headmaster used to go to see Mr Goodwin, the farmer at Paul's Hill Farm and talk to him about when the hop-picking would be finished and when he should start school. But we mainly went down to the farm at Ramshurst and worked there. Little Barden Farm had hopfields and the field behind Garden Cottages used to be a hopfield too in our mother's time. It belonged to Great Barnetts. There used to be a special bin called the Church Bin. If you put hops in the money went to the Church. We didn't have Londoners down in Leigh but you would see their little huts in other places". They both remember Great Barnetts as a working farm in the 1920's and remember driving the cows in and watching the hops being harvested. Their grandfather used to dry the hops in what is today the oast at Moat Farm. Those parts of the farm belonged to Roddy Rogers. And sometimes as children, they used to go and collect acorns for the pigs. "The farmer used to give us sixpence a gallon for them".

ENTERTAINMENT

"There were lots of things to do in the village in the 1920's and 1930's" – "all sorts of clubs and societies you could join and lots of things to do with yourself at home like jam making and knitting". The sisters still have the old Singer sewing machine that they inherited from their mother and Kath has always done knitting, crocheting and lacemaking. "I love it. I do the lacemaking that is crochet work – not the pillow lace. We used to send off for linen – real Irish linen. It was ten shillings which was quite a lot in those days – you only got a pound a week. But it was worth it. Tonbridge was where you bought most of your clothes – if you didn't make them yourself which you usually did – and Flynns was very good for hats. You could take hats back and get them to remodel them into a new fashion."

"You usually got around by bicycle – there was not so much traffic as there is now – and we'd cycle to all the villages on Saturday evenings for dances with our dresses and our black satin shoes in a case on the back of the bike. I've still got my black satin shoes. The only village we didn't like was Penshurst – it was snooty".

"I'd also cycle to Doctor Wood in Penshurst to get Miss Hicks' medicine. Miss Hicks' whippet would come too. He never got in the way."

One day, when cycling back to the village, one of the sisters found a man exposing himself by the railway bridge "all in broad daylight". Quite soon after, they both went to the cinema in Tonbridge by train. On the way home, they noticed the same man on Tonbridge station getting on to their train. They told the guard who looked after them. "We told the policeman, Mr Post, all about it too. You could tell him everything. He was at No. 1 Forge Square. That was always the policeman's house".

In the summer there would be family outings to Hastings to visit their relatives and at one time they went to Studland for a holiday each year.

In the 1920's and 1930's Leigh had a very good troupe of dancers. They would tour all the local villages (except Penshurst) in the summer. Dorothy remembers that each year they sent off to John Lewis to get the material for the new dresses that they would make themselves. There was a Girl Guides troop too that used to meet in the Old School House, although the sisters did not join it.

Quite often in the 1930's there was an annual open air play, organized by Mrs Bickersteth at Pauls Hill (now Pauls Hill House). The Women's Institute was also very active throughout the period between the Wars and Dorothy was very involved for quite a time – only packing it in when she felt she got no thanks! But she did win a ten shilling prize and an award for a special cake on one occasion. In the early twenties, there was also a Mothers Meeting which was run by Mrs Walton. However, it was not until after the Second World War that the Golden Years Club was started, mainly by Margaret Wells. As well as events in the village, there would be summer outings to places like the Warnock Gardens in Polegate.

Ladies and girls did not go into the pubs but the Fautly children were friendly with the family who ran the Bat & Ball which had a sweet shop at the front, "and in the summer we sometimes went to The Brickmakers to have tea in the outside patio at the back".

Dorothy was particularly keen on music. "I was taught the piano by Mrs Ingram in the front room of Oak Cottage on the Green". There was a Leigh Choral Society which was very active. Joan and Elspeth, Lord Hollenden's two daughters, used to come regularly and loved it. Dorothy remembers singing the Messiah in St Nicholas' Church in Sevenoaks. "And once a year we combined with all the other local choral societies in the Pump Rooms or the Assembly Hall in Tunbridge Wells". One year, Sir Malcolm Sargent – then a young man – came to conduct. "He was very cheerful and everyone liked him because he was so encouraging."

Len Walton who lived with his wife, Lilian, in the High Street at No. 3 Oak Cottages, was a great person in the Choral Society – he loved singing. The sisters always remember him on his bike and "when he'd cycle past in the rain he'd say 'fishy weather'".

> *The Waltons had been in service at one of the great stately homes and Lilian was a highly skilled needlewoman – in the 1960's she embroidered children's dresses for Fortnum and Mason, one of which was sold to Princess Margaret.*

The boys and young men used to play cricket and football. Because a good number of homes only had a tin bath for washing (once a week), they often used to go up to the Small Village Hall to get a bath after a game of football. "I think it cost 6d". The women and girls could play tennis in the big garden behind Elizabeth Cottage (where Wildhatch is now) and badminton in the Large Village Hall, although neither of the sisters used to belong to the clubs.

At Christmas there were three dances, one for the Conservatives, one to raise money for the hospital, which was always Boxing night, and one arranged by the W.I. There was also a children's Christmas party and Lord

Hollenden used to provide presents. The sisters remember that at one time they used to receive clothes but there were complaints that the dresses were the wrong size, so Lord Hollenden changed the presents to toys. Kath had a doll she was given until she died.

"Of course, there was the start of the wireless. I think Mr Randerson at Inglenook – the old vicarage stables – had the first crystal set with a cats whisker but we had one too a bit later".

HEALTH

"The doctors and medical services were not so good before the Health Service. You had to pay for everything – even having a baby." Everyone wanted a good local hospital. The Kent & Sussex Hospital was originally where Noakes is now in Tunbridge Wells – just above Five Ways, with the Tonbridge Cottage Hospital up Quarry Hill in Baltic Road.

"We built the Kent & Sussex Hospital." This is the sisters' view of what everyone did in those days to get the new hospital on its present site. The community all round Tonbridge and Tunbridge Wells wanted the new hospital so they had to rely to a large extent on voluntary fund raising. One of the main ways was the annual 'Hospital Sunday' in Tonbridge in the summer. There were big parades with banners and all the firms locally, including Southern Railway, used to join in. There was usually a Leigh village dance in the winter too and the Fautly's have a 1933 newspaper cutting with a photo of the Leigh Dancers and 'the jolly company who attended the dance' to raise money for 'Help The Hospital'. Their sister, Ivy, in Chippenham still has the big china doll – all the way from Canada – that she won in a hospital raffle and Kath had a brooch with a peanut on it that she bought to help raise money. They would also make things for the hospital – including little flannel jackets – white for the babies and red for the children – and they embroidered slippers for the patients. "Mrs Davies at the W.I. cut out the patterns". Rich people used to endow a bed in the hospital. Kath had her appendix out in a bed which had been given by a lady in Rusthall. Another occasion when the family had to make use of the hospital was when brother Fred put his hip out chasing the cattle in the slaughter house field, where The Crandalls is now. "He had a limp ever after". There was also an isolation hospital in Capel. One of the children had to go there when they had pneumonia.

However, the main way that ordinary people paid for hospitals and doctors were the 'medical clubs' – "a kind of insurance: it used to cost tuppence a week". "And there were 'coal clubs' and 'clothing clubs' too."

The surgery in the village after and including the time of the First World War was in Park House, where Doctor Fraser lived for many years. To get to the surgery you went through the garden doorway with the brick arch in the corner nearest the church and formed a queue. Later Doctor Barclay lived in the village at Applegarth. "He was a lad". He went into the army but died young of cancer.

Dr Davidson was the main doctor for the village during the Second World War, and after him, Dr Glaisher had a surgery in the Old School House. "It was not an ideal place – when there was heavy rain the water would come in at the front door and run out at the back."

During the Second World War, Kath and Dorothy particularly remember seeing their first doodle bug when they were in Folkstone. There was also the German plane that crashed into a haystack near Old Kennards. The Spitfire which had shot it down flew off straight away – they later heard it was short of fuel. "The body of the German pilot was put in a sack and wheeled up to the Churchyard in a barrow to be buried". They heard a rumour that his medals disappeared. "I was pleased when many years later someone paid to have his body sent back to Germany for a burial at home".

After Dunkirk, troop trains came through Leigh. "Dunkirk was meant to be secret but people got to know." Dorothy was working in the hospital by then but Kath remembered that sometimes the troops threw out letters from the trains in order to get them posted. They also remember the large anti-aircraft guns in the field opposite Barnetts Mead in Powder Mill Lane.

THEN AND NOW

Looking back at the period between the two World Wars both sisters feel that the village is very different now. "You knew everyone then – it was one big family – everyone helped one another out. Our mother would have helped anyone". When they were children and starting to grow up "they were happy times. Everything was settled – simpler. You knew where you were then", even if perhaps in those days "you were a bit more superstitious about things". Both sisters feel that before the Second World War there was more active involvement by nearly everyone in the Church. "And you only got fruit and vegetables in their season. We only had celery for example at its proper time – and we only had oranges at Christmas. Everything had its proper season". "Lots of people had bees then. Old Miss Hicks had them. She had a sort of corrugated paper thing that puffed smoke at them. If they went off too far, she'd ring a bell and they'd come back".

"It's all too big nowadays. There's too many cars. Everyone's in a rush and you don't know most of the people – and some who you do, don't talk to you". And the Church services seem more for the young – "we like the proper Prayer Book services". "Maybe we didn't have much then, but we had a wonderful time".

"When you were in service, you always used to call people 'Mr' or 'Mrs', although you called the children by their Christian names. When the girls grew up and got married, you had to start called them 'Mrs'. But I remember one lady who I'd known as a little girl saying to me last year 'Kathleen, we've known each other well over fifty years now. I've always called you Kathleen. I think you should use my Christian name now' and I said 'yes'".

Harry and Jack Lucas

Lower Green from the railway arch c1920.

arry and Jack Lucas and their younger brother Bernard were all born in the village. Both their father and his father lived in the village virtually all their lives. Harry remembers his grandfather "who must have been ninety, had a bee in his bonnet about telling me things he remembered about the village when he was young: but I wanted to go out and play football. I always regret that I didn't listen more but I do remember some of the things he told me. I'm not sure whether he was born in the village but he worked at the brickyards in Lower Green – it must have about 1860 – amongst other jobs. But you seemed to do a variety of things in those days. He did tell me about how he had to re-do Budgeon Cottage in Lower Green when he moved in. It had just an earth floor, a ladder to get to the top floor and a piece of material on a string to divide the top floor into two, one half for him and his wife and one half for all the children. It had no gutters or anything like that. He brought reject bricks home with him and gradually laid a floor with them."

Harry was born in 1918 in the cottage – now pulled down – which was next to Budgeon Cottage. Jack was born there two years later. "We walked everywhere as kids. It meant that you knew everyone in a way that you don't now. You hardly saw a car when we were at school. The boys used to bowl their hoops along the middle of the road and the girls had their spinning tops.

No cars ever got in the way. The hoops were metal and were made in the forge. The biggest was about four feet high and the bigger you had them, the bigger man you were. And lots of the children would walk miles to and from school – all the Charcott and Causeway children came until they were eleven; and they walked from Powder Mills too."

However, both brothers particularly remember one vehicle which came through the village regularly – the timber tug. "When they cut the trees, they would drag them out of the woods with horses. It was Baltic Sawmills in Baltic Road, Tonbridge by the Medway which came to collect them. There was this special wagon with two wheels in the front and a long pole joining up to the back two wheels. The man who drove it was called Robin and we knew him quite well. He always stopped his two horses at the horse trough on the Green and we used to shout out to him and run across to get a ride – up to a dozen of us sometimes. Then in the evening he'd come back again with the oak tree or whatever it was and stop at the horse trough again."

Jack and Harry have vivid memories of the village in which they spent the whole of the 1920s and 1930s. They talk about the village as a walk through the village from the station, up the High Street and along to the Green and the Church, both adding half sentences to the others recollections.

"The sewage works past the Station had been built by the Hall Place Estate before the end of the century but my grandfather used to tell about the problems" says Harry. "Unfortunately, when the sewers were laid, there wasn't running water in the houses, so you were expected to go and get a bucket of water from your well or your pump and throw it down the toilet. But, of course, you didn't always do that if you just had a pee. Anyway, there wasn't enough water to flush everything down to the works and my grandfather was paid 1/6d each Saturday to go round with a horse and cart with a load of water cans on the back which he put down all the manholes. Virtually every house had its own well, usually with a pump, although some houses shared one. The main village pump – the one outside Pump Cottage – wasn't a well in our time but before then you had to get water from it when you lived at the Square. It had water from the waterworks. The two water fountains in the Hall Place wall did too. They had big knobs on them and when you turned them the water flowed out – sort of flowed, not gushed you know. They were gravity fed from Hall Place. They took the pump away during the war and covered it over. It had a stone trough in front of it. That's gone too. Sad, really. We ought to get them back some-time." Harry also remembers another problem which concerns the newly built WC which was built to be used by the Budgeon Cottages and the two cottages next to them. However, this time it was not a problem of water. "The trouble was that the shed with the joint WC in it backed on to the allotments and when any of the ladies from the four cottages walked up to it, they felt that they were being looked at by the old gentlemen digging the allotments. So they insisted that the hedge should be allowed to grow up to six foot by the WC. There is still one bit of that hedge which is much higher than the rest."

"Of course a fair number of homes had earth closets until well after the War – that's the Second World War" says Jack. "But there was only one two holer that I've heard of and that was at Elizabeth Cottage. And I think they had eleven in the family, so they needed it".

Starting at the bottom of Station Road or Halt Road as Lower Green was called then, Jack and Harry remember the station being run in a very different way in those days. "For one thing, it had a station master, George Gravett – or rather he was the station master, porter and signalman and he lit the gas lights into the bargain. He was there for years. It must have been from around 1920 to about 1960. If you wanted to go on holiday, you'd ask George to collect all your baggage and he'd come along with his bicycle and wheel it along with the cases on the handlebars all through the village for sixpence. He had a special use for his trolley, too. You know the kind – with long handles and two wheels with a metal front bit. If a lot of people got off a train, he'd use it to make people go through the barrier one at a time so he could take their tickets by lowering it up and down between each of them. In those days a ticket from Leigh to Tonbridge was five old pence return and then it was fourpence single from Tonbridge down to Tunbridge Wells. The majority of people used the train – not many went by bus – and it was particularly crowded on Saturday afternoons because everyone worked a five and a half day week in those days and they wanted to do their shopping and things on Saturday afternoon."

"Lower Green itself was very different then. As you went up from the station there was just the rough pasture on the right where sometimes Mr Goodwin at Pauls Hill Farm, or the Barkaways, used to graze a few bullocks but most of the time it was unused really – just rough ground with lots of the old ponds there from the time of the brickworks. The field was owned by Arthur and Elsie Friend – the children of the man who had once owned the bakery. They sold the field to a man who agreed to convert the stable and cart shed at the bottom of the field into a bungalow for them to live in. (It's the family of the man who bought the field, Reg Hillier, who built the new houses at the waterworks)."

Steam train arrives at The Halt, Leigh - probably 1912.

"There were some really beautiful fir trees in a row along the edge of the road although it was really more a track then. We used to call the deep pond down by the railway line "the wellie" and we used to go fishing for efts – newts they usually call them now. We'd get a worm and tie it on a bit of string. The newts never seemed to let go, and we'd put them in a jam jar and see how many we could get".

"There seemed to be two different types: one had a reddish bit on its front and was more spiky but I never looked it up to see if they were just male and female or whether they really were different types" says Harry, although Jack reckons the newts had the reddish chest and a flatter tail and the efts were plainer.

"At one time, there was a small-holding on the left as you came through the bridge. It was farmed by the landlord of the Brickmakers Arms, Mr Coomber. There were just a few sheds and barns with a horse or two and a few cows and sheep. Father used to do odd jobs for Coomber". Harry has some extra memories. "At the back there was a chaff cutter for cutting up hay to feed the animals – the kind you stuffed into those coconut matting nosebags horses used to have. It could be worked by turning a handle or you could use a horse who went round and round. I cut the top of my thumb off in it. And for a short time there was a fish and chip shop in a caravan thing in front of the barns. It wasn't there long. The man – he was a village man – he used to faint while he was cooking which couldn't have helped."

When Jack was about six or seven he remembers a cart delivering old sleepers to put up the workshop opposite. "It became a bicycle shop run by George Bennett. If you had a problem with your bike, he'd get anything for you. If he hadn't got it in the shop, he'd ring up and it would probably be delivered on the next train from Tonbridge. He also used to charge up the accumulators that you had for radios in those days. It cost sixpence to recharge each one and the children used to be sent along with them. They were in a sort of glass container with acid in. But you had three types of battery to run a radio in those days. As well as the accumulator, there were the grid batteries about six inches long, three inches high and an inch wide with a bitumen top and pairs of brass screws on it. When one part of the grid battery ran out you moved the two wires along to the next pair. But you also had an HT battery – that was High Tension – which were great big things you had to leave on a shelf beside the wireless set. The first wireless set that Mother and Father had in Forge Square was made by a man who lived in the Hall Place Bothy. Mr Pringle – the old head gardener – gave me a crystal set in the mid thirties – he was retired by then."

Going on past their cottage and Budgeon Cottages on the left of Lower Green, you came to the Bakery. It was a shop at the front with the big bake house at the back. Jack remembers a link with their mother's father. "He was a bricklayer in Tunbridge Wells and used to come over to repair the bakery oven. The pointing round the stone slabs in it got worn out with the heat and had to be replaced. It always had to be on a Sunday because Friday was the big baking day – ready for Saturday shopping and the delivery round. On Sunday the oven wasn't being used and had cooled down. Grandfather used to get out a big red handkerchief and tie a knot in each corner and put it over his head. Then he used to crawl in."

Harry has other memories of Mr Belton who had taken over from Mr Friend as the main village baker. "As children, we were always on the look out for extra money for doing odd jobs. I got a job delivering the bread. I was given this bike with a big basket on the back as well as the front. One day, I forgot it had a big basket on the back and I threw my leg over, hit the basket and fell off into the edge of the pond. Belton was a great icer of cakes. He was famous for it. The big hotels in Tunbridge Wells would order cakes for special occasions and Christmas. He delivered them by horse and cart. I remember going with him once. It was really just the farm cart with some straw in the bottom to make it soft and newspapers over the top of the cakes – lots of them. After Mr Belton there was Mr Phipps at the Bakery – he ran the Chapel. There was one regular delivery I do remember – we had to take a dozen or so loaves up to the Church porch and put them in a basket there for the poor. People could only have them after they had been to the service though. They were big loaves then – four pounds. There was another baker who was used by some people in the village, Mr Grayland. He was in Charcott and used to deliver all over the place – Lower Street and so on. Mother used to have him."

Delivery of food and goods was expected. The Sainsburys' man used to come up from Tonbridge. "He had brown overalls and a peaked cap. And there was a man, Mr Putwain, who had a van which came round with soap – you had long blocks of it and cut bits off – and enamel jugs and basins, scrubbing brushes and brooms, paraffin for the oil lamp and so on. You've got to realise that in the 1920s and 1930s not many people had electric lighting. We were lucky and had gas lights from the Estate works in the four houses we lived in but lots of people had paraffin lamps. I can remember when our Aunt Polly – she wasn't our real Aunt – she and her husband Jack Stolton were some sort of relative – when she got electricity. It was quite something. They lived in the cottage on the corner of the Green and Green Lane and it cost £12 to install – a lot of money in those days. Then there was a man from Tonbridge who came round with a cart every Sunday afternoon, ringing a bell, selling muffins and crumpets. And, of course, there was the rag and bone man – he took everything."

Next door to the bakery was Bombers Cottage which meant the milkman – or the main village milkman. "The milk round was bought in the middle of the 1930's by Mr Faircloth. He had a wooden leg. He used to do a delivery early in the morning with his horse and special cart and do another round in the afternoon at about four. He used to let us ride the horse after he'd finished – we'd fight over it – when he'd be taking the horse back to the field behind the houses they'd just built at the top of Penshurst Road – behind where Fred Whibley used to live. But there were lots of other people who used to provide a bit of milk to the village too. There was a farmer with a small-holding at the top of what became Greenview Avenue before he sold it off for houses. He was called Mr Warder and he built a dairy on the bottom of Greenview Avenue behind the little green cricket pavilion. But it didn't seem to last. I think people wanted it delivered. Old Bert Taylor at Little Barnetts Farm used to bring round milk and there was Mr Fredericks with a small-holding opposite Mr Carp in Lower Street who came round too. He'd got one of those bikes with a big basket on the front. Then there was Winnie Taylor. Her father had a small holding at Cinder Hill. She had deformed arms. She came round once with some eggs for us but she dropped them. My father swore at her......."

"By the side of Brickmakers – it's now the antique shop – there was the snob. Lewis Brooker used to sit in there with the top of the stable door open and mend shoes. He was great friends with Mr Bennett at the cycle shop. He was liked by everyone. It had once been the main village butcher's shop before it was the shoemenders – according to our grandfather. It must have been in the middle of the eighteen hundreds. There was a cart which was kept behind the shop for deliveries. You'd go in and leave an order, and by the next day the shoes would have been collected, repaired and returned. There were other people who used to mend shoes in the village too – there was Mr Porter in the High Street by the Bat who used to do a bit."

Opposite, at the top of Lower Green, there was nothing except the waterworks, the Scout Hut, and the two Waterworks Cottages – one now lived in by Jack and his wife, Elsie. "We think that our cottage was the foreman's cottage because it has two extra windows which overlook the waterworks. The track didn't get called Kiln Lane until well after the war, when the Post Office wanted a name for it. At the bottom of the lane, there really is an old brick kiln. It's covered up with earth now but it got partly uncovered when they started on the Well Close houses.

Next door to the waterworks was the Scout hut. "The Scout Troop was run by Mr Russell – I expect everyone has told you about him. We were both in the Boy Scouts – practically every boy in the village was. You could join when you were ten and there were four patrols, with ten or twelve boys in each. When you were fourteen you could go into the Rovers. That was run by Dick Wood. His real name was Harry but he was always called Dick. The Troop got so big that Mr Russell had another bit built on to the Scout Hut – it was corrugated iron. Lady Hollenden came and opened it. It cost a penny a week to join the Scouts but when you got to fourteen, you could pay tuppence a week and play snooker. There was a threequarter size table that had a gas light with a big green shade and we had darts and a portable wireless. On Sunday afternoons at 2.30, there was a bible class which was run by Daisy Walton."

Harry continues. "The big event of the year was the annual trip to Studland Bay. It cost thirteen and six for the two weeks or a pound if you were over fourteen which was jolly good value if you think about it. They hired a lorry from Mr Banks in Four Elms to take all the equipment – the tents, the cookers and so on – down in advance. Then we all got on a special train which stopped at Leigh just for the Scouts and went down to Bournemouth. When we got to Bournemouth, we caught a bus to Sandbanks Ferry which took us across Poole Harbour. Then it was Shanks'

Pony – which, take it from me, was a long way – it must have been three miles to the camp – and carrying our kitbags. Daisy Walton came with Mr Russell – she did a lot to help – and any of the parents who wanted to could come down in the middle weekend. There was a special train for them too.

The Scouts used to put on a play during the Easter holiday in the Large Village Hall. It was written by Daisy Walton and we all acted in it. They tried to get everyone involved in it, even the Rovers. The Large Village Hall had a stage in those days and we did the play for two nights. It was packed out. The money went towards the Summer Camp, although maybe Mr Russell helped with the finances – I'm not sure. In the interval Mr Russell would show films of the previous summer's camp – he was a keen cine photographer. We've got copies of some of those films still in the Parish Council safe.

The building at the top of Kiln Lane which is now part of the garage was first built to house the fire engine at the beginning of the Second World War."

Turning left along the High Street, in the middle of the row of houses commissioned by Samuel Morley, there was the entrance – there still is – to the allotments, the land still owned by the Morley Trust. Harry, always an allotment enthusiast, remembers "Charlie Ingram from Oak Cottage – he was brilliant – his allotment was next to mine". He also remembers the not so good allotment holders; and those whose initial enthusiasm never led to much.

Up the road on the corner was a field in a sort of hollow, called Donkeys Field. Both brothers remember it well. "Originally, it did have donkeys from Hall Place grazing there. They were to pull little carts I suppose – probably for the children. But, gradually, it became the unofficial rubbish dump for the village. It was on the edge of the village in the 1920's. You'd see old men with handcarts and wheelbarrows going up there with their rubbish. I think a lot of the Hall Place rubbish went there too. There were only occasional Council rubbish carts in those days. The trouble was that the butcher used to send up all the offal from the slaughter house and there was the most terrible stink. The good thing though from the point of view of all us lads was all the rats. We used to go up there and see how many we could hit over the head with our sticks."

"In the late 1930s, Mr Whitehead, the butcher built a garage next door to the Donkey Field for his brother. It was taken over by Mr Moon and it was always called Moon's Garage from then until the 1960's. During the war Mr Moon expanded and built a corrugated iron extension on the back with an engineering workshop which was said to be making bits for Spitfires. He had about six men who worked on the lathes and things. Maurice Martin in Garden Cottages was there."

In the mid 1920s, the Lucas family moved from the Lower Green cottage to the cottage by the stable block at Hall Place. Mr Lucas had a new job as a groom there. The two brothers remember skating on the lake. "All the village went and they even came over from the Causeway. They had paraffin lamps all round the lake in the evenings to light it all up. It seemed to freeze over almost every year. It must have been colder in those days. They always broke the ice at one end to let the fish breath. Denis Stolton's grandfather, Jack, used to claim that one winter he had skated from Ensfield Bridge down to Tonbridge but I've never seen the Medway frozen like that. I reckon the Medway used to flood more pre-war than now. One summer they drained the Hall Place lake to clean it out – it was quite a job. As kids, we used to go up what was called the 'Milk Walk' – it was almost a road between Hall Place and Home Farm – it was tarmaced – to collect milk and eggs: actually it was usually the skimmed milk left after they had separated off the cream to make butter. There was this machine where you turned a handle and we were allowed to have a go. I think that we got special treatment because Dad was at the stables. We were charged a penny for a half gallon can. Sometimes we walked up there: other times we went up with father in the horse and cart. He would take up boxes of vegetables and wooden baskets of eggs from Home Farm, go on to the Hall Place laundry on the corner by the Bid Brook to collect the clean laundry in a big hamper and take it all to Hildenborough Station for Lord Hollenden's London house. Then we'd collect the hamper of dirty washing which we'd take back, picking up the milk, eggs and butter for Hall Place on the way back."

Harry explains that the Hall Place's deer herd created one annual problem. "As you probably know, Lady Hollenden was very fond of animals. As children we would pick up conkers and she would pay us. Then in the cold weather, she'd go out and feed them to the deer. The trouble was that if you had a herd of more than a certain size, you had to have a special government licence, so each year some of them had to be killed off. So each year they would pack Lady Hollenden off to Devon. The gamekeepers did the shooting but after the first one had been killed, it all got a bit difficult. The deer knew what was happening and it took a good two weeks. Occasionally, you'd get one of the deer who'd jump straight over the six foot fence. Then, when Lady Hollenden came back, she'd be terribly upset. You know the little old building in the woods up behind the gamekeeper's cottage. It used to be a chapel and apparently Lady Hollenden used to go up there with flowers. Lord Hollenden used to be in London from Monday to Friday , so I think she didn't know what to do with herself."

The Hall Place pheasant shoots used to involve many people in the village. The men used to go out as beaters but Harry and Jack and a dozen or so others of their age were used as 'Stop Boys'. "You had to report to Home Farm or Charcott Corner or Hall Place or the gamekeeper's bungalow or the Blue Anchor (the pub down past the end of Lower Street) – whichever was nearest the wood where they were shooting – at eight in the morning. Then you got taken out and put in your place and you wouldn't see anyone until midday, when you'd be brought two sandwiches they'd had made at the Brickmakers Arms – one ham and one cheese – plus a stone bottle of ginger beer. Then you stayed on till about four o'clock when it was getting dark. You got one and sixpence a day at Leigh but if you went over to Redleaf for a Penshurst Estate shoot you got two shillings – but no lunch. You've got to remember that in those days, Lord Hollenden owned Penshurst Place's shooting. Fred Maddox was the head gamekeeper – he was quite a character – and they'd have shoots on the two estates alternate weeks. Sometimes the guns would all meet at Penshurst Place, go in for a quick drink and then go and shoot a few ducks on the lake before they started on the pheasants."

Jack has some other memories connected with the shooting. "When I left school at fourteen – it must have been 1935 – the first job that I got was cleaning out chickens – they started as day old chicks. It was in a shed behind one of the new houses up Penshurst Road. I found that I was meant to work seven days a week for ten shillings and when my mother found out, she said I shouldn't go back after one week of it. So when North, the Head Gamekeeper asked 'Lordie' if he could have a boy, North must have asked Dad. So I got a job helping the gamekeepers – although I wasn't a proper keeper of course. I had to be up at five or six in the morning and my first job was to clean out the dogs – there were about six of them. Then I'd go out and feed the birds. I'd have a bag of corn on my back and I'd go out whistling to bring the birds out. I'd start at the kennels, then up to the gamekeepers bungalow at the top of Home Farm track, go on through the woods and right to Black Hoath Wood, up by the old aerodrome. We did a lot of trimming back the drives to keep everything tidy and we'd go ferreting a whole day at a time – mainly in the winter. In the winter months, you made traps for the pheasants out of sticks in a pyramid shape and in the early spring you set them out in the corn where the pheasants would be going. When you'd caught them, they would all be put in a big cage thing in Home Wood up by the gamekeepers bungalow, so you could collect the eggs up easily. Then we used to go up to Tonbridge market and buy up broody hens, stuff them in a sack, four or five at a time and bring them back to sit on the pheasant eggs we'd got. We'd also go out into the woods and find all the other nests, collect the eggs to put under the hens too. After the chicks hatched out, we'd take up the coops with the broody hens and the chicks and put them into High Field – up the end of Birdcage Walk. The keepers used to stay up all night to keep the foxes away but I wasn't old enough. They'd put hurricane lamps on poles.

I learned how to make those rabbit snares out of thin brass wire – I'd sit in the shed making hundreds of them if the weather was bad – and as well as putting them out, I'd have to set up clamp traps and gin traps to catch stoats and weasels. You'd be doing that all the year round. I was working with North for twelve months".

Harry too has memories about game keeping. "My wife, Estelle – her father was a gamekeeper. I can remember him talking about all sorts of ways in which you kept the vermin down. If there were too many rabbits around, you had a drop net. It was about fifty foot long and two or three foot high. In the evening, several of you would go out and set it up. Then you'd startle the rabbits and they'd run into the net. You had to be pretty quick to go along and wring their necks or they'd get out".

Around 1936, when Jack was about fifteen, he was offered a job at Hall Place under Mr Pringle, the Head Gardener. "I was a gardener's boy for four years – I did all the jobs but it was mainly in the greenhouses. I'd get the coal out for the stoves which heated the hot water pipes and I cleaned everything. There were about four in the greenhouses, three in the kitchen gardens and four in the pleasure grounds. There were two hard courts for tennis but semi-hard you'd call them now. I'd go up on Sunday mornings with father to brush and roll the courts for the young ladies to play on in the afternoon.

"I left Hall Place gardens the day war broke out – I'd been offered a job gardening in St Albans for a Mr J. B. Joel. He was a racehorse owner and a jeweller – a Jew boy made good really. I even joined the LDV – that was the Local Defence Volunteers that came before the Home Guard. Mr Joel was very keen on it, being Jewish, with Hitler and all that. It was made up of the estate workers. We had broomsticks to practise rifle drills. I met my wife, Elsie, up there. She was a house maid. I got called up in 1941 when I was twenty."

The Lucas family had left the groom's cottage at Hall Place at the end of the nineteen twenties and had moved to No. 2 Forge Square "but father had never liked it there – it didn't really have a garden and father really wanted one. When Oak Cottage in the High Street, right by the allotments came free, father asked the Estate for it and got it. It's hard to picture the way that Hall Place and the Estate ran the village then. It had to be 'Yes Mr Houghton' or 'Yes Sir!' There was a long period when you had to say that. By this time, there was little work for a groom at Hall Place and father moved on to working in the gardens there."

Walking back down the High Street from Donkey Field and the Hall Place entrance opposite, there were two pubs opposite each other – the Brickmakers Arms and the Fleur de Lys. The landlord at the Brickmakers in the Thirties was Mr Thurston. "He had a bullfinch in a cage which he used to hang up outside the main door – in those days you got in by a door in the High Street, " says Jack. "There was an old grandfather clock in there – it didn't work – but when we were lads, we'd sneak in and take it to bits and leave the landlord to put it together again. They had a game called Dadlems. There were nine wooden pins about four inches high on a special table about three foot square with edges round three sides. You had lead weights a bit bigger than a five shilling piece to throw. It used to get taken to all the fetes and things.

The Brickmakers Arms and the Fleur de Lys, 1918.

Tommy Coates was the landlord in the Fleur. He was a character. He used to do a trick with an enamel bowl and a two shilling piece. He'd get the coin and spin it on the bottom. Then he'd slowly begin to circle the bowl until the coin was on its edge going round up by the top, like one of the fairground acts with motor bikes and the Wall of Death. He had another trick too. He'd get a match box and he'd put a bit of cotton wool in it and cut a hole out of the bottom somehow and, when someone came in, he'd get out the match box and say "I've had a bit of an accident this morning: cut part of my finger off but I've put it in this box". Then he'd open it up and his finger would be lying there. I don't know how he did it. My finger wouldn't bend round the way he had his. And he had another trick where he'd hand you change with one hand and then you'd find it wasn't in that hand at all. It all used to cause a bit of amusement – that was the idea I suppose. The other thing about the Fleur was that you could go round to the side door and you could get a drink at any time. The village copper used to get a bit hot on closing times but he used to pop round the side door like the others. The trouble was the two pubs were both owned by the one brewer – Fremlins – and they went and closed one of them down – The Brickmakers."

Moving down the High Street towards the Green you had the various village halls. "The Institute was there, with snooker and various other games. In the large village hall there was badminton and they had plays there. During the period between the wars, they also used the large village hall for shooting. After the last war, the Home Guard wanted to help the soldiers who were coming back and thought it would be a good idea to have a rifle club again. I remember because I was in charge of a couple of rifles which I stored at home and my mother didn't like it. Shooting stopped at 9.30 pm and then we went to the Brickmakers for a drink. I reckon if you took the panelling off at the road end you'd find where the bullets went" says Harry. "The Leigh British Legion was officially formed in 1946 in the bar of the Brickmakers Arms."

The Morley Hall – now called the Large Village Hall – as it was in 1907.

"Next door to the Bat was the shop which sold newspapers and a few groceries, like now but much smaller. It was run by Mr Sherman before the Parrets came and the Parrets were there till the end of the 1970's before Barbara and Alan Johnson took it over. We used to get a penny pocket money each week and directly we'd got it, we would rush off to get sweets, either at the Bat or Mr Sherman's – whichever we thought was the cheapest. You could get twenty aniseed balls and still get a halfpenny change or ten toffees. The first time I saw one of those huge old black and white five pound notes was in there. You didn't often see them". Next door to the Bat on the other side in the first house in the Square was Mr Whitehead the butcher. "He was a bit of a so and so you know. An old devil but he was a good bloke really. He'd be bawling his head off at his people working there – you could hear him from the Green – but he'd take his chaps out to the pub on Saturday night. Stan Wells, who took over the butchers shop on the Green years later after Whitehead had gone, used to work there. He used to lodge with us at No. 2 Forge Square and I remember him getting up at about 4am, to load up the van. They'd deliver out to Chiddingstone Hoath, Weald and Penshurst. He often finished at 8.00 or 9.00 at night. Of course, the meat was just out on big enamel trays and you didn't wrap up anything but no one seemed any the worse for it.

Outside one of the houses in the middle of the Square, there was this sign which was lit up by a gas light, saying 'FIRE'. The house was lived in by Ike Kneller and it was the meeting place for the Leigh Fire Brigade. There was a big hand bell outside. The Fire Brigade was very active in the 1920s and 1930s and during the War. Mr Russell was the Chief Fireman. Until the War, when they built the Fire Station in Lower Green, the head-quarters was in the Hall Place drive on the left. Once a week they had a practice with the 'manual' – that was what they called the pump with two long handles that you had to pull up and down like a see-saw with one man on each end. They went in for lots of competitions and won cups and things. It was all quite a performance to get the crew out. If you had a fire, you would rush down to the Square, and grab the bell. Then you went round ringing the bell to get the fire crew: or Charlie Ingram would stand on the corner by the School and ring it. And then they had to catch the horse. It wasn't very quick.

Eventually, they got a converted lorry and the old pump just rotted away. Bob Jones has got the box that they stored the tools in up at the allot-ments for his gardening things. Doctor Barclay – he lived at Applegarth – was the second in command by then but all the old names were still in the crew – Bert Stubbins, Fred Faircloth, Ike Kneller, Charlie Ingram, and both the Fred Fautlys. I remember them all going off to the big fire at Ramhurst on a Sunday evening before the war. I was on the way to the choir when Dr Barclay came rushing up the path from the lych-gate in his uniform to collect some of the crew who were bellringing."

Leigh Fire Brigade in Forge Square in 1926 when they had won First Prize in the National Tournament at Blackpool and three First Prizes in the SE Tournament.

The Leigh Post Office when it was at the east end of the Square around 1930.

At the far end of the Square, there was the Post Office in the front room looking out on the road. "Mrs Izzard ran it – Tom Izzard was a carpenter – and she used to stand outside on the pavement waiting for the children to come out of school, so that she could send one of the boys off with a telegram. It was the lads – not the girls – and we got sixpence. I once went up to the Blue Anchor pub.

When the Post Office left the Square, it went to the Old Bakery shop for a time before it moved to the Green sometime just before the war."

"Where the Clock Shop and the Hairdresser are now in Orchard House, there was the big grocer, run by Mr Burt who wore a black bowler hat. It was the top class one – where the gentry went. The children used to do odd jobs there too. Things had to be weighed out. The sugar used to be delivered in hundred weight sacks and we weighed out two pounds and put it in those blue paper bags. And the vinegar would come in big wooden barrels and the lads would roll them in. And we'd deliver the groceries on the big delivery bikes, and get sixpence each on Saturday morning – I remember riding out to Killicks Bank. Mr Burt had a man called Mr Eldridge working for him who smoked cigarettes. In the summer, he used a magnifying glass to light them – not matches. We all used to think it interesting as children." The shop became Adin Coates in the mid 1930s. Spencer and Margaret Coates, and their family were there until the mid 1970s.

The village school in the middle and end of the 1920's brings back many memories; but it is often things on the periphery of actual teaching which Jack and Harry mention most. "On the way to school the boys rolled their metal hoops I was telling you about. A few girls had them but they were wooden. We had to hang them up in the Iron Room on hooks. And we'd take them to the top of Church Hill and roll them down. They would go straight across the road – there were never any cars anyway. When the school played Penshurst at cricket, we'd walk there. They would have let you take your bike I suppose but nobody did. You all went together and it was used as a lesson about trees and plants. You wrote it up afterwards in school. You learnt a lot – it all fitted together. On Empire Day, the school used to go up to Hall Place and play games. You used to go walking on three flower pots – you had to move them along one at a time – and we got given Empire Day medals from Lady Hollenden – they were copper coloured with a red ribbon on them. I've still got two of them. I think I'm prouder of them than any war medals", says Jack.

"We all had to go hopping as kids, usually at Mr Goodwin's at Paul's Farm. The school holidays were extended to fit in with it. You had to pick the hops by hand then. Our parents and grandparents had done it as far back as they could remember. We'd get there before 8.00 in the morning – it was damn cold sometimes. When we were small, we had to fill up mother's umbrella with the hops before we could go off and play with the other children. Sometimes, when we were a bit older, we'd go off and climb up the main poles and slide down the wires with our caps between our legs.

After three or four goes, the caps would get a hole in them and we'd get a slap from our Mum. When you were older, everyone had their own basket and you'd collect the hops and then they'd put them in the big family 'bin'. One man held them open and Mr West, who was the sort of foreman, used to push them in. You got paid for how much you'd collected. It was four pence or six pence a bushel. Mr West had a way of pushing the hops down and the women used to shout at him 'don't push it down so hard'; unfortunately, he was deaf."

"It was funny – Mr West and his family lived up at one of Alders Cottages up above Ensfield Bridge, sort of on the west of the village. Then, there was North, the gamekeeper, on the north side of the village. And there was the East family in up by Betty Crawford's house at the end of Hollow Tree Drive, sort of on the east. We always used to say there should have been a Mr South."

Hopping was one of the many ways in which the village helped support the Kent and Sussex Hospital and their own health provision. "Mr Goodwin used to provide a full sized bin which anyone could help fill and the money from it went to the hospital." Mrs Wood, whose husband worked in Hall Place Gardens, ran a hospital fund for many people in the village, including the Lucas family. "You paid a penny a week and then you got free, priority, treatment at the Kent and Sussex Hospital when you needed it."

Hopping at Hutchings Field, Ramhurst Farm c1910

> *Mrs Barbara Bastable remembers a lady from the Compasses who used to come once a year and ask for her 'hate and sixpence' – eight shillings and six pence – for the same kind of hospital insurance fund – tuppence a week for the whole family. When her mother became ill in 1935, a private room was available at the Kent & Sussex Hospital because of the 'insurance' payments.*

At school, the changing seasons brought extra memories. "In the winter, the classroom was heated by a Tortoise stove. It was very efficient. You'd put a couple of shovels of coke in every so often. It was lined with fire bricks and when they had crumbled away, the outside of the stove used to get red hot. It had a little flap door at the bottom and you used to open it to make it blaze up. You had pokers and a special tool to get the clinker out of the bottom."

Harry looks back on Mr Gibbons, the Head, with respect. "You were taught a whole range of subjects; and Mr Gibbons must have been a very clever man to do it all. He taught geography and maths and english and history but he also taught singing – he was very keen on that – and woodwork and gardening. He was strict and he used the cane quite a lot – on your hands – and a thick leather strap on your backside; but I expect we deserved it. I don't remember thinking it was awful. Once his cane broke and I and another boy went to Tonbridge to buy him another one and left it on his desk. He never knew who bought it for him."

Boys and girls mostly had the same main lessons but had some different and extra activities. "Girls did sewing and needlework and boys did woodwork and gardening – it was vegetable gardening really. The Iron Room had proper carpentry tools – benches, handsaws, planes – and you had a choice of what you made". Jack remembers that "I wasn't all that good at it so I decided to make a clothes horse. It was my masterpiece – although really it wasn't very good. Mother used it for ages."

The school garden was up where Meadow Bank is now. Harry explains "It had about six plots, with two boys to a plot for vegetables, and a plot down the middle for fruit and apple and pear trees. In my time, I've grafted lots of roses and apples. I'd go on to the railway embankment and get some of the wild briars and graft on to the top of those. There were lots of Kentish Green apples in those days – everyone had them and I've grafted lots of them. My father, who was very keen on gardening, used to say that they'd fallen off the back of a cart. They are marvellous apples – they keep through to the longest day next year. The only one I know about now was planted by Charlie Ingram in your Oak Cottage back garden. I don't know what's happened to all the rest."

Leigh School, 1931. The headmaster, Walter Gibbons, with the older boys who have their gardening tools.

When the boys came back from the school gardens, they went past the slaughter house on the corner of the green between where the recycling bins and the public convenience are now and saw another part of every day life. "They always used to slaughter on Monday afternoons. Fred Fautly was the head slaughterer. Originally, they used to pole axe them but then they had one of those humane killers. The difficulty came when they had to kill the bullock. He'd be brought down in a cart, not driven down the road like the others. Then they used to put a rope round his neck and they'd all have to pull him in. All the butchers from round about used to come to get their meat, although Hall Place had its own slaughter house up at Home Farm."

The Green was the focus of much activity, whether it was climbing up inside the Oak Tree by Oak Cottage or whether it was soccer, cricket, or just playing with the other boys. Jack remembers that, early in the century, his father had to improvise his cricket on the brick-field because he was not the right class of person to be playing cricket on the Green. Harry's own cricketing career was also unfortunate, if for different reasons. "I joined the Cricket Club but I could never get a game because the team was all Faircloths and Brookers."

In those days it was only the middle bit of the Green that was mowed. "The grass at both ends was kept rough" says Jack "and an old man from Hall Place used to come and scythe it once a year. My grandfather used to say that Oak Cottage had grazing rights for geese and goats – I think it was geese and goats not anything else and John Chapman at Moat Farm says he has got that in his deeds. After the First World War, the unemployed laid a gravel path across the Green from the corner by the school to the end of Greenview Avenue. I can't remember when they grassed it over but you can still see where it went. They also dug the ditch and the raised path outside the old and new Vicarages. I used to play soccer on the Green. There were baths in the Institute and many of the team would rush off after the match to get there first. Most of the houses didn't have baths then."

> *Soon after the Second World War, a new member of the cricket club who came from Lancashire was warned – 'They won't talk to you if you haven't got a watch....'*

"We used to play games on the Green that no-one's heard of now" says Harry. "There was 'Jack, Jack, Strike a Light' – I used to have to get matches from my Mum for that. It was when it was dark and all the boys would be by the school. One boy would go off across the Green. Then we'd shout out, 'Jack Jack Strike a Light' and when he did we'd have to go and find him. Of course by that time he'd moved.... Then there was 'Kit Can' – I think it must have been 'Kick the Can' originally – where you got a cocoa tin and someone kicked it into the grass. Whilst one person looked for it, the rest went off and hid in the grass. Then there was a game where you'd tie a can on to your bike and stuff a rag in it and ride round with it behind you. Quoits were not allowed on the Green – Lord Hollenden wouldn't allow it – but they were played up at the Blue Anchor. There was also a pitch at the bottom of Lower Green on the right too. The quoits were big iron rings about a foot across which you threw to the far end and tried to get over a wooden peg. A lot of people used to play at the weekends. Once a year the Hunt used to meet on the Green. It was a big occasion for us boys. After they set off, we used to listen to where the noise was coming from and then run in that direction. We usually got along as fast as the horses.

Off the Green towards the railway arch and the Medway, it was just a track to Mr Warder's small-holding but in the 1930's he started building the houses up Greenview Avenue. He had fingers in all sorts of things – he had a hairdressers somewhere and the dairy I was telling you about. Anyway, he built the houses and he said that he'd build a road when he'd finished. But he didn't. There was a big row about it. Alf Olerenshaw used to live up there. He had a snob – a shoe repair shop – by Tonbridge station and if you took your shoes up to his house, you'd see him walking to the station with a kit bag over his shoulder with the shoes in and then you'd get them back that evening.

On the other side of the Green there was the Forge with old Charlie Hayter and later the Bullinghams. Charlie Hayter was mainly horse shoes and repairing farm machinery and I remember him sometimes putting the metal tyre on cart wheels. They used to light a fire on a big iron tray with faggots all round to heat the iron tyre up. When they thought it was hot enough, they'd sweep all the faggots off and put the wooden wheel on the tray over the round stone with the hole in it – it's still there – and they'd hammer the hot tyre on. After Charlie Hayter retired, the Bullinghams took over and moved on more to wrought iron things.

When we lived at No. 2 Forge Square, there was Old Ginn – he was Eddie Ginn, the village policeman – next door. He had a big area, down to Moorden and Lower Street and he used to go round on foot or sometimes on his bike. He'd leave his bike where the phone box is now but you never used to know quite where he was. He used to grow his own tobacco on the allotment, then hang it up by the Forge to dry properly. Then he'd make it into big cigars. He couldn't stand gypsies. They used to camp down by the river in the summer and he used to get up in the middle of the night to move them on. Percy Seal – who used to be the landlord of The Brickmakers – lived up at Church Hill House, on the left, before it became a doctors surgery after the war. Percy used to say the house had been a butchers at one stage and you could still see the marks on the floor where they had salted down the meat to preserve it."

Harry remembers the other people on the north side of the Green. "You had Mr Russell in South View, then up the hill where Johnny Burr, the Hall Place Agent lived. He was a funny old boy. The house used to be the old Porcupine Inn and my grandfather used to talk about when they made the Sevenoaks railway tunnel in about 1870, I think it was. It was all built by pick and shovel of course – what a job it must have been – and to keep them working, they gave them free beer. They started from the Sevenoaks end and got the beer from there. But when they got to the Weald end it was too far to bring it from Sevenoaks, so the Porcupine got the contract to deliver the beer from this end. I think the publican's name must have been Martin because there's a stone jar in the village with his name on from around that time. But we've arrived at a position now where no one will remember anything like this. The generation coming now won't care.

Next door, at Park House, there was Dr Fraser. He had one of the first cars in the village, but I remember before that Mr Hobbs, from Leigh Park Farm – that's Barbara Bastable's father – used to drive the Doctor round in a horse and trap. There was a gas light on the little arched gateway you'd go through to get to the surgery and Jack Stolton had the job to go and light it when it got dark. It was Mr Walker's job before him."

Jack remembers one occasion when he was sent to the surgery to collect a bottle of medicine. "Unfortunately, when I was running down the hill, I fell down, the bottle broke and I cut my hand. So I had to go back to the doctor again. After Dr Fraser left around the early 1940's, Dr E A Barclay took over. He lived at Applegarth. He was the Chief of the Fire Brigade after Mr Russell and I remember he had a silver fire helmet when all the ordinary firemen had brass ones. Dr Davidson was the doctor after the war in the same surgery as now, by the Fleur. We really did have everything in the village."

"I've remembered one more thing" says Harry "The postman, Arthur Burchett: if you had a clock that was broken, you'd say to Mr Burchett when he came round with the post 'Can you mend it?' and he'd grunt and put it in his postbag. He was very good at it."

"We moved from Oak Cottage in the High Street to East Lodge, sort of next door to the Porcupine in about 1938," Jack continues. "It was a palace after living in the High Street, although looking back on it now, it was tiny with all the angles in some of the rooms. Three rooms were square but the ones that face the Green were wedge shaped. 'Lordie' – Lord Hollenden – put a flat roof on the open courtyard at the back which helped a lot but it was terrible really."

Harry Lucas outside East Lodge where he and the family were living. 1959.

East Lodge where the Lucas family lived.

By this time Harry was commuting up to Morleys in London. "Before that, I'd been at Duke and Son at Chiddingstone Causeway – although it was always called Dukes of Penshurst. I'd been there since 1932 when I left school at fourteen. They'd started making tennis rackets, and squash and badminton rackets as well as the cricket things and lots of us school leavers went there – Archie Denton, the Halletts, the Jenners and some of the girls too, Elsie Wells, Jane Whitebread, Glad Jones (Mrs Fred Warner she became). There were different departments – the sanding department, the bending department and so on. It was going well until the war started but I thought I ought to leave, so I got the job in London. The trains seemed a lot more efficient than they are now – and cheaper. I've still got my season ticket from 1947 when I went back to work in London after being in the army. It cost £3-3-6d a month from Hildenborough up to London. I used to cycle up to Hildenborough station and leave the bike there and then my father would walk up and collect it and use it during the day."

"The very tall poplars that used to grow along the lane to Church outside the Porcupine and East Lodge were famous in their day. Once, when one of the poplars became rotten and had to come down, they moved the lych-gate and hired a traction engine which they put on the main road. Then someone climbed up the tree with ropes and the traction engine pulled the tree down."

Lych-gate, poplars and Porcupine House – then The Gate House – in 1947.

"The Church was in the middle of village life for us boys." says Jack. "Although you all went for walks on Sunday afternoon – to the pubs often, the Blue Anchor, the Bridge Tavern at the bottom of Rogues Hill in Penshurst, down the straight mile to the Plough at the Powder Mills or the Oak at Lower Haysden – the mornings were very much church for us. Mother and Father weren't really religious – we used to think that it was just to get us out of the way – but Harry and me were both in the choir under Harry Hitchcock – we liked singing. And you got paid too. You got 2/6d a quarter if you'd got good attendance and 2/- if it wasn't such a good attendance. We used to sing in the chapel first at 10.00 o'clock, then you were allowed out ten minutes early if you were in the Church choir and we'd run up to the Church vestry and get our surplices on quickly – they were black with a white thing over – for the 11.00 o'clock service. And quite often there was the 6.30 – 7.30 service in the evening. And there was choir practice for an hour on Monday and Thursday evenings. We were allowed to toll the bell sometimes – there was a rope by the font. It was right up our street as young-sters to do twenty or thirty dongs and then ride up on the rope. I remember them hanging the last bell too, in the mid Thirties, I think it must have been. 'Lordie' paid for it and he was allowed to be the first one to ring it."

Harry remembers that the big day for the choir was the annual outing. "Harry Hitchcock was a cricket man and it was no coincidence that we always went to Hastings in the Cricket Week. We left at 6.30 in the morning by train and Mr Phipps at the bakery used to give us a big wicker hamper of things to eat. It was about two foot by three foot square and two foot high. When we got there, us boys went off and played on the beach or we spent our money – our parents gave us 2/6d – on the penny machines. Mr Hitchcock went off to watch the cricket and came back at lunch time. He always gave each boy a silver threepenny bit."

"The other big occasion for the choir was Christmas Carol singing. The first port of call was Hall Place. They had a water powered organ. We'd sing in a big oblong room and, when we'd finished, we'd all sit on big benches in front of a fire and drink lemonade. Then we'd walk to Great Barnetts – that was the Reverend Walton – then up to the other end of the village to the Bickersteths at Pauls Hill House. After that we'd go to Chilling House – the Limes as it was then – then to Johnny Burr who gave us toffees. When we went to the Post Office – Mr Brooks let us have an orange each out of a barrel. Then we'd go the Williams at Upper Kennards and finish up at about 10 o'clock at Goodwin's farm – Pauls Hill Farm – where we were allowed a sack of apples."

"I can tell you a connection between why I left the choir and my new bike" continues Harry. "When we were kids, we all had these old bikes – almost no one had a new one. We got a frame here, an old wheel there and we put them together ourselves. When I started at fourteen years old at Dukes, I had this very old bike and I said to myself – I'd like a new bike. So I told my mother and she laughed and said she couldn't pay for it and so I'd have to save. I went to see Mr Bennett at the cycle shop and he said it would be £3-19-6d but £4-9-6d if it had a three speed gear. I wanted a three speed so I had to get £4-19-6d. And that's why I left the choir. I'd heard that they wanted someone to pump the church organ and you got four pound a year for that. So I left the choir, pumped the organ and I got my bike. I've still got it."

Jack took over as organ pumper when Harry left the job. "You were nearer the things that happened in those days – nearer the people. You sort of saw everything. I remember when there was a suicide in the river. Mr Faircloth went down to the Powder Mills with a hand cart – and he pulled the body back to the village with a sheet or a tarpaulin or something over it to cover it. When he stopped outside Sherman's shop, we boys – we must have been ten years old – we all nudged each other and said 'there's a body under there.' When people died, the body was put in the front room and left there for several days 'til the funeral. People used to come and pay their respects and the undertaker would come and measure the body so he could go off and make the coffin – made to measure, so-to-speak. Ray Faircloth did it usually but Bert Taylor, down Kiln Lane, did it occasionally."

"When I was very young there was an old man, Jessie Ford, next door in Budgeon Cottage where my grandfather had lived. He was an invalid and he used to sit on a plank outside. He was very small. When he died, there wasn't enough space in the house, so they put him in the wash house out at the back – on the sink. You didn't have chapels of rest in those days."

Harry remembers that there was a bier at the back of the church by the font. "It was covered with a tarpaulin, with four wheels; and the family pulled it by hand along the street, with the mourners walking along behind. I remember once when a farmer died, they brought him along with a horse and cart. But you've got to remember that people were closer to death and things then. The First World War had had a massive effect on the village. Father wouldn't talk about it. He was in one of the Kentish regiments. He got trench fever. Lots of families had lost sons and husbands – you can see all the names on the war memorial. The Bourner family on Forge Square lost three sons. They were devastated.

I remember old Charlie Hayter and watching him in the forge with his old leather apron thing. When anyone died, he'd go up to the church – I went with him once – and he'd ring long, slow rings on a single bell. At the end there was a pause and he'd ring once if a man had died and twice for a woman. Three times was for a child."

The War Memorial

"THEY SHALL NOT GROW OLD, AS WE THAT ARE LEFT GROW OLD:

AGE SHALL NOT WEARY THEM, NOR THE YEARS CONDEMN.

AT THE GOING DOWN OF THE SUN AND IN THE MORNING

WE WILL REMEMBER THEM."

Service of Dedication of the War Memorial – Sunday 12 November 1920. Note the famous hollow oak tree on the far side of the Green which is entirely lop-sided, and Oak Cottage which had four chimneys instead of the present one.

IN MEMORY OF THE BRAVE MEN OF THIS PARISH
WHO GAVE THEIR LIVES IN THE GREAT WAR 1914 – 1919

R. West Kent Regiment	FAIRCLOTH F	JENMAN B
	KILLICK F	MITCHELL G
	SMITH W	TOWNER A
	UPTON H	WOODGATE R
Kings U V P L Regiment	BRAMLETT W	
Essex Regiment	BROOKER J	
London Regiment	BROOKER R	
Suffolk Regiment	HEALY F	
R.F.A.	BOURNER J	BOURNER F
R.G.A.	BOURNER C	YOUNG M
R.A.S.C.	DAVIS J	
Royal Navy	BATCHELOR H	EVEREST S
	UPTON W	
Middlesex Regiment	EVEREST J	HORSEY H
	PARKER F	
Q.R.W. Surrey Regiment	GARNER F	READY V
K.S.L.I.	DAVIES J	
K.R.R. Corps	POCOCK S	
27th Light Cavalry	RUSSELL L	
Dragoon Guards	ROBINSON G	
M.G.C.	BATCHELOR S	TAYLOR J

LIVE YE FOR ENGLAND
AS WE FOR ENGLAND DIED

ALSO IN PROUD MEMORY OF OUR MEN
WHO DIED IN THE 1939-1945 WAR

Hampshire Regiment	HORAN S J L	
Suffolk Regiment	FRASER E G	
Q.O.R.W.K. Regiment	CURTIS J A T	
R.A.F.	CHANDLER L A	PATCHING P W
	SCHOFIELD A H M	
R.A.O.C.	BICKERSTETH E R	HUMPHREY L W C
R.A.	NIXON C G H	NIXON G
R.N.	FLOWER A L	

Bill Crocker and the Leigh United Charities

In 1901, with the agreement of the Charity Commissioners, eight chari-
ties connected with Leigh were amalgamated. The earliest of the eight
had been a bequest by John Pelrett in 1602 and the most recent a bequest
in 1713 from George Children.

The current Clerk to the Trustees is Bill Crocker who has held the post for
ten years. His predecessor, Fred Whibley, held the post from the mid 1940's for
over forty years. Together with the first Clerk, Mr Geoffrey Boby, these three
men have spanned virtually the whole twentieth century helping the Trustees
to help the poor in the village.

Bill Crocker shares a feeling with many of those who have lived in the
village for thirty, forty or even fifty years. "If you were not actually born in
the village, in some ways you're a foreigner. I've only lived in Leigh since
1944. In 1940 my father had been appointed gardener and caretaker to the
country house of the late Lord Hollenden at Matthews Point near
Dartmouth. But because of the run up to D-day, all the people from the
coast area around there were evacuated and my parents, because they were
employees of Lord Hollenden, came to Leigh. They lived in the Bothy at
Hall Place. I was in the Royal Navy but when I returned after three and a
half years in the Middle East in 1944, I had my first sight of Leigh. My
mother explained it was pronounced 'Lie', although the West Country
pronunciation would have been 'Lee'. That was when I met my future wife,
Bertha Hitchcock as she was then, a very attractive Land Girl working at
Hall Place. We were married in 1945 – it was the day Labour won the
Election.

Bertha was born in the village in 1921. Her father was Harry Hitchcock
who was a ball stitcher. Geoff Hitchcock was her brother and there was
Fanny and Steve too. They lived in one half of Budgen Cottage in Lower
Green. They must have been head to toe. When she was young, Bertha was
nicknamed `Sis'. I think it was because she was Geoff's little sister. Archie

Denton always used to call her that – even fifty years later. They all went to the village school. Geoff won a place at Judd and Bertha went to the Convent in Tonbridge – although she wasn't Catholic. Then Bertha went to Constable's College in Pembury Road by the roundabout to learn typing and things. She worked at Wisdens in the Causeway and during the war she got herself into the Land Army at Hall Place, so she could look after her mother – her father, Harry, had died in 1941. After the war she was school secretary for 18 years – with the headmaster who used to throw chalk – and some said he used to rap the children across the knuckles with a ruler.

I remember Bertha talking about the concerts they had in the Large Village Hall between the wars. Her father, Harry Hitchcock – he was an A.I.G.C.M. – was the organist and choirmaster and he used to organise the concerts. He was very good and very enthusiastic. I've got two of the programmes, one from 1926 and one from 1927. They had the Church Choir and an orchestra and outside guest soloists – John Thorne, Mrs Parkinson, Agnes Nicholls CBE, who seems to have been Lady Harty, the wife of Hamilton Harty the composer I suppose, and the Hon. Leila Willoughby. And Celia Macdonald of The Isles OBE is down as playing the piano.

On the Green c1931. Grace Grevatt, Eileen Gibbons, Violet Walker, Daisy Kemp, Muriel Jenner, Violet Chandler, Betty Chandler, Bertha Hitchcock.

The Hitchcock children were all in the church choir – naturally – and I remember Bertha describing how all the choir boys (girls were not normally accepted) had to come to the house in the Square where the Hitchcocks had moved to collect their pay. Bertha used to sit in the corner and count up her pennies. I remember both Geoff and Bertha talking about the scouts and girl guides being taken on camp down to the coast when they were young. The scout master and one of the mistresses used to take them. There was a bit of a joke about what they might get up to together. When Bertha was little, she remembered going up to listen to her father practising on the organ on Saturdays and taking some of the crusts from the 'Sunday Bread' which was left in the porch. There's a good deal about this 'Sunday Bread' and the earlier Quarterly Bread in the Charities Minutes.

I've been Clerk to the Leigh Charities since 1989 but it's much less of a job than it must have been in the first half of the century. I've got the main Minute Book plus all the old rent books and they give a good picture of the village before the Second World War."

In 1901, it was agreed that the first Trustees of the new Leigh United Charities should include the Vicar of Leigh, two representatives of the Leigh Parish Council and, because some of the bequests related both to Leigh and parts of Hildenborough, which had originally been in Leigh when it was a larger parish, a representative of the Hildenborough Parish Council – for the next forty years the Hildenborough Vicar.

However, the two men who were to dominate the running of the Charities in their own different ways for the first forty years were the village doctor, Frank Fraser, and the village headmaster, Geoffrey Boby. What follows uses almost exactly the wording from Mr Boby's carefully written Minute Books. The names of recipients have been excluded at the request of the present Trustees; and a few words and tenses changed to make the meaning clearer.

Doctor Fraser was born in 1857 – so he was forty-four at the time of the first meeting. He was a Scot. He lived with his wife, Constance, in Park House. He was greatly respected and many residents of Leigh over sixty have said "He brought me into the world". His panel patients used to reach the surgery via the side door with the brick arch on the road between Park House and Porcupine House, queuing on the long path outside the house, although almost certainly paying patients were ushered into the sitting room via the front door. The Parish Council chose Dr Fraser, who was at the time its

Deputy Chairman, as a Trustee to the United Charities because they said that he knew every household.

Leonard Martin was the second representative of the Leigh Parish Council on the Trustees. He was fifty-five when this Committee first met. He lived in Leigh and he died in 1917 aged seventy-one and is buried, along with a good number of other Martins, in the churchyard.

In 1901 the Reverend Hugh Collum was Vicar of Leigh. He had become Vicar in 1876, and continued until 1908, thirty-two years, although this was not an unusual length of time to be an Incumbent in those days. His predecessor had served for forty-six years: and the Speldhurst Vicar in the same period had finished his time in office in 1889 after fifty-nine years. Hugh Collum was also highly regarded in the village and there is a memorial plaque to him in the North Transept of the church.

The Reverend James Stone was the Vicar of Hildenborough at the time of the first Trustees' meeting and he served on the committee for fifteen years until his death.

Geoffrey Boby was approaching fifty in 1901. He was the Headmaster at Leigh Church School – as it was then – and was Headmaster until 1919. He was elected as Clerk at the first meeting of the Trustees. He lived in the School House at the time of this first meeting and after his retirement moved to Garden Cottages.

Dr Fraser was unanimously elected as Chairman of the first meeting on 12 October 1901 – and at a large majority of the subsequent meetings. Dr Fraser opened the meeting and, after thanking the group for electing him Chairman, proposed a sub-committee to see to the repairs of their thirteen properties: he rightly assessed that the properties would take up a good deal of the Trustees' time. The meeting also confirmed the arrangements for fifteen people on the Sunday Bread list and fifty people on the Quarterly Bread list, with the distribution only at 4.00 – 4.30 on Sundays. Mr Stone wished it to be confirmed that Hildenborough parishioners who were in great necessity and to whom he gave 'tickets', could present them to tradesmen in Hildenborough.

This first meeting indicated clearly the three major topics that were to be the staple diet for the Trustees for the forthcoming years. First, there were the Charity's cottages and who should live in them. There were four cottages towards the bottom of Lower Green, three on the Green beside South View and two blocks of three cottages each in 'the West End' of the village, as they called it then – where Saxby Wood is now. These cottages were not just always falling into disrepair but were often in danger of lagging behind what was thought of as an acceptable standard as the times changed. Secondly, there was the weekly and quarterly bread and the quarterly and annual gifts in money. Families could apply to be put on the various lists and they could then collect their bread – rather publicly – from the church porch; or collect their money from the School. In 1901, ninety-nine people were on the Annual Gift list at a cost of £43.8.6d, probably the equivalent in today's money of £20 or £25 per person. Additionally, there were seven ladies – all widows – who received five shillings a quarter, about £100 a year each in today's money. And thirdly, villagers could apply for 'tickets' or 'tokens' which could be exchanged for food at the local shops.

It is clear from the Minutes that the Trustees knew a good deal about the circumstances of the individual villagers. And in an era when there were no state and no private pensions (except those given out by Samuel Morley to some of his former employees), help from the United Charities was often important to many of the poorer people in the village. In 1901 income from bequests and stocks was £122.15.8d but there was also the rent from the Charities' cottages.

The implementation of all the Charities' work was left largely to the Clerk, Mr Boby. At the end of the second meeting, after Mr Boby had been reminded about some repairs, he added one of the few comments that actually refer to himself in the Minutes stating stating that the salary he had been offered "was not sufficient considering the large amount of work that he had to do."

The next meeting was not for a year. The question of Mr Boby's salary was the first agenda item and Mr Boby allowed an increase to bring his annual payment up to ten guineas. As a comparison, a five day, all-inclusive holiday in Brighton cost one pound, seventeen shillings at this time.

Mr Collum took the Chair when the meeting was held at the Vicarage on 15 October 1903 and mentioned that Mr Martin wanted to discuss the Quarterly Bread List: Mr Martin felt that it ought to be revised more often than it was – certainly every three or four years: there were people on the list whose circumstances had much changed and who did not even pick up their loaves. He asked that the Clerk put up some notices stating that the list would be reviewed at the next meeting and asking anyone who thought they were eligible to write to the Clerk.

As a result of Mr Martin's suggestion, the Bread List and the Annual gifts were much changed at the meeting two months later. There was an additional matter which – sadly – the Minutes do not fully explain.

However, it is clear that the Trustees knew only too well what the problem was. Dr Fraser said that he had received a letter from one of their tenants complaining about the use of the Nash House. He proposed that the tenant was offered each alternate Tuesday for her washing. This was agreed but it is not clear where the Nash House was, let alone what the difficulty was.

The following year's meeting continued to discuss the usual matters but reviewed a letter of complaint from a Mr Gosling against the baker, Mr Friend, from the bakery in Lower Green. The complaint was not accepted and Mr Friend was allowed to continue to supply the Sunday Bread.

At the next meeting in mid 1905, the Trustees noted with displeasure that some recipients of the Sunday Bread .... "...are in the habit of paying a child to fetch it instead of collecting it themselves" and the Rev Collum suggested that "we ask the Clerk to write to the offenders pointing out that it is the wish of the Trustees that all should fetch the bread themselves unless prevented by sickness or infirmity." Mr Boby then asked about "the tenancy of the cottage lately occupied by Widow H. Her son, Mr H, has made an application for it." The meeting agreed "that it should be allowed on condition that he shall not be allowed to take any lodger and that although the tenancy shall be up to January, he might be called upon to give it up then, should it be required for any widow or poor man with a large family. The rent will be two and sixpence a week."

It was at this meeting that signs of the twentieth century first began to appear. Leigh under the patronage of Samuel Morley had been one of the earlier villages to have a piped water supply rather than the many wells. But Dr Fraser reported – "at length", as Mr Boby noted – about what was happening with respect to the Tonbridge Water Company. The Tonbridge Water Company was intending to supply water to the village: however, the Company was requiring a guarantee from the village that ten percent of households would take their supply.

At the meeting in March 1906, the three questions all reappeared – the supply of water; Mr H. and his agreement not to take a lodger; and the quarterly loaves supplier. Mr Gosling proposed in a second letter that, as he was both a ratepayer and a baker, he should be allowed to supply at least some of the quarterly bread. This was agreed – indeed he was allowed to supply all of it. Mr H. was summoned to the Committee in person and, in what was clearly a stern exchange, asked why he now appeared to have a lodger – a gentleman incidentally. The case was considered and fully discussed and eventually on the proposition of The Reverend James Stone:

"The Trustees are willing that the lodger remains – on condition that the home be conducted as a home should be ..."

As the Trustees were discussing the question of the water supply, the Minutes note that Dr Fraser consulted with a Mr Lees by telephone – a relatively new household item, certainly in a village – about the probable annual water rate. He was told it would be two pence per cottage per week. Mr Stone then proposed that "the Trustees should lay on water to the Lower Green Cottages and the three near the church and that the water rate be defrayed by the Trustees, with the tenants of each cottage paying an additional three pence a week as rent."

To put money, costs and wages into perspective, the two shillings and sixpence being paid for a United Charities cottage was inexpensive. In a country village like Leigh, lodging of a single upstairs room with one evening meal each day and the use of a maid to tidy the room and lay the fire would normally cost four shillings a week. Butter, relatively expensive, cost one shilling and tuppence a pound. Eggs were a shilling a dozen. Five Woodbines were a penny; and a pub lunch – meat with two veg and a fruit tart – cost ninepence. On average, the cost of staples such as food can be multiplied by fifty to arrive at today's prices. However, wages have increased by considerably more in the last century – a senior but young Post Office clerk obtained a pound a week and a labourer eighteen shillings in 1900. Today's wages are around a hundred times more.

After the retirement of Mr Collum in 1906, the new Vicar of Leigh was the Revd Octavius Walton. He was low church and had been the Anglican minister in Jerusalem under the Turks. Sadly, he left no written record of his experiences in the Holy Land. Whilst he was only Vicar until 1918, he returned to the village in 1927 to live at Great Barnetts in his retirement. He died in 1933. His unmarried daughter, Daisy, who built Pippins on the Green after the war, was – as we have seen – much concerned with village activities until her death in 1967.

Over the next three years, the repairs to the cottages and which tenants to choose, the supply of stoves to the cottages and whether existing 'ticket' scheme and the Quarterly Bread could be made more useful to poor villagers continued to be discussed. The original terms of the bequests were consulted and the Charity Commissioners were written to by the Clerk. At one meeting there is an unspecified direction to the Clerk, who was asked by Dr Fraser to "talk to two of the applicants, respecting their misconduct." It was probably only rent arrears because in April 1910, there are full details of two defaulters and Mr Boby's notes – "It is resolved that a month's notice to quit their cottages be given to both of them, to take effect unless half the amount due be paid by 9th May and the other half by 23rd May." However, six months later Dr Fraser noted that one was – "once again in arrears" and the Clerk was asked to give him a month's notice unless the full amount due was paid.

A new subject came up on 26th September 1911. Reverend Walton reported that he had had a letter from Mr Samuel Hope-Morley which stated that Mr Hope-Morley would like to have the three cottages and land near the churchyard and was offering in exchange the two cottages on Leigh Green by the Iron Room together with an undertaking to build another cottage near there. It was agreed that he replied to express the Committee's readiness to take the proposal "into our most favourable consideration".

Church Parade down the High Street, outside the Bat and Ball, June 1907.

To clarify which cottages on the Green they were. The three to be destroyed were built about 1865 by the Vestry to replace the small, thatched picturesque cottages situated in what is now the garden of South View below the Lytchgate. The two to be given to the Trustees were Number 1 and 2 Cherry Tree Cottages on the corner of The Green Lane. The extra, new house became Chestnuts.

The Green and Powder Mill Lane 1906. Note that there is no War Memorial; also the long grass and the smallness of the road, as well as the tent, probably for a special cricket match. The United Charities cottages are on the right between Southview and the Lych-gate, which were demolished by Mr Hope Morley in 1911.

It was at this meeting that Alfred Paget Hedges replaces Leonard Martin as the Leigh Parish Council representative. Mr Hedges was a JP and the recently defeated Liberal MP for Tonbridge after only one term in the Commons. He lived in Upper Kennards with his wife Florence. He came from the Hedges and Butler cigarette family and was the firm's Managing Director. In around 1908 Mr Hedges and Dr Fraser had formed a company that built Garden Cottages. (It was said that Mrs Heath, then the next door neighbour at The Woods, regarded the Hedges as 'Trade' and would not let her daughters converse with the Hedges family over the back of the Heath's designated pew in the church.)

At the meeting on 18th October 1912, Dr Fraser had had more time to consider the suggestion from Samuel Hope Morley – by now the newly ennobled Lord Hollenden. He suggested that the Vicar should see Lord Hollenden and discuss the state of the road leading to the cottages; the water supply; and "whether the smell from the slaughter house by the cottages could be abated."

The Vicar duly consulted Lord Hollenden and, a week later, he reported back on the interview he had had. Lord Hollenden had agreed that he would bring what pressure he could on his tenant who ran the slaughter house and had also suggested that the Medical Officer of Health should see that the nuisance was abated: with regard to the road, his Lordship had said that he was prepared to make a good road right round the Green on condition that the Rural District Council then took it over and kept it in repair ever after; or, failing that, he would make a proper road just to the cottages. The water difficulty was next cleared up with Lord Hollenden saying that if the Trustees laid the water on to those cottages, he would be prepared to help in the expenses.

The legal formalities were progressed with the help of Messrs Biddle and Co, Lord Hollenden's solicitors. The plan for the new cottage was inspected and, after many formalities, Chestnuts was completed – although it was found to be very damp within a year – and regularly for a good number of years afterwards – not least because there had been a large pond in that corner of the village until around 1875.

The Cottage – now called 'The Woods' and owned by the Biddle family – formerly the home of the Heath family.

On the retirement of Mr Hedges as a Trustee at the end of 1915, one of the village's best known figures became a Trustee. Like Dr Fraser he was a Scot. Like Dr Fraser, he had been and would continue to be a power in the village for another twenty-five years. He was John or Johnny Burr, the Hall Place Agent and confidant to the first Lord Hollenden. He lived in what is now called Porcupine House but which was then called The Gate House. At the time of this meeting, he was also Chairman of the Parish Council and there are just very slight hints in Mr Boby's Minutes that the three roles that John Burr held could occasionally clash. Perhaps it was a coincidence but Mr Burr had only one four year term as a Trustee. However, he clearly worked hard during his term and on a good number of occasions was asked to inspect the Trustees' cottages.

It was in May 1916 that the first signs of the War became apparent in the Minutes. Extra money was given to two people "for the duration of the War" – presumably their main breadwinner was away. However, there was another matter, almost certainly raised because of an isolated but tragic event on March 22nd 1916. On that Sunday, three months before the Trustees met, the Germans sent over four seaplanes which bombed Dover, Deal and Ramsgate, killing fourteen people, including four children on their way back from Sunday School, and destroying a number of houses. There was much national debate about compensation for property damage which the Government refused to give. It seems almost certain that it was this raid that prompted Dr Fraser to raise the question of insurance, proposing that the existing amount was increased and that the cottages were insured against aircraft. The total value for the thirteen dwellings for this purpose was £2,300. He also raised a different subject. There had been some cases of consumption – Mrs G. and her daughter at the Powder Mills – and he understood that five pounds was required in order that they might enter a Sanatorium. The Vicar suggested that Dr Fraser should see a Colonel Curtis, with a view of getting some part of the money from the Powder Mill firm, but agreeing to give up to three pounds from the Charity Fund.

The 3rd November 1916 saw the start of a traumatic incident for the United Charities – or rather, that is how it must have seemed at the time. A special meeting was called by the Revd Octavius Walton. He started by assuming all the Trustees had heard "the rumours concerning the conduct of one of the Trustees' cottages [sic], now occupied by Mrs X whose husband is in France in the service of his country. The allegations are, that she had constantly aided Miss Y to elope with a certain wounded soldier and that she had constantly had soldiers drinking in her house." After discussion, Dr Fraser, the Chairman for the meeting, concluded they were all agreed that something must be done; that the husband should be communicated with. He read a draft for the Trustees to consider:

"Dear X. At a Meeting of the Trustees of the Leigh United Charities today, 3rd November 1916, some very serious suspicions were raised on the conduct of your house [sic]. It is not our wish to act in your absence so we must ask you to be present at our adjourned meeting for the purpose on November 17th next. Your Commanding Officer will most probably grant you the necessary leave on your making the request, especially on showing him this registered letter. Please write or better still, telegraph on receipt of this.
     Yours faithfully etc."

There must be some puzzlement today that a group of well-educated men should expect a Commanding Officer to allow a man leave his regiment at the Front almost instantly. The Battle of the Somme was still going on, with extremely heavy casualties for Kentish as well as other units. And the people in the area certainly knew about the battle. During this summer a small crowd had gathered each morning at the fork at the top of Sevenoaks High Street to hear Reveille being sounded. On 1st July, the group was surprised to hear what they thought was thunder on a clear day. It was, in fact, the noise of the first Somme barrage when over a quarter of a million shells were fired at German positions in an hour. Looking at local papers of the time, it seems that the Trustees would also have had indications of the losses the Royal West Kents had just been suffering, although a year earlier there had been some exaggerated bravado at the Regiment's prowess at Ypres – "Never lost a trench during the war and probably never will......."

But back to what happened next at the meeting two weeks later: Mr Burr had received a letter from the soldier in question, although it does not survive and Dr Fraser had been considering the matter. He had consulted with his brother – who was a lawyer – about how the Trustees might stand legally. From his conversations, it appeared that the evidence was not good. He, therefore, proposed that the matter remained in abeyance for the time being. This was agreed and Mr Burr added "that we minute our thanks to Dr Fraser for obtaining legal advice – and free of charge."

There is no further mention of the incident in the meeting that followed five months later in April, or indeed in any subsequent Minutes.

In 1918, Mr Burr's term of office came to an end and Helen Hills – Mrs

Harry Hills – became one of the Trustees representing the Parish Council. She was the aunt of Patrick Hills who lives in Chiddingstone Causeway, known to him as "Aunt Duckie". She lived at the big house at the crossroads past Hildenborough Station, which was called "Crossways" and which she had had built. She had married Henry Hills, late in the last century and started her married life at Bourne Place in Nizels Lane. Although she was widowed very young in 1894, she led a life full of enthusiasms – including support for local sport in general and Chiddingstone Causeway Cricket Club in particular – but she was also much liked and respected in Leigh. At her first Meeting, Dr Fraser delegated her to "find two needy persons in the Hollanden portion of Hildenborough and a suitable recipient for the quarterly bread." Other new faces at the meeting were the village's new Vicar, the Reverend George Weston, who replaced Octavius Walton; and the Reverend A.O. Daniel, the Hildenborough Vicar. As the Trustees reviewed the list of the donations, the new eye of Mr Weston proposed – for the first time – that "all applicants for Charity must fill up a form showing their income."

In September 1919, the Minutes record what was inevitably a tension between two different ways of using the Charities money: should the rents of the cottages be set low – thus helping a small number of poor families very considerably: or should the rents be realistic (if still fairly low) and the resultant rent money be given to all the poor in the parish by way of tokens, quarterly and annual grants and the famous bread? Dr Fraser – as so often – was elected as Chairman. On this occasion, he seemed clear on the matter (although over the next fifteen years, he argued differently). He had received a letter from the Parish Council, asking that one of their tenants' rates be paid by the Trustees. While he expressed sympathy with the tenant in his illness, he could not see a way – as the Trustees of a Charity – to pay rates. The cottages should not be looked upon as Almshouses but as an investment and the rents should be distributed amongst all the poor of the whole parish.

At the next meeting, in July 1920, it was agreed that Mrs Hills should take the Chair. Discussion was of routine matters but included what we would nowadays call cash flow. After they had agreed to raise most rents, Mr Boby had to point – as so often – to extra expenditure needed because of the state of the Charities thirteen properties. There was still surface water at the new cottage on the Green and also a need to have new iron ventilators put in: all the cottages needed to be painted outside – "the same colour as at present" – and that, as the insurance was too low, extra money had to be found for that as well. Because of these problems, four months later, Dr Fraser felt it necessary to propose "that the dole of quarterly bread be stopped." Additionally, the Vicar felt that there could be no annual distribution in January if the accounts were to balance.

The next meetings considered various quotes for various jobs – in one case, the quotes received by Mr Boby varied from £115 to £20; the provision of stoves or kitcheners; and a longstanding Parish Council problem with the sewage. The well at the back of the cottages on Lower Green was not required for the cottagers use, as their water was by now laid on from Tonbridge but the Parish Council's Sewage Committee had found this water very useful for flushing the drains. The Trustees agreed to allow the use to continue.

In May 1923, Mr Boby explained that he had received a proposal from Lady Bright of the Nursing Association "asking that the Parish Nurse should be considered as an applicant for one of the cottages when next a vacancy occurs." The Vicar knew that it again raised the question "as to whether the cottages should be considered as part of the Charities or whether they are to be looked upon as an investment, with the proceeds from them to be distributed to the poor." Dr Fraser, who probably now remembered the wording of some of the seventeenth century bequests and their interpretation by the Trustees, pointed out that "in the past, the Trustees have always given widows and the poor preference. The length of residence in the parish has also been taken into consideration".

Dr Fraser and Mr Boby went off and did their homework and, at the meeting three months later in August 1923, Mr Boby was able to report that "they now had a letter from the Charity Commissioners which stated that they were unable to find anything which would lead them to conclude that the cottages in question were otherwise than ordinary endowments. "They should accordingly be treated as such and should be let at the best rent that can reasonably be obtained." The Charity Commissioners clarification enabled Mrs Hills to recommend that the cottage was let to the Nursing Association "at four shillings a week."

The moral frailty of tenants again appeared in March 1924. "Serious allegations" had been made against one of the tenants, Miss Z. It was alleged that "she has for a long time been in the habit of taking too much drink and that there is undue intimacy between her and a former lodger." After the Trustees had considered the case, the Chairman proposed that "Miss Z should be called in and told that she must give up drinking and inform her former lodger, Mr A that he must keep away from the house. The Trustees are then prepared to allow her to remain in the house." The woman in question was summoned and talked to. And she did give the necessary promises

– although at the next meeting a year later in February 1925, the problem was still around, as Mrs Hill suggested that they agreed "tickets rather than cash be given to the particular tenant."

At the same meeting, Mr Boby said that he "had had a letter from the Assistant Sanitary Inspector ordering that one of our cottages, where there has been a case of scarlet fever, should be thoroughly cleaned."

The concerns of the Trustees were never confined to the centre of the village. People at the Powder Mills and in the northern fringe of the original parish, at Black Hoath, Prices Farm, Killicks Bank, Little Moorden, Moorden itself, the people at the Compasses and Charcot also feature in allocations of help – indeed, in a typical year only a third of the help was to people in the main village.

Income from the various charities which had been united in 1901 sometimes came from the rent on pieces of land. Every few years, there would be a complaint from a farmer or a new landowner querying why he had to pay the United Charities a fee on some land that he thought he owned. Dr Fraser was again Chairman on December 2nd 1929 when a typical query arose. A certain Captain Hawes was disputing the annual charge of two pounds in respect of Kentlands. The Trustees looked up the history, going back to 1895 and initially agreed to get their solicitors, Warners of Tonbridge, to act. However, Mrs Hill suggested a personal approach by her to the Captain. This was accepted and it seems she was successful because the matter is not mentioned again.

The first December meeting in 1933 was unique as Dr Fraser explained, saying that they were all very sorry to hear that the Clerk to the Trustees was in hospital. The Vicar was asked to write to him to send best wishes for a speedy recovery. This was the only occasion in the forty years that Mr Boby served as the Clerk that he missed a meeting. Dr Fraser also had a virtually one hundred percent attendance record – although a week later, the Reverend Leofric Sealy, now the Leigh vicar, gave Dr Fraser's apologies – "he is in India." It was at this meeting that the now recovered Mr Boby first mentioned the question of installing electric lights in some of the cottages. The Vicar agreed "on condition that the work is well done – with steel tubing".

But inspite of the almost continuous work on the various cottages approved by the Trustees and supervised by Mr Boby, major problems continued and in November 1934 Dr Fraser explained the latest cause for concern. He had had three long statements from the Sanitary Inspector relating to repairs which needed to be done at the three cottages on the

Green. Mr Boby had – as so often – done the background work, having met with Mr Cherry, the Inspector. Dr Fraser saw Mr Cherry before the next meeting and asked him to come and talk with the Trustees. At a special meeting on 10th December 1934 Mr Cherry explained that the cottages were not in a bad state of repair and that demolition was out of the question but that each home holder should be provided with a dustbin; that the floor in Widow K's house should be repaired; that brown enamelled sinks should be provided; and that the casements should be made weather tight. It was also agreed that Dr Fraser would meet with Doctor Cave, the Medical Officer of Health, to discuss some of the W.C.s: in the meantime, they would arrange that Miss C and Miss K share one; and Mrs B and family would have the sole use of the other.

There must be some sympathy for the Trustees. Their tenants were constantly saying they could not afford even the uncommercial rents that they were offered, yet the Trustees were meant to make profits which would then be given to the poor.

Little unusual happened as far as the Charities' Minutes are concerned over the next few years – the start of the Second World War is not mentioned. Mrs C H Scott of Hollanden House in Mill Lane, Hildenborough had replaced Mrs Harry Hills who had died in 1937. However, there was a second change of personnel which really represented the end of an era. In June 1940 at a Special Meeting Dr Fraser opened the meeting saying that the chief and only business of this evening's meeting was the appointment of a successor to the Clerk. It was unanimously resolved that the following letter should be sent:

"Dear Mr Boby
I have been instructed by the Trustees to forward to you a copy of a Minute recorded at today's meeting. The Chairman, Dr Fraser, expressed his very sincere regret that Mr Boby, who had served as Clerk for a period of forty years, had been obliged to send in his resignation for reasons of ill health. The Chairman spoke in the highest terms of the very long service rendered by Mr Boby and of all the hard and devoted labours he had put in on behalf of the Charities. It was unanimously resolved by all present that a very sincere note of thanks be passed and forwarded to Mr Boby with the Trustees best wishes for a speedy recovery, and return to the scene of his long labours.
Yours faithfully etc."

Mr Boby was now approaching ninety, living, as he had for many years, in Garden Cottages. Dr Fraser, now aged eighty-three continued to be a Trustee – and usually Chairman – until his retirement to Torquay in 1944. He died there in 1949 and his ashes were returned to the churchyard to be with his wife.

Bill Crocker feels that the work of the Leigh United Charities is still valuable. "The Trustees – that's John Knock, the Leigh Vicar, Michael Phillips – he's the Hildenborough person and Eric Batchelor who's Chairman – still work hard and between us we reckon that we know a good deal about what's going on in the village and who might be needing help. The Charity Commissioners have made us sell off nearly all the houses, so we have just got the investment money to distribute. We help about a hundred and fifty people a year with gas and electricity and things, plus food and a bit of help at Christmas and emergencies. The only properties that we have left are Cherry Tree Cottages on the Green but we do own the land where they built Saxby Wood and West Kent Housing pays us rent for it. So we've comparatively more to spend than in 1900 – £20,000 this year – and we continue to do a lot of work behind the scenes to help people in the parish. So I think all those bequests from three or four hundred years ago are still doing a good job."

Saxby Wood which replaced the two sets of three cottages on the roadside in the High Street.

Ivy Wood

"I got married to Dick Wood in 1973 and we were married for fifteen years until he died in 1988. They were the happiest years of my life. He'd been a widower for about twelve years and I'd known him and his first wife, Edith, altogether for twenty five years – since 1949 – when I moved to Barnetts Road and they were next door. Mrs Wood was very kind to me and helped me when we arrived. There was myself, a tiny baby, my two year old and my husband. I went in front of the Sevenoaks Council committee that allocated the Barnetts Road homes but when we got here, one old man – he was very much in charge of the village in some ways – said "I don't know why they let you come to Leigh". Not very welcoming.

I'd lived on a farm at Kemsing which my father ran for the War Agricultural Committee and I used to ride a horse and seemed to have lots of space there. Barnetts Road seemed small but I'd never had a home of my own before. My grandfather had been a farm manager at Great Hollanden and he knew Mr Burr, the Hall Place agent well. They were both Scots – both great big men. But we only knew the Boyds at Moat Farm and Mrs Matthews when we arrived. Looking back, it was very narrow in the village then – psychologically, I mean. It's expanded now – I like it better now.

Dick was wonderful. He was lovely to be married to. He was kind and intelligent and he was just the same to everyone. He saw the best in everybody. He had been a conscientious objector – not everyone was very nice to him during the War – but soon after he was on the Parish Council and became Chairman too. He wrote about everything – about his childhood and about the earth and its resources and philosophical things – everything. He left school at fourteen but he did his 'O' levels when he was sixty – "Under Milk Wood" and "Far From The Madding Crowd" were the set books. He had a lovely voice too – he was in the church choir for fifty years.

He was really Henry Victor Wood but he was always known as "Dick". He wrote so much about the village and I do hope with all my heart he would like others to share it. Leigh's such a lovely place to live – there can't be anywhere better, can there? So, I'm happy to let it be published.

Victor Harry "Dick" Wood

As well as his personal diaries and some private notes about his beliefs, Dick Wood left three books of his memories of the village which follow. There were also take-offs on Boswell's Life of Johnson and on Cobbett's *Rural Rides*; some articles on rural issues – including fishing and bellringing both of which he loved – which he sent to Fleet Street (without success he says in a note); a very detailed history of Leigh Scouts which he ran for many years; lists of wildflowers he had seen in Leigh (around 175 in 1985); and a selection of poetry and numerous other notes covering subjects as varied as the franking of envelopes and the duties of a Special Constable. Even as he was dying, he was writing about the effects of various drugs that he had been given for his heart condition, so that it would help the doctors and others who had similar medical problems. He was a man of hugely wide interests and the greatest possible charm.

Leigh Scout Troop at Tonbridge Castle in 1926. Those shown in the postcard include Mr Hubert Russell, F. Hawkins, F. Belton, H. Wood, L. Humphrey, J. Upton, D. Lucas, Syd Denton, S. Lambert, Don Thorogood. H. Butler.

THE HOUSE WHERE I WAS BORN

The smallest pair of cottages in Lower Green, possibly in the village, were "Budgeons Cottages". Under the eaves, between the two dwellings a "Sun" Fire insurance plate shone. Underneath that was a rectangular stone with the legend "O & E Budgeon's Gift – 1620". In number One, at the north end I was born on 5 December 1907. I lived there for the first thirty years of my life. The cottage had but four rooms, two upstairs and two down. The front door, only a few yards from the road, opened straight into the living room. The living room had a floor of unevenly laid bricks covered with coconut matting. The ceiling was low with a network of cracks. The one window was less than three feet square, composed of small panes set in a cast-iron frame. There was an open fire grate with a cracked oven on one side. The chimney went straight up to the sky, and, because so much wood was burned, needed frequent sweeping. My father did this with a holly branch on a willow pole.

Until the arrival of gas in the house, in about 1912, all the cooking had to be done on the open stove.

The room was sparsely furnished with a plain deal table with turned legs, a dilapidated sofa, a side table with a wretchedly fitting drawer, a clumsy button-backed upholstered arm chair, and three cheap slatted chairs. In the recesses on each side of the fireplace were cupboards, containing, on one side, cracked cups and saucers, crockery and dry food stores, and on the other side my mother's meagre sewing and mending equipment, and also some glassware, seldom, if ever, used. Under one cupboard was a small chest of drawers containing household linen, dusters, string and flat-irons. Under the other cupboard was a wide shelf holding "our" children's toys, books and games.

The walls of the room were clad in green wallpaper. Over the side-table was an oil-painting – the head and shoulders of the crucified Christ. Over the mantlepiece was a black and white illustration of "The Raising of the Widow's Son of Nain". A rather more cheering picture to my young mind was one from a Christmas number of "The Globe" depicting a postman delivering seasonable mail to a happy household complete with excited dog. In one corner of the room hung a wall clock with bold face, a three feet long pendulum and two brass weights on chains. The hearth-rug was home made, manufactured from strips of old material knotted with a special tool into a hessian backing. While the coconut matting sifted dirt and dust on to the bricks beneath, the rug collected every particle and held much of it even when subjected to the most rigorous shaking and beating by my mother. Two brass candlesticks and some fair-ground ornaments adorned the mantlepiece. During my early years, the room was lit at night by a brass paraffin oil lamp which stood on the table in the middle of the room.

Round about 1912, when gas mains were laid for the newly opened "Leigh Halt", my mother somehow overcame her fear of the unknown, and allowed gas pipes and a meter to be brought into her home. A modest gas bracket with an upright mantle burner and globe was fitted above the mantlepiece, and a point for a gas-ring on a flexible pipe near the hearth. A length of "compo" piping led on to the scullery where a bracket with a fan-flame gave just enough light to make the gloom visible! Now we are there, let us look at the scullery, a room of about eight feet by eight feet, with a floor of bricks on edge, more broken and uneven than those of the living room. The rough-hewn joists and floorboards of the room above served for a ceiling. From one of these joists, we were told, a previous tenant had hanged himself. The walls were of crumbling plaster. The ill-fitting back door with metal latch opened directly on to the back yard. A window, half the size of the living room one, let light onto a shallow stone sink. Over the sink was a brass tap, the sole source of water supply for the cottage. There was no draining board until I, at the age of thirteen, fixed my tiny home-made one. Along one dark wall was a shelf for iron pots and pans. Against another wall was another shelf for galvanised baths and tins of meal and maize for the chickens. An enamel bowl served for washing up and face washing. My father's outdoor garments hung on the back of the door to the living room. A door led from the scullery into the pantry which was lit by the other half of the scullery window. Shelves below the stairs took up most of the room. They contained foodstuff and utensils. Under the shelves on the concrete floor were crocks of hens' eggs preserved in water-glass, and bottles of my father's home made wine and beer. Behind the door were brooms, umbrellas and walking sticks. Back in the living room a door with a latch disclosed the stairs, narrow and steep with threadbare carpet. Above the stairs, there was a shelf with some never-used holiday portmanteaux, some rolls of wallpaper and a gladstone bag. A narrow shelf held the candlesticks used to light our way to bed.

A sharp left turn at the top of the stairs brought one straight in the back bedroom. The low ceiling would have been even lower had it not followed the inside slope of the roof for about eighteen inches. Faded and cracked oilcloth covered the floor. The furnishings were a three quarter size black iron bedstead, a cheap yellow chest-of-drawers and an even cheaper wash-stand with jug and basin. My parents best clothes hung on rails behind the stairs door.

The front bedroom had a tiny fireplace but only once do I remember a fire being lit in it, and that was on an occasion when I was ill. The parting wall between the bedrooms was of crumbling lath and plaster, held up mainly by the wallpaper. There was a green iron double bed with two brass knobs for my parents and a most uncomfortable narrow folding iron chair-bed for me. Another chest-of-drawers, another wash-stand, jug and basin, and a varnished deal chest with iron handles which had accompanied my mother to the various houses where she had been in service. There was some very thin carpet on the floor and chamber pots under the beds. The walls were decorated with Bible texts including "God is Love" and "Jesus Christ is the same yesterday, today and for ever". The "little window where the sun came peeping in at morn" was a repeat of the one in the living room below, and looked out across the road to the trees and ponds of the brickyard. Sleep in these bedrooms was disturbed in more ways than one. Although more than fifty yards from the railway, heavy goods trains which in those days ran largely at night, rocked these upper rooms like earth-tremors. Sparrows and starlings caused a real racket under the tiles. But the worst disturbance surely was that caused by fleas. Looking back it seems as though half our nights were broken by my mother's crying "There's a flea in this bed", followed by a frantic candle-light search by my parents. I couldn't think what all the fuss was about because fleas never bit me, but they brought up great blanes on my father, mother and sister. My parents always swore that the fleas came through the wall from next door. On hot summer nights mosquitoes from the ponds beseiged the bedrooms, entering the open window. Their high-pitched buzz I did take notice of. There was no peace until they were destroyed and the windows firmly closed. One memory of open bedroom windows is that of the dawn call of roosters, each with a crow of different pitch. In those days, every cottage had its chicken run with a dozen or so hens and usually a cockerel.

Let us now visit the outside premises. Between the back doors of the two cottages was a shared wash-house containing nothing but a copper, set in brickwork, with underneath fire hole and flues. There was a wide shelf on which to stand the galvanised baths. Washing day was one of the events of the week chosen by arrangement with our neighbour, Widow Ford. In front of the wash-house was a well with wooden cover and windlass, chain and hook. The water was not, within my memory, used for any purpose, except by Abner Parker when he drew a few buckets full for flushing the sewer. The well contained many frogs and newts. Across the small backyard was the Lodge completely covered with ivy, except for the front which trailed with honeysuckle. Without the ivy, to hold it together, the Lodge would have fallen down. In the ivy were the nests of robin, pied wagtail, wren and hedge-sparrow. The Lodge was used mainly for wood and coal, but contained also mysterious boxes and sacks – probably of potatoes, garden tools, but, in later years, bicycles. The largest two shepherds bullace trees I have every seen stood, one to the side, one to the back of the Lodge. In late autumn they bore large yellow bullaces as big as small hens eggs.

My father was a rough sort of gardener, but his patch was always well stocked with every sort of vegetable, besides strawberries, raspberries, red and white; currants, red, white and black; and several varieties of goose-berry. There was a Victoria plum tree and one or two more of other vari-eties, and apple trees, Bramley, Codlin and Newton Wonder. My father was fond of flowers and always found room for petunias, godetias, clarkia, wallflowers, sweet william, canterbury bells and asters, all growing in the wildest confusion. The hedge facing the road was usually festooned with nasturtiums, while under the hedge were violets and marigolds. Over the garden gate was an archway of pink rambler roses. The tiny patch of garden under the front window held snowdrops and crocus, more violet, london pride and in autumn, chrysanthemums. A pink rose climbed the wall around the window. On one side of the front door was a mass of ever-lasting peas: on the other a grape vine which reached to the eaves. From the tendrils and fruit of the latter, my father made wine. Not far from the back door was a large clump of sunflowers.

At the far end of the back garden, almost as far from the house as possible and screened by a high privet hedge, was the lavatory or "closet" as it was called. It was no more than a tiny brick hut with tiled roof. There was a fixed wooden box set with a round hole and narrow funnel-shaped pan leading straight into the drain beneath. There was no water-trap to prevent smell arising from below. Slops and flushing water had to be carried from the house up the garden path to this tiny abode. The flushing water was often accidentally spilled on the seat or on the newsprint "toilet paper". So with one discomfort and another, as well as the cold in the winter, there was everything to discourage the user from making a prolonged visit.

A small triangular plot of ground beyond the "closet" was the chicken run. One of its high boundary hedges was of Kent Cobnut trees supporting hop bines. My father dried the hops in our oven for his home-made beer, and so we had nuts and beer for Christmas.

There was a small chicken house for about a dozen fowl, and a coop or two for broodies for my father usually, each spring, secured a clutch of fertile eggs to place under a sitting hen for hatching out a brood of chicks. My father used to sit in the run with his birds feeding them with corn from his hand and talking to them. How he managed, when occasion demanded, to chop off their heads on the chopping block I cannot imagine. It must have been agony for him thus to betray his pets.

The idyllic habitation I have been describing was obtained for us for a rent of half-a-crown a week! One then remembers that half-a-crown before 1918 represented one seventh of our total family income. A bargain? Yes, I still think so.

THE BRICKYARD

"Mum, Mum, Harry's fallen in the pond!" cried my sister as she ran. But by the time my Mum arrived, our neighbour, Sid Hitchcock, hearing the cry from his garden, had run across the road and hauled me to safety. I had fallen and lodged behind a willow stump, and was never in danger of drowning.

I do not remember the incident myself and only tell the story from hearsay. But it was my first contact with "The Brickyard", and by no means the last. One had only to cross the road and one was there. At a very early age, I remember seeing Bill Blunt, who lived next door to the Hitchcocks, going to his work as a brickmaker. He went down the path by the ponds which led straight to the Kiln, (or, "Kell" as it was always pronounced), the pug-mill and the sheds. It must have been around 1912, and it was about this period that the works produced its last brick. Beyond the grass verge that ran from the top to bottom of Lower Green on its East Side was a post and wire fence. Behind the fence was a row of conifers, larch and pine planted alternately. Behind them a row of black poplar. In the hollow area beyond were stubbed willows, with here and there a spruce or cypress. The willow trees were to the north of the path already referred to; to the south of the path were the ponds. The path was, in reality, a raised mound to cover an otherwise exposed sewer main. The ponds were known to us children who played around them as the Big Pond, the Little Pond, the Clay Pond, the Effet Pond and the Well Pond. Willow, alder, ash and sallow trees lined their banks. Of these ponds, only the Well Pond next to the railway remains.

Lower Green - during the early 1920s when Mr Belton was the baker. Note the upper door in the bake house at the rear where the flour was hauled up, and the fir trees on the left of the road.

The Big Pond, right in front of our house, had large areas covered with reedmace where moorhens nested, but there were open stretches of water where roach, rudd, tench and sticklebacks swam; also frogs by the thousand and grass snakes by the score. One of the latter once crossed the road and came indoors, to set my mother screaming. The Little Pond had a shoal or two of rudd, and also the Clay Pond, complete with the sunken wreck of George Bennett's model ocean liner which actually had electric lighting! The Effet Pond on the north side of the path held what its name indicates, efts, but it also held, besides tin cans and bottles, a covering in spring of white water crowfoot and yellow bladderwort. I don't know where you will find bladderwort in Leigh today. The Well Pond with its black waters was reputedly of limitless depth, and contained a few roach and rudd, but mostly tench of a very dark green hue, in contrast with the tench in the Hayingfield Pond which were golden, befitting their clayey environment. The Well Pond also had eels.

Eastwards, beyond the ponds, were the remains of the works; the one-horse-power pug-mill, the drying sheds with slipping tiles where swallow built their nests, the moulding shed with a few brick-moulds still lying around, the wooden roof-shaped covers, and the stable and cart shed which was later converted into a dwelling house for Elsie and Arthur Friend. Elsie and Arthur were the daughter and son of Charlie Friend, the baker. Charlie and his wife, besides running their business, kept chicken, ducks and geese in the brickyard. When the brickyard came up for sale in 1921, Charlie bought it.

The Kiln was a brick built structure with fire-holes below and surrounded by a mound of bright red burnt soil. There was also a faggot shed for the fuel which fired the kiln. Beyond the kiln the land lay much as it is today *(1981)* in contour, except that the Hayingfield pond was deep, clear and yellow. The drought of the summer of 1921 caused the Hayingfield pond to dry up. It never recovered to hold fish again, but became overgrown and weed-infested. The other ponds too suffered loss of water. Only the Well Pond remained clear of reeds and tall growing weeds. The whole of this Brickyard area was then a natural `nature' paradise. The fishes I have already referred to. The willow beds were the nesting place of not only thrush, blackbird, chaffinch, robin and wren, but of willow warbler, whitethroat, blackcap, missel-thrush, blue tit, long-tailed tit, great tit, coal tit, greenfinch and spotted flycatcher. The kingfisher also paid visits, but I do not remember that we ever found a nest. Of the nests that we did find, many never survived our constant visiting long enough to produce fully fledged birds. Most children then were egg collectors, and nests were constantly robbed. The finest view I have ever had of crossbills was during one autumn when a flock visited the row of pines and larches in Lower Green and attacked the cones with vicious vigour. They appeared quite unconcerned about the presence of my friends and myself, as we watched them from the distance of a few yards. In May the nightingales sang so loudly and persistently when folk had retired to sleep that, far from Keats "magic casements opening in perilous seas etc.", the windows were banged to, to shut out the unwanted noise. "That blasted nightingale never stops", complained my father.

Away over in the old drying sheds and stable, the swallows and pied wagtails (dishwashers we called them) had their nests. Farther out in the abandoned rushy clay workings, mallard and snipe were comparatively safe from childrens' prying eyes and thieving fingers. Wood pigeon and turtle dove nested in the hawthorn and willow trees in this part of the brickyard. I have no doubt that if somebody had taken trouble with my ornithological education at that time my bird-list would be very much longer. As it is, I can only record what we were told at the time – not always correct – and draw from my later knowledge.

So with butterflies. There were, in profusion, what I now know to be Whites, Hedge Browns, Meadow Browns, Blues, Brimstones, Tortoiseshells,

Speckled Woods, Clouded Yellows, Peacocks, Red Admirals, Walls, Small Coppers, Commas and doubtless many more that do not leap to my memory.

And the flowers! The clearing in the willow bed by the effet pond and the banks of "the path" were, in my memory, a carpet of clover, trefoil, knapweed, bedstraw, vetch, dog violet, yarrow, pea-grass and buttercups. In the damper areas were found meadow-sweet, ragged robin, woody nightshade and celandine.

Yet it was not as a nature reserve that the brickyard meant anything to me. It was our playground, and that was everything. When there, we were safe – almost – from the dreary world of adults. And who were the "we" that possessed this treasure land? "We" were chiefly the Humphrey children who lived in the Lower Waterworks Cottage. Children from other parts of the village sometimes joined us; they were welcome. Frank Humphrey was our undisputed leader; Mabel our sweet Maid Marian; Len, my ever staunch companion; Elsie, Maid Marion's maid, George, not yet old enough to take part in much adventuring; and Doris the baby.

What was the nature of the adventuring? We explored every square yard of the territory, but the ponds gave us most delight. How to get from one boggy island to another, or to a remote moorhen's nest. Never did I arrive home with dry feet. My mother was distraught as she tore off my wet garments. "Harry, you'll catch your death of cold!" she wailed. I could not learn. My feet were wet again the very next day, but I am still alive more than 60 years after. Every climbable tree was climbed and Tarzan never swung from bough to bough with more joy than we did on the resilient willow branches.

Kick-can was the group game that I most enjoyed, and if you don't know what kick-can is I can tell you. A small ring was drawn in the middle of the clearing or in the dusty road by the Waterworks gate. A tin-can was placed in it. A "He" was selected by a rhyming elimination process. The can was thrown as far as possible. While "He" retrieved it and replaced it in the ring, everyone else ran to hide. "He" then went to seek those hiding. When he finds one, he calls his name, runs back to the base and kicks the can out of the ring. But if the hider can run and kick the can before "He", he may run and hide again while "He" retrieves the can and replaces it in the ring. "He's" object is to find all the hiders and kick the can for each of them. When all have been found and are standing round the base, a new "He" takes over. But here is the great thrill of the game. At any time while "He" is seeking, any hider may risk his own life by emerging from his hiding place and run to kick the can from the ring before "He" can do so. As he kicks the can, he cries "SAVED", and all those players standing at the base may run and hide again. The brickyard terrain contained ideal hiding places for such a game.

Fishing and ice games each occupied our time in due season. When the ponds were frozen over with two inches of ice, that was where my heavy hobnail boots came in; they were ideal for sliding. Children with only leather soles came to a halt halfway down the slide, but my hobnails carried me the whole distance. Up the long slide across the Big Pond, and back on another laid parallel to it. "Keep the pot a-boiling", we cried as enthusiastically as did Sam Weller. But Len and I carried our enthusiasm on far too long after the thaw had set in. The ice collapsed under us and we were floundering in the smelly, black icy water. Always timid of heart I muttered, "We're finished, Len!", and prepared to die. Len was of sterner stuff and more practical. Spreading out his arms over the ice he managed to climb out. Seeing him, I too made an effort and found myself dripping on the bank. What my mother said when she beheld her stinking and shivering son, is best forgotten. The next day at school the schoolmaster Mr Nethercot, called the register "Upton", "Yes, sir", "Weeks", "Yes sir", "Wood", "Yes sir". Mr Nethercot looked up in feigned surprise. "What are you doing here Wood? My son came home last night and told me that you were drowned!"

Our fishing brought into being "The Brickyard Angling Society". I was its first and only "Hon. Sec." We constructed a Headquarters using the shelter of a spruce tree and tying in willow boughs to make the walls. The roof was thatched with reeds and the floor strewn with grass and rushes. It really was quite cosy. One day we found a message pinned to our noticeboard indicating that two unknown travellers had spent a comfortable night there.

The only matches we ever played were cricket matches. Cinder Hill children had challenged us. We went to Cinder Hill to play against the Jenners, the Healys, the Foords, Sid Denton and Dolly Gillett. For this was mixed cricket; quite a half of the players were girls. We lost. But there was to be a return match. We prepared the best pitch we could find out beyond the stable. The match had only just begun when Mr Arthur Friend arrived irate to find about twenty children playing far too close to his chicken houses. He soon hustled us all off. I suppose we should have asked him first. There was nothing to do but to retire to the Club H.Q., get out our fishing tackle, catch some fish, make a fire, borrow Len's mum's frying pan, and cook a meal for all the players. I think most of the girls enjoyed the evening thus spent more than they would have done playing cricket. Those fish tasted good!

THE BATTLE OF LEIGH

This must have taken place on a certain Saturday morning in 1917. The enemy was the dreaded Powder Mills army. We knew that they were to attack us (it had all been arranged), and we knew that they were to be led by the feared and ferocious "Jacko" Jempson, with the more amiable and grinning "Shanks" Boxer as his second-in-command.

There were arguments from the start as to who should lead the Leigh forces. "Weasel" Brooker put in his claim on the strength of his many relations serving in Britain's armed forces. Don Day's chief claim was that he was wearing a real soldier's uniform made by his mother. In the end "Weasel" appointed himself Captain, and graciously agreed that Don should be his Lieutenant. Sergeants, corporals and lance-corporals were all awarded their ranks, until there were only Len Humphrey and myself left, so we were made "privates", and felt very proud to have a rank! Captain Brooker said that he had had information that the enemy would attack from the Southeast, so he led the whole of his troops along the Straight Mile to thwart such an attack. As we crossed the railway at the Weir, Weasel laid his ear on one of the rails and declared that he could hear the hordes advancing.

We reached Powder Mills to learn that "Jacko" and his troops had already left for Leigh along the unguarded Powder Mill lane. There was nothing to do but meekly follow them back to our undefended village. They no doubt, had been surprised to find no Leigh army around, and were looking for us. When at last we appeared, "Weasel" ordered "Take up defence positions, so we all scurried up The Forstall and jumped into the deep ditch which was then outside of "Kennards". It was comfortable and comforting in that deep leafy trench, but when the Powder Mill troops came roaring up The Forstall, "Weasel" ordered "retreat to the churchyard". On they came, and "Weasel" again ordered "Retreat to the Triangle". Morale was low, and there were dissenting voices against our Captain who could order nothing but "Retreat".

Everyone feared that it might come to open field warfare out on The Green. Don Day took a contingent across The Green to take up position behind the Iron Room with its thick surrounding shrubbery for hiding. If this failed, the only further strategy was to retreat up Tin Can Lane. But "Weasel" was not finished yet. With only half his troops now he was obliged to order, "Retreat to Donkey Field". Up the High Street we ran, hotly pursued. Half way up Canardy Hill, Lance Corporal Frank Humphrey led Private Len Humphrey and Private Wood into the relatively safe area of the allotments, a place which Powder Mills intelligence was unlikely to know about. From there we crept through the hedge into our back garden and took refuge (and refreshment) amongst the raspberry canes and gooseberry bushes. My dad wasn't at all pleased when he found that the troops had been plundering his soft fruit.

Subsequent arguments ensued as to why the Battle of Leigh appeared to be have been lost. "Weasel's retreat" strategy was bitterly criticised. "Weasel" stoutly defended his action, and pointed out that whereas Powder Mills troop were straggling, tired and weary with a mile and a half to march back to their base, all we had to do was to pop indoors where our Mums had dinner waiting for us. However, with all the experiences gained that day, it never made me into a soldier.

OLD TIMERS

Sixty and seventy years ago in Leigh (1911–1921), everyone had his or her place in the community and knew what it was. Everybody was somebody and was known by everybody else and recognised as such. At the top, as one might put it, was Samuel Hope-Morley, 1st Baron Hollenden, whom some regarded as Lord of the Manor because he lived in the big house – Hall Place. Those who disliked touching their cap and saying "My Lord", took very long steps to avoid meeting him. Almost equally to be avoided was the parson, the Revd Octavius Frank Walton, who was a keen amateur photographer. He had a severe manner with children, and appeared to be much too much in league with a certain gentleman called God who lived above the clouds and whose delight seemed to be in putting all sorts of restrictions upon children, and watching them with an all-seeing eye to record whether they obeyed or disobeyed. The third person in importance in the village was the doctor, Dr. Frank Frazer, solid and serious, but, one suspects, with considerable humanity. I have been told that he assisted in bringing me into the world, but my most personal memory of him is of the occasion when I was bitten by the parson's dog, and was taken to him by my distraught mother. Dr. Frazer cauterized the wound – no anti-tetanus injections in those days – and said that I had been "a brick". Some children even claimed that he had given them a penny when he had had to perform some painful operation on them! Mr Geo H. Boby was the schoolmaster, and of him I have written at greater length elsewhere. He lived of course, in the School House; where else?

Outside Hall Place
Back row from left: Isaac Ingram, J. Wells, Mr J Burr, Mr Bourne (Home Farm),
Charles Hayter (The Forge)
Front row from left: J. "Nimble" Hounsome – Beekeeper, Mrs Water Seal – the Head
Keepers wife, Jack Whibley

The village policeman was PC Austin in his knee-breeches, puttees and with his bicycle. He appeared to spend much of his time cycling around the parish pasting up notices on barn doors about sheep dipping and Swine Fever. He had been known to caution folk about riding bicycles without lights but big crime, I think, never came his way – his very presence was a sufficient deterrent.

Lord Hollenden's agent, who managed the Hall Place Estate, was Johnnie Burr who lived at the Gate House. He was a wild and furious Scot whose greatest interest was in Shire horses, Aberdeen Angus cattle, and in ordering and threatening boys who walked along the tops of stone walls. John Sturgess, a much more civil man, performed the same services for Lord de Lisle on the Penshurst Place estate. He was a Leigh School manager, but he had no great liking for boys who went moorhen's nesting.

The shop-keeping tradesmen in Leigh were William Anderson at the Post Office Stores, where hobnailed boots hung with saucepans and frying pans on hooks in the dingy ceiling; Mr Lindridge owned the General Store, where Bob Hukins, the manager, weighed up your sugar from a sack, and tipped it into a blue paper cone which he had deftly rolled. The newsagent, sweetshop and tobacconist, was owned (yes, actually owned – not rented) by Bradbury Baker, tall and thin, and seemingly well managed by his wife, who, at peak periods of service would call to her husband in the back regions of the shop, "Mr Baker, will you please step forward." The butchers shop was run by Harry Hammond, a lean man who was also a grazier with a farm at Haysden. He was assisted in the shop by his cheerful and chubby nephew, Harry Bowles. They owned a shaggy Old English Sheepdog matted with mud and dung which somebody had appropriately named "Satan". Jack Roots kept the Brickmakers Arms. He looked a grizzly, grumpy sort of man, but my Dad must have liked him, for he was always paying him a visit. He was assisted by his daughter "Pussy" who was married to Larry Coomber. They had the stables and fields at Lower Green, and a horse and van, and pigs. Quoits was played in the Lower Field on Saturdays, while the Leigh Football Club ground was on one of the Penshurst Road fields. Travelling FunFairs and Circuses were pitched on the Lower Field. After Mr Offen left, the Fleur de Lys was run by Dick Smith a cheerful little cockney from the Old Kent Road. Our other village pub, The Bat and Ball, was taken over in about 1914 by Bert Measy, a Sussex man, who combined the work of landlord with cycle repairing at the back of the premises. He sold me my first bike for £2.10s., a monster with two crossbars. Bert's wife served in the bar and sweet-shop, and his daughter Edie was a girl that must have attracted many young male customers. For all that Edie never married.

Charlie Friend was the village baker with bakehouse and shop at Lower Green. He was lean and lanky – his wife round and dumpy. She kept chickens and ducks across the road in the old brickyard, with Leghorns, Black Minorcas, Plymouth Rocks and Khaki Campbells. Percy Martin was the chief baker, and daughter Elsie and son Arthur were roundsmen, driving their horse-drawn vans to outlying parts of the parish and beyond. The appetizing aroma of the bread being drawn hot from the oven at half-past eight each morning is something never to be forgotten.

The farmers of Leigh were well recognised figures, William Goodwin of Paul's, Stevens of Ensfield, Hollamby of Barnetts, Harry Maskell of Ramhurst and Tom King of Leigh Park. Though they had their troubles, and lost money all the time, they could still be seen entering the Fleur-de-Lys by the Saloon Bar door. James Wylie was but farm foreman at the Home Farm, a brawny Scot, with an almost unintelligible accent. But he could climb the ladder to the granary carrying 2 cwt of grain on his shoulder, and, unaided, carry a tarpaulin to the top of a corn stack. He was as strong as many another farmers' horse. Prices Farm was run by Johnnie Burr, with the farmhouse occupied by the shepherd Frankie Bourne and his gentle sister, complete with dairymaid's poke bonnet. A really old-fashioned couple even in those days. Miss Bourne always had time to praise and admire the string of small rudd we had caught in the pond.

To return to the village and its characters. Charlie Hayter was the village blacksmith. He never lacked company, his bright forge fire and his warm personality always attracting visitors. He was not averse himself to a sit down on his bench for a chat, blowing away his own breath and panting like the forge bellows themselves. It was not all chaff and gossip, for Charlie was a fount of country lore and local history.

The Old Forge, Leigh probably in the late 1920s when Charlie Hayter was the smith.

The village wheelwright, carpenter and undertaker was Harry (Potty) Faircloth. He lived in what is now called Pump Cottage and his workshop has now been converted and is called Wheelwrights. He was pretty tubby and not a little deaf, but I think he must have had a very tolerant nature, otherwise he would not have had a whole crowd of village children playing around his premises while he worked. His daughters, Allie and "Babs" invited us to play kick-can in the yard, for it was an ideal place for the game with endless hiding places in the sheds and saw-pit.

Will Ford was the ganger on the Leigh length of the railway. With him were Tom Richards, Tom Hollands and his brother Albert, strong men all. Each day they could be seen going to work in their heavy corduroy trousers, each leg supported below the knee with a leather strap (hames) and at the waist by a wide leather belt which had a sling at the back for carrying their honing rubbers at grass cutting season. It was a sad and tragic day for Leigh when Will and Tom were knocked down and killed while working on the track near Tonbridge Station.

The snob or cobbler was an important member of the village scene. Mr Everest plied his trade in the converted butcher's shop on Church Hill. He was succeeded by Mr Coleman. At a later date – about 1920 – Louis Brooker set up a new shoe repair business, first in a hut in the Fleur de Lys yard, and later across the road in the hut which now houses the Brickmakers Antiques. Lou Brooker, soon to become Clerk to the Parish Council, plied his trade while dispensing news, views, jokes and information to a constant flow of customers.

I think it was about 1910 that Leigh Halt was opened and Bill Bailey was put in charge and worked to the letter of the S.E. & C.R rule-book. Passengers were served with their tickets through the grill between office and waiting room. Before the arrival of a train the gate at the top of the approach was locked: no admittance of late comers. The gate was not unlocked until Mr Bailey had given the signal to the guard for the train to depart. Then the tickets of all arriving passengers were examined and collected. Mr Bailey kept the waiting room, platforms, seats and gas-lamps spotlessly clean. The Revd. O.F. Walton was fond of telling his parishioners that if they had ever wondered about the length of Noah's Ark, it was the exact length of the platforms at Leigh Halt!

Alfred Sales, William Baldwin and "Birdie" Stubbings were three much respected men as they were the men in charge of the Gas-Works and Waterworks supplying Hall Place with gas and water. Water was also supplied to the Home Farm, fountains and horse-trough, and to many houses belonging to the estate. Here again, the whole premises were spotlessly and immaculately kept. Observe the site today *(1981)* – nothing but ruin and desolation under a jungle of brambles.

The Hall Place carpenters of those days were Tom Izzard and Bert Humphrey. Tom was an all round expert craftsman. An example of his work may be seen today in the church. Every Sunday he walked to Penshurst to dine with his brothers; he seemed to prefer their company to that of his wife. If you wanted anything made of wood, strong and solid, then Bert Humphrey was your man. Down in his shed at the end of his garden he would toil by candlelight to earn a few extra shillings to help keep his six children well fed, clothed and shod.

The estate painter was Ike Knellar, whose anecdotes of army life in Imperial India might well have provided the basis for T.V. episodes in "It Ain't Half Hot Mum". Ike's dog, Patch, a white terrier, accompanied him everywhere, and was a favourite throughout the village. Ike really thought he was for the sack on that hot summer day when Johnnie Burr discovered him asleep in the shade of the gasholder he was supposed to be painting. Perhaps even Johnnie liked Ike; everyone else did.

The gamekeepers of Leigh were Walter Seal at "The Kennels", Fred Healy at Old Park House, and Old Titheridge at Tapners, a trio to be instantly recognised, but never to be confronted face to face. Walter Seal sang bass in the church choir on Sundays. Fred Healy, sadly, never returned from the fighting in the Great War. Old Titheridge's best suit of heavy gamekeepers uniform, never worn, was, not very many years ago, sold at a Golden Years Jumble Sale for fifty pence.

The Hall Place Estate bricklayers were Lou Bennet and Jack Smith. Lou had the dry sort of humour that confronted you early on the 24th December with "Well, here's a fine set-out Harry; this morning's Christmas Eve." Jack Smith was dogged and a little perverse. Though his hand-cart had a perfectly good set of handles. Jack always propelled it by pushing on the tailboard. Though a short man, he rode a very high bicycle, because, as he said, he liked to look over the hedges!

There was a choice of at least three milkmen for the people of Leigh. Will Cook who lived in a ramshackle cottage at Kennards Farm served a number of residents mostly in the east of the village, carrying his can on a hook which replaced a missing hand. Abner Parker, a little whiskered man, lived in the house now known as "Bombers". He kept a few cows in Jack Roots' Lower Green fields, carried his cans on a yoke and it caused him no trouble to call twice a day to dip a half pint of milk from his can and pour it into your jug. Old Parker also had the job of looking after the sewerage, and many a quip was made on the likelihood of his getting his two commodities mixed! George Jenner of Park Farm actually had a milk float with a churn for his rounds. It was drawn by a very tired horse which constantly needed George's "C'mon" to keep it moving at all. One day it failed completely, and died in the shafts on Cinder Hill.

Far out of the village in the wilds towards Haysden, in a tiny cottage called the Rushetts, lived Aaron Wickens, the charcoal burner. He had a round of local farms to visit and ply his craft. The charcoal would be needed generally for hop drying. Aaron set up a little tarpaulin shelter on the site where his 'jets' were to be built, and there he stayed night and day till the 'pits' were safely drawn.

Leigh celebrates the coronation of King George V in 1911 when Dick Wood was four years old.

Bill Blunt, Stevie Upton and Pudgy Nichols are the only brickmakers I can remember before the brickyard closed round about 1913. "Pudgy" had charge of the horse that drew the cart and drove the pug-mill. Bill Blunt's house and garden were adorned with window boxes, bird-baths, umbrella stands and other ornaments, all made with colourful broken crockery set in cement.

Leigh had two postmen in those days – Harry Martin and Jack Norman. They did two deliveries a day on bicycles around the parish, after sorting their letters and parcels in a shed behind the Post Office. How proud they looked in their fore and aft peaked caps. There were deliveries on Saturdays, Christmas Days and Bank Holidays.

Tommy Hobbs was the Prudential Insurance Agent, brisk and dapper with impressive grey moustache. He did not scorn to visit the poorest home once a month to collect one penny. He had a cheery word for the people he met, and it was said that the then five church bells ringing round were saying "Here comes Old Tommy Hobbs; here comes Old Tommy Hobbs".

There were one or two upper middle class people living in Leigh, best known of these perhaps was Sir Charles Bright, son of the engineer who laid the first cable across the Atlantic Ocean. He was tallish and dressed usually in green Norfolk jacket, knee-breeches and stockings. Occasionally he would give a magic-lantern lecture in the Village Hall on some scientific subject. Once a year Lady Bright, a magnificent figure in a picture hat, would invite the school children to a garden party at The Grange. Harold Cox was another Norfolk-suited gentleman. He had been a Liberal Member of Parliament, and had then become a Sunday Times journalist. He lived at Old Kennards. The Misses Heath, Maud and Florence, were ladies best remembered for their earlier activity of holding woodcarving classes for the village men. Examples of their pupils' industry are still to be found. I picture these fine ladies driving a smart horse and carriage with rubber tyred wheels.

I have mentioned very few women in my review of village characters, but I hasten to say that there were then just as many noble and worthy women as you would find today – Miss Fanny May for example who lived alone, and "took in" the washing of slightly better-off folk to earn herself an honest living. What a familiar figure she was, carrying her wicker clothes basket piled high with newly ironed clothes. Everyone had a job or position of some sort in the village. Most were farm workers, gardeners or estate labourers, but there were also a good proportion of cricket-ball makers and workers at the Powder Mills – these were the élite. Very, very few travelled to London or elsewhere to earn a living. Today it is the reverse.

MR BOBY

Looking back, one can see that Geo. H. Boby enjoyed being a schoolmaster. He was monarch of all he surveyed and relished it. I can picture him now, with grey hair and whiskers, pince-nez, pinstriped trousers and black swallow-tailed coat. Standing by the blackboard, he would draw up his sleeve to reveal starched cuffs and gold links. With supple movements of the wrist he would demonstrate how to achieve copper-plate writing. For in Standard V we were still learning a good hand! In our copy-books before us was the model line:

"Ebony, a hard, black, ornamental wood",
to be delineated five times before going on to:
"Parallel lines appear to converge as they recede".

As I regard my present crabby scrawl, it all appears to have been so much wasted effort! Perhaps I was wrong to blame the cross-nibbed steel pen, and the inkwell stuffed full of blotting paper, for on the next page I am confronted with:-

"It is the bad workman who complains of his tools".

Mr Boby takes down from the high window ledge the model cubes, cones, pyramids and cylinders and arranges them for our drawing lesson. He moves across to the blackboard again to demonstrate with fine flourish the ellipse, the arc and the "receding parallel lines".

Geo H. does not allow distractions like the sudden appearance of a dozen bees in the classroom to upset his poise but moves stiffly towards the windows to pull the cords that open them, knowing that the bees will soon find their way out. He also knows – cunning old bird – that these same bees had been snapped during the dinner time into a dozen matchboxes and thrust into a dozen jacket pockets, to await a signal for release. It has all been done before and you can't catch old birds with chaff.

Now it is the singing lesson. Mr Boby takes his tuning fork from his waistcoat pocket, strikes it on the desk, upturns it, takes up the sounded note, modulates it, goes to the piano and strikes an Eb. Yes, it is the note he is voicing. He knew he could do it; we knew he could do it. "Today, boys and girls, we are going to learn a new round." (He loved rounds). "It is one which I have never seen written down. It was taught to me when I was a boy at school by my schoolmaster". (This was in 1918, the year before his retirement) "It goes like this:-

"We merry ministrels soft music enjoy
For music doth malice and hatred destroy.
We sing so blithely we drive away care
And with our soft harmony banish despair.
Then, hail sweet music, hail, hail heavenly sound
No pleasure like music on earth can be found".

Thus he taught us with the tune, and I have remembered it with much else that he taught after nearly sixty years. So this round cannot be less than 150 years old.

Our schoolmaster loved words that he could roll off his tongue. "Sit ye down", he would say. "And we will recite the Avoirdupois Table." Avoirdupois was a word he really enjoyed saying. Likewise, the Beer and Wine Measures were recited, though knowledge of the tables was not to be taken as approval for the drinking of beverages which were so measured. But who could resist the chance to enunciate such words as firkin, kilderkin and tierce. Consequently, I can still work out, should you require me to, the number of gallons in a hogshead or a butt.

"And now children, as it is Friday afternoon, the end of another week, we will sing "The Doxology – `Praise God from whom all blessings flow'".

Geo. H. Boby was not only a revered and feared schoolmaster, he was Clerk to the Parish Council, Clerk to the various parish charities, and a lot else beside. There was nothing he could not do in an emergency. When there was no church organist, he would occupy the organ-stool. If riotous mischief were afoot, he could step in and quell it with an authority equal to that of the village policeman. He was consulted by squire, parson and doctor, but one feels certain, he was lackey to none of them.

During the First World War it was whispered that he was a "Pro-German", but whether this was fact, fiction, misunderstanding or pure malicious gossip will never be known. It was probably the consequence of his staunch belief that Beethoven, Bach and Handel were the greatest of composers.

I know of only one instance in which he got caught on the wrong foot. The Parish Council were sitting when one member demanded to know who had planted daffodils on that part of the Green where now stands the War Memorial. Who is this person who takes the law into his own hands and plants bulbs on land where Parish Council notice boards already proclaim that games must not be played on a Sunday; that the riding of bicycles and horses is forbidden? Should there now be another notice, "No flowers to be planted here"? The Clerk stands up and confesses that he is the culprit. Yes, that was the word used by Mr Boby, the schoolmaster who has himself had so many culprits stand before him. Now, there he stands before his accusers, convicted by the words of his own mouth. The sentence? It is sentence enough to have to record his own misdeed in his own scholarly hand in his own Minute Book.

Mr Boby in his capacity as Clerk to one of the many parish Charities, called at Budgen's Cottages every Saturday night to collect the half-a-crown weekly rent. I lived in dread that he would call at the precise time that I was having a bath in a galvanised bath in front of the living room fire. Truly I should have been caught with my trousers down! But I never was. The half-crown was popped into a wash-leather bag and secured with a silver ring. The health and educational progress of my sister and myself were briefly touched upon, assurances given to my mother that nothing yet could be done about the falling plaster on the stairs, and he was away. Awed by Mr Boby during school hours, outside of school hours, I was over-awed.

On a certain day in 1919, Mr Boby, having postponed his retirement to see The War carried to its conclusion, finally laid down his schoolmaster's office and was presented with two golden sovereigns from his pupils.

"PUPPY" JAMES UPTON

"Puppy", alias James Henry Upton, was my schoolboy hero, one year, one month and one day older than I. He had everything that I lacked. He was charming, cheerful and cheeky; I was retiring, reserved and painfully shy. No wonder that I worshipped him when, for some reason I never understood, he took me under his patronage. I suppose the best thing he ever did for me was to invite me to join the Scouts. The second best thing was to persuade my mother to allow me to. My mother was aghast at the idea of bare knees, and convinced that I would die of rheumatic fever. Once in the Scouts the world was mine, where all the delights of fretwork were open to me. Puppy was invited to my home to give me extra tuition in this engaging ploy. After many sessions we produced a pipe rack for my Dad in which his broken clays would have looked singularly out of place. We also made a bracket vase-holder for my mother, which she generously made use of as a spill container, and a standing vase holder for my aunt, for which no use was ever found. My mother's kitchen table, well fretted and drilled, bore evidence of our efforts to its last days.

Leigh Scout troop, mid 1930s.

Puppy also introduced me to saltpetre. After school hours and on Saturdays my new friend worked for the village grocer and was able to obtain some of this interesting commodity. Now our tiny living-room became a firework factory. Charcoal was made in the oven next to our open fire. Squib-cases were made by rolling and sticking brown paper round a pencil. The saltpetre with a little sulphur was put into a cardboard box on the table. The charcoal was added – there was a blinding flash; clouds of choking smoke filled the room. We were lucky to have got away with our eyebrows, let along our eyesight. When the smoke cleared, and my mother had recovered from her hysterics, we held an inquest and surveyed the damage. We realised that we had not allowed our charcoal to cool, and that it must have contained a live spark. As for damage, a deep black hole had been added to the frets on the table. After that incident, Puppy was not such a frequent visitor to our house. Our friendship continued none the less. Puppy was such a versatile genius. It was he who taught me to play the mouth organ, the jews harp and the rattlebones. He himself could play his mother's concertina, his late father's fiddle, and the one stringed fiddle he had made himself from a cigar box. In due season he taught me to swim in the river at Ensfield Bridge. This swimming, again involved earnest nego-tiations with my over-anxious (that is hardly the word for her extreme condition) mother. She was convinced (so my father said) that I should not go into the water until I could swim! Moreover, the coldness of the water would give me pneumonia. But worst of all was the brevity of the slip that Puppy produced for me to wear. It seemed highly immoral, my mother felt, for me to expose such an expanse of my naked body to the gaze of anyone who might be passing. Puppy's swimming instruction was good. His theory was that if you dived under the water and made some breast strokes you would rise to the surface. For me it worked. I needed only to add the leg movements and I was swimming. To Puppy, for his pains, I have been eternally grateful.

On Saturday mornings Puppy had a grocery delivery round. This was done with a horse and van. Looking back it seems madness itself that anyone should trust a horse and van to the hands of the unpredictable Puppy and the timorous Harry Wood. But Puppy, as always, knew exactly how to manage the job, and I beheld him with amazement and something approaching adoration. Mr Harry Draper got the horse and van ready at the stable at the bottom of Lower Green. Then we went to "The Brickmakers" to pick up a few casks and crates of beer for certain customers. Then to the backyard of the shop in the High Street to load the orders and fill up cans of paraffin. Away then to Charcott and the Causeway. That horse had done this round before, long years before Puppy was put in charge. He knew every stopping place better than we did, and hardly needed a shake of the rein to start him moving on to the next customer. And so, although Puppy made that old cob trot all the way home, nothing untoward ever happened to us, no crash, no spill, no accident whatsoever. In the afternoon we delivered groceries to Killicks Bank. Here there was a large family named Jenner who lived in a barn-like house. This family seemed to consist almost entirely of adolescent girls with whom Puppy laughed and chaffed and romped. Puppy knew all about girls. He went to night-school in Tonbridge where he was supposed to be learning a strange system of shorthand called Sloan-Diployan, the secrets of which he endeavoured to pass on to me. At Tonbridge night-school I gathered, girls were an entirely superior breed of creature to our homely and familiar young village females; sophisticated, wildly beautiful, forthcoming, yet at the same time, mysterious, romantic and highly desirable.

On wild and wet Sunday nights Puppy and I would go to the Scout Hut (Puppy was a Patrol Leader and carried a key) and, huddling round the tiny gas fire, read real romance in the pages of books by Ralph Connor, where, in the backwoods of Canada, men were men, and women something divine.

On Sunday mornings we went long walks far beyond our Parish boundaries into the strange territories of Bidborough, Stockland Green and Speldhurst; Nizels Lane, Eggpie Lane and the Weald. After school on weekdays when Puppy's grocery jobs had been completed, our exploration of the neighbourhood was conducted on the grocer's trade bicycle. I sat in the front carrier, and we were away. Puppy was a great explorer. Not for nothing had Puppy's father been in the Navy, and had once been shipwrecked in Arctic regions. He and his comrades had only survived being frozen to death, by Puppy's fathers ingenuity in making a fire by rubbing two pieces of ice together!

Puppy too had ingenious ideas. He had some carbide of calcium, used for producing a light in a bicycle lamp. Puppy dug a hole in the road outside the Scout Hut and placed carbide in the bottom, filled the hole with ashes rammed down hard, poured on water and threw a match. Disappointing! No land-mine explosion as hoped; merely scorched earth.

I last heard of Puppy about four years ago, when he wrote that he was now retired and enjoying every moment of his retirement. He always did enjoy life!

HARRY HENEY

Here was a genius if ever there was one. Henry George Heney was brought up in a magical wonderland called Bullingstone Lane, Poundsbridge, a little way to the south of Leigh beyond Bidborough Ridge, where trout darted endlessly in a silver stream, and it was always high summer. His mother was of farming stock – a Goodwin; his father an Irish schoolmaster.

When he was old enough, he was apprenticed as an engineer with Mr Hall of Tonbridge. Mr Hall taught him well. "Near enough is not good enough; it has got to be right". On one occasion Mr Hall needed to measure something while in an awkward position to reach his own steel rule. "Lend me your rule a moment Harry", he called. Harry confessed that he hadn't got one with him. "You haven't got your rule?" rebuked Mr Hall. "You should never go anywhere without. I take mine to church!" Harry never went anywhere without his rule after that. It was a beautiful little four-fold foot rule made of ivory and tucked into a pocket of his fancy waistcoat. Harry would never have left Halls to become engineer at Hall Place had he not felt it his duty to be at hand to his ailing and ageing mother and aunt who looked after her. They lived in the pretty tile-hung cottage next to the Brickmakers Arms, opposite the fountain in the wall. The windows were diamond-paned, the garden was trim with low box hedges and a shaved lawn, for Harry was the only cottage-dweller in the village to own a lawn mower. Amongst the roses and lavender there also stood such surprising objects, for those days, as a sundial, a bird-bath and feeding table, a hammock, a weather vane and an anemometer, all constructed by the man himself. Best of all, a high white mast with truck and halliard, from which, on important occasions, fluttered the Union Jack. Harry's dress was impeccable; starched collar, sporting tweed jacket, fancy buttoned waistcoat, tailored breeches, soft fawn leggings, and polished brown boots. He was the only villager of artisan class to own a "Burberry".

We children who waited outside the pubs to ask for "fag-ends" knew there would be a prize when the two Harrys – Harry Heney and Harry Mascall (who farmed Ramhurst, and was round and red) emerged from the Fleur de Lys on one side of the road to cross to the "Brickmaker" on the other. For these two gentlemen smoked "Classic" or "B.D.V" which contained "silks", and neither of them had children of their own to make first claim.

It was not until I went to work at Hall Place myself that I came fully to appreciate Harry's real worth. I was the new hand, knowing nothing of engineering. He taught me the fundamentals, how to use simple hand tools; the hammer and chisel and the hacksaw; how to file a flat surface; also, to a degree, the use of the lathe and forge. I still have the odd tool I made for myself in those days, scraper, rimer, cold chisel and square.

The main business of the engineering staff at Hall Place (Harry Heney, Bernard Pankhurst and myself) was the operation and maintenance of the Waterworks, the electricity generating plant and the central heating system and hot water supply for "The House".Everything was kept in immaculate condition. On a desk in the Waterworks engine room stood a brass and steel model of a six inch Nordenfeldt emplacement gun, exact in every detail though enormously scaled down. Only the removal of one vital part prevented it being a lethal weapon requiring a police certificate. Harry had fashioned and built it many years earlier. Now it was one more thing for me to clean and polish! Once a bronze half-bearing from one of the well-pumps was accidentally dropped down the well. No replacement was at hand nor likely to be for days or weeks, and water must be pumped the next day. Harry lost no time and fashioned one from a piece of apple wood, fitted it, and there it remained all the five years that I worked there, and presumably till the works eventually closed down. And nobody ever noticed the difference!

Harry's great joy after working hours was the rural countryside. He was a sportsman, but generally speaking, a loner; our own local Isaac Walton. He knew intimately every reach and pool of the river, where to find the roach, the dace, the chub, the bream, the perch and the pike. And he knew how to catch them. His tackle was of the finest and strongest; his rods and reels mostly by Hardy, but I still have his twelve foot, cane "Millward". If there should be a piece of equipment he needed and could not purchase, be it reel, float or tool for freeing caught-up lines, he made it himself. The hours slipped by so happily for him on the banks of the tree lined Medway. But the activities of the newly formed River Board filled him with rage and dismay as they ripped out the alder trees and wild rose bushes, and robbed him of his sylvan paradise, leaving him only a barren muddy waterway. Harry also enjoyed roving the fields with his twelve-bore double-barrelled sporting gun, shooting the odd rabbit, hare and pigeon. Sometimes he was invited to a "farmer's" shoot and, by what I have heard, claimed a bigger bag than most of the party.

In the hard winter of 1926 Mr Heney got out his shining skates, screwed them firmly to his strong leather boots, and betook himself to Hall Place lake. While a rabble of other folk, including myself, wobbled and floundered on ancient borrowed "boots" or patent "clip-ons", Harry was gliding away cutting fine figures both forward and backward on inside and outside edge. He knew how to grind an edge. How we envied him.

Though at heart a countryman, H.G.H. loved to visit London City. He had a great sense of history, and all the lanes, squares and byways meant much to him. He loved the Lord Mayor's Show, and anything where there was pomp and pageantry. And the Thames with its ships and bridges. He even visited the Theatre sometimes, for I remember after one of his excursions to London, how, for weeks after the air was filled with his whistled tunes from the new "Lilac Time". Harry loved good music, whether of Schubert, Chopin or Handel.

After Harry's mother and aunt died, Harry, thought to be a confirmed bachelor, married Ruth Jempson, a daughter of the landlord of "The Plough". She was a sweet, quiet and homely person. I often visited them in their home, the living room of which somewhat resembled a miniature antique shop. There was an Oak bureau, long-case clock, mercury tube barometer, brass and porcelain on the mantlepiece, a double-barrelled shot gun on the wall, a set of game studies by Thorburn in gold frames, pewter pots, a case of old English silver coins, and a sampler worked by Harry's grandmother in 1814. Let us leave them here in this cosy nest with their treasures around them.

CHARLIE AND HARRY PASSINGHAM

Charlie Passingham lived in the end cottage next to the Village Pump. I can just remember when the tall, green, cast-iron pump with its heavy bulbous handle could draw water from the well beneath it, and Charlie could water his front garden from it.

Charlie was a cricket ball maker, as were so many of the village men in those days, but his chief claim to renown was that he was Verger of the Parish Church. He was handsome in his greying beard and cut-away black coat, and played his part with great dignity, swinging open the great door and conducting each worshipper smoothly to a pew. His appearance was utterly benign; almost divine. No wonder that some years later, towards the end of his term of office, one of my very young nieces returned from her first attendance at a church service and declared, "I saw God, Mum!"

Charlie's wife Charity, is remembered best by school children as a black-draped figure slipping along each dinner time to the "Bat and Ball" with an empty jug and returning with it filled with something brown and frothing over. The jug bar was pretty popular in those days. There were two children, Martha, smart and trim, who remained a spinster to well on in years when she married widower, Jack Stolton.

When Leigh Football Club was reformed in 1919 by the young men returning from the First World War, every player of that almost unbeatable side was a hero to every young lad of the Village. None more so than Harry (or 'Boney") Passingham, the goalkeeper – son of Charlie. He was my special hero. Tall and slim in his white sweater, he was always friendly and genial to us kids hanging around the back of the goal. He was by trade, like so many young men following in father's footsteps a cricket-ball maker at Dukes at Chiddingstone Causeway. But when times became black and work was short in that profession, I remember him as a painter, and also as grave digger and churchyard maintenance man. Harry was also no mean cricketer and played regularly for Leigh, delighting the Saturday afternoon spectators with cheerful batting and very useful medium paced bowling.

He lived with his parents and sister in the cottage next to the village pump. Mary was the dark and beautiful Irish housemaid employed by Dr. Fraser, and it was not long before the village was delighted to observe romance springing up between Harry and Mary. Eventually they married and produced two children, Doreen and Kathleen. Sadly, Kathleen died at an early age.

Mary too died early leaving Harry a widower. Shortly before his own death which he knew was imminent I was talking to him. He said he was not fearing his end as the doctors had promised he would not suffer, with modern drugs available. But he recalled how, before his death, his father lay on his bed groaning day and night in pain. Harry however did not want to talk about himself, but preferred to tell me stories from his own youth in Leigh, one or two of which I here record.

Harry remembered hearing about the blazing tar barrel rolled down Porcupine Hill on each November 5th in order to force the turnpike keeper (the turnpike stood on the Green near to where the War Memorial now stands) to open the turnpike gates free once a year or have them burned down.

Porcupine Hill
with East Lodge
and the Church.

The village stocks, Harry said, were on unconsecrated ground just inside the churchyard. A certain notorious character whose name I have forgotten, approached the Revd. Thomas May on one occasion as he was leaving the church, and offered him a pint of beer! The Revd T. May was offended and sent for the village constable, who arrested Bill (as we will call him) and put him in the stocks. One of Bill's mates passed and saw him and asked what had happened. "I only offered parson a pint of beer," replied Bill. "They can't put you in the stocks for that", cried Bill's mate. "Ah, but they have", answered Bill.

Harry told me how he might have lost his life when he fell in the pugmill in the brickyard. Fortunately, someone stopped the horse and Harry sustained only a broken jaw. Mrs Faircloth, the wheelwright's wife organised the other children to pray for Harry's recovery. Harry Martin – the village postman – heard one girl praying, "Please God, make Boney well again." She was severely corrected by another girl who said "You must say, "Please God make Harry well again."

GATE LEANERS

With the passing of old Mrs Childs, goes the last of our village's gate leaners. I am reminded that less than fifty years ago, it was impossible to walk to the village from Lower Green without passing plump Mrs Blunt leaning with wide-spread elbows on the pointed pales of her cottage gate half way up Lower Green. Her front garden contained a fascinating collection of window boxes, pedestals and other ornamental features, all executed in broken crockery and glass set in cement by her husband, Bill, who worked in the brickyard opposite. Mrs Blunt was only waiting for someone to pass in order to indulge in some friendly gossip, and to watch the world go by – probably Jesse Ford taking a horse from Ensfield Farm to the Forge to be shod.

Into the High Street turning left at the Brickmakers Arms, you would see lean Mrs Young with a pair of pails, crossing the road, ostensibly to draw water at the fountain opposite, but invariably detained, as she had hoped would be the case, by some passer-by with whom to exchange village news and gossip.

Further down the street at her front garden gate next to The Pump, was Charity Passingham. If she was not just popping along to 'The Bat' with a jug for her mid-day pint of stout at the time we schoolchildren were coming home from school or returning with the jug frothing over, she would be leaning on the gate awaiting the appearance of some friendly acquaintance.

Mrs Faircloth, next door in the detached house, wife of the village wheelwright, was usually too busy with her large family to have much time for gate-propping. Mrs Faircloth, when she did have time to observe the world go by, would observe it from a seat in a rustic porch surrounding the front door. But that set her rather far back from the road for intimate conversation with passers-by.

How things have changed. Today, our village folk sit indoors watching the pageant of life on their television sets; then, the life the old people knew and talked about was what they heard and saw as it passed their own front gate. The farm wagon as it passed by, the poorly fed, ill-clad children of the French family who lived up in the wood, the doctor's gig trotting by, prompting the question 'Who is ill down our way?' Perhaps the next passer-by can give some information.

Anything was worth watching to the gate leaners; a gipsy caravan, a drover with a flock of sheep, any sort of stranger, or one of those early motor cars.

But for one event there were no gate leaners – a funeral. For that solemn occasion everyone was within doors, with blinds drawn down, even though a small chink might be left, so that one need not remain in complete ignorance of who the mourners were.

Now we are the mourners, mourning the last of our gate leaners.

SUFFRAGETTES

It must have been around 1912 or 1913 that Suffragettes were a threat, real or imagined to Hall Place, its owner and his household. Consequently, a night watchman was appointed to guard the mansion against these earnest women and their incendiary activities. My father was the unlikely choice for this job. Perhaps someone had heard him relating his nightwatchman experiences on the site in front of Buckingham Palace at the time of the construction of the Queen Victoria Memorial.

"One dark night, very late, this woman came slipping through the Palace gates across to my hut. 'Dick' she says, all agitated, 'Dick, I don't suppose you have a dust of tea you could lend me till I go to the shops; I've run right out and Teddy will be furious if he doesn't get his early morning cup.' Of course I let her have some. Who was she? Oh, it was only the poor Queen"

To return to the Suffragettes. There arrived at our cottage a large white bull-terrier, reputed to be very fierce. His name was Bob, and he was to accompany my father on his nocturnal rounds. Bob was housed in a tub turned on its side and bedded with straw at the end of our garden, and he was secured with a strong chain. My mother pleaded with me not to go anywhere near him. She was more scared of that dog than any Suffragette need have been of my father. My father was also supplied with a bullseye lantern with dark shutter, a hurricane lamp, a police whistle, and a pair of rubber soled boots – a great novelty in those days. Rubber studs, about an inch across, protruded about a quarter of an inch through the leather soles.

"What's the idea of those rubber-soled boots, Dick?" an innocent work-mate asked my father. Dad replied, "Well, if I am doing my rounds and I hear someone about, I can slip away quietly without them hearing me."

My father had the usual night-watchman's hut in the back yard of Hall Place. At regular intervals during the night, he was required to patrol round the house and turn a key in a number of clockwork devices fixed at various points. These recorded the times of his visits.

There is no record that Suffragettes ever visited Hall Place, but if they had I can only imagine my father greeting them as they struck their wicked match, with "Now, now, my dear young woman, what's pretty young thing like you doing in a miserable place like this? Votes? No, that's not what you want. What you want is a nice cup of tea to warm you up. You come along to my hut – I've just put the kettle on – and we'll have it made in no time." What a blessing for my poor mother that Suffragettes never turned up at Hall Place. Dad always had a reputation as a ladies' man.

LEIGH CHURCH SUNDAY SCHOOL

The children of Leigh were well served with religious instruction in the years leading up to and including those of the Great War.

The Village School, as a Church of England establishment, began each day with a hymn and a prayer, followed by Bible and Prayer Book study. By the time Standard VII was reached every boy and girl could be expected to know much of the Old and New Testaments and to be able to recite the whole of the Church Catechism, which included in its content the Ten Commandments and the Apostles Creed. Grace was sung before and after each midday meal, and before every dismissal "Lord keep us safe this night, ..."

On Sunday mornings at 10 o'clock in the School room, was morning Sunday School. Over this presided plump and homely, the Vicar's wife, Mrs O.F. Walton, widely known in her own right as the author of such improving and sentimental children's books as "Christies Old Organ", and "A Peep Behind the Scenes".

Mrs Walton's two grand-daughters, Stella and Diana sat in chairs in front of the class while we village children sat in the rows of desks facing them. Gazing upon their lovely dresses and well groomed appearance, not to mention their perfect manners, I could almost believe that Miss Stella and Miss Diana were angels from heaven. We sang sweet hymns from the "Golden Bells" Collection, and listened to comforting stories about the gentle Jesus.

On Sunday afternoons there was "real" Sunday School held in the day school with classes and teachers. The superintendent teacher at one time was Miss May Hicks, an amply built person with a non nonsense manner, and very wide hat. She was helped by Miss Doris Russell, Miss Ivy Walton, Miss Fanny Hitchcock, Miss Flo Martin and others. Miss Olive Bowles played the piano for the hymns. Missionary causes were supported by the sale of tickets, green ones for a halfpenny and red ones for a penny. My tickets were all green, the most my mother could afford. Children whose parents did not fear for their offspring falling into the sin of pride took home red tickets. Stamps depicting Bible stories were issued and religiously stuck into the albums provided.

Twice a year there were treats. The summer one was usually held in Leigh Park, but the one I best remember was when we all rode in farm wagons behind horses to Penshurst Place. There we had races, and played "The King of the Barbarees" and similar singing games, and had our picnic tea on the very site where, today, Lord de Lisle has provided an adventure playground for the children of his many visitors. The winter treat was held after Christmas in the Village Hall. There stood a large Christmas Tree loaded with presents. The tables were loaded with food seldom seen in our own homes. But we were still told, "You must start with bread and butter". Boys boasted afterwards of how many slices and how much cake they had eaten. There were crackers or "Bon-bons" as they were then called with paper hats and whistles. Sometimes there was an entertainment in the form of a magician or ventriloquist, but sometimes we provided our own entertainment with games such as Oranges and Lemons and The Farmer's in his Den. Then came the presents which were distributed from the tree by Lady Hollenden. During the war the presents were of useful garments, jerseys, shirts, blouses and skirts which delighted our poor parents when our parcels were unwrapped. Then the prizegiving. The prizes were books, popular annuals like "Chatterbox", "The Prize", "Our Darlings", "The

Rosebud Annual" and "Little Folks". Without these magnificent books our supply of good reading matter throughout the year would have been poor indeed. Likewise art. It was in the "Rosebud Annual" that I first met Louis Wain and his cats, and I have loved them ever since.Each prize book had an illuminated label on the inside of the front cover. The typical inscription would be "Leigh Church Sunday School. Presented to Harry Wood for regular attendance and good conduct. 1914". The treat ended with each child being presented, on leaving, with an orange – a real luxury in those days.

It is a sad thing to record that after all the loving care that was given and joy received from the Sunday School, my departure was such a shameful matter. Some of us boys, getting too big for our boots, began to play up the teacher and disrupt the whole class. Miss Hicks called the Vicar who promptly led us to the door and put us outside. I never went back.

THE GREAT WAR

I was approaching seven years old when the Great War began in August, 1914. My recollection of the scene in Leigh is one of marching troops with fife and drum bands, or, better still, a bugle band. They were on recruiting drives for Kitchener's Army. Our nextdoor neighbour, Mrs Ford , told my mother of how her sons were "A-mad to join". Later on the recruiting marches became route marches without bands, but with seemingly endless columns of soldiers marching four-abreast singing and whistling "Pack Up Your Troubles" and "Keep the Home Fires Burning". The troops were followed through the village by children who hoped to beg or find a soldier's button, badge or stripe when they rested on the Green.

In school the lessons reflected the intense patriotism of those early days of the War. Geography was largely delighting in the extent of the areas coloured red on the map of the World. Drawing and painting lessons consisted of producing endless designs depicting Union Jacks and the flags of all Britain's allies. The songs we learned were, "Britannia the Pride of the Ocean", and "God Who Made our Motherland Fragrant, Fair and Free". Sometimes troops in training arrived to practise manoevoures in Penshurst Park where sham fights took place. We children followed to watch and collect the spent brass cartridge cases. To be invited to have a mug of soup at a field kitchen, sent us heavenward.

A volunteer force of "veterans" was formed with Mr Hubert Russell as Captain. They wore grey uniforms with peaked caps, and, on parade carried dummy rifles. They did however practise rifle-shooting with real weapons at butts in Leigh Park between the lake and Birdcage Walk. We used to cheer the troop trains as they passed through Leigh Halt on their way to the Channel ports. We waved to the soldiers and they waved back to us. When the Red Cross trains with their blind windows began to return with such regularity, we children stood silent and wondering on unimaginable suffering within.

In due course our Village Hall and Institute buildings became a military hospital, mainly, I think, for convalescing warriors. Local ladies, including the Vicar's daughters became V.A.D. nurses. Other village women were recruited for domestic duties. The men in "hospital blue", many of them Canadians, were familiar figures about the village. Sometimes they organised amateur entertainments to which we village children were invited. This was my earliest introduction to "the Stage". I was enchanted, and thought they were magnificent with their cheery songs and comic sketches.

In the early days of the war a flying machine overhead sent us racing indoors crying "Aeroplane – aeroplane". Our mothers were brought outside to view this new marvel of science. As the war progressed these frail machines with red, white and blue rings on their wings would frequently make forced landings and send us running to the Green Field, Tapners, Barnetts, Twenty Acres and Leigh Park Farm to get a close up view of the new wonder, and the heroes who flew them.

Then we learned that an aerodrome was to be laid out in the fields beyond the Compasses. Hedges were grubbed and Canadian lumberjacks arrived to fell the many large oak trees on the site and in Blackhoath Wood. We children took our little carts to gather the axemens chucks of wood, and proudly take them home for our mothers fires. Like magic two large hangars appeared opposite Knotley Hall together with administrative and operational buildings. There were also long wooden huts to accommodate the men of the Royal Flying Corps. Exciting wind-socks were set up, and there were lighthouses at Charcott Corner and on the little rise opposite White Post Farm. Aircraft arrived, tiny machines of wood and canvas with wooden propellers and open cockpits. We soon learned to identify the different makes. There were clumsy De Havilands, Vickers with top wing longer than the lower, Farman's with propellers behind the engine, Sopwiths, Bristols, Avroes and occasionally the giant Handley-Page. The pilots and other personnel in their smart light blue uniforms were regarded by us as gods. One other marvel of those days was the motor vehicle on the White Post rise, equipped with "Wireless". We were thrilled to watch the operator with his headphones actually speaking to the pilots flying overhead. I cannot remember that aerial combat with German planes ever took place over Leigh, but there were alarms from time to time. The Fire Station alarm at Tonbridge was sounded to give warning of air raids on London. One night, after one such warning, we were roused from our beds by my mother and taken to a neighbour's house. We watched the searchlights scanning the sky and saw in their beam a Zeppelin. We could hear the drone of its engines. The searchlights escorted it on its way, but it was not intercepted. To me, it was a great adventure to be drinking cocoa and eating a biscuit in candlelight in a neighbour's house in the middle of the night.

The Powder Mill suddenly became a hive of industry. Normally producing a steady supply of gunpowder for sporting purposes, the Curtiss and Harvey works was now called on to produce large amounts of explosives for military use. The workforce was rapidly increased by the employment of young men under military age, and, for the first time, women. They were recruited from the village, Tonbridge and the surrounding district. Most of them cycled to work, and the footpaths were tar surfaced for their convenience, and have remained unofficial cycle tracks ever since. There were sometimes accidental explosions resulting in injury or death. On a night in 1916 a factory building was struck by lightning, and there was a mighty explosion, resulting in the death of some workers. I can remember seeing the boarded fence round the works lying flat, and many other evidences of damage.

On Saturday mornings my mother and I walked through Powder Mills to search the Tonbridge shops for ever-dwindling supplies of food. But whatever foodstuffs might have been difficult or impossible to obtain, there appeared to be no shortage of cigarettes. Strewn all around the works gate at the Powder Mills were dozens of empty packets, discarded by the workers after a last draw before going on their shift. I used to collect the packets, many of them attractively designed and bearing magic names like "Classic", "Monastery", "Waverly" and "Pinewood". Other fruitful sources for the cigarette packet collector were the V.A.D. Hospital refuse heap in the Brickyard, and the Aerodrome "tip" towards Charcott Corner. Arrived at Tonbridge, my mother trailed from one shop to another, joining the queue at "The Maypole" for a few ounces of margarine and cheese, and at the "International" for tea, sugar and bacon, all strictly rationed. Then to certain corner shops to see if they had any black treacle (take your own jar) or oatmeal or flaked maize. Sometimes a fish shop would have red herrings

– an inferior sort of kipper. These severe food shortages of 1917 – 18 obliged our mothers to devise many unusual meals in order to feed their families. Meat was scarce and rationed, but sheeps head, tongue, brains, heart and bones for soup were sometimes obtainable. Bread, also rationed, was a dirty grey colour having potato and other meal mixed with the flour. It was called 'standard' bread. Our fathers brought home rabbits, and even woodpigeons were prized as a supplement to the meat ration. We children, on our birdnesting expeditions, brought home moorhens, wild duck and peewits' eggs. Some artillery horses were stabled near the Iron Room, and the soldiers in charge of them sometimes gave us children some of the food supplied for the horses. This food was locust beans, with hard black pods and sweet flavoured.

We had got so used to living under war conditions that we could scarcely believe it when we were told that the war was to end. On the morning of November 11th 1918, we were told in school of the surrender of the German forces. There was great excitement and rejoicing, and the rest of the day was a holiday. One of the elder boys, Alec Brooker, proposed and arranged for a bonfire on the Green. All the afternoon we scurried around collecting wood and built our fire, and in the evening we celebrated with the biggest blaze that we could achieve at such short notice. The war was over.

TOM BELTON AND THE BAKERY

My first job upon leaving school at fourteen was at the bakery just up the road. Tom Belton had, a year so earlier, left Edenbridge to take over the business from retiring Charlie Friend. He was young and merry with springy hair and dusty eyebrows. But it was his wife, brunette and a little severe who was said to be the brains of the establishment. My father did various odd jobs for Tom, and so, when Ray Jenner left as roundsman, I was told that I was to succeed him. I had no ambition to be a baker or anything else. The job was there, and I was in it. "Looks pretty small!" commented my mother as I set off to work on my first morning. It hardly gave me the self-confidence that I so badly needed then and always. My job was to deliver bread in the village and immediate neighbourhood, while Percy Martin and Cliff Young had rounds covering Penshurst and the Causeway and the wilder parts beyond. I had a box-barrow which I had to pull, and a carrier bicycle. Percy and Cliff had a splendid Ford motor van with painted side-panels depicting corn and poppies. Cliff, with his thick lensed pince-nez, was the driver. Ray was kept on for a few days to teach me the round and to ride the bicycle, an awkward monster with the carrier fixed directly on the handlebars. It was used for delivering to outlying parts of the village. A two-pound loaf of bread in those days, I discovered, cost fourpence halfpenny, and a half gallon of plain flour, ninepence.

And so to meet the customers. When I came to the forge, blacksmith Charlie Hayter greeted me with "Started work then Harry?" "Yes, Mr Hayter", I replied proudly. "Worst days work you ever done", he grumbled. "You'll always have to go on working now, all your life". He was right!

That carrier bike caused me some trouble at first. With its basket piled high with loaves I set out for Ensfield. One day the floods were over the road by Killicks Bank gate. I attempted to ride through them, dropped into an unseen pothole, and – splash – I was floundering in the flood, while my bread was literally cast upon the waters and floating away across the fields. On this same stretch of road near the river, Frank once invited me to take the wheel of the Ford van. I think he assumed I would know what to do. But after about 30 yards we were in the hedge, and my driving career had begun and ended.

After my rounds each day, the first thing to do was to book in all the day's transactions. From my round-book I read out the sad story which Mrs Belton copied into the ledger. Then we emptied my leather cash bag and counted the takings. I recall with sorrow that in all the three years I worked for Mr Belton on no day did the cash on the table tally with what the Ledger said it should be. Always a few pence, sometimes shillings, over or under – usually under. Mrs Belton was pained and sometimes caustic, but nothing seemed to make me money conscious. My next jobs were in the bakehouse, clearing out the ashes, getting in wood and coal for the next days baking, greasing the bread tins, washing up the cake-making utensils and popping up to the back door of the Brickmakers' Arms for Tom's packet of ten "Players" then costing sixpence. Tom was a chain smoker and one suspects that both dough and cake mixture had a tobacco-ash content. On Saturday afternoons I scrubbed the yard and the brick path to the shop, and received my wages for the week, fourteen shillings.

Tom Belton was a great humourist, always ready for a quip and a joke. One day he sent me out to the back garden to see if the sheep were still there. "Sheep" I enquired innocently. "Yes" he replied "I've got a couple of sheep out there". I went to look and returned perplexed. "I can't see them", I said. "They are there all right", he said with twinkling eye. "An ash-sheep and a rubbish-sheep".

Tom drew me aside one day to tell me that "the missus" had informed him that my sales of bread were falling. "You'll have to sell more", he said. "But the customers don't want any more", I told him. "Look here", said Tom, "If they say they don't want any more, you say`you never know what you might want Ma'am'. If they say they can't do with it, you say `I've never known anyone have more than they can do with'.. If they say they haven't a place for it, you say `There's a place for everything in this world Ma`am'. And if they say they can't afford it, you say `If you wait till you can afford it, Ma'am you'll never have it.'" I listened, dumb, to this high-pressure sales talk, anticipating by fifty years the efforts of today's `reps`. Finally, "Tell them that if they keep on eating Belton's bread they'll never die". "But that's not true", I protested. "Nothing truer", replied Tom. "Could you go on eating Belton's bread after you are dead?" There was no answer to that.

On Saturday mornings I had to take about a dozen loaves to the Church, which I placed in the large round-bellied Charity basket on the seat in the porch. This bread was distributed to certain poor of the parish after Morning Service on Sundays. I remember that my sister was one child who was rewarded, (or was it bribed?) with a half-penny for collecting Widow Ford's loaf, and bringing it back in a red handkerchief. Gradually, some recipients of the charity loaf had made unofficial arrangements to have the loaf delivered to their house to save them going, or sending someone to the church to collect it. Soon I was placing only four loaves into the basket, and these were for customers of rival bakers, Grayland of Charcott and Wolf of Hildenborough. Eventually I was approached by one of these to see if arrangements could be made, etc. I said I would have to ask the Boss. What the Boss actually said was, "If they can eat Graylands bread all the week, they will bloody-well have to go to church on Sunday to partake of the true bread – Beltons". But it was only his joke. Charity prevailed. The custom of distributing charity bread after the Morning Service gradually died out and Tom Belton gained another regular customer or two. Tom Belton was once questioned about his own churchgoing. "Why do you always sit in the front pew under the Lectern"? Tom was no humbug. "Good for trade!" he replied breezily. You wouldn't find a more honest answer than that.

Everyone was trusted in those days. The bread, flour and corn that I sold was never checked out or in. I just loaded on to the barrow what I deemed I should need each day. One day I lost my whole load. Returning from a customer's house at Church Hill, my barrow was gone! But there was a group of giggling teen-aged girls. It was meant to be a joke, but I got very angry and slapped the face of one of the girls. The girl told her father, and he reported me to my boss. Next day Mr Belton told me that I must apologise to Mr Reed, the grocer for striking his daughter. Mr Reed was a fellow village trader and a good customer, so it had to be done.

On another occasion I got home from my morning round for a very late dinner. "Gales", Mr Ridge's present charming abode, with lovely laid-out garden, was, in those days Teddy Skinner's ramshackle cottage in a wilderness of trees and bushes. Mrs Skinner, who went out to work, always left a note in the shed as to her requirements. One day, as I put her order in a crock in the shed the wind blew the door shut. I was trapped in pitch darkness with no bobbin on the inside to lift the latch on the outside of the door. After a very long time, my gropings found me a saw, and I had started a long if not impossible task when Mrs Skinner returned at twelve o'clock and released me. And then there was the rest of my round to complete!

Mrs Belton was a woman of intelligence and culture. She used to lend me books, books by David Grayson, a gentle writer on nature, and observer of character. They had their influence. David Grayson was quite a cult at that time with Mrs Belton and her friend Sophie Nicholson who lived next door in a tiny cottage, now extended and called "Bombers". They were great lovers of wild flowers, and they also organised Wednesday night dancing in the Village Institute. To gramophone records we young people did out best to learn the Boston-two-step, the Barn Dance and The Lancers. Sometimes on a Sunday afternoon Mr and Mrs Belton would take me with them on a drive round the countryside – motoring then was a new pastime for the privileged few – proving they were not only "the Boss", but real friends too.

Percy Martin was the chief bread baker, while Tom made the cakes. Percy went in at about seven o'clock each evening to mix the dough for the first batch of bread. He was busy until about ten. Then home to bed and up again about four a.m. to mould the loaves, set them to rise and put them in the oven. Then he would be joined by Tom and Cliff Young to get to work on the second batch. This was drawn by 9 o'clock when he could go home to bed for a few hours before going out on the afternoon round with Cliff. They got home some time before five o'clock. What hours to work! Nobody would stand for that in these days.

TEMPERANCE

Once a year a little man dressed in black, with black Homburg hat came to address the top class of the school on the subject of Temperance. I never had the faintest idea what he was talking about, and never remotely associated his subject with the unfortunate condition in which my father once returned from "the pot-house" as my mother scornfully called "The Brickmaker's Arms". "You've been up that pot-house again, Dick!" she railed. I felt sorry for Dad.

"Learn to control your alcoholic drinks", intoned the little man. Then we were all set to write an essay on the lecture we had heard but never understood. Those who managed to get down something on their paper, some weeks later received an emblazoned certificate in pink or green. But my paper remained blank, so no certificate. The fact that I have remained sober all these years, I attribute, not to the passion with which the little man delivered his lecture, but to the pain and scorn in my mother's voice.

LEIGH FREE CHURCH

The present day Royal British Legion Halls, the Village Hall and the adjoining stone cottage were built round about 1870 by Samuel Morley to serve as Church, Sunday Schools and Minister's house for the promotion of his own particular brand of religious non-conformity. Although so soundly and beautifully constructed the buildings did not last long as places of worship and religious instruction after the death of their founder. By the time I first remember them, forty years after they were built, the large Chapel building had become the Village Hall; the room which had been used for total immersion baptisms (and still has the font under the floor) was the Clubroom and Library of the Men's Institute with portrait of the founder opposite the fireplace. The schoolroom had sunk so low as to become a billiards room; while the cottage where once dwelt the Revd Mr Maxted, the resident minister, now housed the caretaker of the buildings.

The remnants of a once thriving congregation were relegated to a corrugated iron building well behind the magnificent main halls. It was known generally as The Chapel and by the irreverent as The Tin Tabernacle. Within, the walls and pitched ceiling were of well-knotted varnished matchboarding. At the west end was a low platform and reading desk, and a table for celebration of "The Lord's Supper". Above the platform on the wall was the inevitable portrait of Samuel Morley, flanked by framed texts. Beside the platform was an American organ. The rest of the furnishing consisted of wooden benches with backs and a large Tortoise stove which consumed coke, and gave forth sulphurous fumes like unto those which some of the preachers reminded us was the atmosphere of the final destination of sinners. Coconut matting covered the floor, and swan-necked gas lamps jutted from the walls. Services were held each Sunday morning and evening. The minister I best remember was a Mr Downe, tall, grey and of benevolent appearance. At the given hour he would emerge from the vestry by the door at the side of the dais, and take his place at the reading desk to lead the congregation in hymns and prayers, and to give an address. The hymns were those of Sankey and Moody, stirring ones like "When the Roll is Called up Yonder, I'll be there", and sentimental ones such as "Shall we Gather at the River". Miss Hilda Snachell accompanied the hymn-singing on the American organ. Prayers were long and impromptu. "Shall we ask Brother Burfield to lead us in prayer?" says Mr Downe, and Bro "Bob" would offer praise, penitence and petition, with often the most embarrassing and confidential references to other members of the congregation. The address was invariable on the theme of "Are you Saved?" and "Is there a Sinner here tonight?" which sent at least one poor soul away with a very guilty feeling. "There were ninety-and-nine that safely lay in the shelter of the fold," we had been singing "But one was out on the hills away, far off from the gates of gold." They made me feel pretty sure that I was that "one".

Other visiting preachers that I remember were bearded and benevolent Mr Coulstock, and dark and handsome Mr Fred Taylor. Gentle but feeble Mr Hills from Causeway sometimes played the American organ.

Members of the congregation included Mr and Mrs Bob Burfield, Mr Jack Burfield, Mr Snachell and his daughters from Cinder Hill and members of the Taylor and Wells families. The three elderly Crowhurst sisters who lived in one of the now demolished parish cottages where now is Saxby Wood, were staunch chapel supporters.

Mr and Mrs George Hoath, an unhappy and incompatible couple, acted as caretakers, cleaners and verger of the Chapel. On one Sunday morning I met George furiously chasing up the High Street to the fountain in the wall. "In trouble George?" I enquired. "Forgot to get the bally holy-water!" shouted George hotly.

The burial ground, a small triangular plot adjoining the Chapel, today pathetically overgrown and neglected, was once beautifully maintained. Every grave was carefully tended, and many were adorned with those semi-spherical glass gloves containing a collage of china and metal flowers, leaves, angels and sentimental texts, protected by a galvanised wire cage.

Not again shall we see there, a small group of these simple and sincere folk standing around the graveside of a departed brother or sister singing "Safe In The Arms Of Jesus".

MRS BURR

It must have been a year or so after the end of the War, a crowded meeting in the Village Hall, everyone spellbound, Mrs Burr was speaking, quiet and lucid – a magnificent speech. She was only winding up the affairs of the Jam Committee (a body which existed during the War to procure sugar and make jam for the village) and explaining how that it had been decided to use a certain balance of money in hand to procure for the village a piano, but everyone who heard her, wished that they could continue listening to her for much longer than she spoke.

Mrs Burr's chief claim to village memory will rest upon that speech, and her work for the Jam Committee, and afterwards the Women's Institute, of which she was first president.

Today Mrs Burr has passed from our village life. In a manner, she passed a dozen years ago, when a creeping paralysis overtook her; and for all those years the village has extended its sympathetic thoughts to her, and to her husband, through her terrible illness.

The piano in the Small Village Hall, of which Mr Burr is a trustee, is still a valuable amenity.

HOP PICKING

In the early part of this century there was scarcely a farm in and around Leigh that did not grow hops. The Home Farm was the notable exception. Paul's Farm, or "Poles" as we called it, was farmed by "Billy" Goodwin and had its wirework garden opposite the farm across the road, and some smaller polework gardens behind the farm. At one time hops were grown to the south side where the oast house stands. Ensfield Farm, with tenant farmer Stevens, had several fields of hops out towards "The Rushetts" and just over the parish boundary were more hopgardens belonging to Upper Hayesden Farm. Genial, curly headed Alf Faircloth had numerous pole gardens on the south side of Powder Mill Lane, while his brother Charles at Little Barnetts had his pole work on both sides of the road, and also in fields behind the farm at Kennards, which was farmed by Billy Cook. At Ramhurst, Harry Maskell had wirework gardens down by the brook. On the other side of the brook, in Hildenborough parish, were more hopgardens at Meopham Bank. Tom King at Leigh Park Farm had many acres. Hops were also grown at Wickhurst on the other side of the road, and more at Charcott Farm. Another great hop-grower was J Day of Moorden.

It is hard to believe today that nearly all of these acres of hops were picked by local people, only Tom King and J Day employing "Londoners" and itinerant pickers. Almost every working-class family in the parish was engaged on one or other of the farms for the five or six weeks that the picking season lasted. In most hopgardens there were at least three "sets" of about eight bins. Some of the bins were divided into "halves" for a single picker. A mother with a family of children would usually have a whole bin. Three sets would normally pick enough hops each day to provide two loadings for the usual two-kiln oast house. School holidays were geared to "hoppicking". The summer break was usually the last week in August, the whole of September, and sometimes the first week of October. The village folk were mostly employed by Billy Goodwin. Mr Wenham was the measurer I first remember, but he was afterwards superseded by Sam West. The measurer was closely watched by "the booker" Miss Ethel, Billy's daughter, to see that he took full measure each time he dipped the bushel basket into the bin. Miss Ethel also admonished those pickers who left too many leaves in their bin, or did not pick up the hops lying around the bin.

Although Paul's Farm was our nearest hopgarden, my mother chose, for some reason to go hoppicking on the other side of the village at Great and Little Barnetts farms. Charlie Faircloth, lean and serious, at Little Barnetts was the first to have his hops picked, and we then moved back to his brother Alf at Great Barnetts. The hops from both farms were dried in the oast at Great Barnetts by Grandfather Fautly.

I have vivid memories of dewy and frosty early mornings, climbing the stile along the Hildenborough road and crossing the fields to the hopgardens around Billy Cook's Kennards Farm. There were often mushrooms to be gathered, and, later in the day, blackberries. The next garden to be picked was just beyond Little Barnetts Farm, where today cars and lorries fly along the Tonbridge bypass. Then came the garden on the other side of the road opposite the farm, running back to the edge of the marshes. A rugged sandstone cliff provided a wonderful natural adventure playground for the children. Strict mothers kept their offspring close to the bin, picking into boxes, baskets or upturned umbrellas. But my mother did not press me overhard, and I soon drifted off with other boys to the cliffs and wood. These were the days of the Great War, and therefore many of the games were based on military activities. The hopgarden had clods as big as footballs, causing much grumbling amongst the women. But these clods, built into forts and strongpoint, made excellent defences against bombardment from an inexhaustible supply of bombs – more clods.

A make-believe I much enjoyed was to build an aeroplane cockpit in a heap of used poles and bines, and imagine myself one of the new breed of aeroplane pilots. A hop-pole also made a fine implement for vaulting ditches. Hop-poles were not supposed to be played around with, but preserved for use in future seasons, but broken poles could be used to make fires for boiling the dinner-time tea kettle. The hop-poles were about ten feet long, preferably of ash or chestnut, which would last for several seasons. They were set up in the "alleys", two or three to a "hill" with overhead, and sometimes branching, strings. The hop bines climbed the poles and along the stringing. The "bins" were set end to end along an alley about ten hills from the edge of the garden with two hills on both sides of each bin. When "All to work" was called the "pole-puller" in charge of each set put the bines of each pole about two feet from the ground, severed the overhead strings with a sharp hook on a long pole, pulled the pole and delivered it, laden with its aromatic crop to the picker at the bin.

To do this all day for his "set" of perhaps eight bins kept him pretty busy. When the ten hills each side of each half-bin had been pulled and picked, the set would move off to another part of the garden, the pole-puller carrying the bins on his shoulder. The pole-puller also had to hold the "pokes" – loose yellow sacks holding ten bushels – for the measurer.

Charlie Faircloth, did his own measuring. His wife did the booking, marking the bushels taken from each bin and half-bin, and writing the number on each picker's card and in her own ledger. Unlike "Miss Ethel" and later, Mrs Sands at Paul's Farm, she did not seem to see the small basket – "the catch" – that Charlie would often take from a very poor villager.

The "Tally", or rate of pay for picking, was set after work had been in progress for a few days when the farmer could assess roughly what his yield might be. In those far-off days of the Great War the tally might have been set at "eight a shilling". That is, you had to pick eight bushels to earn one shilling. A single picker might expect to pick twenty bushels in a day to earn half-a-crown.

On one occasion – I think it was in 1918 – there were murmurings of dissatisfaction when it was learned that Billy Goodwin's tally was seven a shilling. Charlie Faircloth was approached to see whether he could match this. He couldn't. Led by a forceful lady, Mrs Jack Brooker, a strike was called, and all the women stood solemnly by their bins while Mrs Brooker put the pickers case to Charlie. Charlie looked serious as he left the hop garden. Many of the women, including my mother, would dearly have liked to go on picking, as they recalled how often Charlie had given them "the catch", in contrast with

Billy Goodwin's measurer who always filled the basket. There sat the women, not daring to pick a single hop for fear of Mrs Brooker. In the middle of the afternoon Charlie returned, presumably after seeing his bank manager. "Seven a shilling" he declared, and a big cheer went up, but whether it was for Charlie or for Mrs Brooker and her supporters, I could never be sure.

In hopgardens where there was wirework as at Paul's Farm, Ramhurst and Moorden, the bines were trained up strings, four to a hill, to the permanent overhead wires which had hooks to receive the string. In this case the bines did not have to be cut near the ground but were pulled on until the string broke overhead. This method enabled the work to proceed in a manner different from that in pole work. Instead of the poles being brought to the bins, the bins were moved along the alleys to the hills. At the start of picking, the bins were set side by side along one edge of the garden in alternate alleys. When the four hills next to each bin had been picked, the bin with its contents was moved forward to the next four hills and so on through the garden. Thus, polepullers as such, were not required, and "binmen" as they were called could serve a larger set of pickers. But the binman still had plenty of work rolling up the picked bines, hooking down detached branches from the wires, assisting unathletic pickers in moving their bins, holding pokes for the measurer and loading full pokes on to the waggon. It was the custom on paying-out day to "tip" the binman sixpence or a shilling.

Back to Barnetts. When all of Charlie Faircloth's hops had been picked, pickers, polepullers, bins, pokes, poke waggon, measuring basket, coats, umbrellas, dinner baskets, chairs, boxes, tea kettles, prams, pushchairs and kids would move to the next field which was brother Alf's of Great Barnetts, and picking would start all over again. The only difference was that stocky curly-haired Alf, did the measuring and his young and pretty wife did the booking. It must have been the vision of "Mrs Alf" that first made me aware of feminine beauty. Alf was as renowned as his brother for giving "the catch", and often on a Saturday morning measuring, the basket would scrape up no more than a peck, but Alf gave it full value of a bushel. No wonder he never made a fortune as a farmer!

Towards the end of September, mornings were often frosty. Picking icy hops was agony to the fingers. The open-air life of the hopgarden could provide great contrasts in weather. Blazing hot days compelled pickers to improvise shade by hanging a poke on a hop-pole propped on the end of the bin. Picking continued through rain or shine, though a thunderstorm would send some pickers to the doubtful shelter of a hedge.

At last came a day when the last pole of the garden was pulled, and a great shout went up from the children who were, by this time, sick and tired of the hopgarden. There was usually some horseplay after the final measuring, some of the younger women putting a young polepuller in the bin, or of a young lad being tied up in a poke. Then the pickers trooped to the farm house to be paid. Bin cards were checked with the ledger and each picker received her reward for the many long days of toil, four or five pounds perhaps for four or five weeks' work, but much needed for buying the children winter clothes and shoes for the return to school. But still it might not be quite the end. Brother Bill Faircloth of Warren Farm, Penshurst, might still have hops to be picked though it was now well into October, and some of the pickers were persuaded to go there to help out. Each morning at 7.30 am a horse and waggon loaded with women and young children and babies left Leigh for Penshurst. I can remember Mrs Dodswell amongst the company, breast-feeding her baby on the way. They sang as they travelled as if on an outing. A few more shillings worthily earned.

THE ENGINEERS' DEPARTMENT AT HALL PLACE

After I had worked for three years for Tom Belton, I went into the Engineers' Department at Hall Place. At that time Harry Heney was in charge and Bernard Pankhurst was the second man and I took the place of William Baldwin and we operated from the Waterworks in Kiln Lane. At that time the two estate bricklayers worked from the old Gasworks which adjoined the Waterworks.

We were responsible for the water supply for the house and for the estate houses in the village and also for the electric generating plant at Hall Place and for the central heating at Hall Place. Though gas was no longer made in Leigh we were responsible for seeing that the two gas holders at the old gas works were kept topped up with gas from the Tonbridge main supply. The Old Hall Place gas works supplied Hall Place with gas and the village hall and institute but so far as I know never supplied other houses in the village.

The well was twelve feet in diameter and the borehole was sunk to the Hastings sand level, a hundred and ten feet below ground level. There were no filter beds but water was purified and softened by the Porter-Clark process. The system was to add quicklime to water in a small tank and small quantities of the resulting lime water were then added to the main flow in an agitating cylinder. When the quicklime was introduced choking gaseous fumes were produced, hence the reason for the attractive louvred lantern at the top of the octagonal building. After the lime water had been added to the main flow it was passed through three filters which were cloths about three foot square stretched between plates. Every two weeks the cloths were taken out and washed.

The steam 'Cornish' boiler at the Waterworks drove the well pump which pumped the water from the well to a tank at the top of the filter house. At the same time the steam boiler drove a Blakes direct acting pump which pumped the water from the slate tank into the reservoirs. The larger octagonal building was the filter house, the small octagonal building was the well house and the square buildings adjoining housed the boiler and the engines and the coal store.

There were five reservoirs into which the water was pumped. In the South Tower at Hall Place there were galvanised tanks which supplied Hall Place itself. At the top of the mound adjoining Hall Place there were two concentric tanks, the inner tank was covered and supplied the stables, bothy and stable cottages, the outer tank was not covered and took the surplus water from the inner tank and supplied the gardens. The reservoir immediately behind the Stone House originally supplied the four fountains in the High Street, two in recesses in the wall, one built of granite in the triangle and one which was underneath it. There was a reservoir behind the garden at Park House (and now within the garden extension) from which Gate House and Park House probably had a pumped supply. In my time the water supply from the reservoir behind Stone House had been extended to supply the estate houses in the village. There was also a reservoir in the Granary at Home Farm which supplied Home Farm and also the Laundry.

The waterworks were closed in 1938 when Tonbridge took over the supply of water throughout the village. They had of course already been supplying water from Tonbridge to the non-estate houses in the village and there is a post on the side of the footpath at the Powdermills with a date on it (about 1902) which is probably the date on which the water main was brought from Tonbridge to Leigh.

The village pump in the High Street was still working until about 1914 but was little used.

When I went to work at Hall Place in about 1926, there was already a generating plant supplying a D.C.supply with batteries at 110 volts to Hall Place. The engine room was opposite the Bothy and the engine was a gas engine. It was very noisy and used to make terrific explosions which rocked the village. The gas used to get into the exhaust chamber and explode. I can remember one occasion when it blew off a great slab of stone which came down on a greenhouse. The engine had to run every day except Sunday. It supplied electricity to the house and probably to the stables.

The Square – built in 1889 for Samuel Hope Morley, using architects Ernest George and Peto who had earlier built Forge Square and South View. Tenants from The Square obtained their water from the main village pump, even until 1914.

The gas engine became obsolete in 1927 and a new generating house was built opposite the double doors to the kitchen garden. In this house a Ruston oil engine was installed which burnt crude oil. It provided a D.C. supply with accumulators. I do not remember when Hall Place changed to main electricity but it was likely to be before 1938 because as from that date the only staff in the Engineers Department was Bernard Pankhurst. I had become redundant in 1933 as a result of an economy drive.

The engineers were not concerned with the drainage system which was the responsibility of the bricklayers but the estate owned a steam engine which was towed by a horse and we were responsible for its maintenance. It lived at the Home Farm and was used for annual threshing but it was also taken to the wood lodge to drive the circular saw. It was on one occasion used temporarily at the waterworks to supply steam when the Cornish Boiler was replaced by an upright Coffee Pot Boiler.

We also looked after the steam fire engine which lived in one of the stable buildings in Hall Place. It was called a Merryweather and was horse drawn and consisted of a steam pump. I never remember it being used so I cannot say how long it took to get up steam. Our job was to overhaul it periodically to see that it was in working order. There was also a hand fire engine made by Shaw Mason. It had a manual pump which could be operated by people standing on each side of the engine.

There was also a larger village manual engine which was kept at one time where Healy's Garage now stands and before that in one of the buildings behind the Head Gardener's house. Notwithstanding the existence of this engine, Hall Place had to have its own fire engine which was restricted to use on the estate.

The original sewage scheme was put in by Samuel Morley and probably originally only served Hall Place and the estate cottages. In 1910 it was extended to the other houses in the village and a proper filtering system with filter beds was installed south of the railway line. The engines were Hornsby Oil Engines with hot bulb igntion and they were replaced about 1950 with electric engines. Subsequently the whole sewage works became redundant on the construction of a main sewer to Tonbridge.

LEIGH FIRE BRIGADE

The earliest period that I have heard of, of a Fire Service in Leigh, would have been in the latter part of the 19th century. With Alfred Sales as Superintendent and William Baldwin as Engineer it would have been closely linked with the requirements of Hall Place.

My knowledge of the Brigade in the first decade of the 20th century does not extend beyond the names of some of the firemen, contained in a rhyming dramatic sketch written by Miss Daisy Walton for stage performance by local children around 1912. It appears that a chimney fire had recently occurred at Rose Cottage, a pretty little dwelling standing on the site now occupied by Charlotte Bungalows. It was the home of "Nimble" Hounsome and his family, which included his daughter, Dolly. In the sketch, the house was supposed to be well alight when Leigh Fire Brigade arrived. Scraps of the rhyme which I remember hearing quoted were:

Anderson, our captain's here -
He's the first one to appear. *(A boy in officer's uniform appeared on stage)*
Here comes Baldwin bold and brave;
He our Dolly's life will save. *(Though reports were that Dolly's life was never in danger)*
Next comes Simmonds from the Green
Ne'er a braver man was seen.
Here comes Stubbings, young and old
Both are worth their weight in gold.

I cannot remember anything of the Leigh Brigade during World War I but I believe that "Potty" Faircloth, the village wheelwright, had a leading part in it, and soon after the war I well remember his sons Fred, George, Cecil and Ray together with Bert Humphrey and other firemen – all allotment holders – using the manual fire engine to pump water from the Brickyard ponds, through my father's garden to water the allotments (then always called "The Canadie") in the drought of the summer of 1921. At about this period Hubert Russell took over as Chief Officer of the Brigade, and Fred Faircloth as Second Officer. When Abner Parker died in August 1922, Bernard Pankhurst replaced him as Engineer. Mr Russell was a great showman, and under his leadership during the 1920's, Leigh Fire Brigade became the model for the locality. Fire-drill competitions were introduced between Leigh and neighbouring brigades such as Tonbridge, Falconhurst and Stonewall. The equipment available at that time consisted of a hand-cart with hand-pump and hose for use with local chimney fires, and a Shand-Mason Manual Engine, drawn by one or two horses for larger fires. There were competitions for both hosecart and engine, consisting of a drill to get the hose run out and water on a target in the shortest possible space of time. Mr Russell, an electrical engineer, himself devised the timing apparatus to record to one fifth of a second. The competition standard eventually became so high that the Leigh Brigade were taking part (and often winning) events in Southern Counties Competitions at places such as Oxford and Basingstoke, Bournemouth, and Deal (1925).

Leigh Fire Brigade with the manual at a competition in mid 1920s.

The members of the brigade at that time as I remember, were the four Faircloth brothers, Bernard Pankhurst, Charlie Ingram, Bert Stubbings, Bert Humphrey, Ike Kneller, Fred Faultley and Arthur Davis. All were volunteers prepared at a moments notice to leave their workplace, home or bed, in case of a call to a fire. Joseph Randerson and Bill Sturt were administrative officers not required to attend fires.

The great social event each year was the dinner in the Village Institute Hall to which Mr Russell invited all members of the Brigade and anyone remotely connected with it, such as officers of neighbouring brigades, who all turned up in smartest uniform, though none could outshine Mr Russell in his gleaming silver helmet and epaulets. The dress uniform for all the firemen included a polished brass helmet with comb. (For general duty a flat blue cap was worn.) Other guests to the dinner would include the village grocer for the use of his stable, Mr Burr, the Hall Place Agent, for the use of a building to house the fire-engine, Harry Hitchcock, the church organist to provide music. Thus was I included among the guests for being Assistant Scoutmaster to Mr Russell, one of whose other social activities was that of Scoutmaster. Consequently Mr Russell found it impossible to leave out Miss Daisy Walton, his other Assistant Scoutmaster, though she was the only female in this otherwise all-male gathering.

A sumptuous meal was followed by witty speeches and entertainment by semi-professionals from Tunbridge Wells, such as Lyn Hepworth, Freddie Owles and Violet Godfrey.

The practical fire-fighting of the Leigh Brigade never quite matched up to the silver Cups and Bowls that were won in the competitions, nor to the display of photographs and certificates covering the walls of the Institute billiard room. The real trouble was with equipment, transport and communications. For instance, should you have had your house on fire during a certain period of the 1920's, all you had to do was to go to Ike Kneller's house in The Square where, over the front door was a gas-lamp with the word "FIRE CALL". You knocked on the door and told Ike about your fire (if he was in – if not – find him?). Ike would then get out his bike, and, with a big brass hand-bell cycle around round the village calling out Mr Russell and such firemen as he could find, but making sure first to summon Fred Faultly. Fred lost no time in getting on his bike and cycling to Penshurst Station to get the horses which he normally drove in the shafts of Hills Bros. coal trolley. Then back to Leigh to Hall Place garden stable where the fire engine was kept. The engine by now would be ready to start with as many men as possible sitting back to back on the box that concealed the pump and hose. The horses were hitched to the engine and they were away with the hand-bell ringing. Those firemen who failed to find a seat on the engine, and late comers, followed on their bikes. If your fire had burned itself out while you were waiting they would not blame you. Improvements were gradually made, as for instance the use of a coal lorry to haul the engine in place of horses. Fortunately no serious fire disaster occurred in Leigh as a result of inadequate equipment.

I do not recollect whether the Leigh Brigade were called on when a passenger aircraft from Belgium came down in flames at Southwood in October 1926 and all eight people aboard died, but in any case they could not have arrived in time to do anything useful. They were of much more use in fires caused by spontaneous combustion in overheated haystacks, pumping water into the seat of the fire, while cutting away good hay and containing the fire when it threatened nearby stacks in a stackyard. I remember one such fire at Well Place Farm which lasted for two days before all was finally safe. The firemen were exhausted after a night of work. I was one who went to take a turn on the engine, for the manual required at least eight men on the pump at a time, and they could keep it up only for limited periods. All firemen and helpers were eventually paid for their time when the farmer received his insurance money.

Another fire I remember, occurred on the night of November 12th 1934. I was singing in the choir at Church, when the service was momentarily interrupted by the furious ringing of the fire-bell outside. Charlie Ingram, the verger, leapt from his pew behind the church door and disappeared into the night, leaving choir, congregation, and no doubt parson, with no other thought than "Where is the fire?". It proved to be at Ramhurst; a garage, shed and loft, but by the time Leigh Brigade arrived, despite Charlie's swift exit, the Tonbridge Brigade had been and put out the fire, leaving Leigh in the humiliating position of "standing by".

During the 1930's Mr Randerson, secretary of the brigade, had a new motor car and donated his old "Rover" to the brigade. Ray Faircloth, now succeeding his father as village wheelwright, converted the car into a fire tender to carry equipment, and seat about half-a-dozen firemen. A trailer motor pump was purchased, and the manual engine was no longer required.

Towards the end of the 1930's the Rural District Council built a fire station at the junction of Lower Green and the lane to the waterworks and, with the threat of World War II, local fire brigades increasingly came under the authority of local and national government. Men (and women) were recruited into an Auxiliary Fire Service, and at Leigh a professional Fire Officer from London, George Hanson, was appointed to be in charge. One might say that that was the end of the Leigh Volunteer Fire Brigade.

I'll finish with a story told to me by Louis Brooker, the village "snob" whose shop was next to the "Brickmakers Arms" and opposite the new fire station. The fire call had sounded, and a sufficient number of firemen had turned out. The doors of the station were flung open and out came the fire tender with men seated in position. "STOP" cried Fred Faircloth, the Second Officer in charge. Fred leapt off the machine, and dashed up to the back door of "The Brickmakers" "Quick Marge" called Fred, "A packet of Woodbines and box of matches!"

THE RIVER

Ensfield Bridge is the place where Leigh people are most likely to meet the River Medway. One of my earliest memories is of my father taking me there one summer Sunday morning. There, to my astonished eyes, I saw naked young men (for they wore no costumes in those days) apparently walking on the water. I did not then know that the water, some twenty yards above the bridge, was only a few inches deep, with a firm gravel bottom. Other figures nearer the bridge were splashing, swimming and diving in the silvery water. The water in those far-off days was always silvery, never almost permanently muddy as it is today.

The Ensfield Bridge that I knew was a pleasing brick arch, with brick parapets, octagonal end pillars and stone coping. It served its very useful purpose until 1943, when, on the night of February 4th, it unexpectedly collapsed.

The event that older folk are most likely to recall in connection with the bridge would be in the early years of the century, with the tragic death of Mr Englebert of Meopham Bank. One night people living in Lower Green and Ensfield Road heard the sound of one of those new-fangled motor cars passing their houses. Early next morning, men on their way to work saw that the retaining fence by the north-west pillar of the bridge had been smashed, and parts of a motor-car visible in the water. The alarm was raised, and police and sightseers arrived. Boats and grappling tackle were brought to the scene. Our next door neighbour, Jesse Ford, was summoned to bring his three horses from Ensfield Farm. With great difficulty the car was hauled out of the sixteen feet of water on to the opposite south bank of the river. The driver of the car, Mr Englebert, had of course been drowned.

From the old Ensfield Bridge, looking down the river towards Tonbridge, the banks were lined with trees, mostly ash and alder with here and there a great oak, its branches dappling the water. Alders also grew on the south bank on the Penshurst side of the bridge. On the north bank in summer grew a profusion of wild flowers, purple loosestrife, meadowsweet, willow herb, toadflax and yellow balsam, with here and there a wild rose or a may tree.

Ensfield Bridge c1930 - the old bridge. The river has not yet been dredged and cleaned up.

With the formation of the River Board in the 1930's all this natural beauty was swept away. The trees were cut down and their roots dragged out and thrown on to huge bonfires, leaving the banks bare and unstable. This allowed the earth to be washed into the river bed; the once firm gravel or rocky bottom became silted; the water was thick and discoloured; the Medway had become the Mudway! It has never recovered from this drastic treatment. To return to the days before 1930. Every stretch of the river presented some special feature; shallows where minnows and bleak swarmed; rocky reaches with water lilies concealing pike and perch, reed beds where moorhens nested and water voles busied themselves, and clear open swims with shoals of roach. Dace and chub could always be found in the swiftly running reaches, while bream and eels lurked in deeper waters such as Tapners' Hole. On summer days swifts, swallows and martins darted over the water, while swarms of dragon flies and other insects hovered over the reedbeds and the kingfisher flashed a blue streak to the anglers who sat with rod and line.

I would like to mention some of these fishermen on the banks, of whom, in the `20's and 30's, I was one.

There was Harry Heney, renowned for his high-class rods, reels and fine tackle; Mr Percy, Headmaster of Weald School, who was generally accompanied by his daughter; Alf Miller, a retired schoolmaster from Eggpie Lane; Mr Fuggle, a Gas Company manager from Sevenoaks who gave me my first respectable rod, and Bernard Pankhurst, my daily workmate. Then there was Jack Stolton. On a certain Saturday afternoon, I once saw Jack fishing by the bridge with his very indifferent tackle. He had a bag of about a dozen half-pound roach. No such thing could be seen today.

Round about the turn of the century boring for coal was undertaken near Ensfield Bridge. The bore-hole was situated about 30 yards from the river's southern bank and about the same distance west of the road. No coal-mine for Leigh ever resulted. I have been told that the drill broke and the project was abandoned. We sometimes found portions of the cylindrical borings of varying diameter when we were bathing in the nearby shallows, and many more specimens were turned up by the plough only a few years ago.

A quarter of a mile downstream from Ensfield Bridge, was "Babylons" and "Babylons Bridge". There was no bridge to my knowledge, but probably there had been at some time. Both banks were, and are, protected with walls of great blocks of stone, and the water here rushes over other submerged masonry. A few yards beyond the masonry on each side of the river, and opposite, are three stumps of wood in the water, which may be the remains of the piers of a wooden bridge.

On the south bank the wall is continued at a right-angle to retain a barrier which prevents water from the river entering the western end of a canal which was dug in the early part of the 19th century and with a view to making the River Medway navigable to Penshurst.

It was another project that failed. The owners of the Powder Mills, Curtiss & Harvey, a mile further downstream, objected to the water being diverted from the water wheels of their factory. About a mile of the new canal had been excavated when legal objections halted the work. Our village blacksmith, Mr Charles Hayter, once told me the story of how Curtiss and Harvey's had set a man on the remaining ten yards of land between the dry canal and the river. He was armed with a gun and defied the Navigation Company's workmen to put a pickaxe or shovel into his perch. The matter was eventually settled without bloodshed, and with no drop of water entering the canal.

Fifty yards below Babylon's is the footpath from Leigh Green to Upper Haysden and Bidborough. An iron and concrete footbridge crosses the river to bring one on to the Straight Mile. The Straight Mile is a pleasant walk with many oak trees, and was formed by the excavation of the canal, and would have provided the towpath as far as The Shallows at Lower Haysden. The iron bridge was erected in about 1939 and was preceded by an entirely wooden bridge painted white, and consequently known as the White Bridge. Before this, and before my time, I am told, was "The Ivy Bridge" from which we may imagine its rustic appearance. Less than a mile downstream again, we come to the Six Arches carrying the railway line from Redhill to Tonbridge. The river passes beneath the two middle spans, while the two outer ones on either side provide for flood water. Examination of the underside brickwork of these arches shows clearly that the 1842 single line was built on the north side, and, at a later date the bridge was widened by about one third of its present total width to carry the double rail track. A sharp bend in the river below the Six Arches with "The Mount" on the north bank, takes one under the Tonbridge Bypass.

A few yards beyond the Powder Mills Cut, also on the north side, leaves the main river. "Mallions" footbridge crosses the Cut. Then comes the new (1980) Southern Water Authority Weir. The old weir, which it replaced had served its purpose for just 100 years. Into its brickwork was inserted a stone slab bearing the inscription "C & H. This weir was restored in 1880". The iron gates and winding gear have now gone to the Chalkpit Industrial Museum at Amberly. There was a footway over the apron of the old weir, and steps over the nearby railway embankment. The whole area of and around the old weir hole used to be a popular place in summer for boating, angling, bathing and camping. The parish boundary used to follow the course of the river through the Weir Hole and for some distance beyond, Leigh parish on the north bank, Tonbridge Urban area to the south. It would appear that the new weir and river course are wholly in Leigh Parish.

Returning to where we started our exploration of the river, Ensfield Bridge, let us now look at the present structure. Because of the war the bridge was not rebuilt immediately after the collapse of the old one in 1943, and so, for more than four years there was no direct road link between Leigh Village and Ensfield, Haysden and Bidborough. The Royal Engineers did, however, build a high wooden footbridge. The rebuilding of Ensfield Bridge began in 1946, prisoner-of-war labour being employed. A temporary channel was cut on the north bank, and the natural watercourse dammed off. The river bed was pumped dry so that the new bridge could be erected on the site of the old one.

The new bridge was reopened for traffic on September 27th, 1947.

'VIC'

Dick Wood wrote a number of articles which he sent to newspapers – without success, he says. The following is an example.

We never wanted a dog at all. In fact, for five years the rest of the family fought against my plaintive cry of 'Please let me have a puppy'. But eventually he arrived, a tiny shivering creature – the smallest and weakest of a very mixed litter. It was on a cold December night, and he made straight for the hearth and fire. As he had arrived on my birthday, he was named after me 'Vic'.

He was unsettled and unhappy, and we were all much perturbed by the way he ran blindly about the room, squealing and yelping and falling into fits on the floor. We were told that he was suffering from worms, so we gave him powders, and following advice, shut him in the cold lavatory to await "actions". He gave us a lot of trouble that first week or two, and, looking back, I think we gave him more and I now wonder that he survived our cold un-understanding treatment. Eventually we found that he really did need constant warmth from the fire to restore him to puppily health and joy.

As Vic began to grow we could see that he was going to be a nice little fox terrier. He was mostly white, with a few black patches and some brown markings on head and ears; just what we liked! There followed some of the little problems we had imagined. As soon as he was loose out of doors he was away over neighbours' gardens; fleas – he had to be searched and groomed regularly; more worms – more powders; destructive habits such as tearing up paper and people's slippers in the exuberance of puppyhood. But all these problems and others were solved or modified one by one, and our pleasure in him grew. It was pleasant to take him for walks, at first always on a lead, and we well remember his first walk along the village on the lead, when he dragged back all the time, and upon his return home it was discovered that his little soft paws were sore and bleeding. Try as we might we could never make Vic an obedient puppy out of doors. Off the lead he would scamper away and need a deal of catching; not always by calling or coaxing would he come; trickery had often to be resorted to. Never had he any traffic sense; motor cycles were his aversion, and he would fly at them, and so it was decided that he must never be on the roads off the lead for fear of causing an accident.

But indoors he was entirely obedient and delightful. He loved to bound upstairs every morning, leap upon the bed and snuggle under the clothes with anyone who would welcome him (and who could resist?) He would lick your hand or worry your feet, or enjoy a long tussle with an old slipper. He learned to beg for cake and tit-bits, and later, to shake hands when bidden. He caused much amusement by performing for quite long periods on his hind legs. He even went to his basket when ordered (but soon came out again).

In the Spring I began taking Vic to work with me every morning. At first I kept him there on a long chain, but in time, by his charm, he gained his freedom, and seldom strayed far from me. It was on unfamiliar ground where he always went wild and gave most trouble.

One Sunday evening he ran away and was lost in the woods, and though I searched till well after dark, he was nowhere to be found. The next day, to our relief we heard he had found his way back to his mother's home, to the gamekeeper from whom we had bought him. With joy we received him home again. Another time he was lost on a tobogganing afternoon, and I had to search for him that night in a blizzard. At last he dragged his weary legs home and we heard him pawing at the door. How joyfully he was welcomed. But how can I recount all his adventures; a book would be needed. One thing we did find -it was of no use to punish or even scold the dog for any such misdemeanours as running away. He would cringe and shiver and lie in his basket for hours trembling, his whole body convulsed. He was obviously very highly strung and nervous. But how good tempered and friendly to everyone when things were well! We never knew him to snap at anyone. Neighbours trusted him, and he was friends with all their children. Even Bambi the cat was not really frightened when Vic chased him up the apple tree for at other times they would lie together on the rug before the fire and eat from the same dish. He loved to be nursed by any member of the family, and received many names of endearment, chief of which – I don't know why – was "Pumkins", shortened often to Pum or Pum Boy.

Out of doors, he was a real dog, nosing into every hedge or hole, delighting in every smell, pawing furiously in rat and rabbit holes, chasing, but never catching any moving thing or creature. To my knowledge he only ever caught two rabbits and they were but babies. Yet how he enjoyed life!

All through the next wet cold winter Vic and I struggled to work each day, and when the weather was too bad for hunting rabbits on the railway embankment he would sit in my shed and we would snuggle up to keep warm by my oil-stove. But Spring was coming and soon we should have long, long days out of doors together. I began taking Vic to work in the afternoons as well as the mornings.

On March 7th (1950) I was preparing to go home and looked around for my companion. There he was running along the top of the embankment. He had of late got into the habit of going up there, and I was always concerned to get him down, but, when there, he felt rather like the King of the Castle and very independent of me. The 4.45 train was just starting from the station. I ran into the field calling and whistling. This action usually brought him running to me, but tonight, as the train approached, I was ignored. Vic disappeared from my view across the line, and the train steamed by. I watched for Vic but he did not appear again. I told myself that he was across on the other side and I would see him at the arch. Yet I was anxious as I walked homeward, so instead of going through the arch I went over it on the top. I looked along the line and could see something white lying in the track. It might be a piece of newspaper! I went towards it and knew it was Vic. "He might be injured!" I began to run, but he lay so still I knew he was dead. I walked "Oh well", I tried to tell myself calmly. "It is only a dog". How wrong I was. In the days that followed I found he was not "a dog". He was "my dog". He looked so natural lying there, though his head was completely severed from his body and lying on the other side of the rail. But the expression on his face was eager, happy and natural.

I picked him up and carried him back to my shed, dug a little grave by a small cherry tree, and sadly covered the earth over him. Then, something like only half of myself walked home in a sort of dream to tea, and to await the arrival of the rest of the family to break the unbelievable news. Take away the basket – we shall not need it again. This old slipper, these hidden biscuits, this old coat which served for bedding – his only property. How very happy he was with such few possessions! These practical adjustments are soon made but the mental one is only accentuated by them. "No dog" What is the matter with this house? No dog! At every turn and in every action we are expecting him, but No dog.

For eighteen years I had worked alone and had no companion, nor did I need one. Now – no dog. Where is all that vitality? That life? That beauty of form? That affection and trust? That utter relaxation when sprawled on the rug by the fire? That exuberance when bounding on the Green like a young lamb? Extinguished. Can it be? This poem clothed in flesh and hair, for now all his exasperating ways are forgotten.

The next day I pick up his collar from the railway and fix the little disc with "Vicky" on it to the cherry tree. We long to see the little creature again. Every step I take to work I see him trotting near. We cannot remove the thought of him from our minds. For many days daily activities seem purposeless; one of the family has been removed. We remember stories of silly sentimental people pining for the loss of a pet. Surely though our dog was different. However, there it is. He is gone. We shall not see him again. He had a happy life though, if a short one. We are thankful for that. Good boy Vicky!

And the strange thing is, we never wanted a dog at all.

EIGHTY YEARS OF CHANGE

Shortly before he died in 1988, Dick Wood wrote this for the Parish Magazine.

I feel I must have lived through the most eventful period of history. Two horrifying world wars and all is changed. When I was a boy, some children came to school in nothing but rags and threadbare clothes – some of mine were. The poor were maintained (or not) by charity. Now everyone is entitled to shelter, food and clothing. The horse was the main work source on the farm. A few days ago I read that it is no longer termed an agricultural animal. The internal combustion engine together with electricity has changed everything. Many people never left the place where they were born. I am one such. Now men have been to the moon.

Party politics once seemed important – they now seem irrelevant. What does it matter who does the job, so long as it is done and is usually is.

The behaviour of individuals varies a lot as it always did but those who get into trouble now bring it on themselves. Eighty years ago they were driven to crime by harsh laws and conditions.

All doors are now open to man to go into the future in any direction he chooses. Where will he go from here?

Three farm horses from Great Barnetts on their way back home in 1915.

Vicars of Leigh during the 1900–2000 period

HUGH COLLUM	1876-1906
OCTAVIUS F WALTON	1906-1918
GEORGE E WESTON	1918-1926
LEOFRIC W SEALY	1926-1948
JOHN B EYRE WALKER	1948-1957
JOHN H BOUNDS	1957-1980
CHRISTOPHER MILES	1980-1990
(INTERREGNUM)	1990/91
THOMAS V E OVERTON	1991-1999
(INTERREGNUM)	1999/2000
LIONEL W G KEVIS (Priest in charge)	2000

The Revd 'Bill' Simmonds
and The Sales Family

Some time around 1870, Alfred Sales, a thirty year old, wrote to Samuel Morley from London offering his services. He was taken on as the Engineer to Hall Place and put in charge of the water and gas works which were being built. His story is told by the Reverend W.H.C. (Bill) Simmonds who is Alfred Sales' grandson and who knew Leigh well when he was a child in the 1920's.

"The Sales family have been in the parish of Leigh – not in the village but in the parish – since at least the early 1700's. I have found a mention of John Sales who was Church Warden in 1735. I've done quite a bit of research. Someone suggested that the family was Norman – French and spelt de Sales and may have come over with William The Conqueror from Normandy. 1066 and all that! My grandfather, my mother, my sister and six other Sales are all buried in Leigh churchyard. My wife's grave is there and I hope to be buried there too.

St Mary's and the old churchyard with the new Genner Rooms in the foreground.

The family seem to have lived in the Hollanden part of the parish up by Riding Lane and Mill Lane. At one stage, they owned Little Forge Farm which was up there. Some of them were blacksmiths and I remember my grandfather saying that once they built a velocipede which was a thing with four wheels on a wooden frame. It had four big levers which four men pulled and cranks drove the wheels. It must have gone at a terrific rate – probably forty or fifty miles an hour. The forge was on the corner of Mill Lane where the used car garage is now *(1999)*.

My grandfather, Alfred, was born in 1837 up in Hollanden and he went to Judd School. I remember him telling me that he walked across the fields to school and that he was given a penny for his lunch. He bought a loaf for $\frac{1}{2}$d and some treacle for $\frac{1}{2}$d. Then he pulled out the middle of the loaf and poured in the treacle. When he was fourteen, he ran away to sea. He didn't write to his parents for two years. Later, he qualified as an engineer and married a girl called Mary who came from Norfolk. In the 1860's they were living in London and Mary – my grandmother – didn't like living in a city. She nagged grandfather to get out of London. So he wrote to Samuel Morley and got the job as the Hall Place Estate Engineer – initially supervising the provision of gas which was apparently finished in 1874.

Obviously, they got to know the Morley family very well indeed. Grandfather always said that Samuel was a very humble man in spite of all his wealth – a genuine philanthropist. Grandfather and grandmother had a tied house for life – and a pension too. At first, they lived at Engineer's Cottage, next to The Brickmakers. They must have been there for about forty years. Then they moved to what was then called Park Cottage. The Australians, the Worboys, changed it to what it's called now – The White House. And that's where I knew him. My brother and I used to come down from Clapton in North-East London where the family lived and we stayed with him and Grandmother for a week or two at a time – often it was during the Christmas or Easter holidays – from the First World War until the end of the Twenties when he died and I went out to China as a missionary. I was in Sichuan for twenty-one years.

Engineers Cottages, High Street.

The Revd "Bill" Simmonds and the Sales Family

My mother – she was Emma Jane Sales – was born in 1879 – she lived till she was ninety-seven – and she went to Leigh School under Mr Boby. I knew Mr Boby quite well because my mother was one of his best pupils and she came back to the school as a student teacher. There is a good story about the teacher's exam. Because my mother was not very rich, she had to do a correspondence course which you could do then, with Saturday lessons. When the exam results were published, Mr Boby looked up the list and he couldn't find Mother's name. But she said that he hadn't looked high enough: she'd passed very near the top. After she'd done her trainee teaching with Mr Boby, she went to work at a school in the East End of London. I remember her saying that there were sixty children in a class; and when they did singing, there were a hundred and twenty – all quite different from Leigh and Mr Boby.

She married Frederick John Simmonds, my father – he came from around Oxford – and they had five children. I was the third. Mother's brother, my uncle Benjamin Sales, lived in Leigh and ran the big grocers opposite Park Cottage around the turn of the century before Mr Allchin took it over, I think it must have been. Now *[1998]* it's the clock shop and hairdresser.

Allchins General Store, 1909. Mr J. Allchin was followed by Mr Lindridge, then by Mr Burt and then by Spencer and Margaret Coates.

They had five children too – our cousins – and when we came down we used to be with them all the time. We used to go fishing and walking and swimming in the Medway. The road down to the river – it's called Lower Green now – was just a track then, with gates across past Pauls Hill to stop the cattle. When I was a bit older, my brother Fred and I used to play tennis on the Green where the school had a court until the children came out. I remember once in earlier years – it must have been around the end of the First World War – my cousins, Barry and Norman, and my brother, Fred, and I were going out of the village towards Penshurst. When we got to the railway bridge just past the fork at the end of the village, we started walking along the parapet. Then it grew into a struggle to see if we could push the others off. We agreed that if we fell off it had to be on to the road – not on to the railway track! A man came along and he stopped us. Of course, as soon as he'd gone, we started again. But he went along to my grandfather who went across and told my Aunt Lily. So when we all got home, my cousins found their father had been summoned from London and they got a good hiding. I was lucky. Because my mother wasn't there, my grandfather didn't do anything. He gave us a good ticking off but I didn't get beaten.

I remember Park Cottage well and it's interesting to see the changes. When you went in the front door and turned left there was a small lounge. Behind that, at the back of the house, was grandfather's tool room where he did all his work, with a bench under the little window. You reached the workroom from the kitchen. If you turned right from the front door, it was the dining room. Grandfather had a telescope through which we could see the Quarry Hill Laundry sign above and beyond your Oak Cottage. When my mother realized that grandfather couldn't read small print any longer, she bought him a large print New Testament and Psalms which he enjoyed reading as he looked across the Green. I remember him quoting Psalm 50 Verse 10 – 'All the beasts of the forest are mine and so are the cattle upon a thousand hills'. That verse particularly appealed to him being a countryman. I remember there were the cattle in the fields behind Oak Cottage and there were hardly any cars. You'd remark on the make of a car going along by the Green. Grandfather used to watch the cricket from that window too. He'd sit there and smoke his old clay pipe. I remember my grandfather telling me how, one Sunday afternoon when he was young, he and his brother had been rather bored. They wanted a smoke – so they thought that if they went to the next door neighbour, he might let them have some if they said it was for their father. What they had not reckoned with was that when they'd asked and the neighbour let them in, there sat their father, contentedly smoking with the neighbour. 'You said your father wanted some tobacco from me?' was all he needed to say.

Behind the dining room was a big kitchen where we all ate, with a big range on the right; then outside that was a very cold scullery, with a big sink and a brick floor. There was a cellar where I think grandfather stored apples but I don't remember that we were ever allowed down. The Edwards, who live there now, told me there was a rumour of a passage going from the cellar to the church but I hadn't heard of it before. In the coach house there was the cart – we used to go to our cousins in Tonbridge in it – and hay was stored in the loft. I'm not sure where the horse was kept. Later, my father bought a three wheeled Morgan which went in the coach house when we came to stay. I used to drive us down to Leigh. The milkman used to come to the back door with two pails which he carried on a yoke on his shoulders and he'd measure out your milk into your own jug with a tin measuring can. Looking back on the house, I don't remember that it ever had electricity – which was pretty funny when grandfather was in charge of the Water and Light – but it was lit by gas which I always think gives a wonderful atmosphere. And, of course, the gas mantle gave heat too. It certainly made the room comfortable.

We'd do quite a bit of singing – mother played the piano and Aunt Lily – that was Uncle Benjamin's wife, from the shop – was very keen. And we used to go up to the church services. I always remember coming back from one Easter Service and we were discussing the sermon – some of my family said that the curate should not have used Latin words because the villagers wouldn't understand. I used to go up to the church by myself. I must have been between ten and fourteen and I felt fairly grown up. Grandfather was getting a bit old and shaky by then and didn't usually come. I got to know all the Vicars. There was Mr Weston. He was never very strong – I think that he had TB or something. He was a bachelor and used to preach good sermons. I remember he came round and asked if Billy – that was me – would like to come for a walk. We talked a lot as we went across the field and it was interesting but you can imagine what would be said today – you'd need to have two adults if you were going to take a ten year old boy out for a walk. It's awful to think of our society losing its values.

I remember Mr Sealy and his successor, John Bounds. He took some of our family funerals. Christopher Miles got me to preach and, because I always think of Leigh and cricket, I tried to get cricket into the sermon. The only text that I could think of was Psalm 72 Verse 6 – 'He shall be like the rain coming down on the mown grass'. So I said there were three points to think about. First, the grass and our lawns and the cricket pitch is natural; then secondly, the rain comes – it's supernatural from God – and the grass grows; but thirdly, man controls it – which is all about civilization and the discipline of cricket. So I hope that I was able to say a little about how much I love Leigh and all it has stood for in my life. And, of course, as I told you, I mean to be buried here with my wife, God willing."

Lych-gate and St Marys – before the Genner rooms were built.

May Pearson

(Mrs May Everest)

May Pearson was born in 1914 in Edenbridge. She married, had two children and lived in Charcott nearly all her life.

"My father was a carter at Moorden. My father-in-law, Mr Everest, lived at Pond Cottage, Chiddingstone Causeway and was a bricklayer. You had to train properly in those days. He built the Greyhound pub here in Charcott and the bakery. He helped build St Lukes, the Chiddingstone Causeway Church, too. When they first started the foundations, they put them higher up the hill. Then they found that half the Church would have been in the parish of Leigh – so they had to start again lower down, where it is now. When they were thinking of extending the Greyhound to make a restaurant, I remembered something he said and I told them to look at the deeds. When they did, they found I was right: it says it's got to be kept as a place for working men and they weren't allowed a restaurant.

I went to school in Leigh because my father wouldn't let me go to the Chiddingstone Causeway school – it had a woman as head. Miss Ellis was wonderful and Mr Gibbon was a very good teacher – his word was law. We walked to school, of course.

I was due to leave school when I was fourteen but because my birthday fell just at the wrong time of year, they made me stay on an extra term. By that time, I'd got a job at the Station Inn at the Causeway – it's called the Little Brown Jug now. So I had to do the work there and then go to school. It was a taxi place as well as being a pub but we used to have a lot of airmen at the aerodrome they built at Charcott who used to come to stay if they couldn't land at Croydon. Where the car park is now, there were lots of cabins where they used to sleep. I used to get them breakfast".

Mrs Everest died in 1999. Her daughter, Mrs Eileen Gower, lives in her house in Charcott.

Notice on the Green

up until the early 1930s:

```
NO WHEELED VEHICLES

OR SUNDAY GAMES

ON THE GREEN
```

Privies

"There was a privet hedge
between our house and the
big hedge at the side.
Father planted it specially so
it would shield us when we
went across to the privy.
You could sit in there with
the door open a crack and
see what was going on in
the road."

The Leigh Institute and
The Village Halls

This chapter is derived from the Minute Books in the possession of Jack Lucas.

At the turn of the century Leigh had a "Reading Room and Institute" which seems to have been in an upstairs room at 9 The Square. The balance sheets for 1903, 1904 and 1905 show an organization paid for in part by annual donations from the local gentry and in part by members' subscriptions. Samuel Hope Morley was President. All the well-known village dignitaries were on the committee, Dr Fraser, Mr Boby, Rev. Walton, Mr Hedges M.P., Mr Goodwin, Mr Burr, Mr Hitchcock, Mr Russell and Walter Seal, the Head Gamekeeper. The expenditure lists for these three years give a reasonable idea of what the members – seemingly only twenty to thirty men – were able to do for their five shilling annual subscription. A new bagatelle table was purchased for £6-10-0. Newspapers cost around £5 over the year, with the librarian being paid 15/-. £1 was spent on games; and heating and lighting cost around £7 a year which seems to have included hot water. *[Note: a new bagatelle table, handmade in maple veneer, costs £70 in 2000]*

In 1907, Samuel Hope Morley decided to allow the three village halls to be changed from their former uses (a chapel and baptistery in the case of the smaller two) and to be used for an expanded Institute.

F. W. Streatfield, the first Secretary of the new, Provisional Committee, wrote out a speech which he must have given at the initial meeting of ordinary members. "As you are aware, a meeting of the men of this parish was held in the School Room to consider the advisability of forming The Leigh Institute. This meeting met with such success and the proposed Institute with such approval that it was determined that the scheme be carried into effect. Provisional Committee meetings have been held. A rifle club and a gymnastics club have been instituted. The latter has started with a flourish and great success on Saturday Evening last, thanks to the Kindness and Enterprise of Mr Claude Hope Morley, by an assault of arms and a

Gymnastic Entertainment of a very remarkable description; while on Thursday next General Mackinnon, so well known of fame as the gallant leader of City Imperial Volunteers, will open the rifle range and place the first shot, without the slightest doubt in the centre of the bullseye. In the building that is provided by Mr Morley, there are already signs of the billiard and reading rooms approaching completion and very shortly we hope to see the youths of the parish revelling on the vaulting horse or the parallel bars; those of maturer years completing their hundreds at the anchor stroke; while those among us who, alas! have reached what the poets call "the sear, the yellow leaf", may recline at our ease with the periodicals of the day before us or take our recreation at whatever peaceful games may appeal to our declining years."

One service that Mr Streatfield did not mention was the provision of hot baths. Alf Houghton explains. "In the early days none of the village cottages possessed a bath and the two baths at the Institute were in demand. The trouble was that the bath close to the kitchen range was always hot but the one at the rear of the small hall was installed in an added draughty wooden hut and its remoteness from the boiler meant tepid water. You had to run from a football match to get the hot water".

In 1908, it was agreed to admit ladies up until 6.00 pm and even ladies who were not members could use the baths. Notice had to be given on Friday nights by those wanting a bath on Saturday.

The Institute was open all the days of the week except Sunday, with the Reading Room open from 10.00 a.m. and the main Institute from 5.00 p.m. until 10.00 p.m. In the early days the charge for rifle shooting was 2d for ten shots and billiards was "3d for a game of fifty not exceeding half an hour if any other member if waiting." A second, smaller billiard table was put in the Small Hall for beginners in 1908 and in 1911 badminton was started – for men, although women were allowed soon after.

The Large Village Hall where the Institute played badminton.

In 1914 the Village Halls were turned into a unit for soldiers recuperating from injuries. The equipment was provided by the newly ennobled Lord Hollenden. The Institute was restarted in 1921 and enjoyed its most successful period, with over a hundred members. It was during the next six years that a good number of ladies joined the Committee – Mrs Burr, Mrs Russell, Mrs Wood, Miss Passingham, Mrs Brooker, Mrs Belton and several others. Subscriptions were 6/- for men and 4/- for women. The piano was bought with funds raised by the Leigh Jam Committee led by Mrs Burr. The Institute was much used for dances and for many whist drives; and, with a wooden stage at one end, for regular plays and concerts. In 1926, Alfie Houghton took over bookings.

However, by 1927 membership was down and the Minutes show the Institute was in debt. It was agreed to close during the summer months and there were discussions about forming a working man's club. One of the members, Mr A Stubbins, is minuted as "expressing a wish that Members of the Comittee would attend more frequently in the evenings" and was seconded by Mr Hawkins. Alfie Houghton looking back now agrees. "In my opinion, the conduct of affairs would have been improved by the inclusion of some manual workers in the running of the Institute who actually used the place".

The Institute's membership declined still further during the Thirties. Each year the AGM Minutes recorded a vote of thanks to Lord Hollenden for his support and usually his response where he "wished the Institute better fortune, with a substantially increased membership". Finally, in 1938, the Institute was wound up and in the Second World War, the main Hall was again used for the wounded, with Lady (Muriel Ivy) Hollenden in charge. After the War, the newly formed British Legion Club took over the running of the hall that had been a baptistry fifty years earlier and the running of the Large Hall and the Small Hall was handed over by the Morley Trust to the trusteeship of the Parish Council and a Management Committee who have continued – as always seems to have been the case for the last hundred years – to try to find money for improvements and to encourage new uses for both the large and small Halls. The Legion Committees continue to need a good caretaker/steward – again, as the Minutes show, another long-term problem.

Alfred Houghton

orn 27 December 1905, Alfred Houghton came to Leigh in 1925 to fill the newly created post of Estate Clerk at Hall Place. He became Lord Hollenden's Confidential Secretary at I & R Morley in London five years later, a post he held for 36 years, while still continuing with the Estate work. He has been the Agent to the Hall Place Estate from 1940 onwards, administering a good number of farms, a large number of houses, shops and village buildings as well as Hall Place itself. He has chaired the Parish Council, been a governor of the village school, secretary and keen player for the Cricket Club; and a Special Constable for twenty two years. He continued to look after the Estate until he was ninety three – over sixty years' service to the Hollendens, Hall Place and Leigh. Now an energetic 95 and still a keen vegetable gardener, here are his views on the village and the Estate, particularly in the period before the War.

The Produce Association
prizewinners c.1980.
Alfred Houghton and
Mrs Barbara Bastable.
Alfred was a founder of the
Produce Association
59 years ago.

"I was greeted with unopen arms. It was December 12th, 1925 and I arrived in the dark. It was Hildenborough station with no one to meet me – so I just walked. Incidentally, you probably don't know but Leigh station was called Lyghe Halt in those days. They had fixed me up with lodgings with Mrs Hukins at No. 2, Forge Square and the first evening Mrs Hukins told me that a friend of hers gave me three days at the most with Mr Burr – the Agent. He was there for another 15 years but I saw him out and I took over as Agent in 1940. He was a Scot and lived in what we then called The Gate House – it's Porcupine House now. He scared me stiff at first but he did give me ten shillings to go home to Essex for Christmas.

I had been on a lovely Estate in Hertfordshire – Gilston Park near Harlow. But the fellow I worked for there wouldn't let me do anything. I wanted to learn something each day and I said "I'm not". So when I saw the advert for the Hall Place job, I applied. I wrote my own references – I just went and got them signed. Hall Place didn't choose me – I chose them.

Gilston Park was quite near where my family lived. There were Houghtons in Great Chesterfield for over a hundred years – beginning with my father, Richard, and ending with my brother Harry who died there in 1975. I had four brothers and two sisters – Mabel and Elsie. My father raised all seven of us really well. He was a farm labourer, cum groom, cum gardener, cum poultryman – he did a bit of everything on two farm holdings. He married on eighteen shillings a week but he did us proud – never without a few bob in his pocket. All us boys sang in All Saints Church choir – you should hear me sing – it's always been awful – and two brothers were Communion Servers. When my brother, Alan, and I were choir probationers, we sat in the front pew in the body of the church with an old lady who was supposed to be stone deaf, Grannie Lambert. One Sunday, Alan was really belting out a hymn when Grannie Lambert snapped – 'shut that hell of a row boy, do'. Once all the choir boys struck. We walked out because the Vicar decided not to pay us – it was meant to be about 1/3d a quarter. There was trouble when I got home and normal singing was resumed. Some of the sermons were very long. Good Friday was a day to dread – we had a three hour service. I once said to one of the Leigh Vicars who chided me for not attending church, that I had been to church more often than he had; and when he disputed this, I said "throw in my family and we beat you hands down and when have you attended a three hour Good Friday service?" That killed him off. (His other bleat was that no one doffed their hats or caps nowadays).

All us boys rang or rather tolled the bells because the tower wouldn't stand proper ringing. One Easter Sunday morning I was playing a hymn on the bells. I wasn't musical – never have been – but someone had written out the numbers of the ropes to pull. A lady stepped up behind me, tapped me on the shoulder and said 'young man – do you know what hymn you're playing – it's "Now the Day is Over"'. Mother was a Sunday evening regular: so was my brother Harry right up to his death. Father usually attended church once a year when he hoped one of the hymns would be "Fight the Good Fight".

One of the great joys in the holidays was to play in and around the goods yard of the local station. There was a great deal going on then, with coal, corn, feeding stuffs and the like being delivered into the sidings by the truckload. I remember a favourite trick was to hoist up one of the other boys on the hand-worked crane so that he was high enough off the ground not to dare to jump. We'd leave him there to cool off for a time. Of course, when it happened to you, it was not nearly so funny. There was a hand operated turn-table too which was a source of stolen entertainment. When I went back years later the crane was dismantled and the goods yard disused.

I went to Newport Grammar School near Saffron Walden in Essex as a County Scholar – it was the lowest form of life. The fee paying boys never let me forget my status and some of the masters were real snobs. But when the preps were difficult, the dunces were not slow in seeking help. When I left, aged 16, I had the difficult task of finding a job. I saw an advertisement for a job as assistant estates clerk at Gilston Park. I applied and got it. It meant moving from home but that was what I wanted. The estate was 3,000 acres and the work I had to do there was pretty similar to the kind of things I was expected to do at first at Leigh. Gilston had a TT herd and I learned to sketch each animal on its own card so we could keep accurate records. I won a county prize for the records too.

At Gilston, it meant moving into a new world. I rubbed shoulders with important people, worked with a good bunch of men and took a real part in the life of the village. I was regular at church. On Sunday mornings, I went to St Mary's in the village where the Squire, Arthur Salvin Bowlby, played the organ and the Reverend Lewis preached according to the book – every word of it read. On Sunday evenings, we walked over to St. Botolph's Church in Eastwick where the Reverend Lewis preached extempore, dealing with ordinary subjects. Sometime he made your hair stand on end with the details of his intimate knowledge of our lives. He had a net income of £375 a year for the two parishes, with the house, which was about the same as the Vicar got in Leigh at the time.

My first wage at the Hall Place Estate was £2.10.0d a week. I had £2 in the Post Office and what I stood up in; and I paid Mrs Hukins 22/6d a week which included the washing. It was a good place to have lodging. It was near everything going on.

One of my main jobs at Leigh was to be in charge of the finances for the four Hall Place Estate farms. I started by preparing the first tax claims for farm losses and estate maintenance. But I was expected to be able to do everything. Of course, all the farm hands knew I couldn't. When I arrived a ploughman said 'Walk this horse round the field' – it was huge but I didn't dare say no. Then the bailiff told me to move some bales of hay but they were wet and so heavy that I couldn't do it. I was 19 – only a slip of a boy really. My first job at the harvest was on the threshing machine, taking the sack full of grain off, tieing it up and putting it on the sack-barrow for a man to take away. We started a TT dairy herd just as I arrived. Lord Hollenden – the first one – had had the idea in 1922 and I helped to actually set it up. There were lots of other things. I hated shooting things but I had to do it – pigeons and rabbits. I remember I shot a rabbit. It was only wounded, so I put the gun down to finish it off – and I forgot the gun – I lost it – I did feel a fool. I never did do ferreting. The farms had wheat and mangolds, and there was an orchard at Home Farm and a few hops. I've done everything on a farm – I always say it – but I had a hell of a time to get to know things when I first arrived. I got myself a bike so I could get everywhere – usually I aimed to make it when I wasn't expected. So I'd get to the gamekeeper at 12.45 to make sure there wasn't a smell of a pheasant cooking – whenever was least popular and most inconvenient. I had to look after all the property on the Estate too. You've got to remember that at that time Lord Hollenden owned around a hundred houses and cottages and the Waterworks and the gasometers and the electricity and so on. And there were all the Estate workers. There were still around sixty staff just on the Estate. That didn't include the staff in the house: there were about a dozen of them. There were around eighteen people in the gardens; Home Farm had ten; Gas, Water and Light had three; there were four keepers; three laundry maids up at the Bidbridge Laundry; and fourteen or fifteen other people working to keep up the Estate.

When I arrived, I was taken on by the Hon. Geoffrey Hope-Morley, as he was at the time. The old Lord Hollenden, his father, was nearly eighty and did not have much to do with the Estate by then. He'd been Mr Samuel Hope Morley until he was made the first Lord Hollenden in 1912. He was a real swell. He had been a Director of the Bank of England for forty years and Chairman in 1903 and 1904. When he retired in 1921, the Court of Director said that they 'desire to record their sincere regret at the loss of a colleague of such long experience and to express their feeling of personal regard for one who by his unfailing courtesy has secured the esteem and affection of every Member of the Court.' I've got his bank statement for the end of 1928 and he was worth more than a million – probably one of only six millionaires in the country at the time. And when he died in 1929 the Estate was worth one and a half million. I've got the cutting about the Will from the papers at the time. He left a lot of bequests, including money for all the employees in Morleys and a substantial sum – £500 – to Mr Burr and £100 each to his butler, Ernest Williams; his chauffeur John Eyres; and to the widow of his late keeper, Walter Seal. The housekeeper got £20 and all the Hall Place servants got £10 or £20. I remember we were skating on Hall Place lake when the old Lord died. We had to stop in deference – we were annoyed at the time. I'd never met him and the only time I saw him was when he was in his coffin, through the glass.

Alfred Houghton (right) skating at Hall Place lake c1930

In his day, he'd loved driving his coach and four and he had had lots of horses and carriages. But by the time I got to Hall Place, they had sold all the horses and got rid of four out of the five grooms. So there was the stable block – which probably had room for thirty horses or so – mostly empty, although the carriages were still there. There was a horse-drawn bread delivery van too. We used it for shoots for quite a time and then eventually I sold it to a museum up north somewhere for eighty quid. Not bad.

I could see that the buildings on the Estate were in a poor state. I said to the Hon. Geoffrey Hope-Morley – he became Lord Hollenden in 1929 – "most of these are in ruins" and he let me have a free hand and we put up a whole lot of new barns over the years. Burr didn't do much – there wasn't even a proper accountant employed – I had to prepare everything from what the accountant told me.

The Estate had its own gas, water and light department. We used to pump water from our own well at the waterworks – it was by the entrance gate – to supply Hall Place and many of our houses and cottages – although by the time I arrived some houses were converted to the main water supply. We were still supplying water to some houses until early 1942 when the waterworks was bombed. We had two gasometers down on the same site and we generated our own electricity for Hall Place and many of our houses until mains electricity reached the village. The Estate wasn't on main electricity for some time. I remember that, for a number of years, we didn't get it for my house because I thought if I did, all the Estate houses would want it too. Harry Wood was the boss man at the Gas, Water and Light. He was wonderful: he got things done. And Dick Wood, his son – the most under-rated man in the village – he was lovely too. They had it organised down there so that I couldn't get to them without them seeing me coming – clever.

I never had to deal with any of the domestic staff in Hall Place – well, that was officially anyway – except to pay them. They were all separate. When I arrived, there was a cook, Mrs Savage, who was also the house-keeper. In my eyes, she was always first class and I know her three kitchen staff thought so too. She left on the 25th May 1945 when her wages were £100 a year. (Her replacement was given £182 a year, incidentally). When I came there was also a butler, a footman or two, two chauffeurs and various scullery maids and things – I think about a dozen people plus the laundry people up at Bidbridge and the groom who looked after the childrens' ponies. You got sacked for getting someone in the family way: but a few got away with it over the years.

When I arrived the old Lord Hollenden – that's the first one – had been at Hall Place for forty years and he was always keen on the gardens. He had added a large rose garden and a two hundred and seventy foot long pergola on two sides of it. It used to have sixty-four varieties of roses – ramblers and climbers. But he was in pretty poor health and it was really his son, the Hon. Geoffrey who took on the garden in my time. He loved it. He'd known it from birth and he put his own stamp on the garden and the grounds. He had the three splendid stone bridges built round the lake – replacing old wooden ones. He took a good slice of land from the Deer Park – and there were sixty deer plus the fawns when I arrived – to make the beds on the south side of the lake bigger. He created a new surround to the double hard tennis courts and pavilion, with hedges and shrubs around it.

c.1935. Alfred Houghton standing in front of one of the new bridges built around the lake by Lord Hollenden.

There were fifteen to twenty gardeners in 1925 – 1930 looking after all this and a very large kitchen garden. Altogether there were 20 acres of gardens if you included the $12\frac{1}{2}$ acres of the lake. There were eighteen greenhouses and a large conservatory, with three men doing nothing but the green-houses. They grew oranges, bananas, grapes and nectarines and various other special things. All the boilers for the heating were handstoked. The conservatory was demolished during the Second World War when heating fuel was rationed. Looking back to the 1930 wage bill, the Head Gardener got £3.15.9d a week, George Wood £2.3.9d and most of the ordinary gardeners around £1.14.0d. The Head Gardener, when I arrived, was George Robert Pringle, another Scotsman like Burr. He wore a white shirt with a proper collar and seldom soiled his hands. He had been at Hall Place since 1915. He lived rent free with his sister in the Head Gardeners house at the main entrance – which was much bigger than they required because it had originally been two dwellings. He had a supply of stock stories and one in particular I heard ad nauseam was about Lord Derby whose friend says to him "I hear that you have a new Agent and he's a Scotsman. He'll do you". Lord Derby replied "Maybe he will but he'll see to it that nobody else does". The trouble was that prior to my arrival Pringle was very conscious of being second in command to Mr Burr. I soon gave him cause to change his outlook. His relations with his staff were poor. To give an example – in those days the men worked five and a half days per week, plus weekend duty by rota. Pringle was inflexible and allowed no interchanging at all.

Six or seven of the junior staff lived in the garden bothy. (The main gardener lives there now: it's the place next to my office.) They had the services of a local woman for cooking, cleaning and bed-making duty each morning. For the rest of the time, they fended for themselves, taking it in turn to be responsible for buying the food. Some of the young men were better than others at it and there were unholy rows if the weekly tally, which normally came to 12/- for all of them, came to 12/6d.

Robert Pringle left at the end of 1937. His actual departure was not as unusual as one Head Gardener who was at Hall Place after the war. Neither this man or his wife had been happy in the job – he never had the gardeners' delight of being able to name plants and shrubs and, when cornered, disappeared to study his gardening books. When the couple left, the wife brandished a frying pan. Lord Holldenden merited two downward thwacks and I merited one.

Peter Ferguson replaced Pringle in 1937 and was with us until the end of the war. Even in 1938 he still had a staff of fourteen – much the same as ten or twenty years before. He was very interested in fruit growing and at Home Farm we had a four acre apple orchard which was not doing well. The fruit was poor quality and sparse. The trouble was partly because it was in a frost pocket and partly the amateur pruning by a number of the farm bailiffs. Ferguson was given charge of the orchard. He organized proper cutting of the grass, good pruning, careful use of chemical feeds and, in some years, washing the trees. We ended up producing good crops which were sold picked straight from the orchard. By then it was wartime and we had two local land girls, Bertha Hitchcock – who married Bill Crocker after they had met on the farm – and Peggy Wood. They gave splendid service. Unfortunately, at the end of the war, when Peter Ferguson learnt that the number of gardeners was not going to return to pre-war levels, he lost interest and found himself another job. We're down to two people in the garden now, plus me, and none of us are real gardeners.

It probably sounds as if I was working all the time on Hall Place things, doesn't it? But the fact is that from 1930 on I became the new Lord

Hollenden's Confidential Secretary up in London. I commuted every day for the next thirty-six and a half years. It nearly killed me at the end. I rode my bike up to Hildenborough Station – it cost 1/3d a week to leave it there. Everyone had their own seats on the train and people would move so that you could play cards with your regular group. My office was right outside Lord Hollenden's own room and as well as all the work to do with the business, I & R Morley, there was the work that he did on various committees and charities. He didn't hardly ever go to the Lords – he didn't want to tell everyone what he was an expert at. The charities were mainly to do with the textile industries – things like Russell School and so on. I was also Sub-Editor of the house magazine – 'Threads'. Lord Hollenden was called The Editor but I did it all. And I did all that on top of continuing with the Estate work – which I did mostly on Saturdays and sometimes Sundays.

When Mr Burr left – and I won't go into details about why – in 1940, I took over as Agent – although I did get called up in the middle of the war to fight. I asked to do something where I could use my mind – I got the Artillery.... But my call up was cancelled the day before I was to join because they said the Estate had a prior call. Some people in the village were disappointed.

When I first arrived, the village had everything. It was a lovely place – a very pleasant place to live. There was a resident doctor, Dr Fraser and his son who also became a doctor, the big village grocery which Coates took over in the early 1930s, a baker, a butcher, a milkman, Hayter, – the blacksmith and our own undertaker. There were three public houses. We had our own policeman – I remember quite a few in my time. They were usually next door to me at No. 1, Forge Square. I remember one when I first arrived. He had two sets of identical twins – all boys. They all used the outside toilet in strict order. But having our own policeman meant he was part of the village. I remember once when a plane came down between Leigh and Sevenoaks. The policeman had to write a report and he got a special Commendation for it. You see it was typed. I reckon it was the first typed report they'd had and I typed it. He'd coached me how to do it.

The Village Halls were the centre of social life and there were dances, whist drives and the occasional concert. Badminton was popular because we had a hall with a high roof and, of course, the Green had the cricket and football clubs – although you didn't play on Sundays until after the war. I remember I had to make the change very clear to one newly arrived Vicar. In 1925 I think that we only had about five cars in the village and not many buses either. They were little yellow ones – they held about eight people. If you went to Tunbridge Wells on a Sunday by bus, you walked home from Southborough in the evening. And, of course, the village was so much smaller then – almost no houses along the Penshurst Road, no houses down the left hand side of Lower Green, let alone Well Close. Greenview and Lealands Avenues didn't exist, nor did the Forstall, although Barnetts Road was built.

I always played sport. I loved cricket, although I wasn't much good. I was the Secretary from 1933 to 1937 and from 1952 – 1965 and I did a lot of work I can tell you. I even had to go and catch the pony sometimes to do the mowing. It was usually in the field down behind the butchers in the Square or at Paul's Farm. There was only a Secretary and a Treasurer then, not all the dozens of officials they have now. The Committee used to meet at the Fleur to choose the teams – there were two teams before the War. When we'd nearly finished, I'd think – Hang on my name hasn't come up yet. So I'd say 'You haven't got me playing; if you think I'm going to do all the work and not play, you've got another thing coming.'

It was good being at Mrs Hukins because it was so near the Green. I'd go out on the Green with the other lads and at ten o'clock she'd come and lean on the gate to get me in. But I'd still stay out. I played soccer too and I wasn't much good at that either but I enjoyed it, although I didn't get much time what with working up in London and much of the weekends spent on Estate matters. I like to see Leigh boys playing for the teams – not outsiders. We had some great characters in the teams. You've heard about the two sports families – the Brookers and the Faircloths. They'd had a different type of up-bringing. Sometimes, some of them used to hate the other lot.

Forge Square with No1, for many years the policemans house, on the left; and No2, the home of Mrs Huggins and later the Lucas's in the middle.

I remember one year I had a row at the Cricket AGM with Gibbons, the school teacher. (He was the organist and choirmaster too for many years.) We'd had the Edenbridge match and, when we were losing, Gibbons and another bloke like him had their heads between their knees and were wringing their hands. When the match turned round, you couldn't see their backsides for dust. So I told them. If a man can't lose, he shouldn't play sport. The next day, after the row continued at the AGM, Lord Hollenden – he was the Cricket Club Chairman – said it was all my fault and he wouldn't be coming to the next AGM.

There were lots of other things to do in the village. Charles Hayter – his father ran the forge – and I used to get up at six thirty in the morning and drive down to Ensfield Bridge in his little open Samson sports car to swim in the river. Can you believe that? And when I arrived the Institute wasn't thriving. So I thought – that's just the sort of thing for me to do – me with nothing much else to do! and we got it moving again, although it was a bit of a struggle. It was in the three village halls. There were darts and cards and crib plus a vaulting horse in the Big Hall plus the two different badminton clubs. The afternoon lot – they were the toffs and they had tea and cakes at the intervals when they played – and the evening lots who were younger and, I suppose you'd say, lower class. We played each other once. They were twice our age but they still beat us. The Small Hall had a two-thirds size billiard table – it was on the right as you went in – with a full sized one in what is now the Legion Hall. I think they also had a library but I can't remember – I can't read! Lord Hollenden paid for most of it.

There was a Boy Scouts troop – they used to go on a camp to Studland Bay each summer – run by Mr Russell who was the Church Warden and Treasurer and who lived in South View. He was also in charge of the village fire brigade. He was always blowing his trumpet about his scouts but I told him once when the boys were older, he should let them go – they should be at the Institute. He never spoke to me again.

At one time, there was even some of the gents from London who had a regular Saturday afternoon game of quoits down at the bottom Lower Green on the right before the railway bridge. They used to drink at the Brickmakers Arms.

All the three pubs in Leigh were different. The Brickmakers was a real village pub. You stood amongst the barrels to drink. There were two rooms, one with a dart board and one without. When the Parish Council met in one of them, everyone else would have to go into the other room. At one point, the pub was run by Percy and Marjorie Seal. I remember one day Marjorie was scolding her little daughter and saying that, if she wasn't a good girl, she'd be sold. Tom May, who was in there drinking – he was a very small man but very quick – said "I'll give you five pounds for her and the stuff to make another like her."

Then there was the Fleur – and I used to use the Fleur a lot – and the Bat but you could walk down to the Plough – old Jempson was the landlord – or up to the Gate – I told them they had awful sausages once – like dogs turds – but I was well behaved after that. And there was Bill Sturt at The Blue Anchor past Lower Street – it was so small that you had to stop playing darts when someone opened the door but it had a big open fire. Or you could walk to the Green Rabbit Tea Room on the main road at Hildenborough. If you wanted a smart night out, you'd go to The Old Barn, which was owned by Commander Tomlinson. He was a real character. He had a pet parrot and he used to walk around with it on his shoulder. My daughter, Julie, got married there. They had an airfield behind it for short joy rides. But, if you wanted to arrange a dance in the Big Village Hall, you'd come to me. The charge was a guinea but as often as not the person would catch Lord Hollenden coming out of church and Lord Hollenden would reduce it to half a guinea.

The Old Barn set for tea in the 1930s. The postcard was published by W. Tomlinson, the owner.

One thing was and that was you walked – you walked everywhere. And everyone went for a walk on Sunday afternoon.

On Sunday mornings, of course, there wasn't much else to do other than to go to church. But St Mary's was quite active, partly because the choir was reasonable quality. The first Sunday I went, I was ushered into the Hall Place staff pew – the one with a cushion. But Sunday was meant to be my day off from the official Hall Place work and after that I decided to sit in the pew behind – without a cushion. One good reason was that it was opposite the exit and I was often first away when the Vicar and the choir were just reaching the vestry.

As I was employed by The Hon Geoffrey Hope-Morley, or Lord Hollenden as he became, and as he was a pillar of the church and what was called The Vicar's Warden, I often had to come in contact with the various incumbents that we have had on business matters. They have been a mixed bunch I can tell you.

The Reverend Walton, who had been Vicar until 1918, decided to live in the village after he retired, and his daughter, Miss Daisy Walton, was very active including helping Mr Russell with the Scouts. Then there was a Reverend Weston from 1918 until 1925 but I can't remember meeting him. When I arrived, the church accounts showed an income of £378.11.1d, including the Easter collection of £21.14.5d. Expenditure was £384, with the organist, Mr Gibbons, getting £36 a year, and the choir £3.7.6d, with 40 Saving Certificates costing £31. Over the years I seem to have done more than my fair share of accounts work on this kind of thing. The Reverend F.W.L. Sealy was instituted in 1926. He wasn't married then. I saw a good deal of him and supported his efforts not only for the church but at the school where he was the Chairman. I only ever had one row with him and that was during the War when he was an Air Raid Warden. It was at the height of the daytime blitz on London and we had finished our family lunch early and the children had left to attend Sunday School in the church. The siren went off and in no time at all huge formations of German planes were passing over the village. I was alarmed and I hurried down to the Green. There was the Revd Sealy and many others. I was told that the children were still in the church – without any grown ups. They were frightened. I collected my children and on the way home I told Mr Sealy what I thought of him in a few choice but strong words. He was married in 1940 fairly late in life. After his honeymoon, he looked half dead but he was Vicar of Leigh until 1948. By that time the church's income was £476.15.0d (and its expenditure of £319.4.10d).

When I arrived in Leigh, there was also the Free Church Chapel behind The British Legion. It had been erected in 1907 by Samuel Morley and I've got all the details. It was thirty five foot by twenty plus a ten by eight foot vestry with a porch and a lavatory. The roof was covered by twenty-four gauge corrugated iron and the interior had 'matching' on the walls – (that's the thin tongue and groove boarding) and one inch flooring. The last Minister in the mid-seventies was Rev. A.M. Martin who was really in charge of The Assemblies of God chapel in Tonbridge. During the winter of 1975/6 the Sunday services were stopped due to lack of support and not long after the Friday evening Bible classes were stopped too. The Estate sold the Chapel in 1977 and, as you know, it got burnt down in 1984. Everyone knew who did it but there you are. Incidentally, before you ask, the Estate never owned the Chapel burial ground which had been used since 1875.

Because my four children went to the Village School and because I was a School Manager for many years – a School Governor they'd call them-selves today – I saw a good deal of the teachers and children particularly in the 1930's and 1940's. Walter Gibbons had just taken over as Headmaster when I arrived in Leigh and stayed headmaster until the end of the war. He was a good teacher – perhaps a bit fond of his own importance but he got on with things. Looking back at it, I think that the children of the slightly richer parents got more help and encouragement to better themselves than the poorer children. But it seemed practical at the time. It wouldn't happen now but it didn't seem strange then. Lord Hollenden and I were School Managers with the Reverend Sealy as Chairman, but it didn't really mean much. All the decisions were made before we got there. When Miss Naish was appointed the new headmistress, we were told about it after it had happened – so Lord Hollenden and I both resigned.

I was also on the Parish Council for years. My first recollection of the Council was seeing a bunch of rather elderly men entering the School's building for a meeting. These men – no women – were dedicated and intense. In those days the Hall Place Estate was involved in practically every aspect of Leigh village life, and therefore after most meetings a number of queries would be addressed to the Estate Office. With the agreement of Lord Hollenden, I stood for election to the Council in 1937 and was a winner. This meant that on a variety of subjects I could give the Council a helpful answer on the spot, subject of course to his Lordship's approval (or disapproval occasionally) in a matter of days. Membership of the Council was not onerous as we only met some four times a year, plus the Annual

Meeting. We were not involved in planning which must be the plague of the Council life today. I was Vice-Chairman for four or five years, then Chairman from 1947.

All sorts of things happened during my membership. Cricket was allowed on Sundays on Leigh Green, arrangements were made to mow the whole Green regularly, and the Green was handed over to the Council by the late Lord Hollenden (who in the end had to purchase it off himself for £10. What happened was that we found the Green legally belonged to the family trust who couldn't sell it. So we rang up an estate agent in Sevenoaks and said, look we only get five shillings rent a year from the Parish Council, so what's it worth and they said £10. So Lord Hollenden had to spend £10 and lose the five shillings rent.

Geoffrey, the 2nd Lord Hollenden presents the deeds of the Green to Alfred Houghton which gave the Green to the village.

Later on, politics got openly introduced into the Parish Council – sadly – by four members of the Labour Party – Miss Upfield, Mrs N. Butcher, Dick Wood and Fred Whibley. My disappearance from the Council in 1949 came through politics. A member of the Conservative Association called on me and said that, if I was standing as an Independent, I would not be opposed. I confirmed that I did not approve of involving the Council in politics and would stand as an Independent. But in the event the Conservatives did oppose me and I was not elected. However, the last laugh was mine. Shortly afterwards a vacancy cropped up and I was invited to return to the Council. My turn down was unprintable. In fact, they had done me a good turn. After working in London all day, I was relieved not to have to attend meetings when a half hour meeting tended to last two hours.

I was a Special Constable too. I joined in 1926 soon after I got to Leigh because of the General Strike, although I can't remember actually doing anything during the Strike or much up until the start of war. Then, we were out all the time during the raids. Whitehead, the butcher was the Chief Special Constable, Parrett from the shop was the Special Police Sergeant and I was the Special Constable. I had a good lot of games of cards with the Chief Constable when the raids weren't happening and a good few drinks in the Fleur in our time. We also had the Leigh Specials Pig Club. I've still got a poster. One of the slogans was "Eat What you Can and Pig-can What You Can't".

HELP TO KEEP A PIG

By saving waste food and keeping it dry you help to maintain the supply of meat and edible fats and increase shipping space available for the country's defence.

WHAT TO COLLECT

Remains of :—
Stale bread, cakes, flour, porridge puddings.
Meat, fish, cheese and egg dishes.
Vegetables (cooked and raw) including outside leaves and roots of green vegetables.
Offals from cleaning poultry and rabbits.
Peelings of potatoes, turnips, carrots, etc.
Egg shells.

WHAT TO AVOID

USELESS
Tea leaves and coffee grounds.
Banana, grape-fruit and orange skins.
Paper, cartons, feathers and dead flowers.

DANGEROUS
Soda, soap, salt, and brine.
Glass, metal and crockery.
Rhubarb leaves.

HOW TO COLLECT

Food scraps are best collected in a small covered bucket or a large bowl or colander kept for the purpose. Even a strong paper bag is satisfactory.

" EAT WHAT YOU CAN AND PIG-CAN WHAT YOU CAN'T "

LEIGH "SPECIALS" PIG CLUB

COMMITTEE :-
Chief Special Constable   D. E. **Whitehead** (*Chairman*)
Special Police Sergeant   G. H. **Parrett**
Special Constable   A. **Houghton** (*Secretary*)

" GIVE YOUR SCRAPS TO SAVE YOUR BACON "

Poster from the Second World War to support the Leigh Special Constables Pig Club.

I did a first aid course during the war too. I got through the test by making sure I was the last to go in to the examiners and asking all the others as they came out the answers to questions that I didn't know. In 1949, when I had been a Special for 22 years, I retired and got a long service award which I've still got somewhere.

KENT COUNTY SPECIAL CONSTABULARY.

......................"D".................................Division.

CERTIFIED that....Alfred..HOUGHTON,.................
served in the KENT COUNTY SPECIAL CONSTABULARY from

................1926................to.14th..February,..1949

at.........................Leigh.......................................
During that time he performed, without pay and in a satisfactory manner, all the duties required of him in his capacity as special constable.

Superintendent *Chief Inspector.*

..14th.February,.........191.9

Alfred Houghton's certificate celebrating his years as a Special Constable.

I had met my wife, Doris, at a dance in the Old Barn in 1932. She was Doris Evelyn Francis and her parents lived in Tonbridge. She was the eldest of five daughters. I had lodgings in Barnetts Road by then – worst lodgings I ever had. We were engaged – everyone used to watch everything we did. Even when you pulled the chain, it echoed down the road. We were married two years later or so and I gave the Cricket Club ten shillings to have a drink for us and we moved to our present house, The Firs. We were married and lived at The Firs for sixty four years. It's been the only house that we've had in Leigh. Lord Hollenden gave it to us – sort of over the years – we got the conveyancing formally in 1968.

My wife always hated Hall Place and all therein. You see, when I got back from London at Saturday lunch time, I had to go off to Hall Place and do all the work up there for the rest of the weekend. So she never really saw me and she felt that she had to bring up the children herself. Our oldest boy – he had no fear of anything – he'd be a cricket bat's length from the stumps: but he died swimming in the Weir when he was fourteen and a half – I always picture him as a fighter pilot – you never get over it. Our second son – he's sixty three and a quantity surveyor; and the youngest son he's in simulators – simulated tanks they are now. All the boys went to the village school and then on to Judd. I remember that the youngest was allowed to stay on till he was eighteen but I said to him then that he'd been a better man at sixteen and, if he wanted to give orders one day, he'd better think a bit more for himself. I must say he took it well and he went on to college, worked hard and wiped up all the rest of them. Julie, our daughter, trained as a nurse at the Westminster – she'd been to the village school too and then on to Tonbridge Girls Grammar School. She used to say to me sometimes 'Dad can you lend me some money' and I'd say, 'Yes, as long as you pay me back'. When she paid me back, I'd give her the money but that's the way to do it.

Roger Dadswell – who ran a hairdressers in the Old School House – and Alfred Houghton.

Lord Hollenden was involved with everything in the village, with the church and the school and the cricket club. He did a good deal of day to day work on church things and led on all the main issues. Nobody got away with anything. If they had a hymn he didn't like, he told them so. He was President of the Produce Association. And of course he was the biggest employer in the village – remember he was directly employing over sixty people at Hall Place and on the Estate and there were many older people in the village who had worked at Hall Place and he used to help them if there were problems and there were regular gifts at Christmas which went right back to the time of the old Samuel Morley. In my day, these kinds of presents were still given out up until the middle of the war and I've got lists of most of the years from 1922 to 1942. In 1929, fifty four people got gifts of tea – usually four or five pounds each. In 1929 the Meat List had fifty eight people on it, including five "pensioners" with a total of 225 lbs of meat being given. There are fifty eight names on the 1938 list but, due to the War, the "Pheasant List" was down to twenty five in 1942.

Lord Hollenden used to help out on the hospital side too. It was a strange system compared to today – I used to call it the Department of Health and Social Insecurity. The rich used to give donations to hospitals and charities and in return they were issued with what were called "letters". These letters entitled those who could not afford the hospital fee to get free admission. Often the letters were dispensed with a good grace by the rich but often in a patronizing manner. They were a cheap status symbol. Lord Hollenden and his father, as Chairman of a big City firm, were expected to contribute and they had letters from Great Ormond Street, Moorfields and a number of other London hospitals as well as hospitals in our area – the Royal Surgical Aid Society, the Eye and Ear Hospital and the Kent and Sussex Hospital. Sometimes if you attended a hospital as a "letters patient" you were treated by students. I've got details of the number of "letters" that had to be obtained to get help at one of the Tunbridge Wells hospitals – it took one "letter" to obtain a bandage or an enema, three to get an abdominal belt, twelve to get artificial teeth; forty to fifty for an artificial arm with hand and fifteen to get an artificial nose. People should hang their heads in shame when they compare the N.H.S. which is always there when you want it with what they call 'The Good Old Days'. But Lord Hollenden had these letters from about a dozen hospitals, which he gave to people at Morley's and in the village right up to the start of the N.H.S.

You've got to remember that Lord Hollenden owned most of the houses in the village – even most of the big ones like Park House, where Dr

Fraser lived; Mr Russell's South View; what is now Chilling House but was then The Limes; the Woods where the two Miss Heaths lived; Upper Kennards; and Old Kennards, as well as about fifty cottages and the blacksmiths and most of the shops. He owned the water supply and electricity supply, the Village Green and the Village Halls. He'd lived here virtually all his life and he knew everyone – and liked most of them. He'd call most people by their Christian name which was very unusual for those days. Nearly everyone in the village knew him and they loved him – they would do anything for him, the village people would. They used to call him "The Squire". When he gave the Green and the Village Halls and the Scout Hut to the Village after the war, he said it was because of the fifty years of happy memories at meetings and dances and village events. And although not that many people knew about it, he was a very generous man.

Many of the people in the village grew up with the two daughters as well, Miss Joan and Miss Elspeth. One of my happiest memories of my early days at Hall Place was seeing them in their family home. I remember helping them to master their very first bicycles. I remember trotting beside one of them on her very first pony, with George Hale, the remaining groom, puffing alongside the other. I remember their excitement when fitting out Rookery Nook, a complete miniature house beside the lake. I remember assisting them in their first venture on the frozen lake and being called in as an intercessor when their allowances failed to last the quarter. And I remember many things about them and the family which obviously one wouldn't say in public. Inevitably the girls grew up. Inevitably, they lost their youthful charms and, largely as the result of schooling at a modern domestic science college and travel, they acquired more mature charm and poise.

Lord Hollenden had three wives. The first one was the Hon. Mrs Hillgarth. She cost him a bomb but I didn't really know her – although I used to buy the children's socks and underwear. He married again in 1929 to a Miss Diana Gladstone – she was really Muriel Ivy Gladstone. She loved animals. Her dogs had their own cemetery which she looked after herself. Then there was the old horse 'Diamond' who she doted on – she used to give it cake. She used to spend hours getting chestnuts for the deer in the Park whatever the weather was like. She didn't really have much contact with the village. In 1962 her obituary said that "she was born out of her time and that she would have been more at home a century earlier when Lady Bountifuls and quiet lives were fashionable". She never thought much of me: she didn't like it if I wouldn't back her against her husband but I wouldn't take sides. After all it was Lord Hollenden who employed me. And anyway, you shouldn't get in between a man and his wife.

Lord Hollenden married Anne, his third wife secretly. I was his best man. People used to welcome her when she went around the village. I'm still in touch with her regularly.

I particularly remember the shoots. Both the first Lord Hollenden and the second loved shooting. The first Lord Hollenden had rented a good deal of land – over two and a half thousand acres – off Lord d'Lisle in 1916 and at this time the Hall Place Estate itself had expanded from about four hundred acres to one thousand four hundred acres. When his son took over the Estate properly after his father's death, there was a lot of shooting and a great deal of work for the keepers. There were up to eight keepers around 1916 to look after the shoots at Hall Place and Penshurst Estates and, although it was down to four in the mid and late 1920's, looking at the old staff records, I see it was up to five in 1936 and eight again in 1938. There were even two keepers in the middle of the war. It's down to one now – Donald Hallett. There have been various shooting syndicates over the years. Nowadays, they just have a cup of soup but in the old days it was done properly. The shoot used to visit each of the farms in turn and most of the village acted as beaters. Hall Place used to send out a full meal from the kitchens, with the butler to serve it all. The chauffeur used to go along to help. When I first got to Hall Place, one of the first things I had to do was learn to count the pheasant with Lord Hollenden – Geoffrey that was, the son. He knew more about shooting than the keepers. He had about ten shoots a year, usually starting at 9.00am on a Saturday. There would be eight guns – all big wigs – Lord Cornwallis, people from Penshurst and so on and usually a guest or two down for the day from London. If you didn't behave, you didn't get invited again. The worst thing was to fire from the hip or to fire when the birds were too low. We had an accident once – a long time ago now – a doctor's son killed himself climbing over a fence. He'd forgotten to unload. Lord Hollenden used to count every bird that went down and what the keepers dreaded most was when he'd ask them "What was the pick up?" What Lordie was checking was how many birds had been left on the ground uncollected. We kept a record of every bird shot. The farmer usually got given a brace and Lord Hollenden would give away quite a few birds – including to me. He used to forget how many I'd had some years. Sometimes I got three brace, sometimes six. The surplus got sold. And of course he was very keen on his retrievers. They were always black and nearly always female – the females are supposed to be easier to train. In 1934 we put the shooting rights up for letting – we needed the money – staff wages had already been cut which I didn't agree with – but we got all the rights back eventually.

Most people don't understand about how pheasants are reared. There is always a balance between what the gamekeeper wants and what the farmer wants. The farmer complains that the game are causing tremendous destruction but I think that this is an exaggeration. Anyway, the keepers always insist that the birds are after the insects not the grain. Lord Hollenden probably gave preference to getting good shooting over the farming – and he was never keen on horses like his father. He used to say that his legs were too long to look right on a horse.

But over the last ninety years the farms have taken up quite a lot of time for each of the three Lords – as well as a lot of my time. At the beginning of 1934, Lord Hollenden agreed to accept Burr into partnership to run Home Farm as a limited company. In the first year, it looked as if it had made a profit but this was mainly due to the fact that the in-going valuation was low at £3,220. The outgoing valuation was £4,733.15.0d. In reality losses continued until the partnership was discontinued at the end of 1936. Things go in cycles and I remember that in 1961 I recommended to Lord Hollenden that we formed a limited company and combined all the little farms into two units – one under Roy Bastable and one under William Dicker. It's been a process of change generally but things do go in circles. Between 1900 and 1938 there were three lots of pedigree cattle and then they were done away with three times and so it goes on. I thought that horses had finally had their day by the start of the War. Up until then they did most of the work on the Estate. A stallion would come round once a year. By 1940 we had a little tractor. But you've heard about the shire horse – Diamond. It was during the blitz and a coster from Camberwell called Mr White, contacted Lady Hollenden to ask if Lord Hollenden would keep his horse and work her for her keep. When Diamond arrived she was four years old and in her prime. She was a mare and later she had a foal to prove it. Mac McPherson – who had been the bailiff at Home Farm since the 1920's – was from the horse generation and he loved animals. I remember many occasions when we were carting hay or corn when Mac would inevitably say "Don't over-load Diamond". He needn't have worried. Diamond could shift anything we could put on the wagon. Heaven help the man or boy who had to take the last load home. She knew it was the last load just as well as you did and, if you wanted to arrive at the farm along with her, you had to break into a run – she was always an individualist rather than a team worker. After the war, Mr White asked if Lord Hollenden would buy her. Eventually she changed hands for the then very substantial figure of £90. Gradually she retired from work, with tractors replacing horses at an alarming rate but in the War it would have been difficult without Diamond. By the 1950's she had become a pet and it was not only Lady Hollenden who fed her on cakes and toffees as a treat. People came from miles around – she had lots of admirers. One woman travelled with the laundry van, was dumped at the field, so she could feed Diamond and was picked up on the return journey. Another man

Diamond – in retirement at Home Farm in 1959, aged 24 and valued in the inventory at £8.

used to bring his family of three or four youngsters every Sunday morning. She had a host of admirers – and she knew it.

Mac and, after him, William Dicker were the bailiffs at Home Farm. The Hobbs and Bastable family were up at Leigh Park Farm right back to before my time. But there were small farms too. Mr Corp was up at Lower Street Farm. He was a dairying farmer from Somerset with a critical eye, even if he was the slowest man to react I ever knew. If any change was suggested, he'd say "Why should I? I get a good living as I am". Opposite him was Little Lucy's farm on the other side of Lower Street. It was only 33 acres with about ten cows and it was too small. Then there was Prices Farm with Mr Graham. There was one 'farmer' – he called himself a farmer – I won't say who he was. I said he was a social climber: except no one would let him climb. Then, of course, there was Mr Goodwin who had a bigger farm – Paul's Farm – which was looked after by his bailiff, Fred Sands, who spent 2d every week reading "The Farmer & Stockdealer" and that was about it. Damn good farmer but didn't do much else. But one day, all at once, he got keen on football and we used to go to matches together.

The changes have gone on all the time. It is not just the end of small farms – the number of people on the farms has gone right down too. It used to be twenty cows per man: now one man can do hundreds. It was ten men to look after a hundred acres: then it got to roughly one: now it is much less still. The amount of arable land we had on the Estate went down very considerably between the wars. We started silage in about 1941/42 at Home Farm. From the start of the War after Burr left, I had even more to do with the farms as the Agent. That was as well as looking after all the houses and cottages and other bits of property in the village with all the rents and all the maintenance. Old Farmer Corp would deliver his rent on the exact day every time but not everyone did. I used to go to football with Tim Lee, the coalman. He told me who owed him money and that helped me to know what was going on. The number I've helped out when they had debts – but you didn't say so – though I've still got enemies in the village because of it.

From the 1960's, even before Lord Hollenden died, the Estate began its policy of drastically cutting back its staff and selling its houses, its farms and property. There wasn't anyone in the family who knew or cared much about farming and, with the rents so low, we weren't making any money on the property. In 1964, the last staff at Gas, Water and Light were pensioned off. In 1968, the last five Estate maintenance staff were made redundant. In 1973, the remaining chauffeur was made redundant and the resident domestic staff of the butler, two footmen and the odd man, the cook, two kitchen maids and scullery maid, three housemaids, the lady's maid and the governess were gradually reduced to extinction. And the same thing happened to the deer – all sixty of them went in 1963. They were always getting out when the six foot high fences that you had to have couldn't be fully maintained. Now there are just two the gardeners and two part-time domestic staff – and me – and I'm going to finally retire this March *[1999]* – I've been planning it.

Lord Hollenden died in 1977 and Mr Gordon Hope-Morley, his nephew, succeeded him. By 1979 a new farming venture was set up as a partnership between the new Lord Hollenden and the Bastables with about 1,200 acres, all farmed by just a few men. So there's been quite a change both on the farming side and in the village. Now the Hall Place Estate has no property apart from Hall Place and four small properties which Anne, Lady Hollenden lets for a few pounds a year. The Morley Trust which we set up in 1952 and which used to own things like the Village Halls just has the allotments now – and they're not fully used.

So, if people wanted – and some of them do – they could say it's me that's 'ruined' this village. But things do change anyway and you've got to accept it. I don't know what will happen to Hall Place when the present

Lord Hollenden dies. I don't know if the sons will want it. So there'll be more changes. *[Note: Gordon, the third Lord Hollenden died in 1999. His widow, Sonja, and Robin Hope-Morley still live at Hall Place.]*

Anne, Lady Hollenden once said she was amazed at the range of things that I'd got through on the Estate. I told her it was quite simple and it was all due to her husband, Lord Hollenden. He'd get introduced to something new which took his fancy. Then he'd always finish up saying to me – "unfortunately it's outside your experience", knowing darned well that this would ensure I took on the job for the Estate or the family. He worked me hard but he worked with me.

In 1941 Alfred, aged 35, wrote an ironic portrait about himself in the third person in the I & R Morley house magazine 'Threads'. The article included:

"Alfred Houghton is no respecter of persons, as some who know him will have learnt to their cost. I've heard him say some personal things to people when they rightly deserved it – proper sarcastic he was. Alf puts the wind up some of us when we get a bit above ourselves but he knows the meaning of loyalty and he knows his job in addition; there's the House of Lords work and all Lord Hollenden's committees and charities; then there's the Hall Place Estate... Alf just cannot be idle. And what he doesn't know about agriculture.

Off came his spectacles and I bet no one except his wife, has ever seen him without those on ... I was offering him a fag, as he filled up his shabby looking attaché case with a broken handle which you always see him carrying around on his way to catch his train home to Leigh. As a member of the Parish Council and a school manager there, he speaks his mind as freely down there as he does up at Morleys – he's the sort of chap they'd make Mayor if the place was bigger ... So one way and another, Alf isn't a man: he's a bit of a miracle taken all round!"

Twenty years later in 1960, aged fifty-five, he again wrote anonymously and sardonically about himself:

"We come to the pest of the City's bird population – the Houghton. It has been about a long time – far too long – it is an untidy, friendless, outcast of a bird, despite which it can often be heard to break into diverse lewd songs on an unmistakable cracked note...."

Twenty six years later still, in 1996, Alfred Houghton, Mr Houghton, Alf, or Alfie Houghton (depending on who you are) says:

"If you want a brag from me about me – and I was very proud of it – it was that Lord Hollenden gave me his sole Power of Attorney. I had it for twenty years. He was a millionaire and I was probably earning £350 a year. That's what I call trust and I'd never abuse it. When the family went on holiday, I used to tell them not to worry – "at the worst I'll sell up Hall Place – the Estate and all".

Alfred Houghton by the memorial to his late wife, Doris, who, sadly died on 15th June 1998.

Dorothy Pankhurst

(Mrs Dorothy Goodwin)

Dorothy Pankhurst was born in 1915. She was adopted by Jane and Lillian Pankhurst who lived in Garden Cottages. She went to Leigh School under Mr Nethercott - "a lovely man"; she was married in Leigh Church; and all her four children were baptized there. She now lives in Tonbridge.

"Father – I always called him 'Grandad Pank' – worked for Dr Fraser at Park House for about fifty years, looking after the horse and handsom cab thing that Dr Fraser had. Grandad would drive him round in it, although if the weather was bad, Dr Fraser used to ride his horse out to the patients. Granddad also did the gardening.

Dr Fraser and his wife were a very happy couple. When she died in the late 1920s – it was very sad because she knocked her leg when she got out of the new car and it caused a blood clot. Dr Fraser was heartbroken. There is a memorial in white marble in the churchyard with two lots of hands clasped together.

Mother – Mrs Pankhurst, but I always thought of her as my mother – worked for Dr Fraser for sixteen years, looking after the two boys – Eric and Beaufort. Beaufort went on to be a doctor locally – everybody liked him.

When Grandad retired, Dr Fraser – the old one – allowed Grandad to collect the rents for Garden Cottages and he got paid for it. Eventually, when the young Dr Fraser married and moved to Newton Abbott, mother was invited to stay with the family for three months holiday –all expenses paid. She also collected the rents after Grandad died and I think Dr Beaufort – Dr Beau – gave her a bit of money each quarter to help out when she was old.

By coincidence, some time later, after Dr Fraser had gone, I went to work at Park House. It was for Mrs Twitchell who was the person who looked after the billeting of the refugees in the War.

Barley Bear

" I was born Barbara Faircloth on 9 June 1919 – it was my father who called me Barley when I was little. We were living in Great Barnetts where my father was the farmer – he was a tenant of Lord de Lisle. My mother was Jessie Prikler (she came from Blindley Heath) and my father was Alfred Faircloth. He had been a farmer all his life and his father and grandfather were both farmers too. My uncle, Charles Faircloth, had Little Barnetts. The farms out along Powder Mill Lane were mainly hops. I have a wonderful photo of the Fautley sisters' father drying the hops and I know Kathy Fautly who worked at Great Barnetts used to carry me up and down the stairs when I was a baby. We were at Great Barnetts until 1922 when I was three. Then we took over my grandfather's farm – Charcott Farm. We were there until 1934.

Mr Fautly drying the hops for Alf Faircloth at the Great Barnetts Oast – now Moat Farm – in about 1916.

Great Barnetts, c.1930.

I went to school first at Chiddingstone Causeway. I was only there two years but I think it was good because I met the children in the village. My mother then sent me to a convent in Tonbridge but I knew all the local children and I know a good number still. I used to be called "old Dirty Rags" at school because of my name "Fair-Cloth".

The farm at Charcott was worked by Mr Wells before my grandfather and by Mr and Mrs Porch after us – Mary Porch, their daughter still lives in Charcott. It was mainly hops, although it was a bit of a dairy farm. People from Charcott used to come up each evening to get milk. We had some corn – so you could really say we had a mixed farm. And we had sheep sometimes. The farm was very hard work. My father only had one leg. He had shot his own foot while we were at Great Barnetts. You know how careless the doctors were in those days. It all went wrong and he nearly lost his life. Not the best thing for a farmer to have only one leg. We had an orchard with apples, pears and plums. People were forever stealing the fruit but my father was very easy going – perhaps it helped when you had a wooden leg. There was also a nuttery attached to the house – cobnuts. We used to sell them to Mr Webber who was a nurseryman in Tonbridge by the station with a wonderful garden.

We had about fifteen fields all around Charcott. There was my father and two cowmen: and there was a carter. It was his full time job to look after our lovely big old cart horses – "Capt'n" (it was never "Captain") and "Colonel". They did the ploughing and everything. The cowmen lived in two cottages in the orchard. The two cottages have been joined together and converted and expanded: it's called Jessops now. Violet Austin's father was one of the cowmen and there was Mr Humphrey too and Buck Winter when he was young. So there were four people which sounds a lot now but it was very hard. My father got up to light the fires at five thirty every morning but even when the fires were going, the farm house was terribly cold. There were brick floors and no running water – just a pump in the kitchen. It all seems very primitive now.

The cows were milked by hand and the only machinery that I can remember apart from the carts were a big rake and another machine which cut the corn. The threshing machine was hired in, with very tough men who worked very long hours and who slept rough. They always seemed full of drink – cider. All the village used to come out to help with the hay-making. Some of them would bring their guns for the rabbits.

Bob, Barley and Margaret Faircloth at Charcott Farm in 1923.

At other times of the year gypsies came around – particularly in my grandfather's time. Sometimes they stayed in the orchard quite a long time and their children went to the village school. The men would do all the dirty jobs that no one else wanted to do and the women made clothes pegs and baskets and those wooden flowers. I remember they used to come and ask for water. But in those days nobody minded gypsies – they were just part of country life.

In 1932 the hop market was very bad. We did not get any money for the hops at all. Unfortunately, my father had spent a good deal of money on wiring and we ended up having to leave the farm. It was awful for us. My father had been brought up on a farm and all his family before him. But it was a bad time for many farmers then. Mr Maskell who was at Ramhurst Farm had to leave, too. He was a broken man. He had some sort of job up at the Old Barn Tea Rooms afterwards but he never recovered. It was just too much for him.

So we moved to Bombers Cottage in Leigh and took over the milk round. Bombers seemed so small to us after the farm. There was me aged thirteen, and my sister Margaret who was four years older than me, my brother who was at Judd and our parents. Sadly, in January 1932, only a few months after we had moved to Bombers my mother died. She had always been very delicate – she had asthma. Being a farmer's wife had been hard work, even though she always had help in the farmhouse. She had been looking after Ray Faircloth's wife – Ray was our cousin – because she was ill with pneumonia. Then she seemed to catch it and they both died. In fact, there were three in a row because Mrs Phipps, the baker's wife next door died of it too. I always wondered if it was catching but they said it wasn't. Ray Faircloth made the coffin. He made coffins as a job, as well as being a wheelwright, in the workshop behind Pump Cottage where they lived. I remember one man wheeled my mother's coffin from Bombers to the church on a hearse with two wheels.

So Margaret and I and my father were left to do the milk round twice every morning and we girls had to look after the house too. We would get up at five thirty and go and catch our horse who was in the field up the Penshurst Road beside where Mr and Mrs Whibley lived. The other, newer houses towards the main village had not been built then. One day, I remember the horse being difficult for father to catch but normally it was easy enough. Then we would tie the horse up outside the Fleur and father would push a two wheeled cart with a huge churn on it down to Ethel Goodwin's at Pauls Hill Farm. Fred Sands was the cowman there. Then when it was filled, we would bring it back and transfer the milk to a churn, with a tap, which was on the milk float. The float had a step on the back. Then we would drive the horse round the village and people either came out with their jugs or left them outside the back door. There were no milk bottles when we started – just our pint or half pint measures and you gave people what they asked for – although we got bottles later. We went to all the ordinary houses in the village. We did not go to the big houses or Hall Place, although we did deliver to the Bothy for the gardeners. We did not even go to the vicarage. The local people were always good at paying at the end of each week – all except some of the people who had come to live in the new houses up Lealands Avenue – one of them did a moonlight flit and we did not get paid at all.

We had lived at Bombers for under four years when my father died too. That was in 1938. Margaret and I had to continue to run the milk round all by ourselves – and keep the house going. It was terribly hard work doing everything but we had to do it or we wouldn't have had a house at all. Obviously, we got to know nearly everyone in the village – and all the things that went on – even if I shouldn't tell you about some of them.

Down Lower Green next to us there was the bakery and the baker's shop – they didn't deliver. Mr Belton was there originally, then the Phipps family who we knew well. They had five children. Then the Lakemans came after them. I remember when the little Phipps girl died aged about one. Ray Faircloth made a tiny coffin. I used to make the cushions to go into the coffins – they had sand in them. I put some violets in for the baby.

Barley Bear aged about 17 with the milk round horse, Toby, at the back of the Small Village Hall where there was a field in which the horse sometimes was grazed.

Further down Lower Green on the left, there were only boggy fields until after the War. On the right there was Teddy Thompson's family. He lives in Moorden now but he was a bit of a tearaway then. Mr Thompson, the father, had a motorcycle and sidecar. There were so many in the family that at Sunday lunch when they were all together they often ate out-of-doors. The father had been in the Navy.

Then there was the Humphreys at the waterworks opposite us and the Hoath family next door to them. Tom Coates kept the Fleur de Lys when we went to Bombers. He was a character. He would go off on the train once a week, looking very smart with a button hole. No one knew where he went. He married his barmaid. She was very young – only nineteen or so – and she was so in love with him. I can't remember what happened to them. And of course there was Lou Brooker, the cobbler, in the little shed in front of Bombers. The Brickmakers Arms next door was very much a man's pub.

I seem to remember that Ray Faircloth used to put the iron bands round the outside of the cartwheels that he made – he made all sizes of wheels for all different carts and traps – so there were two wheelwrights in the village because Mr Hayter at the Forge did wheels as well, I think. Mr Winson ran the Post Office on the Green by the Forge. Eventually, we got a motor van for delivering the milk in the late 1930's. At first, we had someone to drive it for us. Then someone said you ought to do it, so I had to quickly learn in order to pass my test.

I could tell you the names of virtually all the people in the village at that time. I remember the men ballmakers all cycling down to Penshurst together each day. It was a man's world. They always expected a meal on the table – dead on time, everyday. Women were expected to do their own things and men were meant to be in charge – on the surface. We were two young girls running the milk round but only because there weren't any men. There was much more of a class divide in those days. You did not mix between the classes. We thought it sad for some of the middle class people. They must have been lonely. We did not have any contact with Lord and Lady Hollenden and The Hall Place family, although we left milk outside the Hall Place workers' cottages. We used to have a lovely time up at Pauls Hill House every summer. They used to put on plays and things. My father used to run the coconut shy.

When I was seven, my mother had advertised for PGs to come and stay at Charcott Farm. That was when I first met my future husband, Philip. He was twelve. Years later, he came back to Leigh and painted a picture of our milk float outside the Fleur. He saw us over the road at Bombers but he was too shy to come and talk with me. But in 1941 he and his brother were staying in the Red Lion in Tonbridge and they came over to see Margaret and me and we were married six months later. The war speeded things up you know. So we have been married for nearly sixty years so far. For a good number of years we lived a bit far out from things at Fissenden, near Chiddingstone but it's good to be back in Leigh now. We had a happy time a Bombers and later at Healthlea on the Penshurst Road where Fred Whibley lived and at Keepers Cottage in Charcott. So I knew people pretty well – even if not as well as when we used to run the milk round and knew everything – well, almost everything."

Cyril Selden

Born 1922, Cyril was the seventh of eleven children. The family lived at Killicks Bank, half way to Penshurst. Cyril went to Leigh School and left at fourteen to work with his father, coppicing wood for fences.

"I loved school. Mr Gibbons, the headmaster, wanted me to stay on but my father said 'no', – I had to come and work with him. So every morning we'd cycle off. Because I was only fourteen and small anyway, I had what was really a fairy cycle and we had to ride all the way to a wood by Pembury Hospital. We set out at about seven thirty, worked through and had a break at about nine, with lunch about twelve. Then we worked till it got dark in the winter and till about five in the summer, although Dad always wanted a little bit more. It was hard work. We'd start by cutting the coppice – it was always chestnut – in November and go through to March. The sap is down then. But from April on you weren't allowed to cut any more.

First you cut the trees down with an axe. Then with hand-bill – what you'd call a bill-hook – you cut off the side branches on a block – it was a three foot stump buried in the ground, with another Y-shaped stump to rest the trunk on as you pulled the tree towards you. As you took off the branches, you threw them on different piles behind you depending on the thickness. At the beginning of each day Father, would come round with a stick with nails in it marking the different lengths and he'd saw the pieces to the right size. The piles were left on their sides until you'd start working on them when they were all brought to the canvas covered shacks on a wheelbarrow. There were six foot and five foot and four foot lengths and so on.

From April, through the summer, we'd make up the fencing and the posts and things. My main job was the shaving. I used an old bagging hook with sacking bound round on each end and you pulled it down the branch towards you with both hands. The top end of the piece you were working on was rested in the 'sprod' – that was a Y-shaped stump about four foot high which was buried in the ground and then the branch rested on a block about two foot high with a groove. I'd take all the knots off first and then work downwards turning the branch round as I went. Then someone else cleaved the wood into two or four, or even three or six, with what was called a 'chit'. That was a sharp strip of metal about a foot long with a ring at one end for a wooden handle. You hit it down into the stake with a mallet – you made the mallets yourself – and then you bent the chit from side to side splitting the wood down. You could adjust it if one side was getting too thin or too thick.

We'd end up with different thicknesses – pea boughs, bean sticks and posts. Then the 'poles' were thicker. One person pointed them. To get them into bundles of twenty-five, we had four stakes in the ground with old bucket handles between them. We'd put a motorbike chain round them to pull it all tight and then tie them up. The spikes were two or three inches wide and farmers mended fences with them. Then there were palings and the bigger posts for the actual fencing. The posts were round and you used them for the ends of the fencing. They were all sent over to the fencing firms. There was Reliant up at Hildenborough station and Cardon's at Charcott.

Cyril Seldon, aged about 15, shaving a post, which rests on the 'sprod', left.

Cyril Selden

One of Cyril Selden's older brothers, probably Bill, working on the various stages of preparing the coppiced timber, c1937.

Using a 'chit' to split the posts.

Tying up the bundles.

Father used to buy bits of coppicing. They came in 'Cants' – it was an area. He used to choose the cheapest – which meant in the most difficult to get to bits usually. We did the woods round Pembury Hospital, and we did Broxham Manor over at Edenbridge and up Riverhill – that was very steep and the trees used to slide down. You really need coppicing to be about ten or twelve years old, perhaps up to fourteen or fifteen; but if it is more than that, the bottoms twist and it's awful to cut. It was hard work but I was happy doing it. In the evenings, when we'd finished for the day, we usually used to hide all the tools in the woods where we were working – under a bush or something. They never got stolen.

Each week we used to start a fire with all the shavings and bark. Sometimes we'd get an old bucket with the ashes in and we'd warm up meat pies which Mum had made or sausage rolls – they were real sausages – but mostly we had jam sandwiches – a loaf each – which Mum had given us and cold tea which was the best thing for quenching thirst.

I suppose you could say the food we had at home was rough, ready and good – you know, wholesome. Sometimes we kids would get sent down to Mr Whitehead, the butcher, for a shillings worth of meat and tuppence of suet and Mum would make a meat pudding for a special tea. Tea was the main meal. The meat pudding was wonderful. It was made in a cloth not in a bowl. She'd also make suet pudding with treacle or brown sugar on it. Mum had a kitchener which was what she had to cook on for all the family. She used that in the winter and then in the summer she used a three-burner Valor paraffin stove. We had a primus too. For breakfast we had bread and marge and we'd soak it in our tea. The bread was brought up by Mr Grayland, the baker in Charcott. At meals, we all sat round a huge table – there would normally be about twelve of us. If you didn't want to eat all your crusts, there was a ledge that ran all the way round under the table and you could hide them there. Down the middle of the table there was a long hazel rod and if you misbehaved you would get a thwack. It was usually from Mother – Dad was usually at the pub. You didn't give any cheek to your parents in those days – there was no back chatting. And if you got caught by the policeman doing something naughty and he gave you a clip and you went home and complained, father would give you another one. It was all much stricter in those days.

We kept a few chickens and we had a pig. We used to go out into the woods to collect acorns for the pig. Mr Whitehead would come up to Killicks Bank and take it away in his old van to the slaughter house on the Green. Us boys used to get sent away when we tried to watch what happened there. Mr Whitehead got half the pig for doing it – or least a good bit of it – but he was a good butcher. Then he kept the meat in the shop till we needed it. (Did you know his shop burnt down before the war? They had to throw all the burning thatch over the Hall Place wall).

We'd get a pheasant or two and we'd catch rabbits in a snare or sometimes when we were working in the woods we'd hear that special squeal from a rabbit and we'd go along knowing it was being hypnotised by a stoat. When we got there, the stoat would go off and you'd pick up the rabbit. There was a funny thing once. I saw a grass snake. It was a big one, about three feet long and it had just eaten a frog – you could see the shape about a foot down. So I picked the snake up and squeezed it and the frog popped out and hopped off. It was quite OK.

We had a big kitchen garden behind the house and grew lots of vegetables. We didn't have new potatoes – it would have been a waste. And we'd go out and collect blackberries for jam which Mum made. We never bought jam. We also had pear trees and apples and a walnut tree at the end of the garden. And some bullis too – they were small yellow damson things – sweet. We were allowed to go and get them off the trees. We'd throw things at the fruit to get it down. But the squirrels got most of the walnuts.

The boys would go down to Mr Faircloth, the milkman with a wooden leg, to collect the milk in a big can and we'd bring it home. During the summer, we'd half bury it in the ground down the garden in a bottle with a stopper to keep it cool. So altogether, we didn't do too badly for food – it kept us happy anyway.

The house was one half of the main cottage up at Killicks Bank. We had the side nearest the track. There were usually ten or twelve at home at any one time because Mum had most of us with only a gap of fifteen months or so. There were five houses up there. There was a very crippled, old man, George Ford – he was bent right over – in the other half of the house. I should think they had to break his legs to get him into his coffin when he died. His sister lived in the cottage too. She wasn't really all there. In the little cottage next to the track there was our second sister with her husband Mr Penfold and in the other double cottage there was Audrey Taylor at one end and the Ottaways at the other, although my eldest brother Bill moved there when he got married. There were also two other cottages – they were even more out in the wilds. They've both gone now. Cooks Pit was where the Fenners lived. That was up the footpath towards Well Place but you went across the field to the right, not left to Well Place. And there was Combe Cot down in the woods between us and the river. Mrs Wyles lived there. She was an old lady and my sister used to go down and sleep in the cottage with her – just being a neighbour, you know. I used to go down and talk till my sister came sometimes.

Doris, who died aged two years and two months of diphtheria, much loved by the family.

The Penshurst Estate who owned all the houses didn't do anything. They said the beams had come from Elizabethan ships but I never knew if it was true. Our house had three bedrooms, one for the five boys, one for the five girls and the biggest one for Mum and Dad. We used to sleep head to toe. You'd look up and see the sky through the tiles and look down through the floorboards and see the ground. You could hear the rats too at night. So it was pretty cold. You didn't get up to dress, you dressed in bed. The boys had cut down clothes from Dad or the bigger boys. The socks had more darns than socks.

We had the loo down the bottom of the garden. It was just a shed with a hole, you know. If it was dark, the older children used to take the younger ones down with a candle in a jam jar.

On Saturday it was the clean-up day. All the children – the girls as well as the boys – had to help. We'd take the big old table outside and scrub and scrub it and clean out all the grooves. We'd scrub the brick scullery floor too and we'd black-lead the grate. Then on Sunday, we had to get all the water for the washing on Monday. We'd get it from the pump or sometimes we'd have to get it bucket by bucket from the well. We'd put it into the big copper and the big tin bath in what we called the pump house. It was down the far end of the cottage by the well. Mum would have a huge wash day every Monday. The clothes and the sheets and everything used to stretch right down the path. Then you'd get into starched sheets – I always remember the feel.

Mum used to go to Tonbridge once a week by train for a big shop. She had to carry everything back from the station. She only had ten shillings a week but she managed.

Even with all the work she had to do with us ten children – and there was little Doris too who died when she was two years and two months old – Mum still had time to play with us. On Sunday afternoons, she'd come out with us in the fields and we'd play cricket or rounders. I don't remember us playing soccer. They were happy days – we seemed to have enough, even if we didn't have much money.

We weren't really naughty. We'd do a bit of scrumping like most boys and we'd sometimes take one of Billy Goodwin's white cabbages which he was growing for the cattle and we'd eat it. So we did get up to a few things. When Dad came home from the pub for his Sunday lunch – we'd have finished ours – he'd have his lunch, then he'd go to sleep at the table and we'd take his tobacco tin. Then we'd roll a cigarette and smoke it in our bedroom. Do you know what we did with the stubs? We had those metal bedsteads with curly tops on them. So we took the tops off and put the stubs in there. The road from the village down to the Ensfield Bridge was just a cart track really, with a gate across it down by The Alders – the double grey cottages. There used to be two road menders, Ernie Grayland and Bill Mitchell. We used to pass them on our way to school and sometimes we'd throw their shovels over the hedge as a joke – but it wasn't very naughty.

The concrete road up to Killick Bank and Well Place Farm wasn't there either. It was just a footpath – not even a track. Us boys had to drag all the coal up from the road across the fields. We used to put a sackful over the bottom V of the bike by the pedals and push it up the hill. My brother George had a cart pulled by a billy-goat and he used that to pull the coal up – but the cart didn't last long.

There was a man we called Old Lamey who brought round fish on his bike and he would have to push his bike up the hill. When we needed the Doctor, he came up the other way. It was the old Dr Wood from Penshurst and he'd come up to Well Place and walk across the field from there. He'd come out any time you sent for him. But Mum looked after most of our illnesses. You could call it an old skill I suppose – like the old crafts. I got pleurisy when I was about thirteen or fourteen. I woke up one night and I said to my brother that I couldn't breathe. My Mum came and she put hot water bottles with boiling hot water in them on my back. It brought me out in great big blisters but all the doctor had to do when he arrived was to lance them. I was quite OK but look at the scars. We had all the old standbys – Vick (I still use it) and Germoline and Dettol and Zambuck. I heard a programme the other day which said Zambuck was Victorian. When I got married just after the war – my wife, Paulette – she was a French girl – had terrible eczema on her arms. My Mum took her in hand and it was cured. It never came back but I never knew what Mum did.

There was a footpath along the river bank from Ensfield Bridge right along to Penshurst but they got it diverted up to Killicks Bank and along the concrete road – a shame really because it was a lovely walk. We used to swim in the river – I learnt to swim there. I remember once I was with my two closest school friends, Howard Faircloth and Neville Ginn and I was walking in a shallow bit. I suddenly went down in a hole in the mud and Howard had to pull me out.

There were lots of other things for children to do. Did you know that Lord Hollenden's two daughters, Elspeth and Joan, used to teach the village boys to dance? And at the Coronation of George VI I think it was, all the children in the Penshurst parish – and Killicks Bank was in Penshurst then – had a meal in the Baron's Hall and then went and played games on Penshurst Place lawns. Then there was the circus each year with a tent and clowns and things. It was in the field near where the sewage works is now, just past Leigh station. One day I was walking home with a trug full of vegetables and a trunk reached over my shoulder into the trug. It was an elephant. It was quite a surprise. You could always go and watch Mr Hayter – Charlie Hayter – at the forge. He always had his tongue sticking out. We had other characters who visited the village. There was the Umbrella Man, who came round on his bicycle and mended umbrellas. And there were the gipsy peg makers. They always used to put their horse drawn caravans – there were usually two or three of them – down by Ensfield Bridge and the old man would cut the pegs from hazel. We used to worry a bit about our wellingtons then. You see, we'd go across the fields in them, carrying our shoes and when we changed into our shoes at the track, we'd leave the wellingtons down there. But they never disappeared.

We did a lot of cycling. Howard Faircloth and I made little trailers for our bikes and we used to go up around the woods collecting firewood. Once, my brother Bill – he was the oldest – he was cycling to the village and he was going down Paul's Hill pretty fast. When he went round the corner by the stables on the right – they're still there – he saw a big carthorse half way across the road. He couldn't stop, so he went right underneath. Another time me and Archie Denton had just ridden over Ensfield Bridge and we heard a whoosh behind us. When we turned round the bridge had collapsed into the river.

Starting to pull out the car that went into the Medway off Ensfield Bridge – the old brick bridge that later fell in too.

Has anyone told you about the drilling for oil? It must have been around 1938. I suppose they were worried about the war coming and petrol. They made a road up from Penshurst and drilled small holes in the field just below Killicks Bank – where the diverted footpath is now. Then they exploded them. Later they built a big derrick up on the hill between Well Place and Killicks Bank. It was big enough to have lights on it for aircraft. It must have gone on for twelve or eighteen months. I don't know if they found anything. I suppose not.

I'd gone to school when I was five. We all used to walk to school. The older ones used to piggy back the little ones. I started at the same time as Miss Ellis. She was wonderful. Mr Gibbons was good too. He was quite strict but we all respected him. He treated his own son – and the policeman's son Neville – just the same as everyone. So they got the cane in just the same way if they did anything wrong. But I think that I only got the cane twice and that was when I had done something I shouldn't have. You know what boys are like. But I had to leave when I was fourteen – although I didn't want to.

After the war, Paulette and I left Killicks Bank and went just across the river to Tapners Cottage – it was part of Lord Hollenden's estate and was really a gamekeepers cottage. Mum moved to Barnetts Road. We were at Tapners Cottage till 1953 when we moved to the prefab in Old Orchard in Charcott. The prefabs were wonderful. No-one liked it much when they built these present flats on the site but they're OK I suppose.

I worked with my father until 1953. He's been wood cutting all his life – so back to the early 1900s – and I don't think anything much changed in the way the work was done in those fifty years. He could have made a lot of money but he drank too much and in 1953 he said he wasn't going to go on. He told me I'd have to go on the dole. I said that I wasn't having that for the rest of my life. The next day Fred Hardy came round from the Smarts Hill Bakery and I asked him whether Mr Brake at the Bakery wanted anyone and for the next thirty-four years I worked for the Bakery doing the deliveries. Quite a change from coppicing but I enjoyed it.

Francis Hamlyn

*F*rancis Hamlyn lives at Westwood Farm between Weald, Leigh and Charcott. He remembers not only the changed landscape over the last seventy years but the different ways that farmers lived and worked in the 1920s and 1930s.*

Carrying the hay.

"When you get older, you look back and remember the way the fields looked in the old days. The hay fiields had cow slips, old rattle grass, red clover, vetch, old hardheads, coxfoot grass and so on. At the time you thought 'what a blooming nuisance' but looking back I like them. There were lots of beautiful grasses – Yorkshire Fog, Timothy Grass – that you just don't see now. Today, it's just different types of rye grass. That's why the hay had such a lovely smell then when you mowed it. Mind you, it didn't have such good food value – although the animals used to like it. The only fields round here now that are what they were, are the two or three little fields that they are keeping specially up Breaches Lane – the first right past Chiddingstone Causeway. The corn we used was different too. To get one ton to an acre was good in 1930. Now it is four tons an acre with the new seeds and fertiliser. It was much taller in those days but much lighter. I started using fertiliser in 1938. Mond, the ICI man, lived at Combe Bank in Sundridge near where we had a farm at one time. He was the one that brought it out.

The field sizes were much smaller until after the war. It is probably the biggest change between the old days and now. If you look at the 1909 map with all the fields, you'll see what I mean. And it was not just hedges being removed which changed things: bulldozers came in after the peanut scheme in East Africa – groundnuts they called them. I bought a bulldozer then and reclaimed fifty acres of rough ground. I've still got it as a keepsake. I remember once when I was ploughing, I came across some great slabs down towards the bottom of the farm drive. I couldn't think what was there until I looked at the old map and found the name of the field. I'd hit the old saw pit. The machinery you used to have on the farm then was built. It really lasted. I spent £7000 on a hay mower a year ago – it's broken down already. And the farm buildings we used in the 1920s and 1930s were the ones that had been used for generations. The first concrete buildings were about 1960. Almost none of the old ones are used for farming now – they've all been converted into houses but it's not automatically a bad thing.

Most of my family were in farming. I was born in a farm on the edge of Dartmoor in 1919. Although we left in 1925 when I was only four and a half, I can still remember what it was like. It often seems that way. Your early memories are clearer than some of the new things. I met an old lady aged 90 at a funeral the other day in Devon. She said I wouldn't remember her but when she was ten or twelve she remembered me as a two year old. My mother was trying to churn the butter and I kept getting under her feet.

So this young girl was asked to push me down the lane in my pram. I said to the old lady 'I can tell you the tune you were singing as we went along – it was 'I'm Forever Blowing Bubbles' 'and she said 'that was my favourite tune'. I remember the day we left too. I've got a complete picture of it – it was all misty. I've still got family down there – a sister at Okehampton and a daughter and son-in-law who run the farm we've got there.

So we came up to Kent. My father's first farm was Scudders Farm in Fawkham, north of Sevenoaks. We were there for two years until 1927 but they were hard times for farmers. I remember my father saying once, 'we've only got a pound left for the month', and my mother saying 'Don't you mind, we've got the chickens outside and the butter'. They had to go round to junk shops to get old furniture.

Hamlyn family picnic, 1927 in Kent.

We had twelve cows and, after we had milked them, we put the milk into two big seventeen gallon churns which we put into the back of our old Model T Ford and drove them to the station to go to Swanley. Mother churned the butter by hand and that got sold too. Looking back on it – talk about hygiene .... but no one died. We had two hundred acres of corn which was all done with a steam plough. You won't know what that was but you used to hire in the men to do it. They would arrive with two big traction engines. One was put at each side of a field with a chain between them which was attached to a five or seven furrow plough. The first engine would pull the plough across, then move up while the second one pulled it back and so on. A man rode on the plough to guide it. The only machinery we had at Scudders was a hay sweep plus a hay spinner which you used if the hay was damp. Then we also had a hay mower – it was four foot six wide and pulled by two horses. The horses weighed damn near a ton each. We had a few sheep too but no pigs. It needed three or four men on the farm to cope with it all.

I always remember the privy at Scudders; I'd never seen a two holer before – one large, one small. It had laurels round the outside which privies often seemed to have and the log pile was stacked out there so the ladies could say they were just going to bring a bit of wood in as an excuse, you see. It was a hard life – particularly at the end of the 1920s. In 1927 we had a reasonable corn crop but we just couldn't sell it: we got nothing, so we had to sell up and leave. We went as a tenant to Overy Green Farm at Sundridge which was owned by Lord Stanhope at Chevening – even if my father didn't like being a tenant farmer. He always wanted his own farm. He got the first year's rent free but then had to pay. In spite of that, he still managed to save £500 each year we were there. Looking back, I just don't know how he did it, remembering just how hard those times were for farmers but by 1936 he was able to put the down payment on Westwood Farm here in Weald. When we moved, I was fifteen or so and was longing to leave school. I was at Judd. I remember to get there from Sundridge, I took the bus which in those days had solid tyres. The buses used to be kept in the old first World War hangars that they had at Sundridge. But I wanted to leave and get on with things.

Raking the hay at Scudders Farm, Fawkham, c1926

At Sundridge, we also had four men on the farm. Two cowmen for the thirty cows, a carter to look after the six horses and an odd man who did a bit of everything. We'd start the milking at 5.30 in the morning and we'd have to be ready for the milk driver who came at 7.30. He also came in the afternoon at 4.20. You could get through eight cows in an hour maximum – usually six an hour – so it was quite a job. I'd crawl out of bed at 5.30, so by nine o'clock I was ready for a really big breakfast – two fried eggs, two slices of bacon, some fried apple and a couple of pieces of fried bread. I still cook it for myself every day, even nowadays. My mother used to cook it for us Monday to Saturday but she wouldn't do it for us on Sundays. She went to the eight o'clock Communion.

I remember going with my father to the Maidstone market. My father bought forty-five heifers off an Irishman. Then a drover brought them all the way to Sundridge along the roads. I helped him and my father gave me a pound note.

We always grew oats for the horses. After you'd cut it, you left it out to dry for three Sundays. Then we had the mangles for the cows. The horses were used to rake the weeds between the rows – they never used to tread on the plants: they knew: very knowledgeable they were. You'd work the horses two hours on and two hours off. But you had to hand hoe the weeds out between the plants. We called it 'thistle dodging': it gave you blisters but I loved it.

Horses started to go out from the mid 1930s, although we still had one old horse in 1950. But by then we had the little Fergie and it could do all the old jobs you had used horses for – digging the mangles, mucking out, hoeing between the rows and so on. But everything got quicker than it used to be. It used to take three or four weeks to do the silage: now it's three or four days. My father bought his first tractor at the Royal Show in 1932. It had a one and a half horse power Lister engine to drive it. Then we got a second-hand Fordson. It was £100 new. It had all steel wheels. I remember when we had just got to Westwood Farm, I got the tractor stuck in the mud and my father said to me "If you'd been using the horses, you wouldn't be in this trouble, would you" and he laughed. And he was right of course.

There was a farm sale when we bought Westwood and I've still got the catalogue. It was 15th October 1936. The main thing father bought was the Fordson tractor which cost £68. But it's interesting to look at some of the other prices that we wrote down on the day. A Guernsey cow went for £6 and two Friesians went for £9-10-0d and £8-15-0d. But a Suffolk – that was a horse – went for £48. Twelve tons of hay went for £40 and three milking pails and stools went for thirty-four shillings.

Fordson tractor 1938 (Note the steel wheels)

When we bought Westwood it had 63 acres of woodland. We started with ten acres of oats (which we got 18cwt an acre from), six acres of wheat, four acres of mangles and two acres of kale. We had thirty six short horn cows, a hundred and one sheep, thirty pigs and a hundred chickens. We did all that with three horses and four men to help who got £2 a week each. And there was no electricity.

In the winter when you were out working, you wore leather leggings on top of your boots. It was practical. Otherwise your trousers got soaked with mud. That was before rubber boots came along. You often wore britches and farmers and the workers often wore waistcoats. If it was raining you didn't worry. You threw a sack over your shoulders and another round your waist and got on with it – the ploughing or whatever. In the summer, you probably didn't have leggings. You just had little leather straps below the knees to keep the trousers out of the dirt – or just a bit of string. You always wore a hat or a cap – whichever you fancied.

In the spring, there was the sowing. We sowed a lot of the grass by hand when I was young – there was no machinery for it. If you were good at it you could use both hands. Horse drills for things like corn came in at the end of the First World War but if it was too wet you still had to sow by hand.

I remember doing it in the field opposite Gaza quite late on and I remember hitching one of the old horse drills to the back of our tractor and making my wife sit on the back to pull the levers at the end of each row.

You cut the hay with a mower which was pulled by two horses. Then you had to turn it by hand with a pitchfork. When it was dry, you had a horse sweep – we had a Cottis Horse Sweep – and that got the hay on to the side of the field where you wanted your hay stack to be. It used two horses, one on each side with a long pole on two big wheels with a rake underneath. Or you could use a hay rake which was pulled along behind a single horse. Then you had an elevator, although originally you would have had to throw all the hay up by hand. The first elevator we had was worked by having a horse walk round but father bought a little one and a half horse power Lister engine around 1934/5 and that drove the elevator.

Cutting the corn

With the corn, we had a binder pulled by two or three horses which cut the corn and bound it into sheaves, ready for hand stacking into stooks – usually ten sheaves to a stook – sometimes eight depending how green it was. You had two sheaves in the middle with four – or three – sheaves down each side. It was more for the wheat than oats because oats took longer to dry – you left the oats out for the three Sundays, as I said earlier. There were stacks of hay and stacks of wheat – with the heads on – and even stacks of flax. When you were thatching the stacks, which was usually around October, you had to make sure it kept the wet out and that the tops would not blow off. You made rope out of straw with a wimble. You know what a wimble is? It is a bit of metal about eighteen inches long like a starting handle for a car. It has a hook on one end which you attached to a piece of straw and went backwards turning the handle with the other person adding more straw as you went along. You ended up with really strong rope – a straw bond. The other thing you made were thatching spars. You split some hazel sticks into four – about two feet long – to make a V – and you used them to peg the straw bonds in place along the top ridge of the stack, with four or five bonds over the top and down the sides. Later in the year, in the winter, you got the thresher round when he was free for a couple of days and he did a stack or two when you needed it. We used to have George Hale when he was up by Penshurst Station. You used to get a lot of rats in a stack. I remember when we caught four hundred and fifteen in one stack of flax.

Making the stack, Westwood Farm, 1932

I was keen to start on things for myself. I went out and bought two pigs for 7/6d each to earn myself a bit of money. I ended up with two hundred. In those days when you had to kill your animals, things were not all that scientific, of course, but they weren't all that bad. The little butchers all had their own slaughterhouses and they would not have done the sort of things that have left us with BSE today. They were too close to their customers. I remember when I was young, old man Gillard had a big fat pig and he was going to kill it. He put a rope round his lower jaw, hoisted him up over a beam in the barn and put a knife under his throat. The pig just threw himself on it. We put him on the cart and put him into a tub to scrub him down and get the hairs off. Then we took him down to the pub – The Chequers – where they made the hams and things. To cure the joints they rubbed in sugar, salt and saltpetre. That was done for two to three weeks. Then you put it in a muslin cover and hung it up. The other way was to put it into a tub of brine. The thing about a pig was that everything was edible.

By this time – it was 1935/6 – farming had started to pick up. We had quotas for corn and things. It was almost like Set-Aside nowadays. Eventually Roy Bastable and I bought a threshing machine between us and we used to hire it out – we did quite nicely. Then, when combines arrived, we bought one of those. We paid for it in a year. Mind you, we worked day and night for it. Then, we got a binder for the straw. We still have machinery that we hire out to other farmers – silage making and sowing maize and hedge cutting – but a silage machine costs £90,000 now and even a machine for sowing maize is £12,000. But of course you can do up to fifty acres a day of silage if you work hard enough and have enough trailers.

We used to have gypsy families to help at certain times of the year. It was mainly the Apseys and the Smiths. They came regularly and we got to know them well – and they got to know me too. We've still got a bit we call Gypsy Corner although they haven't been there for fifteen to twenty years. As well as doing work round the farm, they used to make clothes pegs and things. I remember one night when I was on my way to The Chequers, I saw the back end of a horse in one of my fields eating hay from one of my stacks. I went up to it and I was going to kick its backside when the old gypsy comes round the side of the stack and says 'sorry about that – he's just escaped.' But we both knew. Old Smith is still around I think – making field gates. There aren't any real gypsies now – we call them pikeys.

Down in Devon the harvest was more of a celebration than round here. We'd have a big harvest festival service, then we'd sell all the things given to the church to get some money to give to the poor of the parish, then we'd all have the harvest supper. Everyone used to muck in – the men all dressed as waiters. It's never seemed like that around here.

We never had hops or made cider at Westwood, although we used to get some cider made with the windfalls down in Devon where they had a big press. We never actually picked the apples off the trees. It was just the windfalls, including any old bits of earth, which went into the first pressing. Then what was left was put into alternate layers with oat straw and pressed again, all running down into a granite trough. We used to go back and collect the straw afterwards and feed the cows with it. They used to love it but if they got too much of it they would get drunk. My father used to make a lot of cider. You would give it to the farm workers as part of their wages. They had an old horse walking round in circles to work the press. I remember when I was about three or four, my parents had some friends over and my father told me to collect a jug full. I tried a bit and thought "Cor, this is nice". They found me later on a sofa feeling very sick.

We used to have the hunt come across Westwood in the 1930s and I've never stopped them. But the number of foxes they've killed I could count with the fingers of one hand. The hounds don't tear the foxes to pieces like some people say. I've been right beside them when it happened. Once the fox is killed the hounds just leave it.

Westwood Farm, 1935

We had sheep at certain times of year. You'd buy them in August or September and use them to mop up the spare grass. You'd sell them in the spring. Some farmers round here used to breed their own flocks. I remember there were two farmers, George Porch up at Charcott Farm and Bert Corp at Lower Street, who used to swap rams. Mr Porch led his ram up to Bert Corp's field of sheep. Bert's ram was in the field too. The two rams looked at each other and charged; both broke their necks. "Well I'm buggered" Bert said, "I didn't think they would do that." That was all he said. The older Mr Porch had been farming for a long time. His son – the young Mr Porch – had a hard time. He died milking – he was not very old.

The other farmers round here were Mr Hobbs at Leigh Park Farm – Barbara Bastable's father; Harry White at Wickhurst; there was Mr Latter and Mr Thompson who had Newhouse Farm, Dale Farm and St Augustines. Mr Latter lived at Weald Place and he had money – it was from Hodder and Stoughton – and Thompson was the manager. Sidney Bernstein bought Coppins Farm in 1935 – they said he wasn't very rich in those days and was able to get it by not building a cinema in Tonbridge – they said rich people there paid him not to build the cinema!

Then there was Mr Trotter opposite me; he was a character. He heard the Ministry wanted to build the Gaza Barracks on his land. So he ploughed the fields quickly and planted apples because they had to give him more compensation for an orchard. He used to train polo ponies on the airfield at Charcott too.

Then there was Hatchland Farm. That was particularly important to me. It's at the bottom of Baylis Hill above Weald. It was farmed by another Mr Bastable – he was Roy's uncle. He had a daughter, Winifred, and when I started taking her out she was 19 and I was 17. She'd been pulling mangles all day. It was 20th November 1936 and I went down to Weald to play badminton. I put my bike on top of hers and I went in and said "Could someone move their bike". I had to have her back home by ten o'clock in the evening or there was trouble. We got married in 1942 when I was 23 and we were married until she died in 1991, forty nine years. We were married on Boxing Day. We'd meant to get married in October but I was too busy. We didn't book anything for the honeymoon. We just caught a train to London, we asked a chap about hotels – told him what we wanted – and we spent two days in London. Then we went down to Devon. Farmers' daughters know what they are letting themselves in for. You wouldn't marry if they didn't would you? They work as long hours as you do. My wife would do the chickens although she wouldn't do the cows. But my daughter does the cows and my mother milked the cows. My wife would always help at haymaking. Sadly, we lost our first child because she was pitching the hay.

There was always lots of entertainment if you wanted it. The pub I went to quite a lot, as well as The Chequers up the road to Weald, was The Fox and Hounds up by Toys Hill. It's exactly the same now as it was when

I was courting. A pint of beer cost a few pence and a game of darts cost you tuppence but you got a free pint if you won, so you'd stay on then. We had a whist drive once a week usually, and an occasional dance. I wasn't much of one for dances but we'd have parties for birthdays with lots of other farmers round and have a game of billiards – several of the farmers had tables – or a game of cards – ha'penny nap often. Sometimes farmers would play cards very seriously. I remember when I went visiting my family in Devon. I couldn't at first think why some farmers had a single field in the middle of another farm. They used to play for a field. I've won enough money myself to pay for a trip to Devon and back. Always remember never to play with your back to a mirror – I learnt the hard way. We didn't go out to restaurants like today. I was fond of reading and you could get a book from the lending library in Sevenoaks for tuppence a week. It was where Tesco is now. Then there was the pictures in Sevenoaks. We went every Thursday. It was called the Majestic in the early thirties, then became the Odeon. The first film they had was 'When Knights Were Bold' with Jack Buchanan. The second I saw was 'The Street Singer' at the Ritz in Tunbridge Wells. I went to both the cinemas. They would have films on for three days, then there was a new one. You had a floor show at the start of the film and at the Ritz in Tunbridge Wells you got coffee and biscuits in the middle too – all for one and three pence cash.

We had the old Tin Lizzy Ford and then in 1930 father bought a Singer 8 – new. He let me use it. Towards the end of the thirties I bought an Austin Big Seven. It cost £149-10-0d and I sold it in 1950 for £365. I drove it up to the Glasgow Show. There was nothing on the roads. We were driving up the A1 and there was a Morris. We were driving nose to nose for miles and nothing came the other way. That was fun. We saw the Queen Elizabeth being built on the Clyde. Then there was shooting: I would supply the land and some of the lads would rear the birds. They'd hatch them at home usually, then put them in the incubator and when they were big enough, they'd bring them up here. We'd have two or three shoots a year – and we still do – I've got one this weekend – but I'm a bit different from some of those people who want to shoot as many birds as they can. I'm happy with two or three a day.

I always went to church. I'd been confirmed in Sundridge Church. My father was chapel and my mother was church, so I was brought up happy with both. In Devon I went to chapel and later in the day I'd go to church. Once someone said "Why are you at chapel – you go to church" and I said "It's all God's house isn't it" and I was accepted after that.

In 1942 when I got married, my father said he wouldn't have two women in the same house. So we had the cottage in the wood. It only had a bucket – not even an earth closet. Later we put in a WC but we hadn't got running water to it at first. My father died at the end of the war and eventually we moved into the main house, selling the cottage to one of the land girls that we had had at the farm during the war for £1,500. That was in 1948. It was sold for £215,000 the other day but I wasn't jealous – what's the point. My father left half the farm to me and half to my sister. So I went to the bank and borrowed the money and bought her out.

Nowadays, it's unusual to pass a farm on to a son or a grandson. It's a bit sad. There must have been fourteen farms in this area producing milk before the war. Soon there'll be only one – me. But I'm lucky. I've got my son and his wife; and their son does the arable and the cows – he won a cup last year – and one daughter who does the chickens and another who runs the farm in Devon. I'm reluctant to give advice. I know that's wrong in some ways but I sit back and I chew a bit and I don't say anything. It's the only way they'll learn. I've seen too many farmers who tell their sons what to do all the time. Then, when they die, it all goes wrong.

We started a Westwood in the mid-1930s with the a hundred and seventy three acres. That took four men and the family plus the extra workers at special times of the year. In the wartime we had two men, two landgirls, two horses and a tractor. The landgirls were wonderful: you have to take your hat off to them. They were mainly from the suburbs and didn't know anything about farming or manual work but I can still see them doing the milking. They worked really hard – then they'd go off to the NAAFI at Gaza. It closed at ten o'clock at night and then they'd walk back to the farm in the dark. There was no danger, no molesting then. We lost one or two of them – they got married and that sort of thing – but they were a real help. We were doing wheat, oats, potatoes, mangles, kale and flax too.

By 1950, we also had some pigs and sheep but we were managing on three men and two tractors. The labourers got £1-12-00 a week and the cowman £2. We started cleaning up the cattle herd then. Only nine out of thirty-six passed the TB test, so we got rid of the lot and bought some pedigree Friesians.

In the 1970s and 1980s, we bought part of the Priory land and part of Wickhurst Farm, some land over at Westerham, some of the Long Barn fields in Weald, some land off Mrs Page and Scabharbour Farm. We own three hundred acres now and farm a further two hundred plus acres. We work all this with the family and three men – although the men do get £16,000 – £18,000 a year. We've got two thousand chickens now. We started with a hundred free range hens in 1943. There's three stages really. You had free range. Then you could have deep litter. You get the most deaths that way. And now we've got battery hens which has the least deaths – it was only 4% the other day. Whatever people say, I like a battery egg to eat because you know what the hen's eaten. It hasn't been mucking around in the dirt.

The yields you get from everything have changed massively – it's not just the chickens and the corn and wheat. It's the same with the milk. I got fined £7,000 last year for producing too much – can you believe that. At 1p a litre I'm still getting £10,000 a year but the farmer in New Zealand was producing five hundred litres a day more than us. In New Zealand, where I went last year for a holiday, I saw one man milking two hundred and thirty cows – he started at three o'clock and we were having tea at ten past five.

Maybe the biggest change is the paperwork. I've done it all till now. The biggest headache is the EEC. Every field. And they change everything each year. But I'm getting crafty. I've started sliding it towards my son. I've got the one son, Frederick and three daughters – and most of them have come into farming. I'm just the bottle washer but there are so few farms nowadays compared to what there were that you've got to give them an opportunity. I think it's easier for the farmers that are left.

Nowadays there are cars everywhere – I wouldn't let kids out on a bicycle now. We used to walk three miles from one place to another and back again and think nothing of it. My father used to love Devon because it was all the old local people who were still there. Nowadays round here there are lots of people who haven't been born in the area and who don't work in it.

Things have changed since the 1920s and 1930s. The countryside is different and the farmers have done a good deal of it themselves. But it's not all that different to look at. It's not the same as it was but everything changes. I have removed a few hedges in my time but a forty acre block is about right. At that size it's not too monotonous when you work it. And I like my wildlife too.

I remember after the war when I cleared the thirty acres of what had been woodland. It was a bit unusual. You see, when I was in the Home Guard, I did a course on demolition – nitro-glycerine and all that. They had cut down four hundred ash trees on the farm during the war to make the frames for Mosquitoes – the aircraft – and it left all the stumps. So after the war, I drove up to the ICI depot at Slade Green and picked up a box of gelignite and fuses and taught myself how to blow the stumps out. I soon learnt how much to use – I had to use nine sticks for some of them. The police used to rush round at first to see what was happening. The most difficult was one that was on the edge of the road. Do you know how I did it? I put bales round it on the edge of the road to absorb the blast. Then I put a good lot of jelly under it and Roy ran one way up the road to stop the traffic and I went the other. When it went off, it blew the stump right across the road into Mr Park's field – so there was no trouble. All that was part of changing the countryside a bit too – taking out those woodlands with nitro-glycerine.

Francis Hamlyn in 1995 dressed in his old Home Guard hat

Lord Hollenden

*L*ord Hollenden was born Gordon Hope-Morley just before the beginning of the First World War – he could remember seeing Zeppelins flying over Hyde Park. He went to Eton and joined the family firm of I and R Morley in 1933, eventually becoming Chairman. He ended an adventurous Second World War in Norway where he met his future wife, Sonja. They had three sons, Ian, Andrew and Robin. On the death of his Uncle, Geoffrey, the 2nd Baron, in 1977, he succeeded to the title of Lord Hollenden, moving to Hall Place in the late 1970s. He was a keen shooting man; and particularly enjoyed the family shoot which took place to celebrate his 85th birthday. He was an experienced fisherman and a keen supporter of cricket, as well as involving himself in a number of national charities. The irritating business of

old age – his failing sight and reduced mobility – irked him but he remained cheerful and debonair. Underneath the gentlemanly and courteous exterior lay a man of quiet, perceptive wit and great charm. He did not feel that, in this era, he had to involve himself in every aspect of village life but he did care about Hall Place and the village.

"When I was a child in short trousers in the early 1920's, the family used to come down to Hall Place from London for Christmas. It was usually every other year because we went to Hampden – my mother's family place – in alternate years. I remember my grandfather well – he was the first Lord Hollenden. I had to give him a peck on the cheek when we arrived and he had a little white pointed beard. I always remember that it smelt of lavender – Yardleys, I expect. I was very fond of him. He was always very kind to me. In fact, if I had to describe him, I'd say he was a 'kindly man'. But he was a very unusual man in a number of ways too. He was a Governor of the Bank of England for years and he was also a Master Mariner for both steam and sail. He had a large J Class sailing yacht which he raced every year at Cowes and a big motor yacht called 'Laura' after his wife. He was also a great carriage driver – where you have a special carriage and four horses and race them round a course. He was President of that Association. He was a short man and always wore one of those high white collars that go right up your neck. His father, the first Samuel Morley, (although grandfather was Samuel too), had been offered a peerage by Gladstone but he turned it down very firmly. So when they offered one to grandfather, I think he felt that he couldn't go on saying 'No'. I, and some of the other young ones in the family, used to call him 'The Gaffer' amongst ourselves. I was sad when he died in 1925 – I was eleven then. I adored my grandmother who lived until 1945, when she was a very old lady. She was a great old lady. I can still see her sitting in her boudoir at the other end of the house – the end that we had to finally pull down in the 1970s because it had been so badly damaged in the fire during the last war.

It was just the family at Christmas – not a huge party. Grandfather and grandmother, their two sons – my father and his older brother, Geoffrey, who became the second Lord Hollenden in 1925 – and the two families. My uncle had two daughters, Joan and Elspeth, my cousins. So it wasn't a huge party but it was still all very formal. The whole of the life at Hall Place was very formal. I was continuously told not to make too much noise. My nanny came, of course. She would make sure my hair was brushed and hands washed and so on. Some years later, when I was at Eton, she came down to school, presented me with a yo-yo and took me out to tea. I've got two great nephews and nieces who came down to Hall Place the other weekend and I see yo-yos are back in fashion. Nanny came from the East End. Eventually, she went to America and became rich.

Of course, we were taken to church at Christmas. Grandfather was very strict. You've got to remember that the Estate owned the Green and he forbade cricket and football to be played on Sundays. Basically, you couldn't be active on Sundays. You had to go to church. You were noted if you didn't – and severely reprimanded. He had the right of appointing the Vicar too. (I was told I had it although I don't think it was quite true: but I don't think it would have been right and proper – I might have appointed anyone: a drunk or whatever!) I was always told that Samuel Morley couldn't bear to drive past the Porcupine Inn in his carriage and see the men swaying around outside and full of beer, so he bought it and closed it. Then he got a deputation from the village saying that people did like a drink, so he said all right – he was a kind man – and he built them a pub – the Fleur I guess it was but I don't know. All so he could get to Hall Place in peace. I still remember my uncle driving up to the gateway there late at night and going "Toot, Toot" and Harry Lucas' mother rushing out – tottered out – and opening the big gates. Samuel Morley was very non-conformist and, when I eventually inherited the Estate, there were still lots of old chapels all around the place which I apparently owned. There is the old one up in the woods but it's falling down and the gipsies took all the lead off the roof. Even if we did it up, it would just get vandalized.

Hall Place c1920/1930

I don't remember us having to perform any Christmas songs or set pieces, or having any special Christmas games when I was down here as a child. The carol singers used to come up every year and, when they'd finished, they'd be given a hot drink – something filthy I suspect! I think that we had turkey and plum pudding for Christmas Day but I'm not quite sure. The place was alive with staff then – I think there were eighty-two on the payroll, including all the gardeners and people – but you really only saw the butler and a couple of footmen. There must have been lots of staff out in the kitchen but I never went there. Oh, and there was the 'odd man'. He used to take the buckets of coal round to all the fires. There were fires burning everywhere. All the rooms downstairs. All the bedrooms. My uncle – the one that became the next Lord – damn near set the house on fire lots of times. He used to keep throwing on extra logs to make the fires blaze and they would roar away with sparks flaming up the chimney. You couldn't tell him all the heat was going up the chimney.

I remember there was a marvellous Dutch grandfather clock in the corner of the dining room. (We've had to make that room into the snooker room now: it's so big we couldn't find a dining table large enough; and the heating .....) The clock had sailing ships on it which moved. Unfortunately, when we came here, it had been sold off, like nearly everything else. It was sad.

Another relative who we used to meet – although he didn't come down for Christmas – was Great Uncle Claude, who was my grandmother's brother. He was very tall and always wore a frock coat and those high choker collars, with a top hat in winter and a brown bowler hat in summer. He used to give my father a pot of stem ginger every Christmas and no one ever liked to tell him that father loathed ginger. But it did come in the most wonderful, blue patterned, china pot. He was a remarkable man. He was riding in Rotten Row on his ninetieth birthday when he fell off. But he walked all the way home although it was about two miles – in his top hat too I expect! When I was twenty-one and got given an MG Magnet sports car, he said he wanted a ride. I said 'how are we going to get you in and out' – complete with his top hat – but we did and I drove him home. He said it was the best thing that he'd done for years.

In the 1930s, when I was older, I used to come down here for the shoots. They were all private then of course – just your friends – not like today when people pay to belong to a shoot. The local pundits used to come – people like the de Lisles: we had the shooting rights over the whole of Penshurst Estate anyway – and the Bathursts who lived at Paul's Hill House before the Bickersteths. (The Bickersteth's son became a Bishop). You'd have seven or eight guns each day – nowadays it all fairly much the same – sometimes nine guns now – and we'd have lunch up at the kennels. The butler used to arrive to make sure that it was all laid out properly. It was not really necessary but that was how it was done in those days. Then, at the end of the shoot, all the guns had to come back to Hall Place for tea. It was an enormous meal – terrific – mountains of food. I suspect that it was a bit of a bore for most of the guns who probably wanted to get home and out of their wet clothes.

My Uncle Geoffrey, the second Lord Hollenden from 1925 until he died in 1977 was very different from my father. They had a different way of life really – different likes and dislikes too – but they were devoted to each other. Uncle was what you called then 'a gay spark' when he was younger – although I suppose you can't use the word 'gay' nowadays. He was always a generous host and very interested in everything – every movement – in the village.

He really created the Hall Place gardens as they are today. I remember in my grandfather's day there was a huge conservatory hot house – it really was hot – and they grew pineapples and oranges and things. Uncle was always adding and adding. He'd have got to Hildenborough if he'd gone on any longer. He had a particular interest in trees and a good eye for planting colour-wise too. Of course, he had a huge number of gardeners before the War – many, many more than we do nowadays, when I've only got the two – Tim Bance who's in the Bothy, which used to house lots of the young gardeners in the 1920s and 1930s, and John Porter in the Lodge by the church. Uncle was very proud of the gardens and I remember my mother used to pull his leg about the lake. She would be sitting in the window having a meal and she'd say 'Geoffrey, I really think your pond is getting larger'. Uncle used to get furious that she called it a pond. He was very keen on his peacocks too – there's still part of the outbuildings called the Peacock House – they used to be all gathered in there for the winter. He asked me once would I want them when I took over Hall Place but I never liked them. Filthy noise they make and they start directly it gets light. So I said no. I don't know what he did with them – he probably ate them!

One of his wives – he had lots of them you know – Lady Diana, was very keen on the deer that they had in the Park. She used to spend all her time feeding them. She was the grand-daughter of Gladstone. She was very quiet. She used to use the chapel in the woods. She used to take all sorts of odd people under her wing. Did you hear about "Rasputin" – that's what he used to be called. I think he was a Vicar or something who had run out of cash or something. She let him live in the Gate House. He was a strange character.

When we agreed to take over the Estate – it was around 1976 – my Uncle moved to his house in Devon. We came to live in the Stables here for two or three years. It was at that time that we arranged that one half of the building – the bits that got damaged in the fire – should be pulled down. But it still leaves us with a massive house and the huge gardens. There used to be two large bronze deer outside the front of the house. Some time after the war, someone came along in the middle of the night. No one noticed for several days that they'd gone. And we had a lovely, huge old iron gate which was stolen too. It would have taken three men at least to lift it off. Another time two iron urns went too. We thought we'd seen them later in Tunbridge Wells but we couldn't do anything – there were no distinguishing marks. It has made us a bit unwilling to open the gardens. We did it last year but that was after a gap of seven years. We have had to close off the whole of the top floor where I used to have a room when I came down at Christmas as a child; we don't have any living-in staff; and the garden staff, as I told you, has been cut down to the two men.

Of course the village has changed too. Hardly anyone's using the allotments. I've resigned from the Morley Trust that owns them. I've given the village the Pump and the carriageway up to the church by the Porcupine – you can't have these little bits here and there – the village should have them and look after them. It's the same with the allotments. They should be used properly. They should certainly never be built on. The village has got too big – in my view: that's the big change. There are too many houses. Too much of everything. It's more like a small town than a village now and I don't like the change – but that's just my view.

Sonja, Lady Hollenden, widow of the 3rd Lord Hollenden, with Miss Joan Hope-Morley, daughter of the 2nd Lord Hollenden. Taken outside Hall Place front door.

Dick (Richard) Selling

Dick Selling was born in Pluckley in 1934. His father was a farm worker and in 1944 he moved to Leigh to work for Miss Goodwin at Paul's Hill Farm. The family lived in the Penshurst Road and Dick went to Leigh School where "I used to rule the Village! I was always getting into fights!" He remembers Mr Gibbons – "he used to smack our backsides": and also Miss Ellis. "When they organized her ninety-ninth birthday party, I hadn't seen her for fifty years – but she recognized me even without my red hair".

"I can tell you about game-keeping and about ferreting. I've still got ferrets. They're not vicious. I'd put them down my trousers if someone bet me. I've had a few nips over the years but the only time it was nasty was with a young-ster, when he was frightened, and he grabbed for the nearest thing – which was my nose. It's difficult to get them to let go once they've got their teeth in.

Dick Selling with a pigeon belonging to Mr Clarke, the Head Keeper.

I'd left school at thirteen, spent six months at Wisdens, then I got employed as an underkeeper at Hall Place. I'd been a beater before – old George Faircloth used to take me up on the cross bar of his bike – and I used to go up to the Kennels on Saturdays with Peter Clarke, the son of the Head Keeper, George Clarke. There were five of us looking after the Hall Place shoot but that included the Penshurst Estate as well in those days. George Clarke took over as Head Keeper when Mr North retired. Then there was Ray Playfoot – he'd been there for years – and the other keepers who looked after the Penshurst part of the estate, Arthur Murray and Mr Rhodes who were under Mr Clarke. The oldest gamekeeper in the village was Fred Maddox – he was a strong old boy, with his white hair and big white beard. He had a twelve bore which had a hole up the barrel big enough to put an acorn in – a real ramshackle thing but he still used to shoot with it.

My first job in the mornings was to go out with a feeding bag full of corn. I'd start round Prices' Wood and Black Hoath Wood, then the Willow Beds down by Leigh Park Farm and end up at the Kennels. Then I'd clean the dogs out. There were about eight of them, including two terriers, two spaniels and a couple of labradors, plus Ray had one but no one touched it. He was so obedient. Ray would tell it to sit and the dog would stay sitting in the field all day unless he told it to move.

After that you'd go off ferreting until two or three in the afternoon and when you got back to the Kennels you'd paunch the rabbits and take them down to the butcher, Mr Whitehead. You had to have broken the necks properly because Mr Whitehead wouldn't accept them if they were bruised. There used to be lots of rabbits in those days. When we had rough shoots, I've seen as many as two to three hundred hanging up on the rides.

We kept quite a lot of ferrets. We'd go out with the bitch ferrets and the dog ferret 'Jacko'. The dog ferret is bigger and you'd use them as the 'line-ferret'. That's so that if one of the other ferrets has killed a rabbit down in the warren and wouldn't come out – we called it 'getting laid up' – you'd put the dog ferret down and measure where he'd got to on the line and then you dig. It could be a long way down too, over four feet sometimes. We had a seven foot long spade, with a hook on the other end of the handle for getting the line out. You'd start by netting up all the holes. Then you'd put one of the bitch ferrets into the middle of the warren and work outwards. When the rabbits came up into the nets you had to be very quick to grab them and break their necks, otherwise they got away.

Ferreting today is so easy. You can buy a special collar for the ferrets which works with hearing aid batteries. If you've lost a ferret, you have a box which you move around and it tells you where the ferret's got to. It even tells you how far down it is.

Sometimes the ferret will move when you start digging for it. We used to end up, laid in the mud, with our ear on the ground, to try to hear what was going on. We used to get completely covered sometimes.

At one stage we ended up with over a hundred ferrets up at the Kennels. Quite a lot them belonged to poachers who we'd disturbed and they hadn't been able to get their ferrets out in time.

We spent a lot of time after the poachers. We were often out nearly all night in the winter months. We used to meet Mr Stevens, the Leigh village policeman, at The Priory at two o'clock in the morning and I'd get home just as my father was leaving for work. All for four pounds ten a week; and no overtime.

If you caught a poacher, you could take what they had caught but you weren't allowed to take their ferrets: they were classed as pets. Most of the poachers were from Croydon: I don't know why. There weren't many locals ....! We'd set up alarm guns too. A wire was connected to a thing which was connected to two twelve bore cartridges and they went off if any one walked into the wire. They used to have man traps too which they put out in the rides. I've seen them but they were never used in my time. Most of the poachers were up at the Charcott end. One day when it had been snowing, we followed some footsteps. They led to a caravan up by the old Blue Anchor. We fetched Mr Stevens and went back. Mr Clarke knocked on the door and a very large lady came out and she hit him with an iron bar. So we went and got the Sergeant from Tonbridge and, do you know, she hit him too. When we did get in there, there were two young men and rows of pheasants. They didn't turn up for the Court case but they caught them eventually – in Orpington. When they got to Court and were convicted, the old lady rushed up to the Judge's bench and smashed her hand down so hard that the water bottle and glass bounced up and down. We used to get some rough old scuffles. Usually we went in pairs. Mr Murray – the Penshurst keeper – if you sent him after a poacher, he'd hit them first. So when we got to Court, the poacher would get fined, then they fined Mr Murray for assault, so we stopped sending him.

From February and March on, you started rearing the pheasants. Every morning, you had to collect up the eggs. We probably had a hundred pheasants – including the cocks and there were about sixty or seventy eggs, even eighty, each day. We'd gather the eggs in the trugs and sort out the good shaped ones, see they were clean or wash them; then the next morning we'd put them under the broody hens. We had about sixty or seventy of them in nesting coups all over the woods which I'd have to shut up each evening. The eggs stayed under the hens for twenty one days; and when the chicks hatched, we'd take them up to the rearing field with the broody hens. We'd have to boil up wheat and eggs and go out and shoot rabbits and grind it all up to make the feed. In the summer, we'd have three or four months when we cleared up the woods and the rides ready for the shoots.

All the time we were having to control the vermin. I've a good smell for a fox – the pheasants make a special noise to tell you there's a fox about. And, at the end of the summer into the autumn, we'd put lanterns up at night down the rides to scare the foxes off. We also used to poison them with a very strong poison. I don't know what it was. It was a white powder they kept under lock and key – which we used on magpies and jays too. Sprinkle it inside a dead rabbit and leave it out. Then there were gin traps for stoats and weasels as well as foxes. You're not allowed any of this kind of thing nowadays.

Ray and I used to collect the dead birds and animals as perks. We'd sell the magpie feathers for ladies hats and we'd skin the moles and foxes and things. A gin trap didn't harm the fur. It just caught them by the legs or feet.

The partridge shoots started before the pheasant shoots – about September. They were wild birds really which we helped to rear. You had to find the nests first – not easy, they're just scraped in the grass by a hedge or a ditch. You look alongside a road or a path usually as they like company. Then you mark it and take one egg away, putting a china one in its place. You take all the eggs you've collected back in the trug and they go under broody hens. The whole idea is to stop the foxes and the other vermin getting the partridges and the eggs. Each day or so you go round and take another egg. Then when the chicks just start to peck out of their shells, you go back to the nest, you tickle the mother with a stick to get her off and pop the eggs back in.

We used to have the shoots most Saturdays – either at Hall Place or Penshurst. From September on it was the partridges and then from October to the end of January it was the pheasants. Mainly they were guests of Lord Hollenden. All gentlemen – some were very nice; some not so nice. It meant a long weekend because, on Friday, we'd put up the sticks with the numbers on – one to seven or one to eight – to show where the guns were going to go. On Saturday we'd be at the start of the shoot by eight and the shoot would go on till lunch which they usually held back at Hall Place. We got a sandwich and a baked potato and a beer. Then you got on with the shoot and finished at half past three or so. Then you'd clear up, collect the pheasants and take them all up to the gamekeeper's room at Hall Place, put them in braces (that's a cock and a hen), and give out the tickets to the guns to say how many birds and what type had been shot. It wasn't only partridges and pheasants. Sometimes, they'd shoot the wild duck on the lake. They could be fifteen or sixteen hundred pheasants some Saturdays. The guns would have a brace or two each. Lord Hollenden would have some to take up to his London house. And the rest would go off to Mr Whitehead. On the Saturday night, I'd clean Lord Hollenden's gun. Then on Sunday morning, you'd be out looking for injured birds with the dogs. Occasionally, Mr Clarke would get given a tip which he'd share out on Monday, but it wasn't often.

I expect you know about the old chapel in the main road. Mrs Clarke used to clean and look after it. They'd have services there most Sundays. Lord Hollenden used to come. There were about half a dozen people usually and we were told not to go past it on a Sunday. It's sad to see what a state it is in now.

I was up at Hall Place for four years at the end of the 1940s; then I went back after I'd done three and a half years in the Army, remaining there until the end of the 1960s when Lord Hollenden retired to Devon and a syndicate took over. That put us all out of a job and they got Donald Hallett to take over part-time.

Donald Hallet

Gamekeeping

*D*onald Hallett's father, Bill, came to Leigh in 1939 and moved to their present house, Cherry Tree Cottage on the Green with his wife Grace in 1947. Donald was born there in 1953, went to Leigh School and then, after college, he started as an apprentice joiner, while at the same time working as part-time gamekeeper on Hall Place Estate. He moved to The Kennels – in the woods behind Home Farm in 1979.

"The Kennels was built in the 1850's by Farmer Bailey. Everyone thinks Samuel Morley built everything in Leigh but Farmer Bailey built quite a few houses. The Kennels was originally very small – just the four-roomed bungalow, but it got built on in the Thirties or Forties. It's called The Kennels because the Head Gamekeeper lived here and he had his dogs in the kennels out at the back. I still keep my dogs there today. Quite a few people come up to me and say they've lived here – there was one person who'd been an evacuee here during the war.

The woods and the estate have declined over the years – it used to be a model shooting estate. Originally all the woodlands were planted for shooting – farming was secondary. Everything revolved round the shoots. The rhododendrons, which you see everywhere, and the laurels were all planted to warm the covers. When it was sold in 1870, it was advertised as a sporting estate.

In the old days – really it was up until the old Lord retired down to Devon in the mid-1960s – there was great local rivalry between the Estates. The more influential people you could get, the more Lords, the better. Lord Hollenden used to invite members of the Queen Mother's family, the Bowes Lyons, and Lord Cornwallis, as well as Lord de Lisle and Lord Kindersley. They were all guests: no one paid. It was for the aristocrats and the gentry. The old Lord – he was a character. He was a big man. He used a 28 bore in later life which was unusual – a very small bore. He knew as much about a keeper's job and the shoot as the keepers. He loved it. He'd been brought up with it all his life. He would expect a good bag each day – two to three hundred birds – just to impress really. But he was like that about the gardens too – he knew as much as the gardeners and took a real pride in the gardens and was a very knowledgeable plantsman.

I used to go beating when I was a lad – about ten or eleven. All the boys in the village did it. We got 2/6d a day and a bottle of beer. So I'm self taught really, although I learnt lots of things from the Head Gamekeeper here, Johnny Bryant: and also from Bill Hubbard, the Head Keeper at Penshurst – I was almost in his pocket. When the old Lord Hollenden went down to Devon, the shoot was handed over to a paying syndicate and, in 1970, they asked me to help. It was a part-time job at first. I used to buy in a few birds at seven weeks old and then, in July, I'd put them into pens in Home Wood. It was run by Mr Eric Sutton from Plaxtol to start with and, by the mid Eighties, we got it to the best it had ever been, providing quality sport. I'd been getting more experience all the time. When the new Lord Hollenden arrived, he took it over but soon after we had the hurricane. That was 1987. So much went then. It devastated everything – we are still having to clear up from it now. We almost had to start again. Nowadays, I'm really more into game farming – supplying birds to other shoots. That's my main job but I also manage and work the woodland on the Estate.

When the shooting ends on 1 February, the first thing is to start considering next year's stock. That's particularly important. I go to great lengths – anywhere in the country – to get the best birds to breed from. They've got to be physically right – the right weight, the plumage, the eyes. Bad stock can go over into the next generation and affect the whole stock if you're not careful. It's helpful to bring in outside stock to change the blood – particularly the cocks. I'm using some blue-back pheasants. They come from Michigan in the USA originally. You'll have seen them around. They're a wilder pheasant. You need them to be good at flying to be good sporting birds – to make it harder to shoot. That's what you've got to have. Not just birds that can hardly walk – let alone fly.

Around the start of March, the birds are penned for a month. I put them in the aviary in the woods one year and in the field by the Kennels the next – to let the land recover. There are usually eight hens to a cock. By the end of the month the first eggs arrive.

We collect the eggs on a daily basis. I've got a lad, from Penshurst, who works for me full time. The eggs are all washed and checked and disinfected. There's quite a high disease risk if you're not careful. We store the eggs for up to a week in the cool, around 50°–55°, and the right humidity.

You don't want them in the warm yet or the germ starts developing. Then on the setting day – I do it on Friday – you set the best eggs in the incubator. Mostly it's a thousand eggs a week, with a success rate of 65% – 75% with luck, although if the weather isn't right – too humid, things like that – things can go wrong.

So by the third Friday, you've got up to three thousand eggs in the incubator and the eggs from the first Friday go into the hatcher – the 'still air hatcher' with much more humidity – for three days. Then on the twenty fourth day, the eggs hatch. They're either sold as day-old chicks or we rear them into poults, which are sold at six or seven weeks old. The day-olds go off by rail or whatever and the others go out into the field to the brooder houses – you've seen them in the fields. Some of the shoots buy poults from me or other game farms.

A number of birds will be provided here for Hall Place but it's not the done thing to disclose numbers to the shooting party. It's bad form. I've never disclosed it and I've never been asked. If I was asked, I'd just say, 'same as last year'.

About the beginning of August you release the birds you're keeping into the large pens in the woods to acclimatize them so they can cope with the rigours of life and the awful British weather. They're protected from foxes and other vermin with electric fences round the outside and we're feeding them all the time. This is when they learn to fly but they get back in again through little funnels on the ground round the edges of the wire netting. That's until they can look after themselves. The more they know an area the wilder they become, which is what you want. By September their main aim is to get away – they get the wander lust – and, although we're still feeding them, I have to go round 'dogging in' with my two dogs – I've got two spaniels. I go round all the ditches and hedges especially near the roads to push the birds back to the centre of the shoot.

All this time, I'm continuing to control the vermin. Pigeon shooting is done all the year round. The chap that works for me has ferrets and we do quite a bit of ferreting to keep down the rabbits in January and February. In the spring we use traps – only the humane ones – especially for mink around the lake. The mink are so adaptable – they don't need water. But we get stoats and weasels and rats, too. The foxes are mainly controlled by rifle. I try to be humane and sensible – to keep everything in check – not just to go out and kill everything. I'm not a supporter of fox hunting: I'm not against it either. I allow the hunt to come but only after the end of the shooting season but I'm not all that keen and they rarely come anyway.

The deer are more widespread nowadays. They used to be confined in the deer park at Hall Place. Now they're only minimally controlled but they can cause a lot of damage to the crops and woodlands. They can be particularly troublesome in the autumn when the bucks are rutting. They've just uprooted fifty or sixty young trees I planted. They have to be controlled – for their own good really. Badgers – well, I don't talk about them. I don't want people arriving with dogs. But I go and watch them. I'm good news for badgers.

The Shoots start at the end of October for the pheasants. It used to be earlier when there were partridges here – they were wild – but modern farming has meant the end of them. We have eight or ten shoots with nine guns at each from the syndicate. We meet at about nine o'clock at Hall Place but, of course, I've been organizing the whole thing well in advance and I'd have done a pre-shoot plan which I'd have discussed beforehand – where to go and so on. (The most recent Lord Hollenden would come up here to the Kennels to have his glass of whiskey). I have got all the beaters organized too. The guns draw lots for who is going to be where for the first shoot from one to nine, with number one on the left and number nine on the right, and after each drive – there are four or five drives a day – each person moves up two places. The middle is the best place to be so everyone has a turn. On one occasion, the host who was new to the job, held the numbers the wrong way up so everyone could see them, but he's learnt now!

We go off at nine thirty promptly and the beaters start off. I've got a team of regular beaters. Nowadays it can be anyone. It used to be the village lads like me. Now I've got a policeman, a doctor, a solicitor and so on. They get £15 a day plus beer – not 2/6p. I also have two 'pickers up' who are instructed by me, mainly to make sure that there are no wounded birds left.

The Guns are slightly different from what they used to be under the old Lord Hollenden. It's people who can afford to shoot rather than country people, although we still get some of the old, gentry type who treat us the same as they treat anyone, although I remember one elderly Lord who was both pompous and a gentleman.

The guns get their lunch – it's not at Hall Place but in the room behind Alfie Houghton's old office – and the beaters have lunch at the Kennels. You get varied numbers of birds from small to large – usually a hundred but up to a hundred and fifty birds. We finish most days at the Kennels. The guns get a brace each and the rest I sell. I used to do the plucking myself but nowadays I get all that done outside, what with all the health regulations and things.

I organize a Beaters' Day at the end of the season, which is always fun.

I learnt to shoot when I was young. I taught myself. I did lots of rifle shooting but no competitions. But I had two arms then. When I lost my arm, I had to adapt with the shooting – and with the joinery which I still do – I have a workshop down at the stables in Hall Place. My remaining arm got a lot stronger and I started clay pigeon shooting competitions. There's no allowances made for having one arm. It's on equal terms. I won a European medal a few years ago. The majority of other competitors are very supportive but some people get a bit rattled at competitions if they get beaten by someone with one arm. I feel like saying 'you can tie one arm behind your back if you want'.

Miss Winifred Ellis

Schoolteacher

(with extracts from the school log by Mr Walter Gibbons)

Miss *iss Winifred Ellis was born in 1898. These conversations took place in autumn 1997. Miss Ellis is now about to celebrate her hundred and second birthday. At a recent Millennium School Reunion, she remembered all her former pupils with great accuracy, together with most of their subsequent careers.*

Miss Ellis, aged 22 in 1920, just before she went to Goldsmiths College. At this age, Miss Ellis says her hair was so long that she could sit on it.

"I'm in my ninety-ninth year. I taught at Leigh School from 1927 until 1946. I cycled from my home in Weald every day for those nineteen years. I've never owned a car. I enjoyed the cycling. I think that it did something for my constitution".

The Leigh Church School log, kept with great attention to detail by the Headmaster, Walter Gibbons, records that on 1 February 1927 'Miss Winifred Ellis, born 10.10.1898, uncertified teacher, began duty here today as Infants teacher.'

The reason why Miss Ellis is noted as uncertificated was because two years teacher training was necessary to receive a certificate and "I had typhoid while I was in the middle of my training. I was at Goldsmiths College – one of the best places. I think I caught typhoid off someone there and I had trouble with my leg, so I was not able to complete the full second year course. So when I started teaching, I had to do about two years work before I could receive my formal qualification. I'd wanted to teach since I was about six years old. There were a good number of teachers in my family, although my father didn't think I would qualify.

I always think of myself as coming from Weald. My mother and grandmother were born in the village. Grandfather used to own thirty or forty acres of land on this side of Weald and they lived in a very old house in the village – fifteenth century I think it was – made from ship timbers. My father was born at Chiddingstone Hoath. He had had to leave school early but he used to buy lots of second-hand books. He even taught himself Greek from a Greek lexicon he bought. When he died there was a huge collection of books. I've just given the Greek lexicon to a friend who is doing a PhD. It's very old but he says it's very good, with all sorts of unusual things in it.

I started teaching at St Mark's in Tunbridge Wells on the Frant Road. One day I saw an advertisement for the post at Leigh School. As we were moving from Tunbridge Wells to Weald to build a bungalow, Leigh School was much nearer. So I said to my father that I wanted to go to see the Headmaster and he said he would come with me. So we walked and when we got to Leigh, I did not know the name of the Headmaster so I went and asked at the off-licence. Then I went and knocked on Mr Gibbons' door – he lived in the school house on the left hand side – and he said I could come in. I explained why I had not yet obtained my certificate and why I wanted the job and he asked me to get my application to him within so many days. I think that there were about thirty applicants but I was on the short list of four or five. At the interview – they were funny old boys, the managers – they asked me all sorts of questions. Old Mr Goodwin, who was a farmer asked what my father did. So I said farming. Then he said 'what do you do on the farm' and I said I didn't help on the farm – although actually I did put in a good number of hours haymaking each year. They asked if I was a member of the Church of England. I said that I wasn't a member of any particular denomination. I said that I would teach the children about the Church of England but that I would prefer not to teach any doctrine. Then Mr Gibbons said he'd do it, so that got over that one and I got the job. Later Mr Gibbons asked whether I could take over the Infants and I said I could – definitely. But they were good, the school managers. Mr Sealy, the Vicar, was Chairman for many years. He used to come in every week and sit in for a lesson – not just the religious lessons either. He liked being with the children. He was very friendly.

From the first moment I saw the Green, I thought – 'what a lovely place: what a lovely place for children to play'. The Infants class ranged from four year olds till they had turned seven. I enjoyed every minute. In my time at Leigh School I never had any trouble with discipline. I think my reputation may have been as rather strict but I think that I was always fair.

I still remember most of the children by name and quite a few still keep in touch with me. The children were like a family to me. For instance, just round the Green there were Ann Faircloth, Doreen Passingham who married one of the Brookers, Molly Hayter from the Forge, Mary Stubbins and Doris Ingram from Oak Cottage whose mother used to teach music and whose grandfather, Ike Ingram, the great Kent cricketer, used to come and show the boys how to use a bat. Then there was Dennis Stolton – he was a proper little rascal". [A schoolboy of the same age remembers some workmen digging a trench to the Iron Room. When they went off for their lunch, Dennis filled it in as a joke].

"Then there was Jimmy Fitzjohn, Roger Dadswell – he became a hair-dresser, and John Knock, whose mother I knew very well because she taught in the Infants later. John was a thin little boy and he had the most terrible asthma. It could come on so suddenly. There was Audrey Latter – she was Audrey Fautly then. There was all the Selden family – Bubbles, Joyce and Cyril and lots more too. Cyril was very clever at maths. There was Bessie and Lionel Clark. Lionel did not come from a well-to-do family but he was clever. He learnt to read very quickly. He went to work at Hall Place in the gardens. The Head Gardener encouraged him to go on and take the exams. He ended up with the highest degree you can get in horticulture. Then there was Nicholas Butcher. He came in late one day. I asked him where he had been and he said he'd been having a drink in The Bat ...!

I introduced quite a lot of things. Some of them weren't approved of completely but I'd got many new ideas from Goldsmiths College. I did some individual teaching but there was a good deal of blackboard work. Reading was my pet subject. Once they could read, it opened up all the world. We used to use Janet and John books for reading and I supplemented the main books with all sorts of odds and ends that I collected. I started our own library.

I remember one boy, Alec, was left-handed. His father thought he should use his right hand for writing and I had a big argument with Mr Gibbons – I didn't have many in all the nineteen years. Alec was writing his name on the blackboard when Mr Gibbons came in. 'Why isn't he using his right hand? He must try'. So Alec tried but he moved the chalk back to his left hand. Mr Gibbons said 'You must try to make him' and I said 'I haven't got time – there are five in the class who are left-handed'. Anyway we had been told in College not to force them to change. So I didn't.

With writing, I taught pure script – circles and straight lines. The Marion Richardson ideas came later. I worked out my own numbers scheme and I remember the School Inspectors were quite impressed. I loved Nature Study. I introduced a nature table and the children used to make a nature calendar each month. When the children brought nature things to school, we'd draw them and make notes. I loved handwork too. I took Arts and Crafts at Goldsmiths College. We did all sorts of things for Christmas especially. I started the children using poster paints – they were new then – and we used large pieces of paper, not small ones.

It was a Church School when I arrived. It changed to being a County Council School in 1936 when it was felt it was becoming too expensive for the Church to maintain. There was an annual scripture examination in front of a person called the Correspondent and for many years – it was about fifty years – it was J. M. Sturges. One Inspector who was a vicar told me that I had a marvellous imagination because I had told the story about the man who went to Jericho in my own way. The older children had a written examination – ours was just an oral one. After the religious inspection, the rest of the day was always a holiday".

The School Log, as well as noting the annual May visits of Mr Sturges, also gives the annual reports of the Diocesan Inspector. The entry for 23 May 1927 has – 'The infants answered very well on all their stories and said the texts connected with them with understanding. They have been well taught and on good lines. The three groups of the Upper School have worked well at the subjects of 'worship', 'faith' and 'The Messiah' and certainly their knowledge of them reaches a high standard. The church teaching is distinctly sound all through and the sacramental teaching of the upper group exceptionally so. In all classes the repetition was a strong feature and written work of the school deserves a word of special praise ...' Reports from other years include many phrases mentioning the school's high standards, both on general education but particularly religious education, such as 'The subjects taken were 'The Church as a Society' and 'Duty' in the two junior groups: and in the top class a very wide syllabus on Duty ...'; and 'I noticed with what reverence the opening prayer were said. Some large picture (such as Nelson's) would be a boon to the infants' and 'In the third class the children had a good idea of the meaning of the Baptismal Covenant ...'

Miss Ellis remembers that another annual occasion – Empire Day. "Empire Day was a big event. We went up to the garden at Hall Place for sports or sometimes we went to Mrs Bickersteth's at Paul's Hill because the children had a half day holiday".

Throughout the 1920's and 1930's, the School Log gives an outline of the events on 24 May – Empire Day. For example – 'Children assembled at 2.00 pm. Sang patriotic songs and National anthem in the playground and marched past and saluted the Union Jack'. 'In the afternoon children assembled and sang Empire songs, National Anthem etc and were addressed by the Headmaster. They then proceeded to Hall Place where they were entertained to sports and tea by the Hon. Geoffrey Hope-Morley. Medals (sixteen) were given in each class for essays on 'My Favourite Empire Builder' and 'My Favourite Part of the Empire'.' 'The scholars saluted the flag at assembly and an Empire Service was held in the school, followed by a short pageant of Empire acted by the senior children. The latter part of the afternoon was given to organized games'. 'An Empire Service was conducted by the Headmaster and took the following form – Hymn, O God Our Help in Ages Past; Prayers for the Empire, Jerusalem (C.H.H. Parry); The Children's Song (Kipling); Short talk by Headmaster on Service; Song, England (by C.H.H. Parry); Recitation, The Glory of the Garden (Kipling); Song, England Our Motherland (Bridges); The National Anthem and School Prayer'.

Mr Gibbons was very keen on music, as Miss Ellis recalls. "He had a choir and the school went in for competitions and things. The Infants hadn't got any instruments except for things to tap. So we used to tap things and sing". The School Logs confirm the range of music and associated cultural activities. 'The School choir competed in the East Sussex and West Kent Music Festival at Tunbridge Wells and was successful in winning the following trophies – The Drewe Challenge Shield for Sight Reading; the Challenge Shield for Sight Reading and the Camden Challenge Banner for Open Event; and a School Inspector's report noted 'Drawing and singing merit a word of praise'. In 1926 'Shakespeare Day was commemorated today by lessons and essays on Shakespeare and his works. A prize was given in the first class for the best knowledge of Shakespeare'. 'An exhibition of the children's work was held this evening when between 200 and 300 parents and others were present. The exhibition consisted of all the scholars books, samples of writing and arithmetic, handicraft in all branches, raffia, toy making, cane, cardboard, woodwork, needlework – plain and decorative – drawing specimens in pen and ink, pencil, pastel and watercolour, etc.' 'A short programme of folk songs and dances and other songs concluded the afternoon.

The School Logs note how the older children used to go on outings. Miss Ellis remembers when "they went to Hampton Court and I went too. The boat coming back to London was held up and we missed the train from Charing Cross. We went round Penshurst Place too. The children had to write a composition about the visits.

The Hurdy Gurdy Man – on the Green taken one lunch time in about 1928 by Miss Ellis. Note the monkey on the back of the horse. "The children loved it. I had to ask them to stand back to take the photo."

I never taught the boys and girls in different ways but perhaps the girls would plod on at things longer than boys. A boy was more likely to give up. And girls did seem to learn to read more quickly".

However, the School Log does show – indirectly – that the boys and girls were taught different subjects for part of the time – not least to equip them for their likely roles in adult life. Great attention was paid in the Log over the training of gardening and, to a lesser extent, woodwork which, although the Log does not say so, were for boys only. There were comments on how the weather had affected the vegetables but in particular there are the glowing reports by both the Schools Inspector and, more particularly, the Horticultural Superintendent, Mr W P Wright. 'Good crops of turnips and potatoes have been produced. The other vegetables were late; this result is unavoidable owing to the water-logged conditions during the winter and early spring. The garden has been kept in an exemplary condition throughout the season. Flowers were represented by excellent clumps of annuals. Conditions of tools – well kept. Method of Correlation – diaries are kept. Plans of the garden and cropping are drawn to scale. Well written notes are made on soils, on pruning, on manners and on other subjects. The notes are well illustrated with sketches. General remarks – the cleanliness of the garden has been an outstanding feature. The results are distinctly creditable to the school'. In 1928 a new site in The Green Lane was obtained for the school garden which was less water-logged. Mr Wright approved – 'There is every sign that when the new garden is established that the subject will reach a high standard'.

Miss Ellis remembers how the school broke up specially for hop-picking. "It was one of the main industries round here. The poorer families depended on the money – which helped buy the clothes for winter. People were much poorer then. It's not like nowadays".

Hop-picking started around 20 August approximately and the summer holiday which usually lasted till the end of September was timed to coincide with the hop-picking. Even the School Log showed that occasionally some children were still needed for the hop-picking after the school term had recommenced. The Christmas holiday was only ten to fourteen days, starting about 20 December. There was an Easter/Spring holiday of about two weeks and a mid-term holiday break for two weeks at the end of June/early July.

"When children were ill there was always Dr Fraser in Park House", continues Miss Ellis. "The nurse who is mentioned in the School Log just came in for what the staff called the 'Bug Hunt'. It was only occasional and if any of the children had nits, they had to be excluded for so many days. I remember one little boy – he got into trouble later – the nurse let out a shout 'he's alive' ...."

The School Log not only records the visits of the District Nurse and what seem to have been twice yearly inspections by an outside doctor, but also the bouts of measles, mumps, scarlet fever and 'flu – 'Nearly half the children on the roll are suffering from mumps;' and 'the year started with very low attendance due to heavy snow and influenza'. In 1945 'diphtheria immunisation was carried out in the school today.' Teachers' sickness was also noted. Even Miss Ellis was noted as away, although only once – with a scalded hand, which had happened one day in school. Another teacher was absent – clearly for a long period – 'owing to being ordered complete rest consequent on a nervous breakdown'.

"When you live in a village there is always a bit of scandal, isn't there. I knew nearly everyone in the village but I wouldn't want to make any personal references. Maybe I can tell you one story which made me laugh. There was one father who did the gardening for a big house. The owner went on holiday and when he came back, he said 'now's the time to dig up the potatoes'. But when they did, there were only the leaves. The potatoes had all gone."

Miss Ellis remembers that they did not have school lunches till the War. "Before the War, the children would go home for a meal or the children would bring their own food if they lived outside the village. They all walked from home to school – sometimes quite a long way. They could arrive very wet if the weather was bad and we would dry all the clothes on the fire guard around the Essen stove in the middle of the room. I remember Mrs Fredericks who had the dairy farm in Lower Street and whom I knew well: she asked me to cook an egg for her twins, Dick and John, because they could not get home easily. There was Sam, the older brother too. And if the Medway was liable to flood down at Ensfield Bridge, which it did quite often, then Mrs Selden used to come rushing to the school from Killicks Bank to collect her children before the river got too high. She used to write a really nice note if one of the children was not going to come to school."

"Of course, I remember the teachers as well as the children. I succeeded Miss Strong with the Infants. She was lovely. I think she became ill. When I arrived, there was Gladys Hookway – I was very friendly with her – and Miss Hayhoe. Mr Gibbons was a good headmaster. All the time you got on with your work, you didn't hear anything – not even praise. But if things weren't just right .... but I never really had any problems with him, because he knew I could stand up for myself. He was stern really – strict, you know. He was there a long time.

There was no particular help for the poor families that I remember. We had some Scholarships each year but we should have had more. I wouldn't say Mr Gibbons was unfair about the Scholarships. He had to make the recommendations. But I know he'd feel some of the poorer children would not benefit from a scholarship because they might not be able to complete school."

One of the most unusual events of the school's life happened on Sunday 1 September 1939. The school which varied from 113 – 120 children between 1926 and 1931 and then gradually reduced to 80 – 90 over the following ten years, suddenly found itself dealing with a large group of Roman Catholic evacuee children from Kensington, complete with their own, quite clearly, extremely forthright teachers who were nuns. Miss Ellis remembers how they all assembled on the Sunday to receive the newcomers. "There were 230 of them, plus their nuns and priest, Father Hatherway. We had some great fun with the evacuees but it wasn't always easy. We had the school in the morning and the evacuees had it in the afternoons. Their head infants teacher was a nice little person but I didn't always get on with her. I remember one incident in particular when I had been out to do some shopping. I went back to the school room and found her going through my cupboards. She said she was looking for a lost book of verse. I said she should have asked me and that I'd looked already. There was another, more amusing incident. All the evacuees' teachers used to come to my room for tea. One day, one of them came in and said 'I can't stop for more than a moment: I have left Monica performing an act of contrition; and she rushed out. She came back after a few minutes absolutely livid and said 'Would you credit it: I have just found Monica dancing a can-can'. I try to be unbiased about other denominations. The old priest wouldn't say good morning to me or my children and I got tired of it. I suppose I mustn't be critical but it was difficult with two schools sharing. Eventually I went to Mr Gibbons and I said. 'If they don't go, I will' and he said 'don't become aerated'. They moved down to the Village Hall soon afterwards".

Five years later, towards the end of the war, the School Log records for 21 December 1945 that 'The Revd F L W Sealy visited the school during the afternoon to bid farewell to Miss W N Ellis who has been infants teacher here since 1 February 1927. The Correspondent on behalf of the children presented a parting gift to Miss Ellis'. "I remember being given my leaving present ... I left Leigh School very sadly. It had been a wonderful time but the shock of the terrible incident was the reason I left".

Mr Gibbons's School Log outlines briefly what was perhaps the single, most traumatic incident in Leigh during the whole century. 'July 3 1944. The School reopened this morning after the mid-summer holidays. At about 9.50 am a fatal accident occurred in the main classroom. One of the boys, James Longchurch and a girl, Joan Chandler, lost their lives owing to the explosion of a cannon shell which the boy had brought to school. Immediately the school closed for the day and on the advice of the Chairman of Managers decided not to open tomorrow (4th).

July 5. The Coroner's Inquest on the above was held in school today. The Coroner found that it was a case of accidental death in both cases. The Coroner expressed his sympathy with the bereaved parents and the Headmaster whom he also exonerated from any suspicion of negligence. (The school closed today).'

Six months later, in the School Log of 21 December, Walter Gibbons records his own impending departure as Headmaster. His final entry concluded, 'Mr Sealy presented the Headmaster with a parting gift ... I shall relinquish the headmastership of this school which I have held for twenty years and five months. Owing to reorganization, I have been transferred to the Tonbridge Modern Boys School. I wish to place on record the very sincere regret that I have on leaving this school, also the very sympathetic consideration by the Managers, the excellent co-operation by the present and past members of the staff and the very good relations between myself and the parents of the children. I leave with most pleasant memories of all concerned.'

Miss Ellis moved to Cobden Road Infants School in Sevenoaks. "After Leigh, it seemed a terrible place. There were eighty children with only one assistant with me in a large hut owned by the St Johns Ambulance. The two classes were separated by a curtain. It took a long time to make up my mind to stay but I did and I ended up as Deputy Head. It was a challenge I needed and I did enjoy it really. I was still teaching reading to children who had problems when I was nearly eighty – I decided I'd wear out, not rust out.

"When we moved back to Weald in 1926 my father and my brother – he's 94 now – built a bungalow. Then later – it was 1939 – I had my present bungalow built next door and I've loved it here all that time. I particularly love the garden and the orchard that I've made. If it isn't properly kept up when I've gone, I'll come back and haunt the owner."

Miss Ellis at her 100th Birthday Party in Weald, 10 October 1998.

Miss Ellis has always been held in the greatest possible respect by all the children that she taught. Of the many stories told in the village about her, one told by John Knock is typical – "I was about five at the time: I went up to Miss Ellis and said one of the boys had done something wrong. She gave me a very good explanation of the difference between telling tales and telling lies. I've never forgotten it. I'll always remember her for all she did for us".

Bert Stubbins

ert Stubbins was a kind and gentle man who told witty stories. He was born at the turn of the century in the right hand half of what is now Old Chimneys. His father and mother, Albert Stubbins (who was called Bert Senior) and his wife, Frannie, played an active part in village life as did Bert Junior. In the 1930s after Bert Senior and his wife had died, Lord de Lisle offered to sell the half of Old Chimneys for £100 but the family could not afford it.

The east end of the Green c.1910. Note the long grass; the notice board; and the fact that Old Chimneys – where Bert Stubbins was born– in those days was rendered. Both Old Chimneys and Old Wood Cottages to its left were two homes.

Bert (Junior), who had lived in Ivy Cottage, 4 Barden Cottages, on the Green, since 1919, was a cricket ball maker and a very enthusiastic bell ringer. He was also part of the Leigh Fire Brigade when they had a horse drawn fire engine. He used to tell stories about the problems he had when there was a fire alarm and he had to go out to try to catch the horse. Sometimes, it took ages if the horse was feeling unco-operative which Bert always said made getting to a fire quickly a bit difficult. He would also tell a story about Mr Goodwin, the farmer at Pauls Hill who owned Ivy Cottage and the land behind it. Bert was therefore his tenant, as well as a friend. Before Lealands Avenue was built, there was a field running down to the back of Ivy Cottage and there was a water trough for the cattle at the back of Bert's hedge. Bert used to fill it up everyday for Mr Goodwin before he went to work. Mr Goodwin looked after his tenants and when he was very old and thought to be dying, he asked Bert to come and see him. Bert explained that he thought he was in luck and that he might get a bit of reward for all his years of watering the cattle. When he got there, old Mr Goodwin was lying in his bed. He looked at Bert and said, "You've been a good tenant and I'm glad you're doing well. I've been thinking of putting your rent up two and six".

Bellringing – New Year 1969 with Julie Fuller, aged 10 with Bert Stubbings.

Evelyn Coomber

(Mrs Evelyn Hall)

Evelyn Coomber and her sister Joan were the daughters of Lawrence Coomber and his wife, Lorna. Mrs Coomber's parents, Jack and Ellen Roots, ran the Brickmakers Arms before, during and after the first World War. Both sisters live in Tonbridge.

"When I got to the Brickmakers Arms, I was three years old. It was 1914 and Dad had got called up for the War. We had lived in a house in Tonbridge – I think the rent was three pounds a week – and Mum said 'if I stay in Tonbridge, I won't have any money unless I have soldiers billeted on me, which I don't want'. So she scooped me up and went back to her parents, who ran the pub. Before that, Grandfather Roots had had a little business laying pipes – sewage pipes I suppose they were – with another man, old Mr Pratt, but something had happened. Grandfather was certainly at the Brickmakers in 1910 because Mum and Dad got married from there.

The Brickmakers Arms c1920. Note the motorcycle and sidecar which almost certainly belonged to Mr H.H. Camburm, the well-known photographer of postcards.

My earliest memory – and you'll laugh – was that, to get the beer, you had to bend right down. You see the beer barrels – firkins I think they were – were on little trestles on the floor – not like today with all these engines and things for the beer. You had large and small barrels and they were delivered in a horse and cart from the brewer, Kenwood and Court in Hadlow. The brewery was the big building on the left in Hadlow which they've converted into flats. There were three types of beer, 'mild' which was the cheapest; 'bitter' which was seven pence a pint; and 'old' which was very strong – Mum used to put it in the Christmas puddings. People used to ask for a 'pint of twos' which meant half of mild and half of bitter. So you'd put a bit more mild than bitter – there's a trick in every trade! Some of the old codgers would say 'cor, you've put too much mild in this'. We didn't sell cider – the Plough was the place for that – Mr Jempson that was – he was there for ages.

We had sawdust on the floor and one of the two bars had spittoons – horrible things – and there were open fireplaces and just lino on the floor. There wasn't any difference between the two bars – one wasn't posher than the other but there was a piano in one. We used to have piano lessons on it from Mr Harry Hitchcock, the church organist. Each of the three village pubs had its own people who were its regulars – all locals and nearly all men in those days. There was a bunch of boys from Charcott who played darts every Friday. They walked over of course – you walked everywhere in those days. We had shove-halfpenny and skittles as well as darts. We served bread and cheese and pickles – it was the only food we served in the pub – that's all you did in those days. It cost fourpence. The pub was open from 10.00am to 2.00pm and 6.00pm to 10.00pm. On Sundays we didn't open till twelve.

The Brickmakers was only a beer house – we didn't have a licence for spirits – and you couldn't really make a living from it. That's why Dad, when he took the pub over in the early 1920s, wanted to move as soon as he could. Kenward and Court got taken over by Style and Winch from Maidstone and, to help out, they built us a big tea room the far side of the courtyard, behind Mr Brooker's snob. It had a little wash room and toilets for men and women. We could have as many as a hundred people. We charged 1/3d for bread and butter, tea and jam. Mum used to make cakes – seed cakes and so on – which she used to take down the road to Mr Belton at the bakery. Mum used to shake sugar on the cakes – like you do – but Mr Belton used to say 'if you go on putting sugar on the top, I won't bake them'. The sugar used to catch fire, you see. We'd also buy a big tray of fancy cakes each weekend. The Grammar School boys used to come from Tonbridge on Sundays and we'd usually do them poached eggs on toast. I helped in the tea room a lot but I didn't serve in the bar – I wasn't old enough to work in the pub.

Partly because it was so difficult to earn a living out of the pub, Grandfather and then later, Dad had a little farm down at the end of Lower Green which he rented off Lord de Lisle. We sold off the milk and eggs and things. Grandad had pigs and we'd cook up little potatoes for them overnight on the kitchener.

When father came home from the War, he never really talked about it – except once. That was years and years later when my son was doing his National Service and was complaining about his bed and his blankets and things. My father just said 'Good Lord, you should have been in my war in the trenches.......' I just remember what happened in Leigh during the War – although I was only seven when the war ended. I remember looking out of my bedroom window and seeing a zeppelin going over. I can see it now. And I remember when the Powder Mills blew up. There was a huge noise and I looked out of the window at this light. It was really big. A man called Batchelor was killed. It was very sad. At one time there were soldiers invalided to the Large Village Hall and when the War was over there were these two bath places with hot water. At the pub we only had the tin bath which hung on the wall and when I'd had a bath in the kitchen, I had to go through one of the bars to get to the stairs. So Mum used to take me to the Village Hall sometimes for a proper bath. It cost 6d and ladies went on Friday and the men on Saturdays.

VAD nurses outside the large Village Hall in the First World War

For breakfast, we nearly always had porridge. I had it with sugar – although Grandfather had salt on it. You made it in a double saucepan on the kitchener overnight. And tea and toast – and, of course, home-made jam and marmalade which Mum had done. Dinner – which was in the middle of the day – was the main meal. You had meat pudding or meat pies and sometimes roast meat. And, of course, lots of home grown vegetables from the big garden at the back. There was no starters in those days – you hadn't heard of them. But you had sponge pudding or rice pudding – all sorts of things like that and custard of course. Then, at the start of the evening, you had tea.

I went to the Village School and when you got to the top, some of you went down to Tonbridge for the Scholarship Day. It was quite a strain. If you passed the written exam, you went back for an oral exam. In the oral exam they asked me the colour of the stamps. I thought it strange.

School photograph, 1920.
Back: R.P. Nethercot, T. Groves, G. Boakes, N. Healy, C. Pocock, F. Gower, F. Humphrey, A. Jenner, J. Turnbull
Middle: E. Ford, J. Martin, R. Horam, H. Wood, E. Killick, K. Ford, R. Batchelor, J. Upton, C. Weeks, L. Clarke, E. Boakes
Front: T. Foord, M. Brooker, K. Ford, I. Dadswell, K. Fautley, G. Foord, M. Humphrey, M. Pearson

When we were teenagers, we had dances and – of course – fell in love with local boys. Mr Houghton – Alfie he was always called – I always remember his girl friend. She was from Tonbridge and she was a dress-maker. She had a different dress every time she came over. We were very impressed – and she was very pretty too – really beautiful. I was madly in love with one boy but when we moved, he met someone else. I also remember my first perm. It must have been at the end of the 1920s when I was about seventeen. It was at Mr Warder's hairdressing shop in the Parade in Tonbridge – Mr Warder lived in Lealands Avenue and built the houses up there and Greenview Avenue. Anyway, he and his daughter, Joyce, had this new electric machine for perms. Mr Warder had to take an exam to make sure he could work it properly. I was a bit wary about it.

In about 1929, Dad got offered The Flying Dutchman in Hildenborough and so Nellie and I – my sister was eight years younger than me – and my parents went up there and I continued to help them in the pub until I was married in 1938. The Brickmakers was made into a house in 1951.

I haven't been back to Leigh really – just driven through – although I did meet the lady who lives in Brickmakers in the street once and she said to ring up and come over. But I never did. I'm glad to hear it still a lovely village. It was when I left – but that must be seventy years ago".

Joan Coomber

(Mrs 'Nellie' Helen Joan Standen)

"I was born in 'The Brickmakers Arms' in 1920. There weren't any bricks being made in Leigh at the time but it wasn't that long before. One of my best friend, Doris Humphries, her father had worked in the brickyards – so it was probably only a few years earlier. My first memory is sitting in my pram surrounded by yellow dusters which my mother had put there while she gave me ginger biscuits. My mother was Lorna Roots before she married father and her parents ran The Brickmakers Arms. Father – he was Lawrence Coomber – moved in to help at the pub when he came back from the First World War and took over as Landlord a bit before Grandfather Roots died in the early 1920s.

One of my other early memories was when Father cut his finger – it was almost cut off – when he was chopping wood in the yard. Mother rushed him up to Dr Fraser's – it seemed a long way, all up the long path from the road – and Dr Fraser sewed it on again. But Father's first finger was always crooked after that.

The pub's main entrance was in the High Street – not where it is now in Lower Green. You went in to the bar straight ahead of you and then, on the right, there was the kitchen. It was all lit by gas lights, with a chain on each to turn them on and off. There were spittoons all round the bar – people chewed tobacco, so you had to have somewhere to spit. They were about nine inches across and two inches deep with sawdust in them. There was a cellar down below where the beer was stored and things like venison were hung – I don't know whether it was blackmarket or not.

At the back across the little courtyard there was a big shed which we used as a tea room. The boys from Tonbridge School – it was called "Skinners" in those days – were allowed to go out for a walk on Sunday afternoons. So they used to walk across the water fields and come to have poached eggs on toast and things. My sister, Evelyn – she was older than me – used to complain about the work she had to do. Mum and Dad used to do lots of beaters' lunches, which got taken up to the Penshurst Woods in wicker containers when there was a shoot – just sandwiches and a drink – beer probably.

We also had a field at the bottom of Lower Green on the right where we kept chickens and a cow. I'm not sure whether Father sold any of the things from it or just used the vegetables and eggs and so on in the pub but I do remember Mum took me down in my push chair once and the old cow chased us. Mum had to run like the clappers.

I went to school in Leigh but only till I was nine when father moved to be landlord of 'The Flying Dutchman'. I got the nickname "Nellie" there, which I loathed. (So I'm Nellie to my husband but Joan to everyone else). I remember Mr Gibbons. He was a tall man, rather stern. He was very keen on sport. I remember us all running round on the Green but we weren't allowed on the cricket pitch: that was fenced off. You'd see the cattle being driven across the Green to the slaughter house while you'd play but we didn't hear anything when they got there.

I used to have music lessons at home with Mr Harry Hitchcock. My mum was good at the piano – I think that she taught it when she was young. But I hated them. So one day when I was due to have a lesson, I hung around on the Green until the lesson was meant to be over. But when I got back, Mr Hitchcock was still in the pub having a drink.

There were always things to do in the village. Everyone did a lot of walking, although there were two bus companies that came to Leigh – 'Redcar' buses and 'Autocar' buses. They came twice a day and competed against each other. But people often walked up to Hildenborough to get a bus. It cost a penny to get from Hildenborough to Tonbridge. My husband, Frank, used to go camping at Killicks Bank in the 1920s although he lived in Tonbridge. The Institute had film shows – they were just slides – and I remember my sister, Evelyn, taking me to the public baths at the Institute – it was in the building behind the Large Village Hall – on Friday nights. It was a strange place. I was quite frightened – it was really eerie.

When I got in the way at the pub, Mum used to send me to Mr Brooker, the shoemaker, next door in the little hut. He always kept the door open. He was really nice. Next door to him there was Mr. Belton, the baker. Mum used to take our Christmas cakes to be baked there. The Tengroves, who I still know, must have taken over the bakery in the mid-1930s. And of course there was Mr Whitehead, the butcher in the High Street. You also got the Muffin Man who came round on Sundays with a basket on his head. Then you could get winkles from another man who came round on Sundays. That was a real treat. They were ready to eat and I remember sitting there with an ordinary pin. They were small shells – black – and you took off the black cap and then got the winkle out with the pin.

When Christmas came, we'd have a pillow case at the end of the bed and a little stocking. We didn't open the pub until seven in the evening and we just had an ordinary Christmas really. We opened our presents – a pram or a doll or something – and played games. We didn't have turkey – you didn't in those days – we had a chicken or a sirloin of beef which father loved.

I left Hildenborough School at fourteen and became an apprentice hairdresser. Then I met Frank and we married in 1940. He was named Frank after a Tonbridge Magistrate. Frank worked at the Flint Glass factory in Stocks Green Road by the bungalows. It made test tubes and things for the Army. It was owned by Frank Wooley, the Kent cricketer. When the war ended, they did away with it. It employed a lot of people in its day and we had three of the workers as lodgers at the Flying Dutchman for several years in the war.

We never had any trouble with the policemen – not at The Brickmakers or The Dutchman. Mr Ginn in Leigh was happy-go-lucky, a very nice man. And Harry Phipps was the same. Sometimes three of them all used to come on their bikes and meet at the pub. They often used to pop in round the back to get themselves a pint – a bit out of hours probably – but it didn't seem to matter.

The Brickmakers Arms, with celebrations, almost certainly at the end of the First World War – see the Japanese flag, Japan being one of our allies. J Roots was the landlord from early in the century until the early 1920s.

Doris Walder

(Mrs Doris Foy)

Doris Walder was born in 1916 and moved to Leigh when she was ten. Here she talks about the twenty years that she was with her family in Leigh.

"My father didn't come from Leigh and we didn't have any family connections with the village. Father used to run a hairdressing shop in Tonbridge but, when he sold the shop and the rest of the terrace he'd been able to acquire, he and my mother bought this land behind the Green in 1926 and they started a small farm there which they called Green View Farm. Originally, there was just a track up to it, with a stile at the side of the old cricket pavilion. They built the farm house on the rise at the top right of what is now Lealands Avenue, with a view over the fields one way and the Green the other. Father built the cow sheds himself. We had mainly cows – although we had a few pigs as well – and Father started a dairy behind the cricket pavilion. We had about four men on the farm. We had a tennis court beside the house too.

I didn't go to the village school – I was too old when we arrived. I went to the County School in Tonbridge. I went by train every day. But I do remember the Leigh Headmaster, Mr Gibbon. He was very much part of the village. He used to play cricket every Saturday and was captain of the team, I think. At our school, we used to have a cricket match between the fathers and the school; and because Mr Gibbon's daughter was at the school, he was playing for the fathers. Unfortunately, I bowled him out first ball – but perhaps we shouldn't tell that story!

When I was in my teens, my father started building houses in what became Green View Avenue. My sister had one of them – next to the top on the right. Then, when he wanted to start building Lealands Avenue, some of the farm buildings were knocked down (although the house and some of the other buildings are still there), but that was not until later and by then I had moved away. In the end, father had built forty houses. I don't think everyone liked it at the time but then I don't think anyone who builds is very popular when they actually do it.

I first met my future husband, Peter, in 1930 when I was fourteen. His father, Mr Foy, was at Great Barnetts Farm and Pete went to Kent Farm Institute to study farming when he left school. But when he had finished, he really wanted to go into the Air Force and he became a pilot in 1938. We were married in 1940 and he was off at the war so I only saw him occasionally for the next few years. He used to fly over Great Barnetts to let us know he needed picking up at the landing strip. He ended up as a test pilot at Boscombe Down, although I was still living with my parents until 1947 when Peter and I moved to a farm in Guestling. He wanted to farm by then.

I still remember lots of the village people – quite a few are still there – the characters – Betty Crawford, Phyllis Upfield, Peggy and Spencer Coates, the Parretts, Alfie Houghton – you could set your watch when he walked down to the Fleur each lunchtime – the Reverend Sealy and lots of the others".

Mrs Foy died in 1999, leaving three sons and a daughter.

Green View Avenue, Leigh in the early 1930s.

❀

Miss Phyllis Upfield

*M*iss Phyllis Upfield has lived in Green View Avenue for sixty-four
years. In 1935, she and her parents had been living in Beckenham.

"We came to Leigh when my parents were looking for a piece of land where
they could build a retirement home. I was twenty something and I was
working for the London County Council, so we needed somewhere which
was near enough to a station so I could commute. We had almost settled
on a plot in Penhurst Road and we were beginning to walk from it to
Tonbridge Station to catch the train back to Beckenham. We came up the
track from the Green and we saw this piece of land for sale at the end of
Green View Avenue with a note to apply to the newsagent. My father
thought it would be too expensive; but I said if we didn't enquire we would
never know. So we went back to the village shop and obtained the name of
the vendor. It was someone who had been trying to sell for years – not Mr
Walder – and who was glad to sell to my father for something like £110.
Apparently, no one wanted to live next to a wood! At that time, there was
this wood of large trees with a pond at the bottom between this house and
the railway line where they built Wyndhams Avenue and Wyndham Close
after the War. You could hardly walk in it without stepping on primroses
and violets.

My brother designed the house and then we had an architect to look
after the actual building. We had a local builder – Woodhams. I don't recall
any problems. After we moved in, I was able to cycle to the station
everyday. I did it for twenty three years. There was hardly any traffic when
I started and not very much when I finished in 1959 but I thought I'd buy
a car, mainly because of the weather in the winter.

Most of the homes up Green View Avenue had already been built when
we arrived but there was no house next door and only a small bungalow
opposite. There was, as now, a mixture of people – some who had been born

in Leigh, some from the outside; some professional people, some pensioners. There wasn't a proper road up, and, when our furniture van arrived, it got stuck in the mud. They had to get a tractor the next day to pull it out. There were lots of negotiations with the Rural District Council over the years but the Council wouldn't take on the road unless the residents were prepared to pay. It wasn't until 1952 that it was all agreed and the road and pavements were made up. When we moved here, Lealands Avenue hadn't been built and half way up the track to our house there was a gate and cattle grazing right down to the cricket pavillion and Barden Cottages. When Mr Walder did build in Lealands Avenue, a concrete road was put in.

Green View Avenue, in the early 1930s.

Over the years all the gaps down Green View Avenue have been filled in. When Frank Hawkins married Joyce – Joyce Walder – they built a small house next door and later they expanded it. Then the Bennetts expanded it more and then the Bromleys even more still. It's typical not only of this road but the whole of Leigh, I suppose. The postman said the other day 'No one leaves Leigh: they just build on'.

One of the many recent extensions in the village, in this case, an undetectable match with the original Barnetts Road style.

From the start, we regularly went to church. The vicar then was the Reverend Sealy. He was very easy going. Late in life, he married an opera singer and she started the choir which was an excellent innovation. The trouble was that she had a very powerful voice but she always sang just slightly flat. Father became the church treasurer before the War; and after the War, I was treasurer for twenty years from 1957. The Reverend Sealy had been succeeded by the Reverend Eyre Walker. He was a great contrast to the Reverend Sealy – very pleasant but very much under the thumb of his family – particularly his rather fearsome mother. He was only here for a relatively short time before moving to a parish in Liverpool. John Bounds took over in 1957. He was an immensely sincere man who worked very hard. When he arrived he was very deaf and it was very difficult for him to listen to people. He had an operation later.

Over the years, I got to know Lord Hollenden pretty well – that was the one who died in the 1970s. During the War, I remember him giving me a lift from Sevenoaks Station on several occasions when I was coming home from work and the trains were not running properly: and when I was a firewatcher – nearly everyone was during the War – I usually used to hand over to him and Lady Hollenden on the Green in the middle of the night. I got to know him better when I was church treasurer. He took a great interest in the church. He could be stern – he certainly voiced his opinion, even when he was fairly old which he was in the 1950s and 1960s – and I remember that when we were looking for a vicar in the mid-1950s, Lord Holenden arrived at the PCC and said he had met John Bounds and approved of him. I don't think the other churchwarden had been much consulted! I would describe him as cheerful, friendly and autocratic, with a sort of paternal instinct for the village. I remember when one of the main bellringers had an accident: Lord Hollenden said 'I have forbidden Bernard Pankhurst to ring the bells'. He probably helped keep the church fairly middle of the road – broad – in those days, although it may be more to do with the Church's 'patron' – the Trust that Lawrence Biddle talks about in his book – who have a say in the appointment of new vicars: they are basically on the low church side. In the 1930s, nearly everyone went to Matins at eleven o'clock. There was Evensong at six thirty but I think more people used to go to that in the 1920s and earlier than did in my day. Things are different today: if you look in the Parish Magazine there are a wide range of services – family services with their own music group and so on, with different types of people catered for. When the PCC was talking to prospective vicars, I remember asking Christopher Miles what role he would see for women in the Leigh church. I think he made a friendly remark about flower arranging or something but he ended up by saying that he could never see a lady vicar in Leigh. (Probably most of the PCC agreed in those days!). Winifred Genner preached probably the best sermons I've ever heard in Leigh. She would have loved to have been a vicar and she would have done it wonderfully .... Nowadays, I go to the eight o'clock service – I prefer the Book of Common Prayer – but that does not mean I'm against the other services for other people.

Just after the War, I was elected to the Parish Council. I don't think there was a ballot or anything: we just went along to the parish meeting and there was a show of hands. I can't remember exactly who was on the Council but there was Charlie Ingram who lived in your house, Mrs Margaret Butcher from Bombers, Dick Wood, Mr Grayland, Fred Whibley – who I think was a councillor before he became Parish Clerk for many years – probably Alfred Houghton and maybe Margaret Wells – or perhaps she came on a bit later. Most of the people were Labour supporters, but I don't remember any political type arguments – or any major differences of opinion really. The main thing that I do remember is all the organization for the Festival of Britain in 1951. We did a whole lot of things – it lasted all week. We had the wrought iron village sign made and put up on the Green and we ended with a big pageant. Lady Page, who was one of the leading lights behind things, invited all the workers along to her home, Old Kennards, to a lunch. I had a very smart coat and hat with a Liberty silk frock underneath – and certainly a handbag and a pair of gloves. One dressed so differently in those days. And, of course, there was still rationing too. The girl who presented Lady Page with a bunch of flowers that day was Fred Whibley's daughter, Katherine. She went to the village school, then got a scholarship to the grammar school, went to university and ended up in Geneva working for the United Nations or something. That probably would not have happened very often before 1945.

Katherine Whibley presents flowers to Lady Page at the end of the festival of Britain week. On the left of the picture is Mrs Humphries of Upper Kennards and on the right, Phyllis Upfield.

But, looking back over the years, although some aspects have changed, Leigh is still the ideal village, dominated by the village green and over-looked by the centuries-old church, whilst its inhabitants have always been really friendly and neighbourly. And things have not changed that much. When I came to Leigh, I could ask Mr Coates to send all the groceries up – you could ask for anything – and they would be delivered to the coal shed when I was at work. Last year, when I had my cataract operation, I was talking to Alan Johnson at the shop and worrying about not being able to drive and he told me not to worry: he gave me a notebook and told me to write any orders down anytime. And so the groceries still get delivered if you need it!

Jack Simmons and The Titanic

In the 1960s, one old villager mentioned Jack Simmons. Jack had lived with his parents in Oak Cottage on the Green and had drowned on the Titanic on 12 April 1912. The local paper of the day explained that Jack had formerly been a cricket ball maker with Messrs. Duke & Son, and was making his way to America with Mrs Helen Twomey from Tonbridge who had obtained a new position with the Bishop of Indianapolis. The villager said that they were on their honeymoon, although that may not have been quite accurate, and that Jack was always called Sniffy Simmons because he always sniffed between phrases. He described the memorial service where Jack's mother wore black but she had a red flower in her hat. The body was not recovered but Jack is remembered on his parents' tombstone in Leigh churchyard.

Doris Ingram

(Mrs Doris Dale)

"**M**y father and mother, Charles and Ethel Ingram, and my brother Reg moved from Cinder Hill to Oak Cottage on the Green in 1921. I was born there in the front bedroom two years later. It was the start of a wonderfully happy childhood.

Mother and Dad rented the cottage from Lord Hollenden for over 40 years. The Simmonds family occupied it before us. Their 18 year old son, Jack, was drowned on the Titanic. I think the Simmonds must have had a small-holding there, because there was a brick pig-sty across the yard and a large hook in the kitchen ceiling from which pigs were hung for curing.

In the 1870s, Samuel Morley employed labourers from elsewhere to do building work for him at Hall Place and they used to use the local public houses much too often – so he turned Oak Cottage into a reading room and held Bible Classes there to 'keep them off the streets'.

When we went there as tenants, the rear door opened into the kitchen which was always a hive of industry. There was a large sink under the window and a copper on the left, a large scrubbed table, a mangle; and on the end wall a large cupboard for towels, tea cloths, dusters, tablecloths, etc. – everything we used in the kitchen. One of my earliest memories is of my father chopping logs and bringing them to the door and my mother stoking up the fire which blazed under the copper.

The copper was used for the Monday Washing Day – it was always on Mondays. I used to love Mondays because we always had 'a quick meal' so that mother didn't have to cook a large dinner. I remember the smell of toasted cheese with slices of home-grown onions on the top which greeted me when I had run across the Green from school. The clothes, sheets, towels etc were washed in the copper, then put in a tub of clean water and swished round with a wooden 'Peggy'. When this was done, the white sheets and pillow cases went into a tub of "Recketts Blue" and they came out sparkling clean and then put through the mangle and hung on lines across the yard. How I loved turning the mangle, how I wish I had it today – a few years ago I saw an identical one in an antique shop in Rye, valued at £140!

I can remember a bread oven on the rear wall of the house but it was never used by our family and it was filled in by Lord Hollenden. I presume the Simmonds baked their own bread – many people did in those days.

At the far end of the kitchen there was a walk-in pantry with a small window overlooking the yard. It had deep shelves on which my industrious mother stood countless bottles of jam, chutney, marmalade and jars of preserved fruit, mainly apples and plums from the garden. She was really good at preserving – later she won many prizes at local shows which caused a little jealousy, as you can imagine.

The downstairs rooms had brick floors with linoleum and coconut matting in the kitchen. The 'lino' in the living room and piano room had rugs which we all helped to make with 'wool thrums' sewn into canvas. My brother, Reg, was very good at this and came up with some really nice designs. These rugs lasted so long – never faded; of course, they could be made while listening to our favourite radio programmes, although I remember crying when the crystal set was thrown out.

Mother cooked on the kitchener in the living room before we moved on to a gas cooker in the kitchen – the cakes which came out of the lovely oven were mouth-watering. The kitchener was eventually replaced by an open fire which was made of bricks from the Chiddingstone Causeway Brick Company. In the living room there was the dining table which was covered with a red cloth, with a Windsor chair at each end and two dining chairs at the side. There were also two armchairs, a small sofa, a sideboard and a chiffonier with a mirror and shelves where mother kept various favourite ornaments and vases, and things like that.

There was, of course, no bathroom at Oak Cottage so a galvanised bath which hung on the rear outside wall was used on Friday nights. The copper fire was lit and the bath water heated and baths for us all went ahead – I can still feel the glow from the fire as I enjoyed my bath and playing with model boats. Somehow a modern shower today is nothing in comparison. After each bath, the water was thrown out into the yard and a drain took it away.

Mother taught the piano in the "Piano Room". Some of her pupils attained Royal Academy of Music certificates. She formed a W.I. choir who used to practise at Oak Cottage and great fun was had by all. She conducted – I accompanied them later in her life.

We went upstairs through the piano room door. The bedrooms were furnished in the usual way and the two largest contained washstands with marble tops and matching bowls and jugs. When I was little my room was the one with the arched window but when grandfather Ike came to live with us before the war, the box room was converted into a room for me. I was allowed to have my friends up there to play.

We were very much a Leigh family. My grandfather and great grandfather are buried in the churchyard. Old Ike was a very good cricketer and in fact kept wicket for Kent on several occasions, and he loved to go out on the Green and tell the young cricketers exactly what they were doing wrong! He was quite a character though and a familiar sight sitting on the seat under the oak tree puffing on his old pipe.

Ike Ingram outside Oak Cottage on the Green.

Children in those days had so much more freedom than they do today. 'Our gang' would be off down the fields to what we called 'The Shallows' by the Straight Mile. The water was safe to paddle in and there were plenty of trees to climb. Our schooldays were really wonderful. Our headmaster, Mr Gibbons, taught every subject, plus music, gardening, sport – a wonderful teacher. Most of us could read before we started school – our parents encouraged us – we were all literate and numerate by the time we reached the age of seven. 'Spelling Bees' helped so much, learning our tables by rote, and learning and reciting poetry – real poetry, not the rubbish they call poetry today which is nearly all prose anyway. Our desks were in rows, all facing the teacher, so much better than sitting in circles as they do today. Our School Choir won many prizes at music festivals in the old Pump Room on the Pantiles in Tunbridge Wells.

After school 'our gang' would meet at The Forge. We loved to see Mr Hayter, the blacksmith at work, with the sparks flying and the huge fire blazing. Magical days.

In 1914, father worked at the Power Mills but then he was sent to France like so many other men and experienced the dreadful carnage of that war. He hated to talk about it, but he was gassed and almost died but was carried back to the field hospital by Tom Lomas, his friend from Derbyshire. He saved dad's life and came to visit us every year until he died. A marvellous man.

My best friend was Mary Stubbings who lived next door in Barden Cottages. I used to climb through the hedge to play with Mary in their summer house. Alas, she and two other good friends, Barbara Faircloth and Bertha Hitchcock all died far too young but I will always remember them and the fun we had.

After the First World War, my father worked for Dukes, the cricket ball factory in Chiddingstone Causeway and stayed there until retirement. During the Depression he worked as a gardener for Lord Hollenden and also was a regular beater and loader on the Estate shoots at weekends.

The bungalow behind the Cricket Pavilion was originally the village dairy. The milk was delivered on a vehicle similar to an ice-cream cart. The milk was ladled into our jugs. I remember too Mr Putwain who called on a cycle, pulling a cart. He sold paraffin. And another caller was the muffin man with his tray of muffins which he carried on his head! And on Boat Race Day a man used to come to the school selling light and dark blue rosettes which we children could buy. There was great rivalry on that special day.

But my most vivid memory is of my mother pushing me round the lanes in my push-chair, gradually filling the space around me with leaves and lovely wild flowers which grew in profusion in the hedgerows.

When I see the traffic which pollutes our High Street now, I remember with nostalgia toddling along with my dolls pram in the middle of the road with not a car in sight. Happy days indeed."

1929. Leigh Cricket Club v South Nutfield. On the bench are Charlie and Ike Ingram with Bert Stubbins. The two girls are Doris Ingram and Mary Stubbins.

Mrs Vera Ingram

" I moved to Leigh at the end of the war but I was born in Nottingham in 1916. My father had died when I was two or three and I still remember the straw that they put down in the street for the funeral. I caught polio when I was a baby. I had met my future husband, Reg – Reg Ingram – during the War when he came to work in Nottingham, while Morleys was being bombed in London. We got married in 1946 and we came back to Leigh where Reg lived with his parents in your Oak Cottage.

Oak Cottage and the Oak in the snow – 1998.

So I became part of the Ingram family. I called Reg's father, Charlie Ingram, 'Dad' and still think of him like that. As well as Charlie Ingram and his wife, Ethel, there was also Charlie's father, Ike, who was living in Oak Cottage when I arrived. There were lots of Isaacs and Ikes in the family who all lived in Leigh in the 1800s. There was one who carved a cribbage board in 1805 which I've still got. Then he had a son – I don't know his name – who had a son called Isaac who carved a plaque my daughter in Suffolk has. And his son was Ike – Charlie's father – who carved various things including the hymn boards in the church and a mirror frame and a picture frame. My two daughters both have one. His carving tools are with my daughter in Australia. The Ike I knew – he was very old by then – used to sit in front of the old green corrugated iron cricket pavilion and criticise everything anyone did on the field – almost ball by ball. His friend, Mr Randerson, he was very different, an engineer I think, but they must have been the same age – anyway, he lived in what used to be the Old Vicarage stables – it's called Inglenook now. He was very kind to Reg and me about finding a house. He used to come around the Green to Oak Cottage and he and Grandfather would both light up their pipes and puff away. Oak Cottage didn't have much air at the best of times, so you can imagine what it was like. The stables was a funny old place. Miss Randerson, his sister, used to ask us round. His bedroom was marvellous and so was his sitting room, although you had to be invited in – but the rest of the house ....! I don't know what you could make of it as a house nowadays.

Charlie and my Mum-in-law were completely part of the village – not just because the family had been here for generations – they did every-thing. Charlie was a great gardener. The only rival he had for his fruit and veg at the Produce Association shows was Mr Faircloth – he was from another of the really old families – and there was a good deal of barracking between the two. Charlie was a bellringer for many, many years and he was also the Verger in the church for thirty-two years from the mid-Thirties until 1967. Twice a week he used to climb those very steep steps up the church tower to wind the clock. And he even dug the graves if there wasn't a grave-digger.

Ethel was a leading light of the Afternoon W.I. Years later, Reg told me that although I could go to the Evening W.I. – which anyway I had helped to start with Bertha Hitchcock in 1964 – I mustn't let Ethel know! There was quite a bit of rivalry. Ethel was a great jam maker too. She used to do marmalade for the Church every month and there was always a sort of waiting list. When she was very old, she had a heart attack and the Vicar,

John Henry Bounds, called round and said he hoped she would be up in time to do the next lot of marmalade! She cleaned the church for a good number of years too. When she was getting on a bit, her children and grandchildren, including mine, used to go and help. She used to scrub six pews each week – with cold water because there wasn't any hot – and polish the six pews she had scrubbed the previous week. I remember once the Vicar, Mr Eyre Walker, came in and was thanking Mum for her hard work. My daughter, Angela, who was only little but was helping, said "My Granny's a very old lady: she shouldn't be doing this". I don't know what the Vicar thought.

Reg and I only lived in Oak Cottage for a few months – you can imagine it was very claustrophobic – then we moved to rooms in Tonbridge: and we were the first people into the prefabs where Meadow Bank is now. That was in 1948 when I was expecting my first baby, Angela. They brought ten pre-fabs along to start with but there was a hold up because of the drains. The Council blamed the German prisoners-of-war for digging the foundations all wrong; but we reckoned that the Council must have had people overseeing them. It took six months to put it right. But, when we did get in, they were wonderful. We had a fridge – no one else had one in those days unless you were very rich – and a heated towel rail. And it had hot running water to the copper in the kitchen and a lovely big airing cupboard which was all heated. All for eighteen and six a week. I remember asking myself 'Is this really all ours? Is this really our home?' When they pulled them down, we were the first people to move into Crandalls in 1982.

The children went to the village school when Miss Naish had taken over from Mr Gibbons in 1946. When they got a bit older, I worked at the school. I did everything. I was the dinner lady and then the school secretary and I did all the accounts – because I had done accounts at Players in Nottingham. To start with Miss Naish had to come over from Pembury. She had a car but she hated driving, so she biked everywhere else because Mr Gibbons was still living in the school house. She was a great headmistress and she did so much for the village too. She was on the Parish Council (she chaired it for quite a time) and President of the W.I. She retired to Green View Avenue. I only stayed on for a year under the new Head – Jerry Davies – who was only there for two or three years anyway. He had a very different way of teaching to Miss Naish.

Another person who did a lot for the village was Nurse Ogden. In those days the village had a nurse – she was responsible for Leigh and Weald –

and Nurse Ogden arrived just after the War and looked after everyone, the old and the young. She was a midwife as well as the District Nurse. She was a wonderful, wonderful lady but too sympathetic. If you cried, she cried with you. She lived in Powder Mill Lane but went to the pre-fabs when the owners wanted the Bungalow. She was ninety one when she died.

When Charlie – Dad – retired as the Verger, they gave him a cheque for £75. When he and Ethel died a few years later – it was within a year or two of each other – they were just starting the Memorial Wall in the church-yard. The family wanted to have a plaque for them but it didn't happen for various reasons I won't go into. So when my Reg died, we agreed that the Ingram family should have at least one name on the wall. The family have been such a part of the village for so long and soon no one will have heard of them. When it went up, Mrs Thompsett who used to look after that bit of the graveyard and keep it tidy, came to me and said – 'He's got Tim Lee on one side and Rosie Jones on the other – so he'll be all right'."

Butchers in Leigh

Over the last hundred years there have been five main butchers in the village. At the turn of the century Harry Hammond had a butcher's shop in Southdown House next to the Bat & Ball until after the First World War. Clarence Malpass took the shop over, selling it in 1922 to Mr Whitehead who ran the business until his retirement in 1959 – a service to the community of thirty five years. After a short gap, Stan Wells and his wife, Margaret, moved the butcher's to the newly made shop on the Green beside Forge Cottage, which they ran for over twenty years – once again a central feature of village life. In the last seventeen years of the century the shop on the Green was taken over by Bernard Groves who retired in 1998. It seems unlikely that there will be a butcher in Leigh again, with small village shops struggling to survive everywhere. Planning permission has been given for the premises to be used as a house or a holiday home.

It is said that the small shop next to the Brickmakers – later Mr Brooker's snob – was once a butcher and early in the century or at the end of the last century, it seems there was also a butcher's shop in the annex to Church Hill House. After it was a butcher's, it became the workshop of Mr Playfoot who made hand made boots – famous because they would last for years. At one stage, Mr Bourne, the shepherd for the estate lived there and after the Second World War the annex was used as the surgery for two Dr Woods – father and then the son.

R A "Bob" Whitehead

Bob Whitehead was born in 1924, the son of Mr Donald Whitehead, the Leigh butcher.

"My father was Donald to a few close friends but he was generally known as Mr Whitehead – that was the custom in those days. I was brought up to call men 'sir' and women 'madam', unless I knew them by name when they could be addressed as 'Mr Blank' or 'Mrs Blank'. In those days, a great many men liked to be called 'sir' by those they thought their inferiors in the pecking order. Compared to then, forms of address are more relaxed nowadays. Father had taken over the shop in 1922. I lived in the village until I was twenty five – not long by many people's standards in the village. I went to a private school in Tonbridge and then to Judd. My ambition was to be a locomotive engineer but I had to leave it for health reasons and I went into quantity surveying and the building industry, although my life-long hobby has been steam engines. I used to have one parked beside the slaughter house, sometimes together with the County Council steam rollers. In 1986, Hall Place hosted a steam engine rally."

In 1949 Bob Whitehead married Jean Pankhurst. "We decided there was no way we could live in Leigh: there were just too many relations in the village – everywhere you turned! Although Jean wasn't born in the village, she was often here as a child because she had grandparents in Garden Cottages and an aunt and uncle in Chestnuts on the Green: and then she and her family moved to Leigh in 1940.

Bob Whitehead's traction engine – a 7 horse compound general purpose engine, built in 1904 by Fowler of Leeds. The photo was taken outside the Post Office in August 1956 by another traction engine expert, Bill Love.

I didn't work in the butcher's shop itself much but I made a lot of sausages and I helped in the slaughterhouse. One of my earliest memories of the shop was the ice man. He used to come once or twice a week from Tunbridge Wells in an ex-American army F.W.D. lorry and filled the big ice boxes. That was before electricity. It must have been in 1929 that the Tonbridge Urban District Council laid on electricity. The cable came across the fields by the Powder Mills. Up until then the houses were mostly lit by gas. Chestnuts was lit by gas at least until the War.

Father had few interests or hobbies and spent much of his time at work. He was often in the shop at five o'clock in the morning. He never sold anything but the best – he was always careful about the meat he bought. Someone once said that Father would see some sheep or cattle being driven through the village and buy them on the hoof but it was never like that. He examined every animal before he bought it. He'd buy from Home Farm – where the farm foreman was named McPherson (always referred to as 'Mac'); or from John Day at Moorden Farm; or George Day at Hale Oak; or James Day at Larkins Farm, Chiddingstone; or George Hale at Somerden; or Miss Ethel Goodwin at Paul's Farm, where the foreman was Freddie Sands. He also brought from Cedric Streeton who is still farming at Hawden Farm over at Hildenborough at eighty six. Father was always fussy about cleanliness in the shop and in the slaughterhouse too.

He had a loud voice; and quite a short-fused temper. He used to sack most of the people who worked for him regularly but no one took any notice: they just came in normally the day after and nothing further was said – till the next time. He had the small farm at the bottom of Lower Green and there were three fields which went with the butchers between the slaughterhouse and the railway. (They put the prefabs up there after the War and then Crandalls and Meadowbank in the 1990s). The top field had a pond in it; then there was an orchard; and then there was the bottom field. I remember during the War, a bomb landed in the top field and blew a big oak tree to bits. We went down, expecting the cows in the field to all be cats' meat but they were all gathered round the hole in a circle looking into it to see what had happened. There was a cowshed up there and I remember standing outside the door one time when Father and Ron Hoath, the cowman, were helping with the delivery of the calf of a Jersey cow, which was giving some problems. I overheard Father say – 'I'm just about fed up with you, Ron!' and Ron said 'You're lucky Governor: I've been fed up with you for years'. He had a good number of people working for him at any one time and most of them were with him for years.

The Butcher's shop c1980. From right to left: Stan Wells, Margaret Wells, Fred Fautly and David Hallett.

Stan Wells must have come to work for father about 1930. His father had a butcher's shop in Ashford, Kent. Stan lodged in Green View Avenue until he married Margaret. He worked for my father for twenty years before he went to work with his brother at the Post Office on the Green. A couple of years after father retired, Stan started his own butcher's on the Green. He had terrible arthritis. Then there was Bill Faircloth (actually he was christened Percy) and Bob Card. Ron Hoath started work with my father as a cowman when father had the Lower Green Farm but, after father gave that up, Ron stayed on as an odd job man and cleaner until he joined the Pioneer Corps early in the War. There were others who came and went. Roy Jenner came as an apprentice. He left to join Dewhursts, I think it was and did well with them. Others, whose names I can remember were Tommy Mockford, Douglas Lincoln and Darky Saunders and one man who was a most capable butcher but who left hurriedly one Saturday, believing that he had got a village girl into the pudding club – a false alarm as it turned out – but we never saw him again. Stan Wells's brother, Bill, also worked for my father until he joined the Army in the early years of the War. Then there was Arthur Hall who made the sausages. He had his own place out at the back called the Sausage House. The sausage mill was originally driven by an engine in an outside lean-to, with a belt through a hole in the wall. Then when electricity came, the engine was first replaced by an electric motor, but later by a self-contained electric mincing machine. I remember the 1939 Christmas when I was helping Arthur. It was before the rationing started. I made over a ton of sausages – it was seven to the pound. We reckoned with what Arthur made, we had made thirty thousand sausages over the ten to fourteen days of Christmas and the New Year, even if they weren't all for Leigh because some went over to father's other shop at Redhill where one of the men had been called up.

Fred Fautly was the slaughterman and shopman for many years in the 1920s and 1930s but early on he did one of the delivery rounds too. Originally, father had a horse and two wheel cart, plus a trade-bike with a carrier on the front for the village deliveries. I remember once father heard a horse coming lickety-spit down the High Street and he said 'listen to the speed of that.' When the horse went rushing past, he saw it was our horse and cart but no Fred. The horse went straight through the village, up towards Hildenborough Station with father peddling after it on the bike. He caught it at Lucys Farm in Lower Street. It had its head over the open half door of the stable. By that time Fred had arrived back at the shop all red-faced : he'd left the horse outside Lightfoots Cottages and a car had gone past or something and had frightened it. Later Father got a motor bike with a side car for deliveries and a Morris Minor van. Then he got a bigger Morris van and, by the start of the War, he had four vans. There used to be three main delivery rounds a week, although some people used to expect a delivery every day. When I was a young boy, I used to go out in the van with Fred. I don't expect he was that pleased but he never said anything and we remained friends until he died. He taught me most of what bit I know of the meat-trade. In later years, Fred was in the shop with father.

We used to deliver over a wide area. One round went to Hildenborough – although there was another butcher there: another went to Penshurst and Poundsbridge; and one went to Bough Beech and the Causeway. Father never went to Ide Hill because he was friendly with the butcher there; but there was a sort of armed truce with the butcher in Penshurst. The Penshurst butcher, Harold Thompsett, was much older than Father and gradually allowed the business to slip away from him. He and my Father were quite good friends, even though trade rivals. That was the case with most of the butchers in the adjoining villages.

The Square with Southdown House, for many years where the Leigh butchers shop was situated.

We supplied a good many of the people in Leigh, including Hall Place. We had some peculiar customers, too. I won't tell you the names but some of them were very difficult. Some liked to throw their weight about: but they didn't fare very well with Father. I remember one lady complained that the meat she'd had was tough and Father said 'Madam, I always say the Lord sends the meat and the Devil sends the cook'. Another lady asked how much a leg of lamb was and when Father told her, she said that it was cheaper at Sainsburys in Tunbridge Wells. 'Then that', said Father, 'is the place to go'. But he could be kind to people if he knew they hadn't much money. There was a charcoal burner over in a cottage between Haysden and Ensfield Bridge – it's not there now – and his wife used to send her son over for six pennies worth of 'hodsends' as she used to call it. (She really meant odds and ends). Father used to be a bit generous with what he sent her. He used to play jokes too. Peter Foy, the younger son of the farmer at Great Barnett's, borrowed his brother's motor bike – he was very keen on things like that – and parked it outside the shop. Whilst he was away, Father slipped out and put a mutton cloth up the exhaust. When young Peter came back, he couldn't get it started and had to go off home, looking very crestfallen. When he was out of sight, Father and Fred, who was in the shop with him, removed the mutton cloth and started the bike. They telephoned Peter and told him they had managed to get it going. Later, Peter went into the RAF and he used to tell the story of how in the early days of the War, he'd been flying back over Holland from a raid. He saw a group of Germans but he'd run out of bombs and ammunition. So he emptied his chemical toilet on them.

Monday was the main slaughtering day for Fred and one or two of the others. After slaughtering and dressing (that's removing the hide), the cattle were cut in half down the spine, and the offal and paunch were removed. Then the halves would be hauled up into the roof to cool over night. Monday wasn't a busy day in the shop: most people had bought their weekend joint and they used that up on Monday. So the shop was only open half day and Father would go up to the Sevenoaks market.

Before the days of stainless steel, the shop had hundreds of hooks and rails and Monday morning was the time to burnish them all. The blocks would all be scraped down daily and they are still cleaned in the same way, with a block scraper and fresh sawdust. A few years ago the 'health police' tried to have all wooden blocks replaced by plastic work surfaces. But the research showed that the cuts in the plastic caused by the use of the knives produced minute indentations that harboured bacteria; but the natural enzymes in a wooden block and the sawdust tended to destroy them. And, of course, the saws and the knives were cleaned down every night and we had to clean out the vans after every day's work.

On Tuesdays, the cattle carcasses were then 'parted' into hind and fore quarters and taken along to the shop along with the pig and sheep carcasses. The quarters of the meat were then 'broken up' into their main parts but nothing was cut up into individual joints until it was ordered. Father did nearly all of that. Trussing was a separate operation, and covered boning, if required, rolling, skewering and stringing – all the tasks that were needed to convert a mere lump of meat into a joint for the table.

We were shut on Wednesday afternoons with Friday and Saturdays the big days, getting everyone their weekend orders. We did quite a bit of poultry too and game intermittently. (There were times when Father didn't bid high enough for the Hall Place contract).

On Saturday evenings, we often didn't get back from the rounds till seven o'clock but then the big scrub down of the week had started in the afternoon. There was a copper at the back of the Sausage House and we'd boil it up – probably several times – and scrub everything with the hot water and washing soda – even the tiles and bricks under the overhang at the front – they're still there – everything. We cleaned down the deal racks and stands which had been used for holding the trussed joints in the refrigerator over the Friday night. All wicker baskets were scrubbed and rinsed and all the tools washed. All the marble work tops and slabs in the shop were cleaned and the bench and slab in the 'Sausage House' were done. All the pavings were scrubbed and the Sausage House floor. After the vans returned, they were scrubbed inside and the racks and divisions inside were taken out and scrubbed. Eventually, the copper was abolished and the hot water came from a coke-fired boiler. But we still finished really late. Then it was Monday and start all over again.

The only time it was worse was Christmas when none of us got to bed at all the night before Christmas Eve and pretty late on Christmas Eve itself, too.

I think that it is difficult to describe to someone who wasn't there exactly how a way of life felt without sounding patronizing – about the people in particular. The villagers were not bumpkins – they were often very intelligent. Had they lived in another era, many of those who were artisans when I was young would have had greater educational opportunities. I can think of one man who worked for my father as a farm-hand who was heavily interested in the archaeological finds in the Middle East and very knowledgeable about it all. Had people like him lived today, they might have ended up with directorships or professorships.

Leigh Special Constables in the 1930s. Chief Special Constable and Chairman, DE Whitehead is in the middle – the most imposing figure – whilst Alfred Houghton is behing him (with glasses). Many other local notables are also present including the Head Gardener at Hall Place, Mr Ferguson (second right front row); Mr Parrett (to the right of Mr Whitehead); Mr Warder (back left) and Harry Lucas Senior (to the right of A. Houghton).

A Child's Memory of
Mr Whitehead

One villager in his sixties has his memories of Mr Whitehead, the butcher. "He was a huge man. You'd be sent by your parents to collect the meat and you'd see this enormous man above you with his cleaver in his hand. He used to terrify us kids – but I don't think he did it deliberately. He'd weigh the meat, then he would call out to his wife 'two pounds four ounces, Mrs Whitehead' and she'd call back – she was in a little office at the back with a glass window – 'two pounds four ounces, Mr Whitehead'. But I still remember how frightened I was – and it was a long time ago now".

❋

Betty Crawford

"We came to Leigh in 1933 when I was twenty. It was just my mother, my brother Eddie, and me.

What happened was my father, who had been a doctor, had become very ill. We were living in Keighley in the West Riding where I'd grown up. Father died fairly soon after he had retired and we went to Switzerland. It was all very romantic how my mother and father first met. A girl in Keighley, who later became my godmother, had this pen friend in Switzerland. Eventually, the Swiss girl – my mother – came over to stay with her and thought England was so wonderful that she came back to live. She was a nurse and she met my father who was a young doctor. Very romantic.

Anyway after father died, mother and I went to live with her family in Switzerland – I was about fifteen so I learnt to speak fluent French. We were there about four years and then we came back to England. We decided to settle in the South – more appetising somehow – and we wandered all round Kent and were shown all sorts of places they thought we might like until we came upon Leigh. There was a farmer called Mr Warder who was starting to build houses down what became Green View Avenue – there were lots of objections from the village – and we bought ten acres off him at the top of Hollow Trees Drive.

My brother Eddie, who was two years older than me and had been out to Kenya farming, had our wooden house designed like a Swiss chalet by a London architect. It was mainly made of wood and all low to make mother feel at home. Hollow Trees Drive was just a clay track when we arrived and we got an old boy, Bert Seal, to dig it all up and put down that heavy gravel stuff. There was only one other house down the track at that time – Arthreda – where Arthur and Edith Burchett lived. He was the village postman and delivered everything on his bike. (I expect you realise that the name of the house was half Arthur and half Edith).

I had done a course at Liverpool Physical Training College, so when we arrived here, I obtained a post teaching P.T. and swimming at Fosse Bank

School. In those days it was in the High Street near Tonbridge School – next door to what was the Capital Bingo Hall. I was there for three or four years and then I got a job at a boys' school near Elstree. By that time – it was about 1937 – I had just bought a little tiny Morris – and each weekend I used to drive home all round the outskirts of London by the quieter roads as I had only just started driving. It took two hours. In 1939 I came back and taught French and P.E. at Hilden Oaks. I was there for twenty eight years until 1958 and even after that I gave private French lessons. It was funny: my mother never lost her French accent, even though she lived in England for nearly seventy years. She used to know all the English expressions but they always sounded different when she said them. She was in Barclays Bank one day and they asked her how she would like the money and she said 'Just as it comes' and they all roared with laughter.

I think Leigh was more active then – everybody was in those days. There was all the sports, tennis and the badminton in the large village hall. Of course, it was proper badminton, not your back garden type. You had to be invited to be a member – you had to be very careful who you invited. It was rather snooty. We used to have tea. Then there was the Mother's Union and the W.I. – I think the W.I. was probably just like it is today – people coming to talk to them. A group of eight or ten of us had a music hall act, called 'Firebrands'. Vivienne Humphries, who lived in Kennards, really started it. We adapted music from Jack Hulbert and Cicely Courtneidge – things like 'There's Something about a Sailor' – and we performed all over the place, Tonbridge and Sevenoaks as well as in the Large Hall.

Mrs Bickersteth up at Paul's Hill House ran the Conservatives – nowadays it's always a man – and she used to organise lots of things in the village. She had a crippled leg and her daughter, Anne, had too. There was a big dance each year – we'd go up each week well before and make artificial flowers. Once we made a whole bank of rhododendrons. It was great fun. She gave a big garden party in the summer and once I dressed up with a scarf and was a fortune teller. I heard one man saying 'Isn't it astonishing that an outside woman knows all about us'. He really hadn't recognised me. Mrs Bickersteth also organised a play and there was a Christmas dinner party for the important men in the village – the MP and Lord de Lisle and Lord Hollanden and so on. The food was prepared by caterers and brought to the large village hall and all the women went along to serve. It was like the Savoy or the Ritz – a really magnificent meal. Lord Hollanden seemed to enjoy it all. He was always very amiable – always very lively really. On Poppy Day, he and Lady Diana used to invite me to breakfast because I'd been doing the Poppy collection. Lord Kindersley used to open up Ramhurst Manor for dances too.

I knew the Bickersteth children very well although they were younger than me. There was Margaret, Anne and the son, John. John was only eight when we arrived and at one dinner party he presented me with two bouquets. Mrs Bickersteth said 'Oh John what have you done, Miss Crawford was only meant to have one'. Some years later, the family inherited a big estate in Kent. It even had a church and eventually, when John was ordained, he became vicar of the church.

The church here, St Marys, was very much part of the village. We went a lot – although Eddie and I did not join the choir until later. The Vicar was Reverend Sealy. He was very kind and pleasant. When we first came to the village, he used to ask me to play tennis and took me out quite a bit. I think that he would have liked to marry me but I was only twenty and he was forty seven.

Eddie and I were always very keen on singing. I joined the choir during the War – it was almost a female unit then – and I and Eddie were in it for years – I still am. Mr Gibbons, the school teacher was the organist when we arrived and was there until the mid-1940s when that terrible tragedy with the bomb in the school happened. Mr Gibbons got blamed by some people for not taking it off the boy but what can you say. Others blamed other people.

A coloured postcard from an original by A.M. Quinton, painted after the demolition of the Charity houses in 1911. Note South View was, at the time, thatched.

We had the Leigh Choral Society before the war. I always remember Len Walton loving it so much and Doris Dale and her parents the Ingrams – Mrs Ingram taught the piano – and Nancy Biddle conducted it at one time: but there was also the West Kent and Sussex Music Society which used to meet in a hall at the end of the Pantiles. It's shops now. We used to perform one main work – say by Handel or Mozart – and some female part songs and some male part songs – plus some male and female combined. We sometimes had famous conductors to the big concerts. We used to go on outings too. We'd book a coach and go up to London or Brighton or Eastbourne to ballet or concerts or plays or even skating. It was all very enjoyable – I was secretary for ages.

One of the things that you could do in the 1930s that you can't do now was take a joy flight in a plane. There was a small airfield behind the Old Barn Tea Room on the way up to Hildenborough – 'Oceans of Cream' we used to call it because it had that on the side of the oast house – and I remember I went up once with Eddie.

The two Miss Heaths – they lived at The Woods – were always trying to keep people busy. They were great characters. They were elderly but very sweet. I remember Maud saying 'we must keep the young people entertained'. One of them – I can't remember if it was Maud or Florence – used to take wood work classes. They had a car and a chauffeur. To have a car was unusual then – there were probably only ten cars in the village when we arrived and I think probably only two chauffeurs – the Miss Heaths and Vivienne Phillips. I think that not having a car meant that you had to entertain yourself much more. You walked a lot and I remember cycling a lot particularly during the war when you had to wear a tin hat or you got ticked off.

The village had its own doctor's surgery. We always went to Dr Barclay who had his practice where the doctor's surgery still is now. It was a sort of what you would call a group practice nowadays – maybe one of the first. I think Dr Fraser, who lived in Park House, was part of the group. When Dr Barclay built Applegarth at the end of Hollow Trees Drive I remember the very elderly Miss Hicks who lived at the cottage opposite – where James and Alison Cook live now – was not pleased. She said that she didn't want a dirty old man watching her all the time!

Life was fairly straightforward in those days. You rang up if you wanted any shopping and it was delivered. We had maids – they were Swiss girls who came over and I remember they always used to long for Hall Place lake to freeze over. Looking back to the village as we found it in 1933, I think

my first word would be 'badminton'. I loved it. But thinking more generally, I find the village more friendly now. Then, I was always 'Miss
Crawford'. Now everyone calls me 'Betty'. It was much more 'us 'and 'them'
in those days. There were lots of people with their noses in the air. You
didn't mix with people who weren't your class. You could only play tennis
with your own group. Nowadays it's much more friendly with coffee
parties and chats and the church things – all together really.

Maurice Martin

I came to Leigh in 1932 when I was six with my mother, my father and my younger brother, David. My father had looked after a huge great farm on the Eridge Estate in the 1920s and 1930s with his father but he suffered a lot – like most of the farmers at that time – and he had to give it up. He was offered Little Barnetts – which was split in half then and owned by the Kent County Council to be let to ex-servicemen from the First World War. Father had been in the Army. Mr May had been the farmer there before us. Father wanted to get away from hops but when he arrived to see the farm, he said "Blow Me": there were hops right up to the windows – the old style hops growing up a single pole. No wires or anything. There were four acres of them, with shared use of the Oast at Great Barnetts. But that was too small to be viable, so father did away with them and we had twelve to fourteen milking cows on the seventy acres. They all had to be milked by hand. Mum and Dad did it. I helped with the feeding but mainly with the mucking out in the mornings – because in those days you had the cows inside nearly every night – especially in the winter. It was really hard work. I didn't go much on farming – on the milking anyway, I tell you. You know those machines they had on the pier – Test Your Grip. I reckon the milkmen were the strongest. I had to do the milking when father died in 1953. I don't know how I did it all but I had to until the farm was re-let. The most we ever got was three and six a gallon. It was a better price in winter than summer. Once, one of the cows swam across the Medway. It was a right performance. We had to go all the way down to Haysden to lead it back.

We grew a few potatoes and sold them for seven and six a sack. You got a free hessian sack when you bought them with Blue Cross Cake printed on it. It was the cattle feed – made by Sillcocks or Bibbys, I think.

We kept chickens – for eggs mainly. We'd only have a proper chicken to eat a few times a year, although sometimes we'd have a `boiler' which had grown too old to lay. You'd have to boil them for hours, then roast them a bit. But we did have a proper chicken on Boxing Day. We went ferreting in the morning – my uncle came down for the rabbits: that was the highlight of the day. Then we had a big lunch.

My mother was knowledgeable about the farm work – she did a lot of work with father as well as all the food and things in the house. She did good variations of rabbit. We had rabbit two or three times a week. It was nice but I'd get a bit bored with it – although I would eat one now. We'd have an occasional pheasant too when we didn't think anyone was looking.

Once we had a pig – only once. It was during the war. What a performance. Mr Whitehead, the butcher, killed it and prepared it. He had half which he paid us for and he made us some sausages from it too but they were a bit too rich. We had to go round borrowing all those big earthenware pots you had in those days for all the meat we salted down. We had pork for ever and a day – we got bored with it – but it was real pork – not like the white stuff that you get nowadays.

Little Barnetts was very hard. It was too much really for one man and not enough for two. Farming was hard in those days – grandfather died in his sixties and father died aged fifty-six. I didn't fancy it. My grandfather, that was mother's father, Sylvester Edwards, came to live with us at Little Barnetts for four or five years. He'd been a farmer too but he had also done coppicing and made rustic furniture as well but he was retired by then. He had farmed at Hartfield in the Ashdown Forest. I read in a book once that the Edwards had been the dominant family there in the early 1800s. He had ten children. Ike Ingram used to walk past Little Barnetts when he was an old man and he and grandfather used to chat for hours. I don't know what they talked about: Grandfather was an outdoor man and Mr Ingram was an indoor man – he was a ball maker. Mr Ingram always had a corn-cob pipe, although that's an American expression really – probably you'd say a cherry wood pipe. He gave me his fishing rod when he was very old. It was a lovely one – one of those split cane ones.

The man next door – he farmed the smaller half of Little Barnetts – was Bert Taylor. He had four or five cows and did a milk round with a bike with a can on the front. He'd do one delivery to the village and one to the Powder Mills each day. His cows weren't much good – and one was a bag of bones. So when he got the periodic postcard from the Ministry to say the vet was coming to check for TB, that particular cow was tied up as far away as possible out of sight until the vet had gone. He had a horse called Nobby. During the last war, Nobby was in the field with the army searchlight people. The trouble was they used to feed him bread and he got fat and lazy. When Bert got him into the shafts of the mower for that year's haymaking, Nobby started to sweat before he even moved.

Bert was a thrifty bloke. He scrimped and saved all his life. He was a one man outfit, so come the haying season, he needed some help. One year Mr Hurley, a South African who lived at Homelands, helped him. It was hard work doing haymaking for Bert because Bert did it properly. He'd put poles up either end where they were building the rick so they could put a rope with a canvas sheet across if it was going to rain. Anyway, at the end of it all, Mr Hurley came to old Bert expecting to be paid but Bert just said "well done – I'll do the same for you some time". Mr Hurley never did get paid.

Old Bert must have made a lot of money because in the end he owned two or three houses in Lealands Avenue and a few at the Powder Mills. He was married and it was his wife who did all the hard work, mucking out and things, while he delivered the milk, talking and chatting away. When they retired, she died first, quite soon after. I used to think to myself, there's no justice in this world!

I went to Leigh School – with Miss Ellis in the Infants and then on up to Mr Gibbons. I hoped to go on to technical school but because of the war they'd cut all the places back and I couldn't. So at fourteen I went to Moon's Garage – where Fairlawns mowers is now. Mr Moon had worked for Mr Whitehead who built the garage to start with and, when Mr Whitehead wasn't doing too well, Mr Moon bought it off him. Of course, it was Mr Moon who did the books for Mr Whitehead, so probably he made it look as if it was all going badly! (That's a joke by the way – I think). Anyway Mr Moon had worked in the Monotype factory in Redhill or Horley or somewhere, so he was very conversant with machinery.

When it was just a garage I remember a funny story. It was at the start of the war and Mr Moon said to me, "I want you to go up to The Porcupine to Miss Hope-Morley and do as she says." When I got there I had to take all four wheels off her car, jack the car up on the blocks and hide the wheels under her bed. "They're not going to commandeer my car" she said. It was a Hillman Minx. She became Mrs Bavington-Smith. Miss Walton laid her car up too. Once a month I had to go down to her house and turn it over a few times. It was a Rover – EKL 54. That was at Great Barnetts where she lived with her sister's family – the Cecils. Of course, I knew Miss Walton well because I'd been in the Scouts.

At the beginning of the war we had this lovely old Armstrong Sidley breakdown lorry, with a crane on the back and a brass radiator. But they commandeered that. Took off the crane.

We used to put some of the old cars that were no good in the Donkey Field. It was a great big hole. All our old metal went in there. It must have been a clay pit or something once, probably for making bricks.

From 1941, Mr Moon started making parts for the war effort. All the machinery was driven by belts – it was like they've got in the British Museum. He started with four or five people and eventually it was up to nine or ten. Originally, there was me and Don Grayland who was the foreman – he'd been here since 1938 – and two others who were in the Territorials but they joined up at the start of the war. We ended up with a good lot. There was Joan Smith and Vi Chandler – who lives in Tonbridge; the two Hollands sisters from Cinder Hill; Nora Mills – you remember Mrs Mills from Greenview Avenue who ran the Sunday School; Jean Dadswell and Marion Gooch who married a Canadian airforce pilot; Elsie Winson whose father kept the old Post Office; Sidney Clayton – he came from Penshurst but I still see him; Maurice Wells whose father was the main preacher at the Chapel; Mrs Brunger but she came from Hildenborough; and Mrs Ronalds was in charge of the money. She was quite a stickler. And, of course, there was Barbara Faircloth, who I married later.

The workshops at Moons Garage during the Second World War when they were making parts for the war effort including for Spitfires. Left to right: Gladys Grevitt, Jean Dadswell, Mrs Brunger, Elsie Winson, Hazel Hollands.

I was deferred from the Army once. Then I was called up in July 1945 but the Germans heard I was coming, so they gave up. But I went overseas to Ireland, then to Gibraltar, then Palestine and ended up in Egypt and then I came back to Moons.

You asked about the Forge. In my time that was the Bullingham family – father and son – old Mr Bullingham – he was a clever chap – and his son who worked in an aircraft factory during the last war. The young Mr Bullingham lived in Powder Mill Lane in Hildenborough when his father lived in the forge itself. I remember when the dynamo on his Austin 7 went, he got a huge one – it was off an aircraft I think. It was almost as big as the engine. I had several Austin 7's. I used to drive across the fields in one of them.

After the war, I married Barbara. She lived in half of Old Wood Cottage with her parents. The whole cottage was owned by Miss Haviland who lived in Old Chimneys next door. She'd bought Old Chimneys after Mr Card converted it in the 1930s. The other half of Old Wood Cottage was for her chauffeur/gardener. Unfortunately Miss Haviland sold the whole cottage – it went for £2,300 to the Dixons – I'd loved to have bought it. You'll have heard all about the Faircloth family. In the 1930s when we came here, they dominated the village. The old grandfather was the wheelwright – with his workshop down the lane at the side of the village halls. He had three boys, George who used to live in Graham Marchant's house, The Cottage, next to Orchard House; Ray, a carpenter who lived in Forge Square and who had a small workshop down Kiln Lane; and Fred who was Barbara's father. He was the Chief Officer in the Leigh Fire Brigade. I've got a good photograph of all the firemen. There were lots of other Faircloths but quite a few of them emigrated – to Penshurst. I think there was a Faircloth who ran the Porcupine Inn years ago. Barbara's brother Billy, married Rita. Now that Rita's gone – it's strange – there are no Faircloths in the village at all now.

The Cottage, High Street (one of the Devey houses).

The Gatehouse - once the Porcupine Inn and then the home of Johnnie Burr, the Hall Place estate agent. After his death in 1940, it was lived in by Lord Hollenden's daughter before being sold by the Estate after the war. It is now called Porcupine House.

Doreen Passingham

Mrs Doreen Brooker

Leigh's such a lovely village. I hope it doesn't get too big. Hildenborough used to be like us – a real village – but it isn't now – it's really just a part of Tonbridge. I was born in Leigh – it was in number six Garden Cottages – in 1926. It was wonderful then. I wish I could explain it but I can't really. You could go down to the weir, past Mr Martin's wood – that's Maurice Martin's father who had Little Barnetts. It was called 'The Periwinkle Shore'. It was a sort of Lido. Everyone swam and went picnicking there. The Benn Boys' Club from the East End used to come too and camp in tents in the summer. I remember one young man had no legs but he walked on his hands and he could go ever so fast. He was a good swimmer too. Of course the Lido went when they built the flood barrier twenty years or so back.

We all used to go for long walks – there was a feeling that the war was over – for ever. I'd go primrose-ing and bring them back to my mother. I didn't have any pocket money – if I had a penny, I thought I was a million-aire. If you saw a car, it was an event. Tree trunks were pulled through the village on a special cart with horses and, until the end of the 1940s, I remember them driving cattle or sheep along the High Street and down the lanes to the market in Tonbridge. It would be the farmer with his dog and two other men to make sure the animals didn't get into people's gardens. Pigs went in a little trailer with a net over it, pulled by a horse. I never went in a car until I was in my twenties – so that was after the Second World War – and we always walked to dances. I remember we were excited when Alan Cobham's Flying Circus came to the airfield at Charcott. The planes were only tied together with bits of string in those days. We went to see the Duke of Gloucester playing polo there too. I read comics like Pegs Paper on the Green – but I hid them from my parents. There were lots of children in Garden Cottages and we used to use the grass in the middle to play cricket and tennis. We'd get into trouble when the ball went into people's gardens. There was a little boy called John May who was very keen on planes – those balsa wood and tissue paper models – and we'd have our own flying pageants with our own tents and things.

My grandparents – that's my father's father and mother – were very much part of my life. They were Charles and Charity Passingham and they lived in the third white cottage past "The Bat". The Passingham family were part of the village. My grandmother – I think she had been in service and she had lovely copperplate writing – was one of three sisters and their names were Faith, Hope and Charity. You won't believe what their surname was. It was Hope. So I had a great aunt who was Hope Hope, although I don't remember much about that side of the family, except Faith married a railway man and they lived in the big house on the forecourt of Hildenborough Station.

The cottage on the right, called West Cottage, where Doreen's grandparents lived.

My sister, Kathleen, and I used to visit Grandfather and Grandmother all the time. The house was all shining and sparkling. It had a lovely feeling – a real old fashioned cottage. I can still see it all. You never see a house like that today – they're all so modern. Downstairs, it had coconut matting which was spotless on the floors and starched lace curtains tied back with blue ribbons. The front room was only used on high days and holidays. The living room was at the back with the brass tongs all shining and a fringed lace edging round the mantle piece. You could almost see through the china. The pantry had a marble slab to keep the food cool with crocheted covers with beads on them over the bowls and a muslin umbrella thing over the meat. I can still see it all now. Upstairs there were scrubbed wooden floors with mats and everything was white – the sheets and lace curtains all starched. Outside there were roses all round the porch and there was white everywhere on the steps and the stones in the garden. We'd go in there after grandmother had been baking and she'd give us something. Even after father had married, he'd call in to get a cake from her on his way home.

Grandfather was very tall and calm and serious looking. He looked exactly like Edward VII, with a lovely full beard and white hair – a lovely looking man. He was the verger and he wore a frock coat on Sundays. He played cricket for Leigh. He was really a ball-maker, although I can't remember if he was a quilter or a stitcher, but I think that he had to do lots of other jobs as well in his time. He was still working after he fell ill in 1935 – he had to go on working because you didn't get a pension in those days. He died of cancer but it could just as easily have been TB or diphtheria which often killed people in those days. I was heartbroken when he and later my grandmother died. They must have worked so hard through their lives. I think they looked much older then. But we felt very close to them and they seemed a natural part of our life. I'm sad that I never see any grandparents with the children where I live now in the new houses in Meadow Bank. I expect they live too far away – or something. But it is sad.

My father was Harry Passingham. He was really Henry Charles but he was always called Harry. He was a gentle man and I really adored him – I felt extremely close to him – I think girls always do feel close to their father. He was born in Leigh in 1888 and went to the Village School under Mr Boby who he thought was excellent. He went to church when grandfather was verger and went to Bible classes under Miss Daisy Walton. He was the Leigh goalkeeper – really very good – and played cricket – a bowler – until he was well into his fifties. Before the First World War, he had worked for Jack Gillet who was a painter and decorator in Leigh. Then he joined up – in the Royal Engineers. But he never used to talk about the War. I don't think any of them felt they could describe what it was like – so they didn't say anything. When Father came back from the Army, there wasn't any building work, so he became a ball maker. After the General Strike, father never had a full week's work for fifteen years or so until the Second World War. He did a bit of ball making for Dukes. He dug the graves in the churchyard and cut the grass there. He moved stone at Burslems – the mason's in Tunbridge Wells. He did some coppicing and he went out as a beater for the pheasant shoots. If you didn't work, you didn't get paid and you couldn't pay the rent. So he'd often do one job in the day and come back and do odd jobs for people in the village in the evenings. He had three allotments too, so mother never had to buy fruit or vegetables.

Mother – she was Mary – came over from County Kildare when she was a young girl in about 1911 when there was no work in Ireland. She went to work for Sir Hugh Cassells in Cadogan Square. Sir Hugh owned Swaylands and in the First World War it was turned into a military hospital and she came to work there. She was going out with a soldier but he got killed in the war. (Strange really because the same thing happened to me in the last war). After the war, she left to work for Dr Fraser. Father had had his eye on her for some time and they married in 1924 from Dr Fraser's house, although because Mother was a Catholic, it was in the Registry Office in Sevenoaks. Dr Fraser had built Garden Cottages, so they were able to get one of the houses there.

Mother was a bit strict. Really she was very Irish – black hair, green eyes, very forceful and a flaming temper – although I don't think she ever went back home except for the funeral of her mother and father. I think she had two sisters and two, much older brothers. One brother was a policeman and one had been in the IRA before it became the Irish Free State.

After I started school, Mother worked for Mr & Mrs Humphries at Kennards. You stayed at home when your children were young in those days. She always went hopping down at Goodwin's farm at Paul's Hill. She loved it – I couldn't stand it, I don't know why – it seemed like slave labour to me but the women did it to buy winter clothes for the children. And the hops did have a wonderful smell. People would come on the train from Tonbridge to do hopping at Goodwin's but there weren't any gipsies or Londoners who did the hopping in Leigh. There were so many hop fields then. All up Powdermill Lane and at Mr Days over at Chiddingstone Causeway as well as Paul's Hill. Did you know the hop always goes round the string the same way. It's meant to reach the top of the wires by the end of June. You had a stiltman with a long hook to put the strings up for the hops.

Father had taught me my ABC and numbers before I went to school. I was at the village school when Mr Gibbons was the Head. I thought he was really good. He was a brilliant musician too. He had three children of his own there – Brian Gibbons was really clever. The Infants class was taught by Miss Ellis. Then the middle class was Miss Hookway. She was so good looking – all the boys used to love her. There was Miss Baker and Miss Buxton too. Then the top class was taken by Mr Gibbons himself. Looking back, I feel that the village school really taught me. I still love reading and I go to the mobile library when it comes to Leigh and the Tonbridge library. At school we read books like 'The Deerslayer' and we learnt poems like 'Hiawatha' by heart and had to recite them to the class. I still remember some of them –

'Our England is a garden, full of stately views:
Of borders, beds and shrubberies, of lawns and avenues.'

Mr Gibbons always had a prayer at the end of the day before we went home and the Reverend Sealy used to come to the school to take morning prayers – it was a Church of England School then. Mr Sealy – he wasn't married when he first came to the village – had a Chow dog. It had a blue tongue.

In those days there was a great deal of division of classes. Mr Gibbons would think that he was above the normal people but probably the doctor and the vicar and so on thought that they were above Mr Gibbons.

I remember everyone in all the houses. Miss Heath at 'The Woods' – even until she died, she wore Edwardian style clothes – she had a parasol. The Bickersteths gave a wonderful summer party each year – and one at Christmas too. Every child got a present. Their son, John, became a bishop. Lady Hollenden – I liked her – she was gentle. She was Gladstone's grand-daughter. She was very shy but she did talk to everyone – took an interest in everyone. In 1935, when it was George V's Silver Jubilee, there was a big celebration at Hall Place. We had a pram race – all the prams were deco-rated and there was a mile race where Dick Wood beat Bob Faircloth on the line. In the winter, we had skating up at Hall Place lake too. There was Mr Benjamin in what's called The White House now – he was after Mr Sales. And up in Park House, there was Dr Fraser. I told you that Mother worked there for four or five years before I was born. Dr Fraser delivered both me and my sister Kathleen, who was eighteen months younger than me. Kathleen was born prematurely and was always delicate. It was sad: she died when she was fourteen of a burst appendix. Dr Fraser was ahead of his time. He not only built Garden Cottages but he started 'The Doctor's Club'. It was separate from the Hospital Clubs for the Kent and Sussex Hospital and went to pay for your doctor's bills. He had two fantastic sons, Beaufort who was a doctor too, and Eric. Dr Fraser was a lovely doctor but he didn't suffer fools gladly – if you didn't really have anything wrong with you .... But often you'd go to the village nurse first: that was Nurse Christian – she was lovely. She lived in the bungalow down Powdermill Lane. Her prede-cessor was a battleaxe. I think that the village nurse was sort of attached to Dr. Fraser but I'm not quite sure how. After Dr. Fraser retired, we had

Dr Barclay who built Applegarth. The school had its own doctor who came, once a year I think it was, to test the children's hearing and eyesight. And there was the school nurse who came I suppose once a term – you've heard what she was looking for – nits and things.

The policeman I remember best was Mr Ginn. Now he was strict. He'd give any of the boys who were up to no good a telling off. The policeman had capes in those days, and he'd sort of flick them with it. He had a son Neville who was an epileptic. He'd sort of throw his head up in the air and have a spasm. It must have been very frightening for him. People didn't understand in those days and some of the children .... But I was friends with him. He was very artistic. He became a dress designer or something. After Mr Ginn, there was Mr Cornelius and he was replaced by Mr Stevens. The policemen always lived at No 1. Forge Square until they built the police house in The Green Lane well after the war.

Mr Gillie ran 'The Bat', Mr Thurston 'The Brickmakers Arms' and Tommy Coates 'The Fleur'. Grandfather used to pop down to The Bat quite often and I remember my Grandmother going down with a big jug for beer regularly.

Then there were all the shops. You could go to Mr Brooks at the old Post Office on The Green. You'd give him your shopping list and he'd deliver it all.

The Post Office on the Green when it was run by Mr Brook's predecessor, Mr Anderson. (Note the spelling 'Lyghe' on the postcard but Leigh on the shop).

There was so much to do in the village. You've probably heard about the plays and the concerts and the dances. And all the sport for the men. There was a lot of singing. Dick Wood had a lovely voice and so did Eddie Crawford. I liked Eddie very much. He had a red sports car and an Airedale dog. At home, we had a wireless to listen to from the middle of the 1930s. It was a Cossar and it worked off mains electricity, not the battery things you got from Mr Bennett. We'd listen to Radio Luxembourg. Then, later, I remember having In Town Tonight and Music Hall and there was Toy Town and Uncle Mac on Children's Hour. We didn't have electricity until the mid-1930s – only oil lamps – and when we did have the power put on, the tenants had to pay to have it installed which was quite hard as there wasn't a lot of money around in those days.

I remember when war was declared in 1939, mother just sat down and cried – she couldn't believe that there was going to be another war. When the war started, I was only fourteen and I got a job as a cashier in the Tudor Cafe in Tonbridge. Later, I helped dish out the ration books and things for the Ministry of Food in Sevenoaks. When I was eighteen, I got engaged but he was killed just after the D-Day landings. After the war ended, the Ministry said that they would only keep on the official Civil Servants, so I went to work at Knotley Hall. It was the Childrens Aid Society at that time – under Mr Ron Spense who was very good. Later Barnardos took it over and we thought they wasted money on some things – although Lord Bernstein did give the money for a nice swimming pool. He also gave some money in the early 1960s to help with Charlotte Cottages for the old people in Leigh. They were named after his wife's mother who was Charlotte – she's buried in the churchyard with her daughter, Sandra – Lady Bernstein: I was looking at the grave the other day.

Charlotte Cottages, built in the early 1960s as sheltered housing with financial help from Lord Bernstein at Coppins Farm.

With my father being keen on cricket, I used to watch and, for a long time, I was the scorer – it was over ten years. John Knock always talks about my copper plate handwriting in the score books. So, I met Tony – my husband, Tony Brooker – partly through cricket, although of course I'd known the family all my life. The Brookers were very much part of the village in the 1920s and 1930s. You've heard how they used to say the village could have had a cricket team just made up of Brookers.

Tony's father was Ernest Brooker. He'd fought in the First World War and before that he'd been working in the cricket ball factory in Woodside Road off Quarry Hill in Tonbridge. There was a laundry there – they only pulled it down a few years ago – and he met a Tonbridge girl, Gertrude whom he married. They lived in Garden Cottages for a bit, then they moved to No. 3 Park Cottage – it is called The Stone House now – but it was three separate cottages then. By this time he was a stitcher with Dukes at the Causeway and he worked there until he died young – before I was married. Ernest had a good number of brothers. There was Lewis – the cobbler in Lower Green who had a son Jack. There was Stan and his sister Minnie who both lived by the Fleur de Lys in their parents old house. Then there was Monty but I'm not quite sure if he was a brother or not. I think they were all cricketers.

The Stone House – formerly Nos. 1, 2 and 3 Park Cottages – each of which had their own well inside their own part of the building.

Ernest and Gertrude had seven children. Alec was the eldest, then Marjorie, then Ken who had a lovely singing voice – you've heard about all the choirs – then Joan and Roy – they're both still alive. Roy was a brilliant goalkeeper and he went to have a trial for Kent for cricket but the war got in the way. Tony – who I married – was the youngest and he had a twin Eric but he died when he was a few days old – you didn't get all the help during child-birth that you get nowadays .

I'm glad I'm not a teenager today, I tell you that. We could go everywhere when I was young – we didn't worry about being mugged and things – you trusted everybody. It's sad it's not like that now – especially for the children. Then it was a wonderful village. We had such a happy time. Everything and everyone was very close, although that meant everyone knew everyone else's business.

When we were young, all the girls used to collect autographs – I remember one which I always like that one girl wrote in my book:-

I dreamt I did die and to Heaven did go
And where did you come from they wanted to know?
And when I said "Leigh", didn't they stare
They said come right inside, you're the first one from there.

❀

John Banks –
Garden Cottages

"The firm I work for, Worrin and Lawson, are the managing agents for the current owners of Garden Cottages, Tonbridge & District Properties Ltd who bought twenty six cottages from the original owners and builders, the Kent Cottage Company, in February 1945. Since then, four of the cottages have been sold. Some of the tenants are still in the houses they have been in since well before 1945.

There are problems tracing the history of the cottages because there was a big flood in our offices and the Deeds were very badly damaged by water but we do have some records. On 2 August 1905 Kent Cottage Company Ltd, signed a building agreement with Lord de Lisle and took a Lease of the land down Powder Mill Lane. Building probably started in 1906 or 1907. We know nothing of Kent Cottage Company Ltd except to say that they would seem to have finished building work by 30 April 1914 when they took a conveyance of the freehold of the twenty six cottages from Lord de Lisle. Kent Cottage Company bought some extra land – it could have been the allotments at the back – in 1924. The company's registered office was variously shown at Park House, Applegarth and 3 Garden Cottages, Leigh. We have no idea as to the reason for this or as to who was in occupation of those properties at that time. Tonbridge and District Properties Ltd acquired all the land when they purchased the properties in 1945.

It has always been quite a difficult balancing act for Tonbridge and District Properties Ltd between keeping the rents low – which we try to do, particularly for the people who have been there for years – and keeping everything up to scratch. The circular road around the cottages was never designed for cars let alone a good number of cars per house.

Tonbridge and District Properties Ltd is a property investment company which operates all its properties on a strictly commercial basis and is free to sell or otherwise deal with the properties as it sees fit. We have no idea why some people sometimes seem to think the cottages have a charitable status – it is not the case. But we do try to help as much as we can."

Mollie Hayter

Mrs M Maidman – The Forge

"One of my grandfathers was the village blacksmith and farrier and the other was the Leigh carpenter, wheelwright and undertaker. The blacksmith was Charlie Hayter with the Forge on the Green. He lived and brought up three children in Forge House. The eldest was Charles Hayter; then there was my father William Hayter who was always called Bill; and then there was my aunt Alice. You have seen the photo of Grandfather shoeing a horse with the local boys looking on. I think the two small boys in the middle are Stan and Archie Denton – but I'd love to know who the others are.

Charlie Hayter c1930 shoeing a horse at The Forge

When Grandfather – Dana as we always called him – wasn't busy shoeing horses or repairing farm equipment, and so on, he'd sit in the end window looking out and keeping an eye on things. In front of the Forge, there was the busy working yard, which was always a jumble. He had originally come from Brenchley but he certainly had the Leigh Forge before the turn of the century because my father was born there in 1896. The hunt used to meet on the Green in front of the Forge. I was always taken out to see the horses as Dana knew most of the huntsmen. As a special treat we were also allowed to sit on the big working horses while they waited to be collected after they had been shod. Grandfather died in the mid-1930s and the Forge was sold to Mr Bullingham.

In the 1920s and 1930s there were lots of Faircloths in the village. My other grandfather, who was one of them, had been the main carpenter in the village but he died about the time I was born so I never knew him. He lived in Ivy House – which someone changed to Pump Cottage – with his workshop and stable at the bottom of the garden (where the bungalow is now). My cousin, Geoff Hitchcock, used to live there. Grandfather and Grandmother Faircloth brought up ten children in Ivy House. As well as Grandfather Faircloth, there was Uncle Fred Faircloth who lived in one half of Old Wood Cottages, his son Bill, who worked at Coates, also Uncle Ray who lived in the bungalow next to the Old Bakery, and Uncle George who first lived at the Causeway next to Wisdens and then moved to The Cottage in the High Street. There were two others sons who moved away and also two daughters, one of which was my mother, Alice Harriet (Ally). There were Faircloths in Penshurst too, but we were brought up to think of them as 'the other side of the family' and we never saw much of them – I never knew why.

Now called Pump Cottage, it was formerly Ivy House.

We were also related to other families in Leigh. The Whibleys were distant cousins and my grandmother and Minnie Whibley were both Martins. Incidentally, my grandmother Faircloth was born in The Porcupine in 1862 when it was still a coaching inn. The Hitchcocks were also relations: my grandmother was one.

My sister, Sally, and I both went to Leigh School where we were very happy – lots of memories and, like everyone else, we remember Miss Ellis with great affection. We still go and see her. My life and time spent at Leigh were very happy – very carefree years.

The two things I remember most from my childhood were both smells – the smell of the burnt hoof when the shoe was put on, and the smell of leather when I went over to Wisdens, the cricket ball factory, where we'd watch the men sewing and shaping the cricket balls. Several of our relations worked as ball makers.

I got to be mad keen on riding and used to go from Great Barnetts Farm with Margaret Foy. Her father owned the farm there. (It's the 1920s house past the big Great Barnetts barns). If we ever rode across the Green, (which we did often), we would be in great trouble with my uncles who said we would damage the cricket ground – they were great sports enthusiasts.

I had been born in 1928 at 11 Council Cottages – it's called Barnetts Road now. Then in 1937, we moved along the road to Kenbar, a house my father had built. It was between Kennards and Great Barnetts – hence the name. He carved the name in oak and it hung above the front door. Years later, long after we'd all moved, I heard from my cousin, Geoff Hitchcock, that the house had new owners who had changed the name: so I rang up to see if I could have the original name plate. But they told me they had just burnt it. They were very apologetic about it and quite upset.

Carthorses on the Green

When Lawrence Biddle first arrived in the village in the late 1950s, he was talking with Bill Hayter whose father, Charlie, had run the forge on the Green until the early thirties. Bill Hayter described how the Green "would be covered with horses on some wet winter days in the early part of the century because the ground was too wet to plough and the farmers had all realized that they had not got round to having their horses re-shod."

The Old Forge, Leigh.

Peter King

Peter King was born and still lives in Plaxtol but has worked all his adult life as a blacksmith in Leigh or, more recently, in Chiddingstone Causeway. For many years he was the Treasurer of the British Artists Blacksmiths Association.

"My grandfather was a farrier with the London and General Omnibus Company at the turn of the century. In those days, they took off the old horse shoes and put two of them together to make a new one – it was called "Doubling Up". There was no way you could waste in those days. My father and three uncles were all blacksmiths too. My father worked at Hyders when it was at Crouch but he worked at the Forge in Leigh too for a year or so after the First World War.

You've got to remember how many forges there were before the Second World War. I suppose they were mainly farriers – a glorified shop really in each village. Even in the 1920s and 1930s there were two in Leigh, the one behind Pump Cottage as well as the main one on the Green. I don't remember the one behind Pump Cottage when it was actually working but all the anvils and tools were in the corner of Tim Lee's coalyard down there and Amos Taylor, I think it was, had taken over the undertaker's business. He had an old Austin Ruby and, because he was quite a tubby gentleman, we were always having to adjust the springs on one side. After the War, Topper Skinner took over the Penshurst forge and it became a garage but one of the conditions of his lease was that he had to shoe a horse at least once a year. Something like that. I think there had been a farrier up at Smarts Hill, too, by the bakery. There was certainly a big forge where Avebury Avenue is now in Tonbridge and forges in Langton and Cowden. Old Mr Skinner had his forge at Charcott – he used to do chimney sweeping as well. Mr Hayter was the smith on the Green here at Leigh. He was there until the mid-1930s and when he died his widow sold all the things – the anvil and so on. Then, after a bit of a gap, Mr Bullingham senior took it over and started almost from scratch. He was a clever man. I remember coming across lots of patents for things that he'd got in a box but the only one I remember now was a stand for a garden fork. Soon after he moved in, he made the sign that's outside the Forge still – although they've let it go all rusty. After the war, his son, Ralph, took over.

After school, I had gone to the Tech in Tunbridge Wells. There were some pretty funny teachers in those days. We had one at the Tech who was brilliant but he went around with a great big book in his hand and then he'd suddenly throw it across the room at someone. And I remember teachers who twisted your ears – boys AND girls – really hard; or flicked you across the face. You couldn't do that today. Anyway, when I was seventeen and I'd finished at the Tech, I became an apprentice with Mr Bullingham at the Forge.

The other people who worked at the Forge then were Gordon McCulloch and Fred Donally. Fred was brilliant at repoussé work – that's work where you raise up a pattern on the sheet of metal by hitting into a pitch block. Then when you have got the main design, you fill it with pitch, turn it over and put in the detailed work from the front.

In those days, in the 1950s, there weren't queues of horses on the Green anymore but I do remember that when the slaughter house reopened after the War, the sheep used to be driven across the Green and it was chaos as they would all escape across the roads.

We made all kinds of things at the Forge. We made all the tools for the little factory down at the old water works in Kiln Lane which made adding machines and a board game called "Counterplay". When Ralph Bullingham sold the Forge, I moved to the back end of Moon's garage for many years in the old Nissen hut.

There is not that much old wrought iron in Leigh. The gate into the Churchyard at the top of Church Hill is nice – I made the lamp above it for John and Hermione Whitehouse in memory of their son, Peter, who died in India – and there are a few bits of railings and gates in the High Street and a few things at Hall Place. But nothing you'd put in a book of famous wrought iron work.

Miss Jill and Miss Wendy Bullingham

In the mid 1930s, Jill and Wendy Bullingham's grandfather, Harold Birdsall Bullingham, took over the Forge in Leigh, and he and his wife, Edith, lived at Forge Cottage until his retirement in 1952. Harold Bullingham's son, Ralph, started helping in the Forge after the war and the family moved to Forge Cottage in 1952. Jill and Wendy still live in the village – a family association with Leigh for over sixty years.

"Grandfather was born in 1879. His father was a wealthy, but strict Victorian photographer. He even had his own yacht. When Grandfather was still a very young man, he worked his passage on a ship to America. The family story says he was a stoker on a liner but we're not sure and maybe he was more on the engineering side. He got a job with Otis, the lift firm and seems to have discovered his talent for inventing things. Before the First World War, he had returned to London and he designed his own make of car, called the Zendik. It was built in Kingston. There was a van version too. He then served with the British Red Cross in France. We've got a caseful of his medals. He took the lease of the Forge in the mid-1930s and started specializing in ornamental wrought ironwork, rather than mainly shoeing horses, which had always been done before. He had a good clientele, including customers in London, making things like candlesticks, light fittings and porch lanterns, basket grates and fire screens and shop signs. He also made the sign that still stands outside the Forge.

Grandfather was a real character. Mrs Blackmore – everyone called her 'Mattie' and she lived at the Old Dairy – used to say that he was one of God's gentlemen. He could usually be seen puffing a pipe – he had a lot of different ones – and wearing his tweed hat. Sometimes the pipe was like a bonfire, but quite often it would go out and he would still be puffing it. At one stage, he used to write off for to Heath and Heather for a special herbal tobacco. The smell used to get everywhere and when we were a bit older we used to buy him ordinary tobacco for Christmas! When we were small and visited him, the Forge was open right up to the top of the roof, with all the tools hanging down from the rafters. On one vist there were nuns – they were Sisters of St Vincent de Paul, with their enormous white headdresses – having prayers with the evacuees on the Green. It was quite a surprise. Our grandparents had one of the evacuees staying with them. She was called Gloria. They adored her and in the end they didn't want to part with her.

Harold Bullingham in the Zendick car that he invented c.1920's.

Harold Bullingham standing beside the Zendick van.

The Forge was closed in the latter part of the Second World War and grandfather went to Malvern to make aeronautical parts. When the war ended, father joined grandfather at the Forge and later took control of the firm. We all moved to Forge Cottage in 1952 when Grandfather retired.

Behind us, there was a pretty weatherboarded white cottage on the right of Church Hill which was pulled down about thirty years ago. A nice old couple called Mr and Mrs Horan lived there in our time. Mr Horan was very keen on bargains and used to go to all the shops in Tonbridge to find the cheapest place to get things. He had a collection of sardines in a cupboard and he'd come in to us and say – 'This week you can get sardines for so much at such and such a shop'. He also made home-made wine from vegetables and fruit and stored it in the shed. Once, when it was very hot, it exploded and blew the windows out of his shed.

Church Hill in the 1960s – before the weatherboarded cottage on the right was demolished and a bungalow of grey artificial brick was erected.

Father began taking on some very large orders. He made numerous light-fittings for London hotels and churches all over the country, including the lights in St Mary's. The modern design was chosen by the vicar, Mr Bounds. He made tabernacle doors for the chapel at the Sacred Heart Convent in Tunbridge Wells and for other churches. He also sent a great deal of work abroad. He made special fittings for a Rajah's palace, light fittings for the new Aden University and for an Officers' Club in Tanganyika. He also exported to Australia, New Zealand, South Africa and America. But he had to turn one order down: it was to make railings and gates for the Palace of King Feisal of Iraq. The dimensions were so large that they couldn't be fitted into a building the size of the Forge.

Father won many first prizes and medals for his work at exhibitions and shows in the South East and London. One of the prizes was for a beautiful firescreen with a galleon in full sail as the centre piece which was done in repoussé, where a picture is beaten into the metal.

Most of the machinery in the Forge at this time was electrically run and of the latest design. Eventually, in 1961, the firm became a limited company and, because of the need for expansion, another workshop was opened at Powdermills. Seven men were employed then and, along with the ornamental work, a mass produced range of office and garden furniture was introduced.

Probably the best known example of father's work is the village sign for the Festival of Britain in 1951, which was designed by Grandfather and made by Father. The original paintings were by me (Wendy). It shows four local scenes surrounded by a wrought-iron design of hops.

Father was forced to retire in 1972 through illness. The Forge was sold and converted into a house. During the years since the 1930s, many homes in Leigh, including Hall Place, would have had something made in the Forge and probably many do even today.

Ralph Bullingham with prizewinning weather vane – from July 1958 when Leigh was much involved with the Best Kept Village Competition.

❁

Joy Castell –
The WI

Joy Castell has lived in Leigh for nearly fifty years and joined the Lyghe Women's Institute – as it is still spelt – in 1955.

There was some research into the W.I. in the village to celebrate its eight-ieth birthday. We found that The Woman's Institute in Leigh, which was started in 1919, had eighty members – all ladies at the beginning. Lord Hollenden allowed the W.I. to use the Small Village Hall for the meetings which were always in the afternoon. Looking at the records of the first full year, 1920, they had classes in folk dancing and dress making – as well as various talks on things like 'Citizenship', 'the Girl Guides' and 'Children's Upbringing' – all much the same as today, except that nowadays it's line dancing rather than folk dancing. They had collections for the Lord Roberts Workshops for the disabled servicemen from the War, and for the Tunbridge Wells Cottage Hospital – they both got regular donations over the coming years. Mrs Edith Burr was the first Secretary.

The records of the meetings in the 1920s show it was a flourishing group, with usually about ten lectures a year but with a variety of extra things – crochet work competitions, usually an annual concert performed by an outside concert party, or a dance – in one case it was a fancy dress dance. There were courses in dressmaking and, one year, in glove making. In 1926, the concert was to raise money for the Village Nurse – we think that it was to help get her a car but we're not quite sure. In 1922, eighty W.I.'s in the area made a patch-work quilt, each one illustrating an aspect of its own village. Our contribution was a sampler. The whole thing was then presented to the Chairman of the West Kent Federation of W.I.s.

So by the time I joined the afternoon W.I. in 1955, it was a long estab-lished village institution. Almost as soon as I joined, Mrs Ingram – Ethel Ingram who lived in your house – roped me in to join the Committee and I've been on it ever since – the longest serving W.I. member in the village I think. Mrs Ingram was the live wire – the Queen Bee if you like – in the

1950s. She was a marvellous person, very active, no inhibitions about anything: she'd just stand up and make a speech or anything. She introduced me to village life really. She got the W.I. choir going and played the piano for it, too. We even had a modicum of success! We did our best anyway! Mrs Ingram walked off with all the prizes in the Produce Show – the preserves and so on. When she became ill in the sixties, Doris Dale, her daughter, took over the piano for the choir – although Doris never actually joined the W.I. – it wasn't her kind of thing. We used to go on the bus to Tunbridge Wells and Maidstone and Rochester and Chatham – all over the place. We went to the County Produce and Craft Shows with exhibits made by our members – jams and preserves, chutney and home-made sweets and cakes, plus all the craft things – hand-sewn garments, embroidery, knitted or crocheted things, paintings – much the same type of things that are put into the Produce Association nowadays. But no flower arrangements – mainly because there was a limit to our carrying ability! Mrs Ingram didn't mind getting on the bus with two big baskets. We were like a crowd of gypsies! Of course, hardly anyone had a car in those days – well, some of the husbands did but the wives didn't. That was why we went by bus. In those days, the talks themselves were fairly similar to the 1920's, health, diet, art, pot plants, current affairs, travel (we usually had slides), the Red Cross, Lifeboats, enamelling, floral things, and I suppose not surprisingly, cooking ideas. And as well as the choir and the choral competitions, we had beetle drives and whist too. In the mid-1960s, an evening W.I. was started and that lasted until four or five years ago.

Looking back to the 1950s, I just remember how young we all were in those days. All of us thirty or forty year olds. We keep saying on the Committee nowadays that we must get young people but it isn't easy. So many of us on the Committee seem to have grown old together. But we did have an afternoon on belly dancing not long ago!"

About Mrs Ethel Ingram

"Mrs Ingram was always doing things for the village. She had a bike but she was always in too much of a hurry to get on it, so she could be seen running across the Green, pushing it. Then sometimes she would leave the bike at someone's house and rush on to something else without it".

And John Knock says "I can't remember the Christian name of Charlie Ingram's wife but I remember her very well. She taught me – and lots of other people – the piano. We always called her Mrs Verger Ingram to differentiate her from the other Mrs Ingram who was called Mrs Dinner Ingram because she did the school dinners".

John Knock –
Cricket and Sport in Leigh

*I*n the summer of 1939 the Knock family, including son John, aged two, moved to Leigh from Bexleyheath. Two more sons, Dick and Geoff, were born at Leigh during the war. The family went on to play an active part in village life. The father, E.J.M., known as "Jim", was a parish councillor in the 1950's and 1960's, whilst the mother – called "Kitty" by her family – taught the infants and juniors at the village school for long periods between 1948 and 1975. "For some reason, I don't know why, the children always called my mother 'Miss Knock', and the unmarried headmistress, "Mrs" Naish says John. John, who still lives in Lealands Avenue, has been committed to sport in the village, helping each succeeding generation. He has many of the cricket and table tennis club records but in addition he has known many of the people who participated in sports up to the Second World War, as well as virtually all those who have picked up a bat or kicked a ball since then. He has also been a long standing parish councillor – now its Chairman, and the trombone player with the 'Village Green Stompers Jazz Band' – formed at Oak Cottage on the Green in 1976. Here, however, he talks mainly about sport in the village.

The Village Green Stompers in its early days – May 1978 – at the Angel football ground, in Tonbridge supporting Leigh who were beaten 4-1 by Capel in the Cup Final.
From left to right: Bob Jones, Tim Asson, David Heritage, Dudley Hurrell, Chris Rowley, John Knock, Ted Holden.

"The Minutes of the Cricket Club that I've got go back to 1919, although I know the Kent archives have got some score books for the late 1800s. There seems a gap for 1900-1918. But, obviously, Leigh had a flourishing club then. Tom Watson's 'History of Cricket in Leigh till 1837' makes it sound as if it was probably being played in Leigh in 1650 , although the Club has taken Tom's more definite date of 1700 as the formal start of Leigh cricket.

Leigh Cricket Club about 1899.
Back row: B. Baker, C. Passingham, T. Johnson, J. Passingham, W. Hollands, F. Martin, B. Martin
Middle row: B. Ingram, W. Seal, I. Ingram, W. Duke, H. Faircloth
Front (sitting): T. Johnson, J. Wheatley

In 1897, the club built a new corrugated iron pavilion. It was paid for by subscription – there's a list in the pavilion now. It included lots of names we still know, and included the Duke family – who claimed in 1811 to have been making cricket balls in Penshurst and Chiddingstone Causeway for two hundred and fifty years. A photograph of the Leigh Cricket XI at the end of the last century shows the eleven players together with three club officials. While all the players are in their whites, some wear wing collars and ties. There is a fine variation of beards and moustaches but several of the team were clearly far too young for such things. Ike Ingram, who was by this time over fifty years old, is the captain and there's another Ingram, Bill. There are two young Passinghams and H. Faircloth – again, all well known village families. Club caps seem to come in a variety of styles and colours and the club mascot – a black and white cocker spaniel – sits in the middle.

In 1919, there are two interesting things in the Club minutes. It was obviously a dry summer because the village fire brigade had to be asked to water the pitch. There was also an application by the Club to the Parish Council to do away with the paths across the green. That was so the foot-ballers could play on the school end of the green rather than play across the cricket square. There were three tracks across the green at this time. One from the Oak Tree to Joey Randerson's corner – that's the corner where Powder Mill Lane turns, by the path up to the vicarage; one from the school corner to Joey Randerson's corner; and one from the end of Greenview Avenue to the old Post Office and the butchers. Presumably, it was this last one that they were worried about. Incidentally, Mr Randerson was an architect who lived at Inglenook – the nearest house to the corner at that time, before they built 'Pippins'. He designed the iron bridge across the Medway when you walk down from Greenview Avenue.

The metal footbridge across the Medway designed by Mr Randerson

In 1920, the club hired a pony and mower to cut the grass once a week; I remember hearing that the pony used to have leather shoes attached to its feet so that it did not mark the pitch. The roller with shafts that's still in the pavilion forecourt was also pulled by a pony. In the 1930s, they bought the Dennis sit-on mower. That's still in the mower shed and used occasionally. It cost £80. The groundsman in the 1930s was Jack Stolton – Dennis Stolton's grandfather. He was a brilliant snooker player.

In 1920 the Minutes show the club hired 'a lorry' for the away matches. I haven't been able to find out whether it was a motorised lorry or a horse drawn one but probably it was motorized by then. Certainly there are good stories about very 'jolly' parties returning from away games. Don Thorogood told me about the time when Monty Brooker and his team were returning from a match and the post match celebrations in what he called 'Ray Faircloth's sort of lorry'. The lorry did not quite make it. It slid into a ditch. Roy Brooker has a host of good stories, too. Once, after a match, Monty was in the pub, down on all fours with a pint of beer perched on his head AND a lady sitting on his back drinking the pint. On another occasion at a match up at Swaylands, Monty could not be found when it was his turn to bat. He'd had a few. He was finally found sitting on a pedestal in the middle of the stately home pond. But as well as being a great character, he was a good cricketer. Another Brooker, Stan, who I only remember as a careful umpire, apparently back in the days when he was a regular bowler, used to sometimes have a few pints before the match. It was said that once when he came on to bowl, he ran up in the wrong direction and had to be repointed by his team mates in the direction of the wicket.

There were a number of Committee discussions in 1930 about seats to be put out round the boundary for the public. I think they were the small wooden slatted ones that are still in the old store of the Large Hall. There weren't many cars then. I remember sitting on the seats when I was little in the 1940s. It felt grander than sitting on the grass. It looked like a county ground in miniature. But they stopped putting the seats out fairly soon after the War.

The grass was long all round the edges of the Green then – not mowed all over as it is now. I remember as a very small child, I would crawl through the grass till I came to the edge of the ground and then I'd lie there watching the game with my head in my hands – looking through the grass.

In 1921 and 1922 the club was fund raising – it always is – and they arranged for some evening dances on the green. The 'orchestra' cost two pounds five shillings but I am not sure what the instruments would have been.

The club wrote requesting the use of the Iron Room for the player's teas in 1923 and I still remember the Iron Room being used up until 1972 when the new pavilion was built. Roy Brooker – the captain – used to get two of the younger members of the team to leave five or ten minutes before the end of the innings to collect the tea urn from Mrs Fitzjohns in the High Street and carry it down to the Iron Room.

In 1931 there was a photograph of cricket on the Green at Leigh in 'The Times'. There's a copy of it in the pavilion. I knew many of the people who played cricket then. The most famous family was the Brookers. At one time, they could have got eleven players out. Someone asked Roy Brooker's father to get a team together just made up of the Brooker family. He refused, saying he played cricket, not entertainment. But there was a properly picked Leigh team which did have eight Brookers in it.

Lewis Brooker was the cobbler right up until the 1950s. His shop was where the antique shop is now in Lower Green, next to the Brickmakers. He was a very good bowler – one of the main ones right through to the war. He used to replace my cricket and football studs for nothing and give me advice on how to bowl at the same time. He was also the parish clerk for a good number of years before Fred Whibley took over in 1956. Fred was a good player too in the thirties and forties – a good bat but a bowler too.

Other Brookers included Ken – he was the next generation. He was an offspinner. He was at the ball factory – and a chorister. And there was Roy, who still lives in Tonbridge. He was a brilliant bat and wicket keeper. He would have almost certainly have played for Kent except for the war. Then there was Tony Brooker, Doreen Brooker's husband. He was the second eleven's wicket keeper. He went into the navy during the war and after he stopped playing he was a regular umpire. He became President of the Club after 'Lordy' – that's what Lord Hollenden was called – stood down when he started to spend more time on his estate in Devon. Doreen was the scorer for many years. Her father was Harry Passingham, another fine Leigh sportsman.

Frank Smith was another great character. He used to stand in the doorway of the Bat with his hands on his hips – he always seemed to be trying to stop people getting in, or out. You'd go in and he'd say "I'll tell you something", so you'd say "What's that, Frank?" and he'd say "I don't know nothing". He was the uncle of Joan Sargeant and Betty Smith in Barnetts Road. He was inclined to come back home from the Bat along the white line in the middle of the road, vaguely watching for cars, saying "I'll have 'em if they come over the line." When he was living at Lightfoots, he got a bit the worse for wear one night and fell into the ditch up the Penshurst Road. He called out 'man lost' until rescued by Tony Sadler and Andrew Whibley. He was a bowler with strong likes and dislikes – including what he thought of other bowlers. It was rumoured that he'd let balls from bowlers he didn't like through his legs. He was a legendary story teller. One of his sayings was – 'if you want to catch a rabbit, shake some pepper on the ground and, when he sneezes, hit him on the head with a hammer'.

Then, of course there was Eric Batchelor and Archie Denton, both stalwarts of the team from the 1930s onwards. Archie was a regular bowler. He worked at the ball factory. Eric was a bowler and a hitter of sixes.

In 1937, the Minutes had two things that made me think that nothing changes. The club had bought some chicken wire to go along the hedge between the Pavilion and Barden Cottages to stop the balls getting lost. And there were complaints that lads were hanging around in the pavilion at night. In 1937, they also bought a flagstaff and flag which was free standing to the left of the pavilion as you looked at it. It was there until the new pavilion was built.

In 1938, the road round the green was widened – I guess mainly because Lealands Avenue and the houses up there had been built. The builders asked the Cricket Club if they could borrow their hose. The Committee rejected the idea. They did not trust them not to bust it. The following year the Club was able to get its water from the mains instead of the Dairy. The Dairy was behind the Pavilion. When we were children we called it Anisons Dairy but it was probably Andersons. It was rather run-down when I was young and it was converted into a bungalow just after the war. Mrs Blackmore – Mattie – lived there until the 1970s.

In the 1930s, they had a chain round the cricket square, not a rope. They also had chains round the War Memorial. But I think that they both got taken away in the war to help the war effort. During the war, cricket was played mainly by older men and boys plus a few people in protected occupations. It was even allowed on Sundays from 1940. In 1939, the pavilion was placed at the disposal of the Special Constabulary – again, it was to help the war effort.

Ike Ingram was the most famous cricketer that Leigh ever had. I remember him almost permanently installed in the front of the old cricket pavilion. I don't think he held us youngsters in much veneration. He'd been a cricket ball maker at Dukes, and around the turn of the century, he'd been part of the team that made a set of balls sent to a special exhibition in Melbourne. One of the set is still in the pavilion. It was presented to Ike for his services to Leigh and Chiddingstone Causeway cricket. Ike had played for Kent as a professional for two seasons in 1879. The high points in his career were an innings of 112 – and a century was very unusual in those days – and two games against Dr W.G. Grace when Ike played for Kent against the England team. Neither Ike nor WG performed all that well in these two matches – both were out for ducks in one match.

CRICKET WEEK

...y, Thursday & Friday, Aug. 7, 8 &...

... v. M.C.C. AND GRO...

KENT.   1st Innings.   2nd Innings.
...am, Esq. c Shaw, b Cottrell 8
...K. Mackinnon, Esq. c Kingscote,
       b W. G. Grace 0
...A. Absolom, Esq. b W. G. Grace 21   not out 15
...rne not out 60
...d Harris c Clarke, b Cottrell 0
...P. Yardley, Esq. c Barnes, b W. G. Grace   3
...hon. Ivo Bligh b Morley 19
...Y. Foord-Kelcey, Esq. run out 28
...S. Jones, Esq. run out 1   not out ....
...C. F. Tufnell, Esq. c Mitchell, b Shaw   12
...Ingram b Shaw 0   c and b Shaw ....
...A. Penn, Esq. c Shaw, b W. G. Grace ... 0   c Mitchell, b Morley ...
       Byes 12, l b 4 16   Byes ....
              Total 218   Total ....

M.C.C. & G.   1st Innings.   2nd Innings.
A. W. Anstruther, Esq. c Bligh, b Penn ... 0   b Foord-Kelcey ....
W. G. Grace, Esq. b Hearne 0   b A. Penn ....
G. A. H. Mitchell, Esq. c Absolom, b Foord-
       Kelcey 31   c Bligh, b Penn ....
A. W. Ridley, Esq. c Hearne, b A. Penn ... 1   c Jones, b Foord-Kelcey
G. B. Cottrell, Esq. c Yardley, b A. Penn   8   c A. Penn b Foord-Kelcey
C. G. Clarke, Esq. c Ingram b A. Penn ... 3   c Absolom, b A. Penn ...
G. St Barnes, Esq. b Foord-Kelcey 5   b Foord-Kelcey ....
Capt. Kingscote hit wicket b A. Penn 5   c Hearne, b Foord-Kelcey
G. A. Webbe, Esq. b Foord-Kelcey 9   not out ....
W. N. Powys, Esq. b Foord-Kelcey 4   b Foord-Kelcey ....
Shaw b Foord-Kelcey 5   c Mackinnon, b A. Penn
...ley not out 4   c sub titue, b A. Penn .
       ...es 4   Byes 1, l b 1 2
              Totals 109   Total 126

Umpires—Willsher and Farrands.

A Press Telegraph is on the ground in communication with all ...
                  the ordinary Charges.

Old cricket scorecard, probably from 1878 when Kent played an MCC team containing W.G. Grace. Ike Ingram playing for Kent was bowled out for a duck, but W.G. Grace was also out for 0.

The Leigh Football Club was formed in the late 1880s. And I know that at some time they had a ground up the Penshurst Road. The Tonbridge League was formed in 1898 with the Leigh Club as a founder member playing a Tonbridge XI and losing 0-12.

Leigh Soccer Club, 1919/1920.
Top row: Tom Izzard (1), Ike Neller (2), Chummy Card (3), C. Friend (4)
George Faircloth (5), William Godwin (6), Harry Passingham (7), Johnny Burr (8)
Mr Evelyn (9), Jack Roots (10), Stan Brooker (11)
Middle Row: H. Martin (1), Ennie French, (2); R.P. Nethercock, Cecil Faircloth (Capt.)
Ray Faircloth (5), Bill Hayter (6), Hollands (Linesman) (7)
Front row: Rob Martin (1), Fred Faircloth (2), Boxer Brooker (3) Charlie Lambert (4)

One of the finest soccer players the village ever had was Billy Hayter who died a very old man in 1984. He worked for I and R Morley up in London.

In 1919/20, Leigh won the Tonbridge and District League Competition. I know about it because there's a photo in the pavilion of the team. So many of the names are the real old village families. There are three Faircloths in the picture – Charlie, Ray and Fred. There's Harry Passingham, Mr Nethercott – the schoolmaster – and one of the Brookers; Mr Card and Mr Martin, who I think was Harry, whose brother Charlie ran the Post Office at Chiddingstone Causeway.

The Village Halls played a big part in peoples' lives – particularly their sporting lives. Not only did the football teams change and wash there but there used to be 'The Institute' there. They had snooker, billiards, table tennis and badminton. Badminton was started in 1911. Table tennis started later – in 1923 – when Mr Nethercott proposed providing a table tennis set at a public meeting. The records show that a table was made by Tom Izzard in the Hall Place workshops from materials supplied by Mr Williams. Local players practised and competed against each other and competed in friendlies against visiting outside teams – much as teams play each other at darts today. I remember Alfie Houghton telling me how he used to teach some of the young players at the end of the 1920s. There was a proper Tonbridge Table Tennis League by the end of the thirties, though the Leigh Club didn't join until 1950.

In the summer there used to be women's stoolball on the Green as there is now, as well as cricket. But Daisy Batchelor is the expert on that. There's also 'mixed' stoolball now; not everyone approves.

And you could play tennis too, on an informal basis. My parents were keen. Mr and Mrs Pucknell – he was an accountant – had a court at the beginning of Lealands Avenue on the left, and there was one behind Elizabeth Cottage on the Green, and one at the Old Vicarage. Dick Wood – who was very keen – told me once that sometimes ordinary people were allowed to use the court at Hall Place too. In fact, the Hollenden family and the estate were generally pretty good to people – even though relations between the Estate and the people in the village can't always have been easy. They had power over a lot of people – sacking and the rent collection for a lot of houses. I remember Alfie Houghton saying once that he always made it a rule never to accept a drink off anyone because you never knew what you might have to say to them the next week. But the Hollendens – and Alfie – did a lot for the village – not just for sport but all general village activities."

Harold Farrington –
Cricket Ball Maker

Although he has lived in Hildenborough for nearly sixty years, Harold Farrington and his wife, Myrtle, have adopted Leigh as a second home, attending the Church here for many years – "We've found real spiritual happiness in St Mary's" – and being seen by Leigh people as one of them. Harold was born in 1922 and, after being in the Army during the Second World War, he became a cricket ball maker in 1946, continuing with two interruptions for the next forty years.

"When I got back from the War, I worked in the butchers, Sainsburys, but there wasn't much meat to sell with rationing and so on. So when I heard they were looking for cricket ball makers, I was keen to try. My first firm was Grey Nichols in Mount Pleasant Road, Hildenborough. I met Ken Mundy there. He's now in charge at the cricket ball making factory/show place at the Whitbread Hop Farm. I worked at Grey Nichols for eight years but then I was made redundant – things weren't going all that well for the English cricket ball makers, with imports coming in from places like Pakistan. There was no redundancy money in those days and I had to get another job quickly – I'd just got married to Myrtle!

The head station master at Tonbridge was a baptist colleague and when he heard I was looking for a job, he offered me the post of leading porter at Hildenborough station. There was a station master, Mr Adams, and two porters, Harry Hogwood and me. We used to do shifts, one from 6.00 am to 2.00 pm and one from 2.00 pm to 10.30 pm which met the last train at 10.15 pm. A three month season to Charing Cross was £11-5-0. I expect it's well over a thousand now; but people earn more I suppose. Being a leading porter meant being assistant station master, selling tickets,

Railway ticket for a dog.

keeping the fire going in the waiting room and generally helping people. I also had to clean the oil lamps above the track all the way to Sevenoaks Tunnel. Sometime, when there was a heavy wind, the gantries would be swaying around – with you on them. I still remember all my regulars – Mr Biddle: he was first class, and Mr Magnus at Porcupine House and lots of others. They were always very kind. They'd get together at Christmas and give me a present to thank me for looking after them. One very foggy night, the train got into the station and people rushed up and said 'Mr Magnus has fallen out'. The train had stopped further up the line and Colonel Hugo, thinking it was the station had opened the door and said 'After you, Magnus', and Mr Magnus had stepped out into the darkness. So I set off up the track and before long I met him – walking along like a Grenadier Guardsman, with his umbrella over one arm and his briefcase and his bowler hat at an angle.

After a few years, I got a job with another cricket ball firm, Ives, in Tonbridge, but that factory closed too, so I went to work for Sullivan's, the butchers. Then around 1962, five of the local cricket ball makers merged to become Tonbridge Sports Industries – it became British Cricket Balls later. They all moved to the Wisden's factory at Chiddingstone Causeway – the far end on the right. As well as Ives and Wisdens plus Grey Nichols, there was Lillywhite Froude who'd come from Lyons Crescent in Tonbridge and Stuart Surridge who were by Tonbridge Station on The Approach. Nearly a hundred people all came together.

There are lots of stages to making a cricket ball and there are a number of specialist jobs in the factory. First, there's 'the quilt makers'. They make the inside of the balls. Then there's the people who cut the leather and stitch the four bits of leather into the two halves – that's what I did. And there are 'the seamers' who put the two halves together which makes the first bits of the seam and 'the stitchers' who put the final two seams on the ball before it is polished and finished.

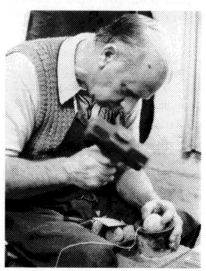

The late Bert Hunt making a five layer cork and worsted quilt. Mid 1970s.

The quilt – the middle of the ball – has an inch of cork to start with. In some factories they had a secret middle which they made in 'The Secret Room' – they still do at Alfred Readers at Teston and British Cricket Balls which is the one at Whitbreads Hop Farm. They're the last two real English cricket ball makers. Then you put on thick layers of cork, bound on tightly with wetted worsted twine. You'd hammer the quilt into a cup to get it evenly round and then bake it in an oven.

Then the job that I did starts. The cow hide comes in white and has to be dyed red. When that's done, I'd cut out four pieces in special, nearly oval shape. You had to cut the edges of the two quarters at an angle so that when they were stitched together, they fitted properly without a gap. When you've got the pieces cut, you have a curved awl and you make a series of holes from about half an inch from one side into the thickness of the leather so that the awl comes out at the edge of the leather. Then you stitch two of the quarters together, making a cup shape, with the stitching on the outside only. When that's done, you turn it inside out so that the stitching doesn't show. I could sew two dozen covers a day.

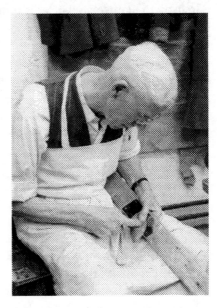

Bill Skinner holeing the cover before sewing the two quarters together. Chiddingstone Causeway, mid 1970s.

The thread you use is traditionally six strands of hemp waxed together. I used to use a straight awl with a wooden knob on the end to do the sewing but some people used a needle. You wound the thread round the awl and pulled it through. To get it tight enough, I wore a half glove made of leather. Myrtle says I used to come home with my hands all cut and sore and that that was the cause of my arthritis. But I don't think it was really. Anyway, once you had finished sewing the halves and turned them inside out, you added a little leaf of thick leather that you'd cut in a sort of ellipse. That was to compensate for where there wasn't any stitching. You glued those in and you put the halves in special hydraulic presses. These had an inner cup and then you screwed another cup over it, so that you got the right shape. It took about a minute maximum in the press.

Harold Farrington 'blocking out' the covers in the hydraulic press. Dukes, Chiddingstone Causeway, mid 1970s.

I had to sharpen my tools two or three times a day – and, though Myrtle used to complain – I'd sharpen them when I go home in the evening, too.

Ken Mundy, the foreman at Dukes and still at British Cricket Balls at the Beltring Oast, weighs the covers and the quilts. Mid 1970s.

When I'd finished my job, the seamer can do his bit, sewing the two half covers that I made round the quilt. At the turn of the century they used to put ninety five stitches on each of the three double circles. Nowadays, even the best balls – they're called Grade A – only have eighty. Afterwards, the stitcher adds the final two rows of stitches to each ball and then the balls go into another press to make sure that they are entirely round before they are polished and finished and stamped.

Barry Crooks doing the final stitiching together of the two halves to make the first part of the seam. Dukes, mid 1970s.

We would each put our own mark on the ball we'd made, so that if there were any complaints, they would know who had made it. The cricket balls I made each had a number seven stamped on.

Quite recently, after my time, there was great rivalry between cricket ball makers and some of them started making the seam bigger to please the bowlers. Everything got so out of hand that the cricket authorities introduced a series of regulations which nowadays apply for all the top quality balls.

Of course, we had to do cheap balls as well. They were made with only two pieces of leather which started as a circle and were then cut to a special shape and put in a press with a thinner, inside part. Then the two halves were sewn on to a solid composition cork core, rather than the proper quilt, although it's still referred to as "the quilt".

Although there had always been out-workers, our Union inside the firms was very strong and it was a closed shop. The Union was not in favour of out-workers because they could make more balls than the people in the factory if they wanted to – and get more money. They were all on piece rates. Charlie Ingram who lived in your cottage from the 1920's was a great union man in Wisdens. There were several quite serious strikes, even in my time. And Myrtle will tell you that after one five week strikes, we were down to our last bit of food.

There were a lot of cricket ball makers in Leigh. Bert Stubbins at Ivy Cottage – he was a volunteer fireman at one stage when they had a horse-drawn fire engine where Healy's Garage was – Leigh Service Garage now; Fred Whibley, who was the Parish Clerk; and lots of others.

When I was about a year and a half from retirement, Wisden's decided to move to a new factory in a development area, where they got a grant. I get a pension from them. It's £3.39 a month which makes us laugh each time it arrives. It's lucky I did another contributory pension as well.

I should tell you about a strange coincidence which took me back into history. I used to teach at the St. John's Church Sunday School, the main Hildenborough Church, and I was telling the children about cricket ball making. There were some boys from the Coles family who lived nearly opposite Mill Garage – the second house up. They said that they'd got something interesting at home that they'd bring to show me. They brought in some old clay pipes and some bits of leather that the family had found under the old floorboards. You could see that all the bits of leather were very near the shape we used for making cricket balls. The Coles traced everything back and it was thought that the house was probably the oldest known cricket ball making place in the country but I've forgotten the details.

It's funny: all over the years Myrtle didn't like cricket. But now she has become a fan – at last.

Dorothy Thompsett

(Mrs Dorothy Gibbs)

"It was quite a surprise when I got to Leigh. I was fifteen. It was 1935 and we had come back from Canada, where we lived on the edge of a lake. Leigh seemed very built up – sort of cramped – and the people seemed very British and snobbish; they didn't want to mix with us: they didn't interfere or anything but they were not very friendly. It takes ages to be accepted – I'm still not sure I'm accepted after more than sixty years. You have to be born in the village I think, like Bernard and Russell, my brothers, who were a lot younger than me. But there were lots of really nice people when I look back on all the people I've known – as well as some who weren't so nice! But I wouldn't like to talk about them – it wouldn't be right somehow.

We moved into one of the double cottages down Lower Green – the ones nearest the bakery – next door to Mr Brooker the shoemender. Then, after I got married in 1937, the rest of the family moved to Barnetts Road – next to Fred Whibley.

My first job was at the Grosvenor Hotel in Tunbridge Wells. That was quite a shock. You see, we didn't have any pubs in Canada. The nearest liquor store would have been a hundred miles away from our farm and, anyway, Father made his own in the woods. So, when I got to this hotel and was told to work behind the bar, I just didn't understand it – about giving change and things – I didn't even know what a sixpence or a shilling was. They were nice people there but, when my Mum found what I was expected to do, she made me give in my notice.

My brother, Ronnie, who was a few years younger than me, got a job working in the gardens at Hall Place. He lived in the bothy up there – there were lots of lads who were up there – Sid Lucas was one of them. When Lord Hollenden was away they had quarts of cider and I used to go up and play cards – gambling, you know.

I got to know Lady Hollenden – that was Lady Diana – mainly because of horses. She was American. She adored her horse who was called Diamond and I had had my own in Canada, so we got on well together, although she wasn't one for chatting in the village. I'd go and give Diamond sugar lumps and she would come with cake. She went to some of the village dances occasionally and I remember once Mr Vince – Harry Vince, who lived in Garden Cottages – was dancing with her. He had his wellingtons or his boots on and he tripped and they fell through the big drum – much to Lady Hollenden's disgust.

I still see Alfie Houghton who, as you know, was the Hall Place agent and I always joke with him and ask him which bush he's been hiding behind. He and his wife had that terrible thing with his son drowned in the weir when the son was doing his King's Scouts. He was a lovely lad. My sister, Betty – she played stoolball for Kent – was down there when it happened. He went under and just never came up. I've swum across the weir lots of times – I'm a strong swimmer – and you could feel a sudden pull in the middle – it was like a hole. I don't think Mrs Houghton went down to the village ever after that.

Lower Green had Mr Bennett's bike shop at the bottom. And there was a large black Nissen hut, further up on that side next to the fire station which was where Mrs Selden lived. Teddy Thompson lived in Lower Green too as a boy when we were first there. He was a character – he was naughty but never nasty with it, you know. I remember him putting firecrackers through the letter box of the Fleur de Lis. But then boys did do things. One day there was smoke coming out of the big oak tree by you. My little brother, Russ, had lit a fire in there and set light to the tree.

During the War, all sorts of things happened. Once we were in the hop garden at Paul's Farm – it was run by Miss Goodwin after her father died – a German plane flew down and shot at us. There were two Spitfires chasing it and I think they shot it down up by the big greenhouses of the Old Barn Tea House – you know, the one that had "Oceans of Cream" written on the Oast House there. The Old Barn was owned by Mr Tomlinson who'd been a Lieutenant Commander in the navy. He was a character. I worked at the glass factory in Stocks Green Road – it made ampoules and glass bottles for medicines – and we had to cycle past the Old Barn on the way home. Mr Tomlinson had a long wire outside and he used to hang up lots of rats that he'd shot in a long line on it. He had lots of geese on that pond by the road for years and years. I remember once they all decided to walk up the road to Hildenborough station. There must have been about forty of them. It held up the cars for a good time. Another German plane came down in a haystack between Sir Arthur and Lady Page's house – that was Old Kennards – and the Old Vicarage. There were bullets going off everywhere. Old Mr Faircloth from Old Wood Cottage – half of it really – was head of the fire brigade then. Everyone was trying to get the body of the pilot out of the plane but they could only get half of it. He was buried in the churchyard but I think years later the body was sent back to Germany to be buried there.

Then you've heard about Mr Hanson who ran the Post Office on the Green. He was Mrs Wells's father. I think that he handed over his licence to run the Post Office – there was something to do with the black-market – but anyway Mrs Wells – as she became – took it over. Then there was the bomb in the School. We were very close to both the families whose children were killed – particularly the Longhursts. He was a lovely boy. My husband, Henry, was in the Navy. He lost his leg, so he was invalided out. I think maybe he was the only person in the village to come home like that from the Second World War.

But it is a nice village. We had lots of fun. We used to go to the pub and, on the way home, we'd climb over the school fence and ring the school bell at midnight. Then there was the skating on Hall Place lake. And I remember when my husband and Archie Denton and some of the others had been up to the pub. It must have been near Christmas because on the way back, they thought they'd sing carols at the little old cottage opposite Adin Coates – it had a monkey tree. It's where Charlotte Cottages are now. A little old man with a long white beard lived there and he was looked after by an ex-ATS lady. Anyway she didn't think much of this, so she went upstairs and emptied the chamber pot on them. And there was another time, it was after the war, when my daughter, Lindsey – she was only little – and I were coming home in the dark one evening. We were going past the slaughter house on the corner of the Green and we heard all the lambs baaa-ing. So I put Lindsey on my shoulders and she squeezed in a little window high up and we let all the lambs out. She was standing there in all the manure. Anyway, all the lambs went off down to the station.

It was all quite fun in those days.

"BURNING UP THE OAK TREE"

Russell denies that he ever tried to set fire to the oak tree: he says it was a huge willow tree down by the Iron Room. With a friend, they stuffed some straw into a hollow part of the tree and set light to it. A combination of Bernard Pankhurst and Dennis Stolton thought they had put it out but, much later, it came alight again. Bernard, and friend, were long gone.

❀

Archie Denton

Archie Denton was born in 1917. He had been very much part of the village all his life and he chatted briefly before he died in 1998. His nephew, Keith Denton, has given permission for Archie's recollections to be used.

"My father – he was another Archie – was born in a cottage between Chiddingstone and Chiddingstone Hoath in the late 1800s but he lived in Leigh most of his life and he played cricket for Leigh for ages; then he was the umpire and scorer. I was born in the village and I played cricket – and soccer – for Leigh, too. The cricket club sub used to be three and six a season and you got pads and things thrown in. The first team got the new ones: then they got passed on to the second team. The soccer sub was five shillings a year.

I went to the village school. I started in Mr Nethercott's time but I don't really remember him much. It was Miss Ellis I particularly think of – from the infants' class. She was wonderful. I always remember her riding her bike going back home to Weald. When I got to the top part of the school, the Head was Mr Gibbons. He used to get me to go round the school with the roll call and see who was in each class and who was away.

In those days – the early twenties – the boys played marbles in the road and the girls did hopscotch there too. You could roll a hoop down Church Hill and it would go across the High Street, bounce on the kerb and go right over the school fence into the playground – there were never any cars or anything.

I used to take the Sunday loaves up to the Church porch on a big delivery bike each weekend. There were about twelve of them – all big loaves.

I worked at Wisdens but I wasn't a cricket ball maker – I made tennis rackets. They had screws in them in those days.

We always used to say that you weren't really a local until you'd lived here for fifty years. The village used to have real characters then – there aren't many now."

Keith Denton

Keith Denton was born in 1945 in Tonbridge.

"I never lived in Leigh but I seemed to have spent a good deal of my childhood in the late 1940s and early 1950s in the village because of all the uncles and aunts that I had here – and because I loved it here. My dad was Stan Denton, and he had two brothers, Uncle Gordon – he died young and I never knew him – and Uncle Archie, who I always called 'Uncle Pop'. They had all been brought up in 17 Garden Cottages by their Aunty Rose because their mother had died when they were young. Aunty Rose had been in service and had never married. There was also Uncle Alfie Houghton whose wife, Auntie Doris, was my Mum's sister. And then there was 'Uncle' Fred Sands who was some sort of relative – I'm not sure quite what and who I think was in charge of the farm up at Paul's Hill. And there was 'Uncle' Fred Maddox – he'd been the gamekeeper at Penshurst – and Aunty Alice. They lived in Rose Cottage opposite Adin Coates, the big grocer when I knew them, but they used to live in a little cottage in the middle of the Penshurst Estate – I am not sure which – but it didn't have any proper water or sewage or electricity or anything. They weren't my proper Uncle or Aunt again – just some sort of relations – but I always called them Uncle Fred and Aunty Alice.

So, as we lived in a small flat in Tonbridge, opposite the Star & Garter, I used to love coming to Leigh, which we did almost every weekend, usually Sunday afternoon. At first we came by the 101 Maidstone & District bus but, when I was bigger, Dad and I would cycle and Mum would come by bus.

Garden Cottages with their own little green in front were wonderful. Uncle Arch taught me football and cricket there before I progressed to playing on the proper Green. Number seventeen was only small – and Uncle Arch lived there all his life. Some of my earliest memories are of Christmases there. So many people in such a little house. Downstairs, there was a little scullery and a minute kitchen with a huge range in it and the

Garden Cottage in 1909 when they were new. The right hand cottages had not been completed. They were known in the village as the White City.

front room where all the family squeezed in. We'd all stay the Christmas night – seven of us in this place that was probably tight for three. On Boxing Day, everyone would go up to Aunty Doris and Uncle Alfie at The Firs for a big family party. The Firs seemed like a mansion compared to Garden Cottage. There was an annual children's party too, in the British Legion Hall which I used to go to.

Uncle Arch was a great vegetable gardener. He had his allotment up behind Garden Cottages – everyone used them then. It was all immaculate up there. I used to go up with him to feed the chickens. Nowadays only one or two of the allotments are used – Bernard Thompsett and so on.

When I was a bit older, Uncle Arch and I used to sit and watch the cricket on the Green after tea – all the evenings seemed hot in those days – with the clock striking seven, then half past and both sides trying to win before time was up. Then he'd take me up to the Bat where I'd have a Vimto and some crisps, staying hidden behind the bar, while Uncle Arch had a brown and mild. I was the excuse for an early evening drink! Sometimes we'd go to the Brickmakers: but never the Fleur. (Father never came in the pub – he was the worrier in the family). Then we'd get the ten past eight bus back to Tonbridge.

When I got a bit older – probably about eight or nine – Uncle Arch – 'Uncle Pop' – used to take me to see Jack Cole's pigs. Jack Cole was a huge man who always dressed in a boiler suit and rode a very upright bicycle. He lived in Garden Cottages too and he used to frighten the life out of me. He was the slaughterman and we'd go down to the slaughterhouse at the end of the Green. The pigs made an awful row – all in their pens. Jack had a stun gun thing which I supposed he used for the killings. His allotment was next to Uncle Arch's and he used to spend all his spare time there. He was a great rival to Charlie Ingram at the fruit and vegetable show. Jack always used to ask me whether I'd heard the cuckoo, no matter what time of year it was! It seemed a bit strange.

'Uncle' Fred – that was Fred Maddox – had a great white beard and always wore plus-fours. He and Aunty Alice had lived in Rose Cottage since the early 1940s. It was a lovely cottage, with very low ceilings. Even Uncle Arch had to duck to get under the beams and he was very small. It had a super, overgrown cottage garden, with brick paths. When they wanted to pull it down to put up Charlotte Cottages in the early 1960s, I reckon all they had to do was put a rope round it and pull on it with a tractor!

I remember going up Paul's Hill when I was young in the late autumn evening with other children to see the hops being unloaded and my other 'Uncle Fred', Fred Sands, being responsible for the drying in the Oast up there for Miss Goodwin who ran the farm after her father died. The hop fields were so beautiful.

Leigh seemed to have everything in those days. There were the two groceries and the pubs but there was also Mr. Whitehead, the butcher; and the cycle shop by the railway bridge (did you know that Dorothy Gibbs' husband, 'Gibbo', who was a great friend of Archie's, used to ride a bike even though he only had one leg). The bike had a fixed wheel. There was the garage that the two Healy brothers, Jack and George, owned, as well as Moon's Garage; and there was the hairdresser in the Square which came a bit later, run by Mr Hawkins; and even a watchmender, Mr Birchett, up Hollow Trees Drive. And there was so much to do. Dad was a very keen bellringer when he lived in the village. He used to tell me about the special peal that they did at the end of the War to celebrate.

Uncle Arch had a dog called Ben. He was scruffy – no collar or anything – and he followed Uncle everywhere. But the trouble was, he was very independent. He used to get on the 101 bus and go to Tonbridge. But he always got back somehow."

Ray and June Chadwick
(Mrs June Smith) and Peter Smith

*J*une Chadwick was born in 1932 in Folkestone. Her brother, Ray, was born there five years later. Their grandparents, Victor and Rose Wood and their uncle, Dick Wood, and his wife, Edie, all lived in Leigh. So both children often visited Leigh before the War. In 1940, when their parents split up, the two children moved with their mother to their grandparents' home at Budgen's Cottage, Lower Green.

"Budgen's Cottage was tiny and there were five of us in it," says Ray. "Uncle Harry, that was Dick Wood, and Aunty Edie lived at the top of Barnetts Road and Dick became like a father to me. He was always there but he never imposed. He took me fishing – he was a very keen fisherman – we went out catching rabbits and moles, and he taught me all about nature – about all the birds and flowers. He also wrote sketches for the plays they did in the Village Hall. His job was in charge of the sewage works and he used to bring home the vegetables that he grew there. Mum wasn't all that keen".

June has a different set of memories. "Ray spent a lot of time out with other boys and playing on the Green but I was more with my grandparents and Aunt Edie. Aunt Edie was wonderful. She had been in service in Robertsbridge before she was married and she used to run the Barnetts Road house like that. There was a box room full of plums drying and bottles and bottles of preserves – apple rings and things like that. Because grandfather was the assistant gamekeeper for Hall Place, he used to take me there and all round the copses. One of my first memories in Leigh was trailing after grandfather to feed the pigs at the bottom of Lower Green in the little farm that belonged to Mr. Baldwin. Ray used to ride on the pigs – and I think we both fell out of a cart which used to give us rides down Lower Green. And I remember Mr Gravett, the stationmaster in Lower Green: he was always on his bike and he was always hurtling down the road, trying to catch the train to sell the tickets but he was usually too late:

people had to buy their tickets at Tonbridge. At the other end of Lower Green, there was Mr Brooker who mended shoes in his little shop. I used to go and sit with him. He was very patient. He told me how to mend shoes and showed me how to cut the leather. But grandfather used to mend our shoes – I've still got his last. My best friends were the Bennett sisters – Nina in particular. Nina and I used to go everywhere together. Her father owned the cycle shop down by the station. They lived in the flint house next to the Village Hall. I think Mr Bennett had lived there all his life and I think his father lived in the village before that. Anyway, Mr Bennett had a car – it was very unusual – there were hardly any then – and he'd take me out on Sundays. It was just about the cat's whiskers".

Institute Cottage – where the Bennett family – Mr and Mrs and their two daughters – lived for many years. Mr Bennett owned the bicycle shop at the bottom of Lower Green.

"When we moved to Leigh we were very poor", says Ray. "It was very unusual for that era to have a father who had gone off. And if you were poor, you got treated in very different ways by different people. The Knock family were particularly kind, but not everybody was like that". June agrees: "some of the middle classes didn't want to know you at all. But the gentry – I suppose you'd call them that, although it seems funny today – would talk to you. Lord Hollenden was always around and Lady Hollenden was very nice. Sir Arthur and Lady Page were always very friendly. Lady Page always wore flamboyant clothes and she would come into the Bakery and put cakes she had bought into her hat. And the Babbington Smiths – at the Gatehouse (that was Lord Hollenden's daughter) would always talk to you. I remember going up to Kennards and Upper Kennards and they'd invite us – that was Nina Bennett and me – inside the house and we'd get lemonade and cake. We never got those at home." June's husband, Peter Smith, the son of the baker, remembers going in the van to deliver the bread to Brigadier Kindersley: the Brigadier said 'come and have a look at my new car' and showed him his new Rolls Royce.

In about 1944, the family were getting too big to fit into Budgen Cottage and they moved across the road to a black Nissen hut. "It had been used by the firemen and ARP wardens during the war", explains June. "I think it was owned by the Sevenoaks Rural Council. It had two bedrooms at the back, a bathroom and a kitchen and a room where we could sit at the front". "It was pretty basic: just a curved concrete outside, painted with black pitch or something but with no lining", says Ray "and icicles used to form on the inside and drip down on to the beds. But it did have a bath which we'd never had before".

Both June and Ray went to the village school, with different memories of headmaster, Mr Gibbons, but having the same high regard for Miss Ellis. June was in the class when the mortar bomb exploded. "Joyce Chandler, who was killed, was next to me. All I can remember was that she stood up and I went under the desk. My hands were quite badly burnt. After it, there wasn't any counselling like you'd get today but I don't think it was necessary really: we all got together in our own groups and talked. It must have been much worse for the teachers – they must have felt so responsible. Mr Gibbons left soon after".

June was fourteen when she left school. "Miss Ellis signed my autograph book. She wrote that one must 'keep one's face to the sun so that shadows fall behind you'. I've still got it. I went to work at the Post Office – which had moved to the Green by then. It was owned by Mr Winson and just had the Post Office and a few sweets and things. Mr Winson's daughter, Margaret, got married to Bill Wells and Mr Winson passed the business on to them. They wanted to make it into a proper grocers but because it was just after the War you had to have a permit for that and to get the permit you had to get a petition signed by a certain number of people, saying that you'd use your ration book in the new shop. Anyway, they got permission and they expanded – they built more on the back and Bill and Margaret lived there."

Fairly soon after this, Ray remembers the disaster that struck the Nissen hut. "My mother had been drying a mattress in front of the heater – it had got wet from the condensation. It was so cold, that we went across the road to my grandparents. The mattress must have fallen on the heater because there was an enormous fire. We were lucky the fire station was next door but, you know what they say, the firemen do as much damage with the water as the fire's done and everything in the front part was ruined". However, Mr Winson said to June that "because I'd lost everything, he was going to put my wages up from fifteen shillings to a pound a week. He was a very kind man".

"It must have been about this time when I started bell-ringing", June continues. "I did it for four or five years and I did a bit of hand-bell ringing for special do's as well. Mr Pankhurst – that was Bernard – was the Bell-Captain at the Church and Mr Stubbins – that was Bert Stubbins – was another great ringer. We'd practise every Monday night and Bill Wells, who'd got a new baby at the Post Office by this time, used to get annoyed because he said we'd wake up the baby. The other ringers used to go round different churches but I wasn't too keen – the other bells seemed too heavy. The old story was that most bell-ringers come down from the belfry on Sundays and creep round the back to the pub. In any case, I never knew a bell-ringer who actually went to church. They used to have difficulty to get enough ringers – I expect it's the same now. Each week I'd walk up to Hall Place with grandfather to get his pension which he got from Lord Hollenden. Mr Brooker used to pay it out. It went on until grandfather died. He got the Government one as well, of course, from the Post Office. I don't think that he and my grandmother paid any rent either. I always felt well disposed to Lord Hollenden. He always seems to look after people and he seemed to keep everything in the village together".

June has one other particular memory. "In about 1949, a new baker took over the bakery in Lower Green and that was how I met my husband, Peter. He was the son of the new baker. I went to work there for a bit but I wasn't there long".

Ray and June Chadwick (Mrs June Smith) and Peter Smith

Lower Green including the Bakery under Mr Phipps ownership in 1930s. Mr Phipps followed Mr Belton.

Peter Smith takes up the story. "Mr Lakeman and his wife, who was an artist, had owned the Bakery during the War. His difficulty had been that he could never get any ingredients to make anything apart from bread. All through the war and after it, he just got his ration of flour to make a fixed amount at a fixed price, although he had managed to make some jam tarts once a week. He sold it to F A Smith after the War and then my father bought the Bakery off them. So we were L E Smith & Son who'd bought it from F A Smith and Company. Dad was the baker; mum was in the shop; and there was me doing the deliveries. The supplies – flour and other things – were getting easier when we took over but you still had to work everything out – even how much flour to sprinkle on the board to roll out the dough. June and I got married in 1956 and we moved away, so I only lived in Leigh for five or six years. My father sold the business to another baker, Mr. Trengrove a few years later but I don't think the bakery was around for very long after that".

June, Peter and Ray are agreed that Leigh was a good place to have lived. "I found it a really nice village", says June, "and although we had a hard time and Mum must have found it really difficult, my grandparents and Uncle Dick and Aunty Edie were all lovely. In fact, most of the people were very nice and caring."

Miss Friend
The Baker's Daughter

Diana Wood who lives at the Old Bakery in Lower Green remembers talking to Miss Friend whose father was the baker before and during the early part of the First World War.

Miss Friend remembered how the flour used to come from Hastings by train to Hildenborough Station and they would have to go up and get it with a horse and cart. Then it used to be unloaded from the cart, using the wheel and pully that there used to be up on the wall and pulled up into the doorway at first floor level (now hidden by the 1970s extension). People used to come in on Saturday afternoons with pies and Mr Friend would bake them using the residual heat from when he'd made the bread early on Saturday. Miss Friend also remembered that, when her brother was called up in the First World War, she had to drive the bread round in a pony and trap, including to the prisoner of war camp in Chiddingstone.

Monica Gray

(Mrs Monica Paterson)

An Evacuee at Oak Cottage

*I*n July 1994, a lady was standing outside Oak Cottage on the Green *pointing at the house to a younger lady. The second lady turned out to be the daughter-in-law, who had brought her 16-month old son with her. Invited in for coffee, the older lady told her story – the story of 9-year old Monica Gray who had been evacuated to Leigh throughout the war.*

"Two days before war was declared, nearly all the children in our Catholic school in Kensington were sent 'en bloc' to Leigh. We arrived and were put in the main village hall. People came from Leigh and other villages around to choose the child, or children, they wanted. Farmers, for example, came in and chose older boys because 'they can work on the farm'. I came from Hans Road by Harrods. My mother was a bus conductor and remained one until she was 60. We were proud of our name, 'Gray with an A', which we traced back to Lord Gray. I had two sisters with me. One sister, Joyce, ended up with went to the Sadler family in Barnetts Road. One went to Fordcombe. After spending two days at Old Brickmakers, I was chosen by the Ingram family who lived in Oak Cottage. I lived with them for the next six years until I was 15. I still think of Mr and Mrs Ingram as 'Mum' and 'Dad'. I can't even remember Mrs. Ingram's Christian name.

For the two days before war was actually declared, people in the village with evacuees were not given any money by the Government. So while I was at Old Brickmakers, I ate up the corned beef sandwiches and custard cream biscuits I had brought with me.

Because we were Catholics, it was thought better that we did not go to the Village School. Anyway, we had brought our own teachers with us. We were said by the villagers 'to have no manners'. When we got to the Brickmakers, the legs of all the tables and chairs in the living room had paper wrapped round them. I asked whether it was decoration. 'No. It's because of children from London – to stop the damage', I was told. I told them that my Mum lived opposite Harrods and she had a table like this one in her kitchen.

There was ill-will between the village children and us evacuees. We barely mixed with the village children. There often used to be fights. At an early stage, we were told to play the village children at stool ball but we had only played things like rounders before, so we were beaten easily: but we got better. The second year we practised – and we won. We were very pleased!

My best friend from London was Eva Collins who luckily went to live next door at Ivy Cottage with a brother and sister, Bert Stubbins and Daisy Milliner. We had a string between my bedroom at Oak Cottage which had been 'the box room' and Eva's with a bell on each end. When the German bombers came over, I used to sleep on a mattress in the cupboard under the stairs – the coal hole it was then.

We used to go and play in the yew tree house at Old Kennards which we reached by going up the unmade-up drive of Inglenook and we used to go and pick celandines in the ditch outside the Vicarage. We used to steal apples from Great Barnetts but we never dared take the plums from the Magistrate's house just up Green View Avenue. We used to play in the woods that stretched between Green View Avenue and Leigh station, complete with the marshes and the old brick fields and we used to post letters in the oak tree outside here on the Green. In the winter, when the Medway flooded, we'd put on our wellingtons and see how far we could wade out without the water going over the top. Of course, it always did in the end. When we got back home, 'Mum' would put dried bran in the oven to heat up and then put it in the wellingtons. When the wellingtons were dry, she'd shake out the bran, dry it out and put it away to use the next time.

Some summers I went hopping down Powder Mill Lane in order to earn some money. The money was given to 'Mum' partly towards a new winter coat and partly towards wool which I used to knit my own scarf and gloves but also to knit clothes for the soldiers. When you went hopping, you wore a sort of sacking apron so that the hops didn't stain your dress. It was a terrible stain – sort of browny grey. You could never, ever get it off your clothes and the only way to get the stain off your hands was to rub them with loganberry leaves or runner bean leaves. At the end of hop-picking we'd take home some of the hops and make what was called a hop pillow. You dried the hops in the oven and stuffed it all into a pillow. Then, if you had earache or you couldn't sleep, you were allowed to take the hop pillow up to bed.

I only saw my sister in Fordcombe once during the whole war. With Joyce, my sister in Leigh, we walked to Penshurst and caught the bus to Fordcombe.

Once or twice a year, all the children used to act as beaters for Lord Hollenden's shoots. And Lord Hollenden would invite all the evacuees up to Hall Place at Christmas. I did bell-ringing almost every week. Although 'Dad' was a bellringer, it was Bert next door who taught me very early on Sunday mornings. Once I knew how to do it, on Sunday mornings I would rush to Mass, dash back to breakfast and then go and ring the bells to summon the other religions to their service. It amused me to think of it then and it still does. (Bert also taught me how to roll a fag – but, luckily, I never liked it. He had very strong tobacco).

'Dad', Charlie Ingram was the verger and famous for his fruit and vegetables. He was also well-known for watching every cricket match from his own deck chairs which he placed beside the Oak Tree well before the game started. His father, Ike Ingram – widowed and in his seventies, had come to live at Oak Cottage and lived there until his death half way through the war. Ike was famous, having played cricket for Kent and occasionally it was said for England. There were some of Ike's trophies in the living room on the sideboard and some upstairs in his bedroom. Mrs. Ingram, 'Mum', came from Ringwood in Hampshire. Like 'Dad', she was a pillar of village society. She was famous for her jams which she sold to help the war effort and her cake making, which she cooked on the range in the living room fireplace. I don't know where she got the sugar with the rationing on. She was President of the Women's Institute and one of the main First Aiders. She taught me to knit and sew and darn.

'Dad's' main job was as cricket ball maker for three days a week but he worked at a fencing firm for two and a half days a week. Sometimes I was allowed to go and help make cricket balls with 'Dad'. 'Dad' was a well-known radical and was a strong Labour supporter and the shop steward at the cricket ball factory.

'Mum' and Charlie were a happy couple. Every evening after dinner, Charlie used to sink into his own armchair in the corner opposite the living room window – put his arms behind his head, sigh loudly and happily, and say 'Ah, that was a loverly meal Mum'. The Ingrams had two children, Reg and Doris – she is Doris Dale now – but both of them were a lot older than me.

Oak Cottage seemed very different then, when the Ingrams paid two shillings and sixpence rent a week to Lord Hollenden. There were bricks on the floor on the earth with lino on top and a rug in the living room. Ike had a big leather armchair in the corner by the living room window and Charlie his own chair at the other side of the fire. All along the wall back on to the kitchen was a long sideboard with some kind of sliding or maybe 'rolling' top that opened with a leather strap.

Oak Cottage during the Second World War. The windows are protected with sticky tape to protect against flying glass in the event of a bomb.

The kitchen was smaller than now, with a huge larder in the other half of the room. There was a copper to the left of the kitchen window. 'Mum' used to put lots of Christmas puddings in it all at once. There was a huge mangle and I used to help wring out the washing by feeding the clothes through the rollers. But I used to read books whilst I did it and occasionally I used to get my fingers in the rollers along with the clothes.

What is now the dining room was then 'the Best Room'. It had an upright piano and 'Mum' used to give piano lessons, including lessons for me. She also used to teach the choir but because there were too many people to fit in the Best Room, the choir was in the Living Room, while she played from next door. The Best Room was furnished with chintz covered chairs and you were only allowed to go and sit in there if you were doing something very quiet like reading.

The lavatory was outside in the garden. It was an earth closet and everyone took a bucket of water with them when they went out to it. We used to think the toilet at school used to smell terrible.

The garden was what Charlie did. There weren't many flowers – just fruit and veg which used to win most of the Village prizes. There was a water barrel on the left of the kitchen window and a well a few yards in front of the kitchen window. Round the back there was not only the old Kentish Green apple tree but also a 'bullis tree' – which was a cross between a plum and a damson.

To us, the war seemed part of everyday life. Bombs fell on various parts of the village but the greatest annoyance came when 'the bloody Germans' bombed the cricket pitch. That's what Charlie said.

After leaving Leigh when I was fifteen, I went back to London but I came back every year to see the Ingrams until their deaths in the mid 1960s. It wasn't that I didn't love my real mother – I was always very close to her – perhaps it was partly because I had been away from her between nine and fifteen, which can be pretty difficult, can't it? She used to try to get down to see us at Christmas and maybe once every summer, but it was very difficult to travel around then. Once my father borrowed a car and drove down. It put our reputation up no end.

Looking back, it must have been very difficult for the people in the village. To be told suddenly that you had to have one or two extra people in your house when you were mainly pretty crowded already, and with your own children forced to sleep two or three to a bed .... and the nuns would just march in and demand things .... but, for me now, there are such happy memories of Leigh that I brought my daughter-in-law and grandson down to see the village and to tell them all the things I remembered."

Joyce Gray

(Mrs Joyce Styles)

"When we arrived in Leigh – there must have been about sixty girls plus all our teachers – it took quite a time before they found some of us homes. And sometimes, when you were living in a place, they would just swap you around without anyone asking you. You were just told you were leaving. I remember the first winter was very cold and I was just sent out in the morning to look after myself. I was so cold. It was really awful. I used to go into the Forge, very quietly and sit by the fire. You put Fullers Earth on your chaps – behind your knees: places like that.

My mother in London had an electric fridge, electric lights, a radiogram and a phone. When we came to Leigh, the house I went to didn't have any of them. I had to learn how to trim the wick of an oil light. They must have thought all evacuees were all from the East End slums the way they treated us. But I suppose there were sixty of us suddenly descending on the village: it must have been difficult for them too. When I arrived, I asked if I could ring my mum and they said 'you haven't got a phone – you're lying' and I said 'yes, we have: it's Kensington 8226' and I went to the phone box at the bottom of Church Hill.

The village children would follow behind us and shout at us – 'You're Londoners' and we'd shout back 'You're Liars'. And because we were Catholics, we called the Church of England people 'Prod-y-Dogs'.

We had a proper school uniform with blazers and Panama hats – straw hats. We were told to hold our heads up high. Our school motto was 'It All Depends On Me' and we had lessons in self-control. We had to sit for half an hour with our hands behind our backs without moving.

To make money for the war effort or to help get more school books, we used to do a line of pennies round the Green or collect a mile of books. Things like that. Everyone joined in.

I ended up living with Mr Arthur Sadler and his wife in Barnetts Road. He was the milkman – he worked at Hollanden Farm. They were always kind and I came back and saw them right until they died. I came to Mr Sadler's funeral three or four years ago".

Evacuees

A DOUBLE EVACUATION STORY

While there seems general agreement that the village did not like the evacuees and the evacuees did not like the village, on a personal level it is clear that once individuals on both sides got to know each other properly, many close attachments were formed.

Bernard Lucas, younger brother of Jack and Harry, works in the Sevenoaks Sainsburys. He was recently talking to a customer and mentioned that he had been born and bred in Leigh. The customer said his wife had been evacuated from London to Leigh during the War and had become very close to the couple who looked after her. When the War was over, his wife had stayed in touch with the couple. Nearly fifty years later, when the now widowed lady was getting very old, they had her to live with them – a reverse evacuation.

Elizabeth 'Betty' Clark

(Mrs Betty King)

"I was born in 1930 at 17 Barnetts Road. I was only in the village until I was fourteen and a half, so I wasn't here very long – I couldn't wait to leave – but I remember a lot about the things that happened in Leigh – particularly the school things – and I remember all the things my parents and my grandparents and my aunt told me. The Clarkes and the Taylors – the Taylors were my grandparents on my mother's side – both families had lived around here for a long time. Grandfather Taylor – he was William Taylor – had been at Leigh School and so had my mother. She was taught by Mr Boby: she always spoke very highly of him. And then all of us children went there too. So there were three generations at the school.

Grandfather Clarke used to spell his name with an 'E' but my father and most of my uncles never did – I don't know why but I was a 'Clark' before I married. My father, Charles – he was always called Charles not Charlie – he was born in 1897 in Mayfield but lived in Edenbridge and other places round here most of his life. When the First World War broke out, he went to the recruiting place and lied about his age. But they turned a blind eye at that time. He became a Gunner. He had a terrible time. One day he had been firing for forty-eight hours without a break. He went back behind the lines to his tent for a rest, and just as he lay down, a shell came and in the explosion all his toes were broken. So he was invalided back to England to recover. He told me once that he had met Edith Cavell, so we think that it must have been at the hospital in Brussels on his way back to England. Mother always used to say how wonderful Nurse Cavell was. When he got back to England, they found he was under age but by the time he had recovered he was over the joining up age so he went back to the Front again. He was at the Somme and Paschendaele, and at Cambrai and he got gassed. He was under a pile of dead bodies and was left for dead – and you know you couldn't touch the gassed bodies. His parents were told he had died of wounds whilst in action. There was an obituary in the local paper and the family went into mourning. But he was pulled out and, although he was blind and deaf for a time and he couldn't talk, he recovered and he went back in again. After the war was over, he stayed on when the Army was occupying Germany – we think that he must have been in the Army for five or six years altogether. He ended up in Cologne because I remember telling him I was going over there with my husband on business and he told me how he had been on sentry duty there one night in 1919 when it was bitterly cold and they had no greatcoats. He went to relieve one of the other soldiers and found him upright but leaning against the inside of the sentry box. He'd frozen to death. They got greatcoats after that.

The War Memorial – with posts around it. A postcard sold at Mr A. Izzard's Post Office shop.

When Father came out of the Army, there weren't any jobs. Father had lots of medals – I can just remember them. But he wouldn't talk about them, even though he used to wear them on Armistice Day at the parade at the War Memorial when they marched round the Green. I remember one day my brother was playing with them and father took them away and threw them to the ground in disgust. I never saw them again after that. He said to my mother – "they said we were fighting for a land fit for heroes but ...." He was very disillusioned. Mother told me that, after the War, he used to go off to look for work every morning in his suit and bowler hat – you always had a bowler hat in the 1920s – but he couldn't get anything. Then one day he got offered a job as a labourer – a hod-carrier I suppose you'd say – by a builder, a Mr Snazell, in Tunbridge Wells and he rushed home on his bike to change out of his suit into his working clothes so he could start straight away. He used to cycle to and from Tunbridge Wells every day – the bike had one of those carbide lamps on it that you have to light with a match. One night on his way back from work, he rode into a trench that they had dug in the road on Quarry Hill and he had quite a severe head injury. I remember a policeman coming to Barnetts Road to tell us about it.

My mother was born outside the village – at Killicks Bank. She watched 'Cider with Rosie' on TV once and said that her childhood in the country was just like it. When she moved to Barnetts Road with father, she never got used to having near neighbours – she'd never had them before. They were all very nice but she didn't mix with them much. Later, some of them told me that they used to confide in her because she wasn't a gossip.

When she had been little, they noticed she had a limp. She was eleven months old by then. So they took her along to Doctor Fraser and he said `sit her in a high chair and rest the leg.' But when she was two she hadn't improved and her father was still worried. So he took her to Barts Hospital. He had to sell some things to afford it. It must have been winter because my mother always remembered being told to look at the snow. Anyway, they thought she had a broken hip but I wonder now if it was infantile paralysis. They told her father that Mum would have to have an operation and then have a calliper on her leg and would have to lie on her front for weeks and weeks. Mum had the operation and did try the callipers but she said that it hurt so much, they decided not to go on with it. I saw the callipers in a cupboard once. They must have been extremely painful to wear – I tried them on. So Mum was always disabled and she always walked with a crutch – although she couldn't half walk – she used to go over to her brother at Weald every Christmas. But it did cause her problems and she had great pain and suffering over the years and when she was sixty it became gangrenous and she had to have the bad leg off. But she lived till she was 71.

She was a great character. She had nine children of which three were still-born, so you can see she didn't believe in birth control. It was on religious grounds – she called it a mockery to God. She used to have lots of discussions with me about why she thought birth control was wrong when I was a child. I remember, when I was seven, I wanted to breed some chicks and the hens kept sitting on the eggs but nothing happened. It was all because Grandfather Taylor had shown me a hen with seven chicks out in his woods, just wild – there can't have been any foxes around. And the eggs he had looked just like our eggs at home. Anyway, I went on and on about it. So one Saturday, when the others were out, she locked the doors and she told me everything. She started with the cockerel and went right through to V.D. She was very religious and she quoted the Bible – "the sins of the fathers" and so on – and about deformed children going on for three generations if you went with more than one man. She said that had she not been born handicapped or otherwise she would not have married or have had children because it might have been passed on. But she said her hip had gone wrong when she was little, so it was all right. I remember she explained that babies in mothers' tummies were floating around like a cork. But she never told me about birth control – I had to learn that for myself.

Mother and father married in Chiddingstone Causeway Church – it was July 10th 1926. Father was twenty-nine and mother was twenty-four. There were five boys in father's family and they all joined the Army. Uncle George – he was one of father's brothers – rose from the ranks and he ended up as an Acting Major in the army in India. He sent my parents a whole lot of white silk for the wedding dress. To get it through the customs, he cut out the middle of a book and packed it in very tightly. My grandfather – William Taylor that is – he picked hundreds of rose petals from his marvellous garden for the wedding and threw them down in a carpet in front of my mother and father when they walked out of church.

They lived in a flat in Southborough for a bit and then they moved into Barnetts Road, half way down on the right – the two houses at the end hadn't been built then. I think Father had helped build the house – it was probably Mr Snazell who was the building firm – but he had some sort of advantage in getting the house. Father always helped mother around the house – it's not just a modern thing that young husbands are meant to do. He did lots of chores – he lit the copper for the washing and cleaned it out, he mended the shoes – because we couldn't afford the cobblers – and he did the garden for all our vegetables and things like that. Mother hated the idea of taking anything from the parish and she always made me feel it was shameful to live in a council house. There were a lot of middle class people in Leigh who seemed unaware that council houses and poverty existed. I remember that an old missionary from China, Miss Owen, came to live at the end of Barnetts Road – in a council house. She helped my sister with her school work when she got to the Grammar School and we gathered that Miss Walton, from Great Barnetts was a sort of relative and was rather embarrassed that Miss Owen was in a council house.

Barden Road - then called the Council Cottages, in the mid 1920s before the two pairs of end cottages were built.

There really was poverty then, even if it didn't seem obvious. It was the kind of thing that we talk about in the Third World today but most people don't realize what it was like then. It is amazing how things have changed. When the Second World War started, my father felt he had to join up again to get more money – even after all he'd been through before in the other war. But he wasn't in very long – Mum had another baby to get him back.

When I was three and a half, I had my first experience with a privy. It was at the back of my grandfather's cottage up at Black Hoath. We had a proper toilet at Barnetts Road. The privy just had a bucket beneath a wooden surround in a little hut full of cobwebs and ivy growing through the roof. My aunt, Nellie Taylor, my mother's sister, lived with her father (my grandfather William). He had a few cows and pigs and things up the road at Cinder Hill and the hens in the chestnut wood opposite. He planted an orchard to the right hand side of Black Hoath and he grafted several variety of apples or pears or plums on to the same tree, so that he got a longer fruiting season from them. The garden was really beautiful with wonderful roses and things. He'd planted snowdrops which spelt out his name – William Taylor. Mr Gibbon used to say, if you wanted to see a really beautiful garden, go up to Black Hoath. Grandfather was a tenant of Lord de Lisle and he was allowed to use the land on the other side of the track going up to the railway cutting. He dug a pond in the chestnut wood there with an island in the middle with rhododendrons on it and he had a hut which was his apple store. The house is called Foxwold now.

My aunt Nellie was amazing. She had been born without proper hands – sort of thalidomide really – but she could knit and crochet beautifully. She went to the village school quite normally without anyone fussing and she had a child. She also played the accordion and the organ. She pulled the organ stops out with her teeth. She had long, beautiful yellow hair which I used to wash and brush for ages. She taught me how to plait it and coil it up over her ears like they did in those days – because, of course, she couldn't do it herself. I remember it was a great shock when she cut it off eventually. She also taught me how to skin a rabbit. She had caught it in a snare but she couldn't skin it so I had to learn, even if I was a bit squeamish at first – especially when the eyes popped out. But it was quite a biology lesson. When she was old she came to live at the Alms Cottages on the Green – she still played the mouth organ. She told me once 'some people would have had people like me put down at birth'. But I always thought her amazing.

I was always longing to go to school. I went for an interview when I was three and a half – it was all day. Miss Ellis was an extraordinary teacher. I was an avid reader all through my childhood because of her. I read the books which were meant for grown ups. We weren't supposed to read more than books about children having little adventures and things. I used to take books from the adult library which was next to one of the classrooms when I was doing the milk money and the savings stamps. We used to read poetry sitting under the chestnut trees on the Green. Miss Ellis had the respect of everyone – the parents and the children. She was very strict with us but the children knew she loved them. She had very good discipline but she never used the cane or smacking that I ever saw. I could tell you what she did with boys who stoned frogs. She had a good idea who the culprits probably were and, when the others went home, she kept a group of boys in the classroom. I went home but my mother sent me on an errand, so I crept into the school porch and peered through a crack in the door. The boys were still sitting at their desks. Miss Ellis said "I don't mind staying here all night but I want to know which of you stoned the frogs". Then the largest of the boys started to cry – he was normally one of the toughest boys – and he confessed. Miss Ellis talked to him quietly and dried his eyes. That was all. But he never did anything like it again.

When I first arrived at school, I remember Miss Ellis told all the children – 'There will be NO swearing or I will wash your mouths out with soap'. I was terrified because I didn't know what swearing was and then it was worse because she went behind a screen at the side of the classroom – to wash her hands and I thought that she was going to do whatever it was – I didn't know. When breaktime came, I went up to my older brother, Lionel, and I asked him what swearing was. He couldn't pronounce his 'W's' when he was little, so he explained it by saying it meant 'vicked vords'.

Lionel was named after Lionel Hedges who was the MP who lived in Upper Kennards. I was named Elizabeth after Lady Elizabeth Callender from Crowborough who did good works of some kind or other. All our family were named in that way – I think that it happened in those days. Lionel was clever and there were a number of other clever ones at the school who should have got scholarships if the parents had got enough money to keep them at school after fourteen, but they just had to go off into life. It was not before time that things changed. Lionel was lucky. Mr Gibbon suggested that he became a gardener's boy up at Hall Place. Lionel did so well there that Mr Fergusson, the Head Gardener recommended him for a student job at the Cambridge University Botanical Gardens. Mr Houghton took Lionel up to London – Lionel had never been there before – and put him on the train to Cambridge. I always remember that. In the end, he took all the horticultural qualifications and ended up as a top person in a government horticultural centre in Faversham and the UK representative on a world wide organization for plant breeders rights. I had another brother, Cyril Pagett Clark – I don't know who he was named after – who was Cyril Pagett? Cyril went to the village school too. He was three years younger than me and he was fond of writing plays and stories. But he died when he was forty-six.

School was different then. Miss Ellis really was wonderful. I still go and see her. Mr Gibbons, the headmaster, was a great one for the cane with the boys and he'd pull hair and bang heads together for chattering but maybe it was just like that at the time. He had a rough tongue and could be hard on some of the boys. I remember him saying to the boys "I'll cut off your waterworks". Once Lionel was beaten so much he had to stay away from school. There was a long row about it. Then there was Teddy Thompson – he was always a naughty boy – just naughty, not at all nasty – he kicked a ball into the portrait of Samuel Morley, breaking the glass. He was beaten with the cane and a small cricket bat – but it didn't do any good. I remember once Mr. Gibbons hid behind the door when the boys were coming in from football and he hit them all as they came in. The trouble was I came in too and he whacked me. But one thing I will give him. He did love his music and singing and he did help me. We were doing singing lesson although it was recitation in this case. He sent me to the end of the room and made me face the wall with my back to him. Then he made me recite the prologue to a play – shouting 'Louder, I can't hear you' until the strength of my voice increased. He taught me that. I was lucky: he told one girl that she had a voice like a dead mouse. To our family, he seemed a terrible snob. We felt that he thought it was a waste of time to help the poorer children.

When I was fourteen, I had finished the school curriculum and I was getting bored with the revision, so they let me work in the Adult Library doing the milk money and fixing the stamps in the saving books and things like that. I was there the day the bomb went off. I don't think the full story ever really came out. You can see why. It was in the summer and I had been talking to one of the boys, James Longhurst, before school began. He had a thing – it was like a big torch battery with cardboard round it. He'd been sticking pins in it. He said he'd found a dump with lots of them and the next day he was going to bring in one for each of the boys. I went back to the Library and Mr Gibbons walked up to the telephone box at the bottom of Church Hill – we didn't have one in the school – to give the number for school dinners as he always did. While he was out, there was quite a babble next door and I was talking to Joan Chandler whose desk was just by the Library door. James must have been telling some of the others about what he'd found and it went off and I was thrown back. I must have been stunned because, when I came round, I was across the desk. I thought that I'd lost my legs. I went out to the shelter outside the school like a zombie but I came back into the classroom and saw everything. Joan was sitting still at her desk with wide open, staring eyes. Mr Gibbons was at the far end of the classroom and he shouted at me to go down to the shelter. At the shelter there were some boys who were sitting on another boy who was screaming 'my brother's lost his arm – I must go to him'. Joan Chandler was so pretty. She died of shock. It was so terrible. I had nightmares and sleep-walks. Lots of the children did. There was no counselling or anything to help us. It was so hard to work in the classroom – we went back to school after a week. I still can't talk about the details. There were the two funerals. The flowers that came – they came from everywhere – all the schools around as well as all the village. But nobody shed a tear. We were brought up that way."

Farms in Leigh
1965

*I*n 1965 the WI decided that farming was changing dramatically in Leigh and that it was worth making a survey of what they saw as the few remaining farms. They questioned each of the farmers and produced the tables below for that particular year. The changes up until then were indeed large when compared to 1900 but they have continued in the subsequent thirty-five years.

Leigh Park Farm
(R Bastable)

Milking Cows	140
Beef Cattle	140
Sheep	450
Pigs	170
Pasture: Barley Wheat	

Moat Farm
(D Boyd)

Beef Cattle	28
Sheep	100
Pigs	20
Piglets	320
Pastures: general	

Littles Barnetts Farm
(W L Wanstall)

Milking Cows	42
Young stock	33
Pigs	90
Turkeys	75
Pasture: general	

Ramhurst Manor
(Lord Kindersley,
Manager: Mr Kinch)

Beef Cattle	20
Sheep	60
Turkeys	36
Pasture: Kale	

Paul's Farm
(J Bennett)

Milking Cows	55
Young Stock	48
Beef Cattle	12
Sheep	50
Hens	24
Pasture: temp past: barley, hops, wheat, kale	

Ensfield Farm
(W G Lerwell)

Milking Cows	75
Young Stock	60
Sheep	150
Poultry	1,000
Pasture: Barley, oats	

Southwood Farm
(E Sparrow)

Sheep	100
Pigs	150
Pasture: general	

Home Farm
(Lord Hollenden,
Manager: Mr Dicker)

Milking Cows	120
Pasture: Barley, wheat, oats	

Morals Over a Century

The subject of morals, or immorality, seldom came up directly but was mentioned in passing in a good number of different ways. In no instance, however, whether talking about individuals or making general remarks, was there criticism of women and in only one case, criticism of a man. Everyone was clear that the children of a 'lapse of judgement' were treated no differently to any other child. Several people were initially concerned that names would somehow get into the book (which they would not have done in any case). One person explained the attitude of the village to illegitimacy over the period he knew about – the 1920s onwards. "People – particularly those who have been born in the village and been at the village school – know about most of the facts but it's part of a closed circle: you don't talk about how Mrs So and So was never married or how the husband of So and So was not the father of the child. There was a sort of conflict, if you like, between the initial family disgrace and, yet the definite feeling that, once it had happened, you did not hold it against the mother and certainly not against the child. Anyway, it was quite common". Another said, "it was a nine days wonder – good for a gossip". Another said "think of all those handsome Italian prisoners of war" – which was a reminder that, in a more general way, wartime and post war Britain had a huge number of pregnant brides and that morality (and immorality) are not perhaps as variable as people – perhaps particularly the elderly of each generation – sometimes think. Divorce may be more common for the children of Leigh School today than in 1950 or 1900; but probably passion has not much altered.

One story moved me and I have altered it to relate it at all. Those who knew the two people concerned will probably recognize them: others will not. It was told to me by an 'outsider': he came to the village when he was about twenty, many years ago. As someone not born in the village, he said that he had some difficulty in getting into the cricket club but that when he had used 'the Bat' for a couple of years, he was allowed to join!

However, he realized that he had been accepted – at least in part – by the village when he was invited to a farewell party in the Large Hall for an elderly villager who was leaving the country for a warmer climate. As the new cricket club member drank with some of the team, he noticed the man who was emigrating was in a corner deep in conversation with an even older well-known local. Everyone seemed to be leaving them alone: he remarked what an amazing likeness there was between the two in the corner. Puzzled, his colleagues in the team said 'Didn't you know – it's father saying goodbye to his son'.

Leigh celebrates the coronation of King George V.

Ben Fagg – Bellringing

en Fagg moved to Leigh just after the last war when he married Mary Stubbings. He has been a bellringer ever since. He has also looked after the Scout Troup with Dick Wood and been a Parish Councillor.

"I started learning bell-ringing after D-Day when the Government released the bells. They weren't needed any longer to warn people of invasion by the Germans and the bells returned to their proper purpose of calling people to church.

I'd been in the Army in North Africa and been captured and put in a prisoner of war camp in Italy. When the Italians gave up, we escaped and I came home and married into a family of bellringers in Leigh, although I hadn't known it until one weekend on leave and I found that my wife-to-be, Mary, and my father-in-law, Bert Stubbings, were both ringers. I asked if I could learn, and that evening father-in-law took me up to the belfry, tied up the clapper of one bell to silence it, and began teaching me how to handle it. From then on, wherever I was stationed in England, I found the nearest church with a ring of bells and attended their practice nights. By the time I was demobbed, I was learning to ring rounds and call changes.

So when Leigh became my home, I joined the band – that's what you call a group of bell-ringers. The band at that time included Bert and Mary, Bernard Pankhurst – he was the Captain of the Tower – his wife Lilian and his brother Douglas, Charlie Ingram, Bill Card and Stan Denton. Stan was nicknamed 'Bumps' because he only rang the tenor bell – the biggest – and we could only manage a simple five-bell method. The tenor bell always rings in the last place at the back, which is called 'bumping' it or 'drumming' it in odd bell methods, e.g. 5-7-9-11. (In even bell methods, 6-8-10-12, it changes place with the others.)

A ring of bells usually consists of six, eight, ten or even twelve bells. We've got six in Leigh. The total number of changes without repetition increases exponentially with the addition of each bell, so that with five bells

— 351 —

you can get a hundred and twenty changes; with six, it's a hundred and twenty times six, that's seven hundred and twenty: with seven bells it's five thousand and forty, and so on, so that it would take more than three years of non-stop ringing to ring all the changes you could theoretically get with twelve bells. But just to ring the five thousand and forty changes takes three to four hours, and that has become the accepted statutory number called a peal.

I had to start learning with bell control. There is no time limit for that, you learn at your own speed, which can take a few weeks or even years; no one knows in advance, and there is no competition; getting it right is the important thing. If you're careless or not paying attention, it can be dangerous. And it's nearly as bad to be over-confident. Once you have mastered bell control, you next learn to ring round, the bells speaking in sequence from the treble to the tenor. The middle bells are known by their numbers, but, however many are in the tower, the lightest is called the treble and the heaviest, the tenor. You have to listen to the bells, and particularly to the interval between your bell and the one you're following to get an even beat.

You start 'change ringing' by what are called 'call changes'. The conductor calls the numbers of the two bells he wants to change places and so on through until he calls them back into rounds again. When a call is made, it is acted on two blows later, to give everyone time to make the adjustment without confusion.

In the last century a Cambridge librarian, named Stedman, who was also a Bell Captain thought there must be more than rounds and call changes. He probably hadn't got anything better to do! So he applied his mind to devising a way to make the bells change by a logical method without the need for someone to call. The result is now used universally as the introduction to 'method ringing'. It is known as 'Original' or 'Plain Hunt'. He went on to design more complicated methods, and the science has spread everywhere in England, with a few bands in New Zealand, Australia, Canada and U.S.A., even one Church band from Central Africa, all local native people, who visited Leigh a year or two back, and spent an afternoon practising with our bells.

If you're keen, you can go to any other church and just walk into the Tower and they say 'Are you a ringer?' and you say 'yes' and they say 'come on in'. The main difference in each Tower is size of the bells – the heavier they are, the deeper they are – and the length of the rope – the longer the rope, the more elasticity there is in it. So you have to pick the bell up and then you feel it. Of course, it goes wrong sometimes. There's even an old saying – "you're not a good ringer until you've broken a stay" – a stay's part of the bell's suspension. It holds the bell at rest. The belfry fund will pay for it but, of course, the object of the exercise is not to break one. Actually it's quite hard to do.

So you never know who you'll have. Don't run away with the idea that because Leigh's only got six bells, you'll only have six people there. Sometimes we can't manage the full six for a Sunday morning but sometimes at a practice there's more – last week we had twelve. There's one family from Hadlow who go round to all the churches with their children just to give them experience. It's a sociable thing really. The thing about Leigh which I like is that if anyone makes a mistake it's a laughing matter with us all. Stella Wooldridge – she's the Captain – she's young but the most skilful and Captain by consent. She's a viniculturalist. In other towers, if things go wrong, it's a post-mortem, often taken very seriously.

It is not just a hobby for enthusiasts. Its prime objective is the Anglican equivalent to the muezzin in the Islamic mosque – a call to the faithful to prayer. The Church of England is the only church in the land which is permitted to have bells which speak outside the building. And I have the impression that, at one time, the right to have outside school bells has also been limited to Church of England schools. (Leigh School, which does have an outside bell, used to be a Church school). But I'm not sure if it's true. Our practice nights are fun and social occasions, but they are also training for a service which the bellringers give to the church community in Leigh".

The bellringing team outside the Church porch in the late 1950s. Left to right: Bill Card, Bert Stubbins, Douglas Pankhurst, Bernard Pankhurst, Lil Pankhurst, Charlie Ingram and Stan Denton.

LADY BELL-RINGERS

Before the War, when lady bell-ringers were first allowed in Leigh, it was agreed that the men bell-ringers should always go up the tower first, with the women coming up afterwards. This was because, originally, the circular staircase up the St Mary's Tower only went half way up to the bell-ringing room, with a steep ladder the rest of the way. As one person put it – "it was a question of propriety".

Arthur Lewis

A rthur Lewis was born in Buckinghamshire but has lived in Leigh with
his wife Brenda for nearly thirty years. He is very active as an allot-
ment holder and with the Produce Association and also with the
Scouts. Brenda is also very active in the village, including the W.I. Committee.
Arthur is a bellringer.

"I will be seventy in the year 2000 – we used to talk about it as children
thinking how strange it would be. Brenda and I moved to Leigh in 1970 but
I think we are beginning to be accepted as part of the village now!

I only started bell-ringing about fifteen or twenty years ago. Stella
Wooldridge is the Captain of the Tower now – she's only young – but it's
funny to think that, when Bernard Pankhurst's wife – she was a
Passingham – just wanted to be a ringer in the 1930s, she had to ask
permission because she was a lady. Bernard, who was Captain, and his
older brother Douglas must have both done forty or fifty year bell-ringing
and Bernard was a mainstay – although he was pretty strict and it was said
he frightened the children!

Most bell-ringers have their annual outing – going round visiting six
or seven different towers in an area – like going round the Romney
Marshes or a bit of the Sussex coast. On one outing, we got to Portsmouth
Cathedral – a touch of class about that – but unfortunately there was a stay
that was badly cracked. We knew it wasn't very strong and no one really
wanted to use that bell but eventually someone volunteered. The trouble
was that he pulled off too quickly and broke the stay. He should have let go
but he hung on and he took flight right up towards the top of the tower,
hanging on to the sally. It was all rather embarrassing – especially as a
wedding was scheduled soon after. But it was all sorted out in time.

I don't remember any very scandalous tales about the Leigh bell-
ringers, although there are stories of a drop of ale in the Tower. But I'm
sure it was many years ago when, it is said, it was not uncommon!"

Mary Bounds

John Bounds arrived in Leigh with his wife, Mary and their family, as the new vicar in 1957. John served the parish faithfully until his retirement in 1980, having looked after the parish for nearly a quarter of a century. John died in 1997 and his ashes are in the Churchyard. Here, his wife Mary, who did much to support her husband and care for the village, talks about their arrival.

"It was a long journey from our first parish in Hertfordshire. But we soon settled in. We had so much help from people in the village when we arrived. The Old Vicarage was big but it was ideal for us and the family. We made the dining room into a table tennis room and it became a meeting place for all the young people. We also put a railway layout in one of the attics. The cellars were used by some of the older village boys for growing mushrooms! Very successfully.

The 'Old Vicarage' in the 1930s. It was in fact the new vicarage when it was built at the end of the nineteenth century. The present vicarage was built in the late 1950s.

The Church porch, with the circular stone area in front, laid in memory of the 2nd Lord Hollenden in 1977.

The annual Church Fete in the very big garden was a day everyone looked forward to each year. I can hardly remember any wet days. It was a lot of hard work but it was fun and full of friendship.

After we had been in the village for a few years, it was decided to build a new vicarage in one corner of the garden and sell the old vicarage. The new building did make the housekeeping easier; but it lacked some of the romance of the big old building, as many of the older generation in the village will remember.

One great event was the laying of the 'Friendship Circle' outside the Church porch in 1977 in memory of Lord Hollenden. The idea was that it would be a good meeting place after church to talk and greet friends. It got called 'The Lot of Gossip Circle'! The Memorial Wall was another wonderful idea and reflected on the kindness of the Hollendens and the Kindersleys and the others who helped start the project. The names bring back so many memories – Nora Mills – who ran the Sunday School and Mr Mellor who was a most faithful organist for many years. And all the others. Both the Hollendens and Kindersleys entered into all the social gatherings in the village and there was no feeling of them and us which so helped in the happiness of the village.

But time doesn't stand still and all our little children from the Leigh days are over forty and many of the children John baptized will have children of their own by now."

St. Mary's Leigh

PROPOSAL FOR A WALL OF MEMORY ON THE NORTH SIDE OF THE CHURCHYARD

Leaflet printed in 1977 to explain the idea of a Memorial Wall in which people of the village could buy a space for a plaque in memory of their late relatives. To date a hundred and sixty people are remembered on the Wall, including John Bounds.

Don King

Don King was born in Hildenborough in 1931 "but my family lived in Leigh at various times, certainly as far back as the 1870s or 1880s. My mother – who was a Martin – told me about her grandmother who must have lived in West Lodge. When the Morley family wanted to go to Penshurst Station – and it must have been the only line at that time – they would drive up with the carriage and horses and blow a klaxon horn. Great Granny kept a bonnet and white apron on the back of the lodge door and she'd rush out and open the big gate and make a curtsey. Then the same would happen when the carriage came back – even if it only had a nanny or whatever in it. Great Granny got a loaf of bread a day for that.

The West Gate of Hall Place c1910 where Don King's great grandmother lived.

My mother's still alive aged 95. She remembers when they lived on the Green at Leigh in a bungalow somewhere over near the old cricket pavilion. One night father had been to the Bat and Ball and he was coming back across the Green in the middle of a huge thunderstorm which frightened mother; so she let out a terrific yell. Father heard her and thought it was a burglar or something, so he started running and fell over the chains round the cricket square. It nearly killed him. When he got home, he was ready to do worse to Mum than a burglar.

When I was a boy just at the end of the war, my Dad was often in Leigh. He knew Frank Barkaway who lived at the main Great Barnetts house. Mr Barkaway had two racehorses – he was a dealer – he dealt in everything – a great fat man. My father used to drive these horses round in a cattle truck – it wasn't a proper horse box – with Joe Pointer who used to ride them. Eventually, when one of the horses was being ridden by a proper jockey at Goodwood, the proper jockey found he couldn't control it and it went into a fence and broke a shoulder. It had to be put down. Father was very upset.

Once – when I was only a lad – I was up at Great Barnetts and one of Mr Barkaway's donkeys ran across the road and went into a pond there. It was summer and the pond was very muddy and the donkey got stuck. It took hours to get him out. We put corrugated iron sheets down and I went out and put a rope round its neck. Then everyone hauled it out – it was completely covered with mud.

When I left school I went to work at Hawden Farm. It's between the Powder Mills and the railway line. It was owned by Mr Neville Smith. They still used horses at the end of the war and I started as the waggoner's mate under George Scudder. We had four horses – Darkie, Dolly, Bonnie and Nobby. Mr Smith used to say 'You can't keep a lame horse' – which I didn't like because you ought to look after animals that have done a good job for you. Anyway, George Scudder used to keep on working outside when it was raining after he'd sent me inside. I'd be polishing the horse brasses and he'd still be out in the rain. One day he got pneumonia and quite soon after he died. His widow lived in a farm cottage and she asked if she could stay on. Mr Smith said it was quite all right – she could stay, as long as she was out by the end of the month.

I was only a lad but Mr Smith kept me on and made me the main waggoner. We worked all the hop gardens down there. And there were pigs as well. I'd take them along to the Leigh slaughter house.

Later, I drove coaches for my dad's firm, Kingsway Coaches. I remember picking up the men and women from the Leigh Golden Years

Club where the telephone box is now and taking them up to some of the big houses around here for tea – 'Mountains' where Dr Fraser, the son of the old Dr Fraser who was in Leigh, used to live; and to The Long Barn down Coldharbour Lane to play bowls – places like that.

Then I went out on my own and started to do tree work and demolition. Once I took down a huge chimney in Paddock Wood. I cut it down like a tree. It took me half a day to cut the brick out at just the right place – the walls were two foot thick. It had to land in a gateway between some buildings: and it did. I knocked down the old Redleaf House too. I had skip lorries and I called the firm Kingbins and I've bought quite a bit of farm land at different times. I started as a boy with a bike – an Armstrong – it cost five pounds – and now I'm pretty well-known around here as a farmer – the auctioneers don't even have to ask for our number."

Bonnie and Darkie with Don King and Malcolm Coomber at Hawden Farm about 1946

Don King in 1999.

GROWING UP IN LEIGH IN THE MIDDLE OF THE CENTURY

"Perhaps you've had a romantic picture of the village painted by people who were born in Leigh. But it did not really always nurture its children. Even after the Second World War, I remember it as having a very strict class and social structure out of which one did not stray. Everyone knew everyone else's business – nothing was missed and the village could be a stifling place to grow up in. Many of the younger generation had to get away to find suitable employment. Newcomers who moved in and commuted to London were resented."

Bet and
Joan Smith

(Mrs Joan Sargeant)

*B*et Smith and Joan Sargeant are sisters. They were nearly born in the village. Joan was two and Bet three months when they moved to their present home in Barnetts Road in 1926. But grandfather and grandmother Smith had lived in Leigh, the middle of the three Lightfoots Cottages, since the 1890s when their grandfather worked at Price's Farm, then later at Hall Place.

Lightfoots c1908.

"Grandfather wasn't really a Leigh person. He'd been born in Chiddingstone or somewhere like that. And Granny Smith was born in Wellers Town or Charcott – she had that funny accent. She'd say 'CHA-AIR' instead of 'chair' and 'WATTER' instead of 'water'. She was short and wiry, and even when she was in her seventies, she'd run in the races they had each year in the Park. She'd pull up her long skirts. Of course, we'd egg her on. And she'd play leap-frog too – properly, with all the jumping over people. I always remember her bringing back baskets full of fish from Tonbridge". Grandmother Smith died in 1954 aged 85 but Grandfather Smith had died in 1931. "I can't remember him much", says Bet. "He died of congestion of the lungs. I got it too. I was five. My Aunt Nance saved my life. She came round and gave my mum five pounds for a bottle of brandy. She said she'd rather give it to me now, than for flowers for a grave. Aunt Nance had a parrot. It lived in their flat above Forge Square at the end and, when the doctor or the vicar came, he'd say 'don't you hurt my mother you old bugger' – he didn't like them much. And he'd whistle at girls and watch the football out of the window and yell 'goal' when they scored".

Bet and Joan's father, Cecil Smith, was born in 1899 in Lightfoots, the third son, following William and 'Uncle Frank'. "The older two brothers went to school in the Old School House in Powder Mill Lane which was for boys only and was a penny a week – not the school where it is now. After Dad left school – the one on the Green that had girls – he went to work in the Powder Mills. They sent the gunpowder down the river in barges. Half way through the Great War, he lied about his age and joined the Buffs – the Kent lot – I don't know what their real name was – and he went to France as a cook. He got gassed – mustard gas – and he lost one of his lungs. That was when he learnt about duvets. He was in hospital in Germany and he used to say that you slept on a feather bed and you had a feather bed over you. But he wouldn't ever talk about the War – except to say you had to kill the fleas by pressing the seams of your trousers". Uncle Frank was shell shocked and William, who had gone into the Army earlier, was killed. "Forty years later when Granny was dying, she called out for Will – where was he?"

"After the War, Dad went to Cardon temporary – although he stayed for thirty one years. They were the fencing and gates firm by the station at Chiddingtone Causeway. He started on fencing and was promoted to gates. Mr and Mrs Cardon lived in a house with a tin roof behind where they built Fairlawn, past Lightfoots. Mrs Cardon – she was French – she looked as if she'd fell in a flour bin. She was lovely. When they sold up, Dad went to work in 'O-So-Kool' in Tonbridge who made fridges for caravans and things; then he ended up at Hunter Seal at the Powder Mills. He retired in 1975.

He used to make a few bob by selling the rhubarb he grew in the garden and he used to sharpen saws. It was a shilling for a big one and sixpence for a small one. He'd sharpen shears and scissors too. There was one man who went to his death owning Dad nine pence. I know who it was too. He used to sharpen the butcher's saws – Mr Whitehead that was. Mum never really got on with Mr Whitehead, although he could be quite kind.

He'd weigh up the meat and if it came to four shillings and tuppence, he'd let some people have it for four shillings. But Mrs Whitehead didn't like that. She used to watch him and wouldn't let him get away with a penny.

At home Dad never did the cooking unless Mum was ill. But he always cut the bread and Mum always did the carving. But if anyone wasn't well or needed anything in the night, Dad would say 'You have 'em all day: I'll have 'em all night'. And he'd come and take you downstairs if there was a thunderstorm and you were frightened.

Mum and Dad had got married on 3 June 1923. Mum was Sophie Peacock and she'd been born in Shipbourne. First of all, they went to live in Tonbridge. Then in 1926, they were offered a house either in Garden Cottages or this house in Barnetts Road. They chose this one because it had a proper bathroom and Garden Cottages didn't. And they said there was another thing too – Garden Cottages had a coffin door. That meant you couldn't get a coffin down the stairs – you had to bring the body down first. We can remember all the people that moved into Barnetts Road when they were new – the Clarks, Mrs Lidlow who used to watch everything that went on – she must have wore the lino out – Dolly Ready and so on. Sheila Whitebread's parents moved there a few months later".

Both sisters went to the village school. "Miss Ellis – she was wonderful. She'd used to look after us little ones really properly. When it was cold, we weren't allowed to leave until she'd seen that every one of us had our coats buttoned up properly, and our scarves and mittens on. On Fridays she'd tell us a story. She'd say, 'All sit quiet and close your eyes'. Then she'd bring round a sweet and put it in our hands and she'd start when we all had the sweet in our mouths. I'd like to see my grandchildren having a teacher like her.

In the summer, we used to go for a fortnight's holiday to my Aunt at Hildenborough. We used to skip in the road and Aunty said we couldn't and I said we could and she said we couldn't. So I went home. I was a sod some days. I'd tweak the others. And we used to have a dog and I'd say 'bite Joan, Punch'. And we'd roll out of the door into the snow with a saucepan and fill it up. When it melted, we couldn't understand it". "And Bet used to eat mud too..."

Just before the War, Joan left school. "I was fourteen and I went into service in Tunbridge Wells. It was horrible. I was a between-maid, which meant the worst of everything. I had to help a horrible old cook and had to help upstairs. I wasn't there long – it wasn't what I wanted. I really wanted to be a nanny but Mum didn't want me to. I would have had to have gone to learn in Somerset and she said it was too far away. So I went to work for the most distrustful parson's wife there ever was – down in Tonbridge – not in Leigh. She locked up everything. I did give her a mouthful when I left. So did my Mum. I worked at various places after that during the War."

Once, when the two sisters were outside the Barnetts Road house in the middle of the Battle of Britain, they saw "a ball of fire coming over the roof. It seemed to lift up, it just missed the house and went into the barn in Old Kennards – the Sandeman's house now. It was a German plane. They got the pilot's body out and he was buried in the churchyard". Bet and her friend Kathy Passingham, aged 14 and 12, felt they had to do something. "We used to collect flowers – just wild flowers because we couldn't afford to buy them – and we'd put them on the grave. He was someone's son".

In 1950 Joan went to work at Paul's Hill Farm for Miss Goodwin for five or six years. "I did a bit of everything. I did the milking – on Sundays I had to get up at 4am to do it. Dad used to get up too and give me a cup of tea to see I was all right. And I'd help with the calving and feed the sheep – AND chase them when they got in the hop fields. I'd do the hop picking in my spare time – Mum used to come – she loved it. Then in 1957, I got married to Albert Sargeant – it was in the Tunbridge Wells Registry Office. We went to live in Tunbridge Wells at first; then we came back here to live with Mum and Dad; and then we went to live in Myrtle Cottage which was where Saxby Wood is now. Albert had a grandson, Johnny, who was nearly three when we married. Albert died seven years later – Doctor Glaisher had to come out specially to tell me; no one else would – so I adopted Johnny properly and brought him up."

Bet hated hop picking. "It got your hands so dirty. I left school at fourteen too and I did daily work. It was seven days a week – including Sundays. I got seven and six a week. I gave my Mum five shillings and I had two and a tanner. I can't remember what I spent it on. I worked at Yardley Park School. I remember we had another maid there and we were taking food along to the Headmaster and a heart rolled off the plate all along the corridor. She just picked it up and we put it back on the plate. Once all the children caught chicken pox. Joan came and took me to the cinema and, when we came out, she saw spots all over me and took me home. After that, I joined the airforce and ended up as a batwoman – a whole crowd of us – in Mildenhall with 15 Bomber Squadron. You'd stand outside and count all the planes back home. It was worse when the weather was too bad and they'd get diverted. Then you had to wait till the next day for them to come – or not. After the War, they said we could fly over Germany, so I went the once to look – in the bomb bay. I came out at the end of 1947 and had my twenty first birthday party at home. The Vicar, the Rev. Sealy came.

Pauls Hill Farm and Oast House in the 1950s, worked by Mr William Goodwin and later by his daughter Ethel as tenants of the Penshurst Estate. The farm and outbuildings have now been sold and made into three houses.

Measuring the hops c1930. In the picture are Albert Childs, Sid Dann and Sam West, together with Miss Ethel.

I went back into the WRAF in 1951. I was a corporal. We had Ladies Nights – with the band playing. They were called 'Meadows Nights' when they were all ladies. Usually there was a sergant in charge but sometimes I had to be in charge myself. We had this WRAF officer who was a sod but I remember after one dinner, she came out and said 'I didn't realize Sergeant West wasn't here'. It was the highest compliment I could have got.

I came out of the WRAF after three years and then in 1955 Gordon was born. Now he's out in the States in Rhode Island – Woonsocket – flying all over the country for his job. When I got back to work, Mum looked after Gordon. I went to Elliott and Spears in Hildenborough where Fidelity are now. They made lampshades. Then in 1960 I went to work at Penshurst Place for Lady De Lisle – she was Viscount Gort's daughter and there was a big picture of him over the fireplace. Then around 1970, I went to work at Ramshurst for the old Lord and Lady Kindersley and I'm still there with the next Lady Kindersley. I've seen all her children grow up – and they're still nice".

"Uncle Frank didn't marry. He lived at Lightfoots with Granny until she died; then on his own until he was run down by a car which didn't stop. He went to the Bat on Friday nights; to the Fleur on Saturday nights; and to the Brickmakers on Sunday nights. Granny – his Mum – used to say he'd got to be back home by nine o'clock or she'd come and get him. I don't think she ever did but she give him a right tongue lashing – real tongue pie it was".

Both sisters, totally part of the village, love living here – but they look back on their early years in Leigh as a far superior time. "Things don't change for the better – that's the trouble. We had a really good time in the village when we were young". "Yes, it's worse. You don't know anyone. You go down to the shop and pass dozens of people – no one says good morning – except you! There's no open spaces. Down The Green Lane there was nothing; and in front of our house and behind it there were just fields. They've ruined the village – they've built everywhere". "And the bus service ran every hour right up until ten o'clock and they went to Tunbridge Wells. There were the dear old steam trains – although I used to turn away when I was little because I didn't like the sound of the steam. My Johnny used to stand in the sink at Myrtle Cottage and watch the fire box in the engines. Now the line's electrified".

Both sisters have strong views on religion in the village. Bet remembers the variety of vicars – some of whom she considers better than others. "Mr Eyre Walker was terrific. He was only here seven or eight years just after the

War. He wasn't married. He lived with his mother and father and sister in the big old vicarage. He prepared Joan for confirmation. He visited people. He came round one Boxing Day because Mum was ill and he had a cracker and a piece of cake and a cup of tea. His mother, Elinor, used to have hymn singing before the service on Sunday nights; and Wednesday evenings too. It was really fun. Mr Sealy was smashing too – before the War. But he used to forget names and times. Lots of brides used to have to get him from doing the gardening for weddings. And John and Mary Bounds used to visit people, too. They were here over twenty years. Once I told one of our vicars what I said to the Jehovah's Witnesses the other day – 'I don't need an old church on the hill to talk to the Lord: I can do it on the Green'." Joan agrees.

Bet also has views on gardening. "If I ever win the Lottery – if I did ever move out of my house – it's just going to have a window box and a gardener to do it. But we won't leave Leigh".

Anthony Woodburn's internationally known clock shop which was in Orchard House for twenty years until the late 1990s. The grills were installed after a 'ram-raid'. The shop has now been reconverted wholly into a house.

Eric Batchelor

ric Batchelor was born in Brockley in 1920 but came to the Powder Mills when he was three months' old. In 1949 he moved to Leigh with his wife Daisy and for many years he has been a pillar of the commu-nity – on the Parish Council, participating and organizing its sports clubs and helping with in many other affairs in the village. He is President of the Cricket Club, Chairman of the Football Club, President of Tonbridge and District Table Tennis League, President of the British Legion Club, Chairman of the Leigh United Charities, a trustee of the Crandalls Charity and treasurer or auditor for a good number of other village organizations.

"The thing I am probably proudest about is the new cricket pavilion which took years to fund and a vast amount of effort. Our family spent probably hundreds of hours in fund-raising for the building. I know there are people in the village who don't like the look of it but it's just right for what we need it for – for the cricketers and soccer players and stoolball players. People don't realize the problems there were with the plans. It's used by lots of other village organizations, too. What do the people who complain want? – the old green corrugated shed we had before which most of them never saw?

Eric Batchelor, Kings Scout 1933 – at the Powder Mills.

I'm not really a Leigh person. I'm from the Powder Mills. I didn't actually live in the village until I was twenty nine. My mother died in childbirth, so when I was three months old, we moved back to the Powder Mills where my family had lived for generations. I was brought up by my grandparents on my father's side – my father married again and lived just down the road – and I can trace my forebears back to John Batchelor in 1851 who was a gunpowder maker. He was my great grandfather. My grandfather was in an explosion at the Powder Mills factory during the First World War and, in 1927, one of my uncles and a man called Scott were killed in another explosion. My father was a storeman there, too. But in the early 1930s, with the threat of war, the gunpowder factory was moved to Scotland, leaving many local people – including people in Leigh – unemployed. The factory land and the cottages which went with it were sold off. Later, other businesses came in – Bridge Chemicals, SmithKline French, Ward Adams, Vivien Chemicals and Hunter Seal and so on. A few houses have been built since the last war, but the twenty three original cottages and the two managers houses are still there, although they're all privately owned now.

During the 1920s and 1930s, when I grew up there, the Powder Mills was a thriving little community of its own. There was a forge and iron works and it had its own social club. I learnt my billiards there – it wasn't snooker so much in those days – and we had darts and cards and table tennis. We had our own soccer pitch and a cricket pitch at Meopham Bank on the Hildenborough Road. Each Christmas there was a big party in the Club Room for the children of people who worked at the Powder Mill. We used to play hockey on roller skates down the hill to the Plough – by Rooky Wood. It was always worth telling the girls about the ghost of the Children family from Ramshurst Manor who haunted Rooky Wood – to give them a fright – especially at night when we were playing 'Jack! Jack! Strike A Light'. I had a wooden cart – most of the lads from the Powder Mills did – and we had races down Rooky Wood Hill. As we got older, we'd get our cycles out and go all over the place.

My grandfather died in 1932. So when I was twelve I became the man of the house really – looking after things – the garden, the allotments, and so on – with my grandmother and Aunt Ruth in one of the small cottages. Money was short – my grandmother only had a widow's pension and my Aunt Ruth worked part-time as a cook.

I didn't have much to do with Leigh until I joined the Leigh Scouts when I was about twelve – although we played cricket and soccer against them and Haysden; and I boxed against Leigh once. The Scouts were run by Daisy Walton and Herbie Russell. We had great days in the old Scout Hut. I became a King's Scout. Daisy Walton gave me a box camera for doing it – I've still got it. I carried the Scout banner at Canterbury Cathedral and became a Rover Scout and finally an Assistant Scout Master. The highlight of the year was the summer camp at Studland. When War broke out in 1939, we were down there. Herbie Russell gave me the boys' train tickets and a five pound note and asked me to get them back to Leigh. I think we spent most of the five pounds on crisps.

Most of the Powder Mills children walked to Leigh School until they were eleven but I went to Hildenborough School. I walked down to the railway bridge at Hildenborough, then across the fields to Riding Lane. I didn't get a scholarship to the Judd School at first, so both my grandparents – on my mother's and father's side – agreed to send me to Judd as a fee paying student. To their great relief, after two years I won what they called a Foundation Scholarship. I played lots of sports for the school – cricket, rugby, athletics, boxing. My father was a great sportsman. Some of his genes must have been passed on to me!

When I left Judd, I became an assistant in the Collectors Office in Tunbridge Wells. The job was set up under the Poor Law Act. Under the Act, parents, sons, daughters, and even grandparents were assessed on their means to make a contribution towards the cost of any relative who had received help from the State – either in hospital or money from the Relieving Officer for food and lodging. After this assessment, it was my job to visit and endeavour to collect money from these 'liable relatives'. It was never easy – very often if they saw me coming, the door would not be opened and I would have to try to catch them in the street! I remember often trying to get money from mothers who owed a midwifery fee, too. I found the best time was after hop-picking when money was available. Some of the children could be three or four years old before their mothers were out of debt for the midwife. Others owed money for a contribution towards the cost of relatives being in Pembury Hospital. A Medical Officer from Pembury Hospital looked after what was called 'the sick poor'. Most people bought stamps for health insurance for the doctor or the hospitals but not everyone. The Collector's Office was above the Relieving Officer in Calverley Road, Tunbridge Wells and there would be a weekly queue of people waiting to receive their Poor Law relief benefit – very similar to what's given out by Social Security or the Benefits Agency today. While I worked in the Collector's Office, I was studying to be a Relieving Officer.

Scout leader Herbert "Herbie" Russell in the mid 1930s at Studland Camp.

Miss Daisy Walton, Studland Camp, mid 1930s.

Leigh Scouts at Studland 1933. Pictures taken by Eric Batchelor.

The war came in 1939, together with the air raids. I'll never forget my first sight of the day-light bombers. There appeared to be hundreds of them flying above you – I had never seen so many airplanes. I used to cycle to Tunbridge Wells with another Leigh lad – Ken Eldridge – and we'd watch the dog-fights as we went to work up Castle Hill on the Pembury Road. Daisy and I were courting and I would cycle back with her to Tonbridge. One night when I was returning home along the water fields between Tonbridge and the Powder Mills, a bomber dropped its bombs in front of me. I cycled past a line of bomb craters leading up to the Powder Mills. I was sure that one had dropped in the centre of the Mills. The last one dropped short, but I've never been so scared and frightened.

I was called up in 1941 and went into the R.A.F. I think we were meant to go to Singapore but, as that fell while we were on our way, we finally landed in Cape Town. Over the next few years, I worked on aircraft engines and in my spare time, my sport stood me in great stead – very often we flew to away games.

After I was demobbed, I went back to my old job in Calverley Road, Tunbridge Wells – there were still people to be chased for money – but in 1948, the new National Health Service came into being and the work of a Relieving Officer ceased to exist. So I went to work at the Kent and Sussex Hospital. I was one of the first to work in the NHS. In 1949 we moved to Sherwood Park and, as I had done book-keeping at night school before the war, I started studying to be an accountant. It was hard work, particularly with a wife and two small children and a bent for playing cricket and foot-ball. I had to pay for all my studies; no days off or the cost of your corre-spondence course or your entrance examinations; but I did qualify. I continued to work for the local Health Authority for over thirty years. I enjoyed the work and I was within twenty minutes of playing on Leigh Green. I finished up as Deputy Treasurer, working on a budget of over £60 million a year. I retired when I was sixty three but even after that, I continued to work part time for over twelve years, dealing mainly with stocks, shares, brokers and investment managers.

When I had come out of the Airforce there was nowhere for Daisy and me to live, so we went back to the house in the Powder Mills with my Aunt Ruth – my grandmother having died during the War. We were there two years. Eventually with the help of our District Councillor, Mr Morley, who lived in Penshurst Road, we got a house in the Forstal. I was a founder member of the British Legion and so was Mr Morley, which may have helped. So that was how we came to Leigh. Christopher had been born in 1947 and

John was born just after we got here in 1949. I started playing cricket and soccer for Leigh, and have been a member of the two Clubs ever since.

Soon after I came to actually live in the village – it must have been early 1950s, I joined the Parish Council. We had the meetings in the School Room then. The alms houses on the Green needed extensive repairs and a sub-committee was set up. I found an architect willing to do the work for peanuts and we got all the drawings and costings ready. But when we showed them to the full council, they wittered on and on, altering this and that, until I got totally fed up and resigned. I went back on in the Seventies and was on for nearly twenty years. There's never really been any politics on the Parish Council – or not much – which is the way it should be, although I suppose that there was a general Labour feeling after the War, particularly by Dare Jones. The only real problem was money. The Chairman mainly – but some of the councillors as well – did not like to spend money. They were ratepayers. So not a lot was done around the village. Following some retirements and a change in Chairman, Knocky and myself, both being accountants, ran the small Finance Sub-Committee and saw that the Parish Council eventually built up a sufficient cushion for the Council to spend on most of the things that were needed around the village. But we're not going to get enough to re-do the Village Halls properly, let alone help with a new building for the school. Anyway, it's not the job of the Parish Council or the village people to raise money for a new school building. That's the Kent Education Authority's job, although despite some original doubts, the Parish Council has regularly helped to finance items of equipment for the school. Now it seems to be regarded as an annual grant.

I had helped start the British Legion after the war and the branch and club have kept going to this day, although sometimes it's been hard going. I can't remember ever missing a November Remembrance Day Service at the war memorial. Many times I have read out the Roll of Honour, each time thinking of the men I knew – Charles and Gilbert Nixon from the Powder Mills with whom I played when I was young; Leslie Chandler who became a King's Scout when I did and others from cricket and sport – not to mention my own family losses from the first War. Although I can no longer march, I still stand on the parade. I'd had an uncle – Uncle Horace – in the First World War – in the Navy on H.M.S. Formidable. He came home on leave and they flashed up on the screen in the Tonbridge cinema that everyone in H.M.S. Formidable had to report back to the ship. The ship was sunk in the Channel. When my grandmother got a telegram soon after, she said that she knew about it – she'd seen Uncle Horace at the bottom of the bed on the night he had died. I've still got the telegram.

Thinking about changes in the village in the last fifty years or so, I worry about the lack of local employment, the loss of the farms and the farm cottages and the tied houses. It's turned the village in to a commuter estate. Even the hop gardens have gone – once there were hop gardens all around the village between the wars, giving the chance to nearly all the villagers to earn some extra cash – often for new clothes for the children. It is also sad to see the lack of shops and businesses in the village. In my early days, Leigh had a butcher, a baker, a dairy, three grocers including a newsagent, a separate post office, three shoe repairers, a forge, even a wireless and cycle repair business – not to mention an undertaker, a slaughter house, and a farmer who sold milk from a milk can on his milk round – 'A pint today Mr Taylor'. Buses used to run hourly and all day on Sundays, there was even a price war between Redcars and Autocars before the war and you could travel to Tonbridge for almost nothing. We've had a huge increase in the number of houses that have been built since the last war but the cost of housing has become too high for many of the older villagers' children – they have to move away and they rarely come back. There seems to me to be a lack of community spirit, too – however many organizations you belong to, you never seem to get any volunteers without them being press-ganged.

But having said all that, who'd want to live anywhere else. I wouldn't. You wouldn't. We live in cuckoo land – what I mean by that is we sometimes don't realize what a good place it is to live. There's no great thefts, or robberies or rapes or murders. There may be a bit of petty vandalism sometimes, or climbing over the roofs of cars, or leaving litter around the re-cycling centre, a bit of graffiti, but it's not really the end of the world – although some people in the village may think it is. In my view, we live in a small protected community compared to the outside world – we even have a special village policeman back again. I don't think some of our villagers realize how lucky they are: who would want to leave and see high rise flats at the end of the road – I wouldn't."

Daisy Kemp

(Mrs Daisy Batchelor)

*D*aisy Batchelor (Miss Daisy Kemp) was born in Chiddingstone Causeway in 1920. The family moved to Charcott when she was seven and she went to Leigh School when she was ten until she was fourteen. She married Eric in 1942 and they have lived in The Forstall since 1949. As well as having run her own catering business, she was a founder member of the Leigh W.I. and the Ladies Stoolball team and played stoolball for Kent. She is Vice President of the Royal British Legion – "I've run the Legion's children's Christmas party for forty years" – and is Vice President of the Leigh Cricket Club – "amongst other things, I've organized the team of helpers for the Club's teas for over forty years!".

"It's not the same now as it was in the village. Before the War you knew everyone. You had all been to the village school together. There were hardly any cars – I can only remember the Parretts and Lord Hollenden having cars – so you stayed in the village more; and there was no TV, so you were out in the streets or the countryside much more. You knew all the workmen in the village – people used to come into the village to work: now they go out of it. The village cottages are all turned into town houses now. There are no farms, so no farm workers and no farm cottages. The farms and farm buildings have all been converted. They've built lots of extra roads and houses in the village too, so it's bigger.

I remember before the War when they built Green View Avenue and then Lealands Avenue; and six houses going up along the Penshurst Road beyond the garage made of corrugated iron that Mr Whitehead had put up. Then after the War, they put up the prefabs – on the school gardens. Then the Council put up the original Forstall houses – they were called Airey homes, made of concrete slabs – and Eric and I were one of the first people to move in. That was 1949. They didn't last though and in 1986 we had to move out for eleven months while they knocked them down and built the present ones – out of brick. Wyndham Avenue and Wyndham Close were built, in the early 1950s I guess, and about the same time Mr Brittain was allowed to build all the other houses along the Penshurst Road, as long as half of them were council houses. Then Charlotte Cottages were put up and Donkey Field and Saxby Wood. Then, more recently, there has been the building of Meadow Bank and The Crandalls, with Well Close the latest. So the village has far more houses than in the 1920s and 1930s. The Green did not even have a properly made-up road round it before the War; and there was a cinder path across it from the school to Powder Mill Lane with a mud path which joined it which went across to your cottage – Oak Cottage. And Oak Cottage was always white – not the pink you painted it! There are no hop gardens now: it's not just the sight of them that's gone: we used to work in them in the autumn. There's not the same kind of community spirit there was. People did things together more then. The last time it happened was the Silver Jubilee in 1977 but up until then the village always had a annual sports day for the children and a big dance in the evening – all ages and classes together – it was a team effort, although I suppose there is the SuperStars each year now. But it's not quite the same.

When you were children, everyone was friends. It didn't matter what your parents did. When we lived in Charcott, my father was a stockman for John Day at Camp Hill Farm. The Faircloths lived at Charcott Farm and their field was at the back of our cottages where we played and fished. They were really nice – although it was a bit different when Mr Porch took over. 'Take the swings down' – he said. But he was from Somerset! But he did let us fish in the ponds, with a bent pin and string. The best one we called the top pond. There was a lovely big log you could sit on. We did catch things too – tiddlers – which we put into a jam jar. Then we'd pour them back at the end of the day. Sometimes the beagles used to meet at the Station Inn – it's the Little Brown Jug now – or at The Greyhound and we'd all go off with our sandwiches and lemonade. We were really tired at the end of the day. We'd play hockey in the road at Charcott with a walking stick and a tennis ball and I used to help in the bakery at Charcott which was two doors away from us. And we had iron hoops and skipping ropes: and dolls and prams: and we played 'Jack, Jack, Strike a Light'. We had great fun with our whipping tops too – 'Window Breaker' and 'Carrot Top'. And I was in the girl guides and the choir at St Lukes. Charcott was a very friendly place – I suppose it was much smaller than Leigh and there were no cars and no council houses then. There was a well on the Green.

I went to the Chiddingstone Causeway School until I was ten. Then the Headmistress changed. There was a row and lots of us children started going to Leigh School. We all used to meet at Compass's Corner and walk to Leigh. The Head was Mr Gibbons – 'Gibbo'. Everyone respected him, even though he did use the cane on the boys – but not nastily. It was a small bamboo stick which he used to hang on the blackboard. Teachers did cane the boys in those days. There were one or two boys who were picked on a bit perhaps. I remember one who was a nasty piece of work. I used to sit next to Mary Stubbins – she lived at 4 Barden Cottages. We'd chatter away and Gibbo would come round behind us and knock our heads together. But Gibbo told all the girls that he would play the organ for them when they got married and he did too for me and Eric; and he brought the choir along. He was also the cricket captain, as well as the organist and head-master. I remember we played stoolball at school with Miss Baker. We played nearer the War Memorial than now: and the dancing which we did in Miss Baker's class room and on The Green. I remember all the children from that time. I still see some of them and reminisce over old times.

When I came to leave school at fourteen, I had to think what to do. I wanted to work in a shop. I don't know why. But my father said 'no'. My mother had been a cook and I could cook, so I ended up in domestic service in a house in Penshurst. I lived in and I was paid five shillings a week. I got half day off on Thursday and every other Sunday. I was there for four years, working under a cook. She came in after breakfast, so I had to get up at six thirty to get everything ready – the fires and the breakfast. There were the two parents and the two children plus a nursery maid to cook for. In the winter, I made porridge in a double saucepan and in the summer they had cereals. Then there was eggs and bacon and things, although I particularly remember smoked haddock with poached egg. The plates had to be hot. There was a housemaid and a gardener. Cook was in her fifties and I was only fourteen but we all got on well together. There were no problems. She could cook too – she was a really good cook. Each day she would talk to the lady of the house about what we were going to have to eat, then she would tell the gardener what was wanted. We didn't have a fridge in those days obviously, but you had a larder which was cold, with a marble slab. They always put larders on the north side of a house. We kept flavouring and things for years – not like today with their 'sell-by' dates – what a joke. After breakfast, there was what we called 'Elevenses' and the children had their main meal at lunchtime. Cook would prepare it and I'd take it up to the nursery on a tray. You'd always have a roast for Sunday lunch, which often meant bubble and squeak on Monday, which was always washing day. The grown-ups would have their main meal in the evening, except Sundays. There was soup or something like that: then the main course, chops or steaks or chicken or pies with lots of vegetables; then for sweets you'd have rice puddings or blancmanges or what you'd nowadays call the solid things – jam sponges and so on. The table had to be perfectly laid out – a white damask table cloth and linen napkins.

Of course, you had different food when you were like my parents, a farm worker. Boiled eggs – anything to do with eggs; rabbits because my father was good with his catapult; and coloured chicken – you know what that is? It's pheasant. The chickens were in a run at the bottom of our large vegetable garden, so we had plenty of fresh veg and fruit.

After four years in Penshurst, I got a job as a cook. I was only eighteen but it didn't seem too difficult – I'd always done it really. It was in Tonbridge, just before the War started. There was a mother and daughter plus another daughter who went away to be a physiotherapist and a son, who went off to be in the Navy. When the War broke out, two evacuees came.

The first women to be called up were those born in 1920. So I had to do something for the War effort. Eric said I couldn't join up – we were engaged by then. I'd seen him on the Green when I was seventeen and we got engaged when I was nineteen and married with a Special Licence when I was twenty-one – on a Thursday. It was 12 March 1942.

It was at Leigh Church and Mr Gibbons did play, as promised. It was a Special Licence because Eric only had a short embarkation leave. Anyway, I didn't want to work on a farm and I did want to be in engineering. So I went on a course at the Tunbridge Wells Technical College and I ended up on a centre lathe in an engineering works in Maidstone. We got the blue prints but we never knew what the parts were for. We had to get each part right to the nearest thousandth of an inch with a micrometer. I joined Maidstone Cycling Club too, and did a lot of cycling.

After the War, I was in a catering firm. I worked my way up from the washing up to doing the important cake icing. I did a special course on it. Later, I ran my own catering firm. I gave it up when they wouldn't let you use raw eggs in the Royal Icing. Ridiculous!

I need to tell you about stoolball in the village. Although lots of villages had had ladies teams for years, Leigh didn't seem to have had one. I'd first played stoolball when I was ten on the Causeway cricket ground and I played at Leigh School, and lots of the other women in the village had played it at school too. So in 1951, we started the Leigh Ladies Stoolball Club – almost as an evening out for us all. We left the husbands at home, looking after the post war children. The first year's sub was a shilling. Then, when we joined the League the next year, it became two and six. We won the League twice – 1961 and 1965 and we were runners up in 1966. I was playing for Kent by then, as wicket-keeper, and I'm still Vice President of the Kent League. The teams Leigh play against now are still most of the original ones we played in the 1950s – Edenbridge, Langton, Speldhurst, Groombridge, Bidborough, Chiddingstone and so on. I was captain for about three years but we'd swap it around and I'm still President even now. My best score for Leigh was a hundred and eleven not out in 1954 and Eric gave me a stoolball bat which was specially made for me by Jack Pride in Camden Road. That's really good because you know just what weight you want and what width of handle is right for your hand. We always used to have enough players. Nowadays it's not so easy. It's like the cricket. It's fading.

Stoolball - the Kent team walking out to field against North Sussex on the Green at Leigh in June 1960. There were two Leigh players – Daisy Batchelor and Betty Middleton, second and third from the left. The old green pavillion which had stood from 1897-1971 is in the background.

It's the same with the W.I. We started the Evening W.I. in 1956 because we all had children and couldn't get to the afternoon W.I. We started with twenty members and it got up to fifty. But eventually it was down to fifteen, so we packed up and most of us joined the Afternoon W.I. We had been going for thirty years, so that wasn't bad. We still go for walks and outings.

Everyone in the village has always helped each other. No one really went short in the 1930s, however poor they were, or during the War, or during the rationing, even during the terrible winter in 1946/7 – it really was the worst ever. We were living at 6 Powder Mills, where we were before we moved here to the Forstall. Eric had just been demobbed. It was so cold but Eric and his father went out collecting wood and I sat in front of a roaring fire with half coal and half wood, very pregnant with our first son, Christopher, rubbing my tummy with olive oil to stop the stretch marks! It worked too! Our friends used to come down from London and take kit bags of wood back on the train and very often a rabbit and fruit and vegetables as well. It was like that then.

❋

Colin and MaryAnne Stratton-Brown

*C**olin and MaryAnne Stratton-Brown arrived in Leigh in 1967. Colin had come out of the Navy the year before and was working in the City for a shipping line.*

"Leigh was an accident really. We didn't like the idea of Surrey; and this part of Kent seemed good for commuting. The trains went to Cannon Street, so I didn't even have to use the tube. When we were house-hunting, we spotted a house in Green View Avenue on the market and we thought it would be much nicer than a house on a housing estate. The rates in Leigh were much cheaper than Bromley where we had been living and made up for the extra cost of the annual season ticket. Incidentally, if anyone tells you that the commuting is awful today, it is much better than it was in the late sixties and early seventies. Nowadays, I comment if I have to stand. Back then, I was only able to say 'I had a seat today' once or twice a year. And there are no mystery tours around south London ending up in Victoria as happened on several occasions, including after the Hither Green disaster.

When we arrived, our only car, or the only one that went, was a 1933 Rolls-Royce. Both the grocers, Mr Coates and Mr Wells (who ran the post office store on the Green), called on us shortly after our arrival seeking our custom. Mr Coates took one look at the car and said 'I can see you will be supporting my shop'; as it turned out, we actually supported both. We can just remember the blue paper bags for sugar which Mr Coates was still using. There was a problem with the plumbing and we were advised to contact Vic Fry who lived in Penshurst Road. He had been a qualified Royal Naval plumber and he saw our wedding photograph with me in my Naval uniform. He must have spread the word, because after about three weeks in the village I went to Mr Wells, the butcher – he was brother to the other Mr Wells. Mr Wells said to me, 'As you were a Supply Officer in the Navy, I am sure you would wish to inspect the premises'. So he showed me round the shop including the cold stores at the back. Shortly after this, I was inveigled into the British Legion by John Ponton. They wanted ex-servicemen to join because the number of ex-servicemen determined how many civilians could become associate members and use the Club. So I came to meet many people who had spent most of their lives in the village such as Harry and Jack Lucas. I ended up doing a spell as Treasurer of the Branch and, for a few years, Treasurer of the Club. After we'd been in the village a few weeks, we'd made more contacts than we'd made in Bromley in nine months.

We went to the Church and after nearly a year, I went to the annual church meeting. After the meeting, Phyllis Upfield, while looking at me so I could hear, said to John Bounds 'There is someone who could bring down the average age of the PCC'. So I joined. In addition to being on the PCC, I've been a Churchwarden for a total of fifteen years. The first time, after I had completed seven years, I had to struggle to find someone to take over as it was assumed I would stay on indefinitely. I thought it really ought to rotate. On my third spell as a Churchwarden, I found myself coping with the interregnum between Christopher Miles and Tom Overton. It was a huge amount of work, not only interviewing applicants but also arranging clergy to take those services which required an ordained priest but I was very lucky with all the help given by the lay readers, Winifred Genner, Audrey Price, Harold Farrington and David Sellicks, not only in taking the other services, but also covering pastoral work. One activity was actually fun – the rebuilding of the wall round the church-yard. David Sellicks had found a bricky; and he and I, with help from some teenagers, spent a long time chipping cement off the old bricks so that they could be reused and mixing the cement for the bricky, who was called Dave.

When we first came to live in the village, there was a flourishing Sunday School run by Mary Bounds. In those days, many parents sent their children to Sunday school, even if they themselves only attended church for the festivals. However, in the last few years, the Sunday school is active again, although nowadays it is used mainly by children whose parents are attending church at the same time. There is much more involvement of the laity nowadays – it is not all left to the Vicar. Sidesmen are actually asked to act as sidesmen and to read lessons, rather than this being left to the Churchwardens.

I wish the village still had fresh meat. It is sad that the slaughter house has gone and, recently, the butcher. It is also regrettable that the ditches have been filled in. When we had the big flood in 1968, I wandered down the garden to see where the water was draining to. I found that, in common with the water from the other gardens, it was flowing down Green Lane, crossing the road, and flowing through the policeman's house. So several of us cleared the ditch by his house so the water could flow through the pipe under the road, out through the old ditch, bypassing the house.

Perhaps one of the biggest changes in the village is that there are fewer families where generations have been born and brought up in the village and stayed on all their lives. Nowadays, the next generation often does not want to stay in the village but, even if they do, more often than not, they cannot afford the prices which houses in the village now command. Thinking back to when we arrived, one of the biggest surprises was how feudal the atmosphere seemed to be, even if everyone talked to one another and was friendly. It is completely different today – the feudal feeling is gone – but with still the friendliness; it's one of the main reasons people stay here.

The Green under water at the time of the flood in 1968.

'Bombers' is our third house in Leigh. We like being back in the middle of the village. We can walk nearly everywhere. Bombers was once one of the village dairies and we've dug up two milk bottles from the time when Barley Bear and her sister were running the milk round from here. You can still make out the writing on the bottles. It reads:

'Where are you going to my pretty maid?'
'To Old Bombers Dairy, Sir' she said
M & B Faircloth

Surrounding the inscription is the music for the nursery rhyme and a picture of a girl and a boy. We've showed it to Barley Bear.

MARY ANNE STRATTON BROWN

We moved into the village in 1967 and, almost as soon as we arrived, people called at the house to offer help. We had one baby, Henry, and, soon after, Claire was born. I was very surprised when Dr Evans apologized for asking me to go to the surgery for ante-natal check-ups. He said that, in the past, he would visit mothers in their own homes for their last three months. I didn't expect to be visited at home just because I was pregnant. People suggested baby sitters to us and Dorothy Fautly babysat for the children for years.

People seemed to know each other in the village, even if only by sight. When I walked across the Green with my two week old baby, Robert, in the pram, I was asked if I had had a boy or girl by people I barely knew. The same pram ended its days as part of the collection of old prams used by the Afternoon W.I. members for their annual Mother and Baby race – it had the right sized wheels. The 'Mothers', with their at least ten year old 'Babies', raced around the Green.

When we first arrived, I could push the pram round the roads without any worries and it was the same with the children on their bikes; there was so little traffic. Once, I broke down in our old Rolls turning from the Green into the High Street. I was in the middle of the road with people, including Stan Wells, the butcher, trying to push it but no other cars came along.

In the early 1970s, Anna (Rowley) started a playgroup at Oak Cottage with the help of a group of friends including me. After that, our the children moved on to various schools in the area, with our two boys going to Tonbridge and Claire to Tonbridge Girls' Grammar School. They joined the Brownies and Cubs which they enjoyed, especially 'Bob-a-Job' week. Two of our children took up bellringing when they were old enough and also took part in Superstars on the Green. The children used to help me when I did 'Meals on Wheels'. They loved it and the old people liked seeing the children. It's sad it has stopped.

The village celebrated the Silver Jubilee in 1977 with a number of activities. There was a long procession from Hall Place to the Green, led by the Village Green Stompers, and including a W.I. float which was supplied with refreshment by Len and Dora as it passed the Bat and Ball. There were games and later a bonfire on the Green and finally a dance in the Large Village Hall.

The Silver Jubilee Parade on Saturday 11 June 1977 led by The Village Green Stompers founded for the occasion by Chris Rowley, Ted Holden and John Knock (and still playing twenty three years later).

The Post Office celebrating the Silver Jubilee in 1977 with the proud owner, John Henison. The shop was converted to a house and holiday home in the mid 1990s.

EXHIBITION
Organised by the
Leigh and District Historical Society
in
LEIGH CHURCH
Showing the Church, its history, tythe map,
archives and other documents, stained glass,
monuments and furnishings
OPEN

Wednesday	16th May	2 p.m. – 6.00pm
Thursday	17th May	2 p.m. – 6.00pm
Friday	18th May	2 p.m. – 6.00pm
Saturday	19th May	10 a.m. – 6.00pm
Sunday	20th May	11 a.m. – 5.30pm

ADMISSION FREE

Lawrence Biddle preparing for the Historical Society's exhibition in the Church.

Historical Society exhibition held in Spring 1984.

There has always been plenty to do in the village. I helped with the Playgroup for ten years after it started in the Village Hall in 1974 or 1975. Colin did a spell on the Small Village Hall committee and was persuaded into the Civil Protection scheme in its early days. The Tennis Club started in 1980 and, although we were not founder members, we joined early on and have been members ever since and I've been on the committee. There is also the Historical Society which started about twenty years ago. It has mounted several exhibitions, including one about the Church and a joint one with the Parish Council to commemorate 100 years of the Parish Council. But over the last thirty years we have only done the same as many people in the village. Taking part in activities and knowing people in the village is what makes village life special.

❀

Morgen Witzel

M *orgen Witzel and his wife, Marilyn Livingstone, arrived in the UK from Victoria, British Columbia, in 1987. They had both finished university degrees and thought they probably wanted to settle in England which they had visited before and liked. In their twelve years in Leigh, they have both contributed greatly to the life of the village – Morgen spent five years as a Parish Councillor, in particular working with other councillors to try to resolve some of the traffic problems and co-ordinating the campaign against the railway line expansion; he also worked on the Village Design Statement, wrote the story of Leigh during the Second World War, and was Chairman of the Historical Society.*

"We started out in London where we were both working at the London Business School: but central London, in not very perfect flats, was not ideal. So we started thinking of the country – I'd grown up on a farm. We found Leigh completely by chance. Marilyn was going to work and picked up one of the free papers, New Zealand News UK, to read in the bus. She saw an ad for a flat in the country for someone who 'must be fond of dogs, ducks and owls'. So we came to see the Robinsons and both sides agreed to try it out for six months. All our friends said we were mad: 'it will take you half a day to get to London.' As you know, it doesn't; and, anyway, nowadays we are largely running our own two small businesses from Leigh – something that more and more people are doing, incidentally. And now twelve years later .... We're going to Devon mainly because we can't find anywhere large enough that we can afford round here.

Marilyn got involved in village things before I did. She joined the choir and got involved in church things and I think she joined the Historical Society before I did – although I remember that I gave a talk to the Society about the Parish Council records after I'd done an inventory. I got involved in the Parish Council Centenary Exhibition because of that.

It was Diana Wood and John Whitehouse who suggested that I stood for the Parish Council in 1994. They said that a new, outside perspective would be useful. And I do think it is good to have a mix between the old and the new – the people who have known the village all their lives, people like John Knock and Graham Marchant, plus newcomers like me or Alison Gibbs. I think that there is a good mix now. I've been impressed by the dedication of the Parish Councillors too. It takes a certain stick-to-it-ness, sometimes with little in the way of thanks. I am impressed by how well the council works: we do get a consensus between us – maybe surprisingly – on all the important issues.

Probably the only aspect of being on the Parish Council that I have found frustrating is the lack of co-ordination between ourselves and the officers of Sevenoaks District Council – but not our district councillor, Alison Cook, who is wonderful. The Parish Council is meant to represent the village, and we see the people we represent everyday and know pretty well what needs to be done. But the system nowadays doesn't seem to work as it should. The Parish Councils have virtually no power or authority – and even the District Councils seem to have less and less. If you go back to the original 1894 Local Government Act, it gave responsibility and the relevant authority to local bodies like ours. It was sensible. But a lot of that has got lost. Whitehall seems to think that parish councils aren't up to the job – which is rubbish. I worry that this will in time make people blasé about local government, and that we won't get good parish councillors or district councillors. It will be a tragedy if people feel they can't help or work for their own community.

The Parish Council is very important. We do a lot of work that perhaps few people notice, a lot of day to day minutiae which are nevertheless vital and which concern everybody. At one of my first parish council meetings, one of the items on the agenda was whether there should be street lighting on the High Street. In fact, that had been on the agenda of the very first parish council meeting a hundred years before. And a hundred years ago the Council spent many hours on setting up the Alms Houses on the Green: we still spend a good amount of time on them. So maybe not so much has changed.

The major difference nowadays is that all Parish Councils have to deal with dozens of outside bodies – give their views about the wider world – even if I suspect no one takes any notice. We have regular correspondence with South East bodies – about the Gatwick second runway or the endless saga of the rail line – which has taken a great deal of time – or about the SERPLAN proposals for extra housing; and we have to make comments on the police and health and education. Even with the Village Design Statement we had to consult outside, although it is meant to be the village's view of what it wants.

On the whole, I've found my six years on the council very rewarding. It is a fine village. We have both really enjoyed living here. If you can contribute, you feel it is important. Service on the Parish Council is one way of helping out, and putting something back into a community that has given us so much.

We both feel that a great deal of nonsense is talked about the English being aloof. It's not what we have found here – and not what our friends from other parts of the world have found either. On arrival, we could not have been made more welcome, and our departure, for us at least, will be a very sad day.

Footpath between Paul's Hill and Penshurst.

What People in the Village Think of Leigh Now

At the end of 1997, the group working on a document for the Sevenoaks District Council – a Village Design Statement – sent out a long questionnaire to every house asking for people's views on what Leigh was like and what, if any, things could be improved. There was a very large response, representing over four hundred and fifty people, who had on average been in the village for nearly twenty three years each. Here is a summary of what they said.

Respondents used and valued the amenities in the village. The Post Office/shops were most mentioned, followed closely by footpaths, the Green, the pubs, the garage and the trains. Buses were mentioned by half those who mentioned trains. The School and tennis courts were popular and people particularly welcomed the local tradesmen – electricians, plumbers, decorators and so on.

What was known before the survey was the large number of clubs and organizations in the village (thirty nine) but what was cheering was their popularity with those who responded: many people belonged to three or four. The most popular was The Produce Association, then the Historical Society, with The Legion, the Tennis Club, the Church and the Scouts/Cubs/Guides all attracting a good number of supporters. The range of village organizations was cited overwhelmingly by people as one of the most positive things in Leigh – the glue that holds the community together.

When asked what 'built' features they found most attractive, the buildings in general were much liked, with a large number of specific mentions of the architectural detail – the tile hanging, weatherboarding, the brickwork, the chimneys and the Hall Place wall. People also particularly liked the natural features in and around the village – the Green, the footpaths, the limes along the High Street, the woodlands – although there were concerns that the roadsides, the hedgerows and the footpaths were not kept in a good enough condition and concern that open spaces in the village should not be diminished. Footpaths which were especially liked included the walk to the Medway from Green View Avenue; the Pauls Hill path towards Penshurst; and Birdcage Walk. Views that were most frequently mentioned were the view up towards the Church from the Green and the view coming into the village from Hildenborough but clearly those replying felt we lived in a beautiful village which they all felt must be preserved against unsightly development – either with badly designed house extensions or by extra badly designed buildings.

When asked about the people in the village and their attitude, the sense of community was nearly always mentioned, together with the good social mix and the variety of ages. There were a few comments that there were too many newcomers who moved on quickly or were too 'urban-orientated' and one mention that not many A,B,C1s were born in the village. One or two also said how important they felt it was for children to use the village school.

The questionnaire went on to ask about the future. Inevitably there was a huge range of specific suggestions. However, the principal categories were the need to prohibit or at least restrict further growth (remember that Well Close had just been built), together with the need to preserve the open spaces and the present amenities. Street lighting was largely opposed; church bells were approved; and one person thought there were too many cats!

What was overwhelmingly opposed, however, was traffic – the speed or the volume or both, and parking problems, now and in the future. The unlovely exterior (not the practicality!) of the cricket pavilion and dog fouling were the next biggest concerns but there was a wide range of things in the village which people thought were ugly, ill-designed or badly kept up. There was also some concern that there was not enough for children and/or teenagers to do; some concern about crime and lack of policing; and a whole range of sensible (or totally impossible) individual ideas for improvements in the village.

However, the overwhelming view of those who replied to the questionnaire was that Leigh was a good place in which to live – that it had nearly everything people wanted in a village. When asked to give one word which best described the village, whilst three replies said 'endangered'/'threatened', and one said 'dormitory', and one said 'OK', every other word was positive, ranging from 'idyllic', 'charming' and 'delightful' to an overwhelming majority who used the word 'friendly', with 'pleasant', 'picturesque', 'attractive' and 'community', all collecting a fair number of votes – each in their way demonstrating virtually unanimous support for the village at the end of the century.

Leigh School Children 1999

In the summer of 1999, I went with my wife, a former secondary school art teacher and pre-school playgroup leader, to talk with twenty-six children in the top two years at Leigh School. They came in groups, usually of three, mainly best friends, and talked for about fifteen minutes each – occasionally answering our questions about the village and the school; more often just talking naturally.

Leigh Primary School, Class 4, 1999.
Row 4: Ben Pullen, Andrew Bourne, Daniel Lade, Calvin Draper-Wright, Aaron Munday
Row 3: Tom MacGregor, Simon Taylor, Liam Brooker, Kevin Taylor, Andrew Massingham
Row 2: Ayrton Phillips, Laura Warwick, Sheridon Phillips, Sophie Bresnahan,
Lydia Wright, Alice Marchant, Daniel Hall, Ashley Hall
Front: Eleanor Newton, Emma Child, Chantalle Chin, Tamara Gates, Rebecca Manners,
Lizzie Longhurst, Kyrstie Linstead, Hatti Snellgrove, Jo Holt
Teacher: Miss V. Jenkins.   Headteacher: Mrs T. Wright
L.S.A.s: Mrs S. Nevard, Mrs K. Flint

Sophie Breshahan, Hattie Snelgrove and Tamara Gates. Two of the girls live in Leigh and one in Hildenborough, although she has lived in Leigh.

"My favourite thing at school is singing. We've just done 'The Bumble Snouts' – it's a whole play – with Mrs McBride". "She's excellent". "I was one of the narrators". "So was I". "I played the triangle".

"PE is good. We always do rounders". "We can vote for cricket or rounders but rounders always wins". "We play it together with the boys – they like rounders too". "And we play football on the Green with the boys". "The big children look after the little ones on the Green". "And in the summer, we eat our lunches on the Green". "Some have school dinners but it's mainly the little ones". "The boys are horrid to us sometimes – when we're playing soccer".

"Half the class are leaving this year – they're older. We're staying on". "Some of them are whiz kids – they can do the Maths". "Maths is awful". All three agree "but we've got another year".

"We hate homework". "Miss Jenkins sometimes forgets to give us homework but Y says 'Miss Jenkins, can we have our homework' – ugh".

"We've all got computers and PC's at home". "I love them. They're really fun. You can do card games and mechanics and all sorts of things on them".

Is it a good thing to have school uniform? "Yes, probably". "If you had to wear your own clothes to school, they'd get all dirty." "The uniform's not bad really". "I get all my own clothes at Bluewater". "I get mine from Lakeside – in Thurrock". "I normally get dresses. I don't like trousers. I only wear trousers when it's cold in the winter but I wear shorts sometimes in the summer". "And pedal pushers". "I like clothes".

"Leigh's a lovely village". All three agree. "I've lived in lots of places and Leigh's really the best". "If you haven't got a big garden, you can play on the Green". "But nearly everyone has got a big garden". "Not everyone – but, anyway, I can go out through a hole in our back fence into the fields". "It's not dangerous; there aren't many cars – although you should look out". "The village is just big enough". "It's got the Village Shop where you can get things and Mum can go out to buy the meals at the last minute – that's handy".

Sam Rolfe, Kevin Taylor, Daniel Hall, Eleanor Newton, Alice Marchant and Kirsty Linstead. Only two of this group live in the village itself. The others live in Moorden, Knotley Hall, Cowden and a farm nearby. One has a parent who was born in Leigh which is relatively unusual.

How do the boys get on with the girls? The girls are quite clear. "We play football all together in the winter – the boys and the girls together". "The boys make up the rules – they're always hitting each other and kicking each other". "Yes: but if the boys are awful, we ignore them". "Or you punch them – and then go and tell the teacher". "You've got to stick up for yourself". "One boy tried to break my arm, so I bit him".

And if the girls are awful? "We just walk off and play football".

There is a wide variety of pets at home – "a rabbit": "a rabbit and some gerbils": "some mice and a goldfish": "three guinea pigs": "we used to have a dog and some fish but we haven't now": "yes, we've got a big dog and we did have a goldfish but my brother flushed it down the toilet".

While all the children quite liked the village, they are clear that there are extra things that they would like to see because "It's a bit boring". "There should be slides and swings." "And a climbing frame" "And a paddling pool". "There should be somewhere proper to roller blade". "And there should be a basket ball place – it's better than football".

Leanne Turk, Claire Wells and Katie Stephens. Two of the girls had been born in the village and had family connections with the village – "my mother was born and bred in Leigh".

All three feel that they are lucky to live in Leigh. "We've got the Green". "I really like it – it's lovely and peaceful in the village". "Yes, I like it because it's small". "No it's big really". "It's nice and small compared to a town but it's large for a village with things to do". All three agreed with this last analysis.

"You can play on the Green and ride your bike around. I play stoolball too – my Mum plays". "I play cricket and there is the school netball club and I do swimming at the Swimming Club in Tonbridge. I'm quite keen – I'm the best diver in my group". "I have piano lessons with Diana Day, down Green View Avenue". "And we all play rounders in PE at school".

"I don't have to do anything to help at home. We've got a dishwasher and things – so there's nothing to do". "But we have to keep our rooms tidy – a bit". "I'm not allowed to use the Hoover – I've already broken two".

There are the usual disagreements about subjects they like best at school. "Maths is excellent – we're doing long multiplication". "No, it's awful". "We have the Numeracy Hour each day where we all do things by ourselves".

Eddie Alwood, Dominic Bradford and Frankie Baker. Two of the boys come from outside the village – Penshurst and Edenbridge; the third moved to Leigh five years ago.

"Compared to Penshurst, Leigh's much more fun. I come to Leigh all the time. I don't do anything in Penshurst except live there". "Edenbridge is all right. It's got more shops. But this school's nicer". "Leigh's good when there's something to do but – all the old people – they tick you off when you play football. You have to go on the Green and put down your own goal posts." "I play table tennis – that's with John Knock. And I do cricket, that's with John Knock too. He does lots of things with us". "I play tennis with my Dad". "We do roller blading lots and lots. They say they are going to put a proper place with ramps and things for it in the village." "I do cricket and swimming". "Yes, I do swimming too, and I go fishing with my Dad. We go down to the green bridge or the silver bridge. We fish in the river and in the ponds. We get roach and gudgeon and carp. I caught a ten pound one once. That's the biggest I've caught. And I'm going sea fishing with my sister's boyfriend in Portsmouth. He lives there".

All three like PE best. One likes Art but two do not. Geography and History are "all right". "We did the history of Leigh". There is the Literacy Hour and science is interesting – "We are doing weights and electricity": "and sound waves": "and food chains".

All three are going on to Hayesbrook School. They will continue to be together, to their great relief.

Lizzie Longhurst, Charlotte Stokes and Rebecca Manners. The three girls have very different family connections with Leigh. Rebeccas's grandfather was Dick Wood and her grandmother, Ivy, and family have lived in the village for many years. Another has been here for four years. The third has only been here a short time and is just going to Dubai – to her sadness "but I can write to the others on E-Mail – we've all got PC's at home". "We're all best friends".

"We watch telly a lot – the Cartoon Network or we play POD – it's great." – "My favourite thing is eating and sleeping and biking and eating – and eating!" "The Raymond Playstation is brilliant". "I have to play with boys before my Mum comes home ..... ugh "

"My best subjects are PE and Art: they're better than Maths and English. I like PE because I'm good at rounders". "I like Maths best, then Art. We've just been doing the man with an eye here, then another eye down here – Picasso – he's brilliant". "And we did Sunflowers by Van Gogh". "Yes, English, stuff it: writing's boring. And Maths, stuff it".

"Some people have school dinners". "School dinners are ugh – a lot of the younger ones have school dinners. I have a packed lunch. We have it out on the Green."

"The Green is the best thing about the village". "But it can be boring here". "But there's millions of ghosts here". "No, there aren't any ghosts". "Yes, there are. We've got a big pond by us and there are masses of ghosts there". "When I'm in the shower and I've locked the door, then it opens, and closes again. And IT'S in my room." "It could be an alien".

Andrew Massingham and Daniel Lade.The boys are best friends, even though one lives in Leigh and one in Tonbridge.

"I get three pounds a week pocket money – it gets more as I get older – and I can get extra for doing extra things to help – so, I get 10p for doing the washing up or emptying the dishwasher". "I started getting pocket money when I was seven and I get 35p a week now but I've got lots of brothers and sisters: and I get five pounds a month put into my bank account for saving for special things – I'm saving for a playstation." "We've both got computers and PCs".

"As well as using the computer at home, I practise my clarinet. I have lessons at school on Wednesdays." Others at school are learning the piano and one person does the flute and one has a junior clarinet. "I have my own clarinet. The school don't have any instruments but you can hire them".

"PE is the best thing at school but Art is good". Both agree. "Science is OK but I'm dyslexic, so I get special help with English. The Literacy Hour is all right because you have taped stories". "We get divided into five groups for the Literacy Hour. Miss Jenkins splits us up so that the talkers don't all get together – you know who they are ...." "Yes: W is the funniest person in the school – although you don't always laugh at it" – "and he does swear quite a lot ... "

"If you're bad you get a warning. If you get two warnings you get sent to Mrs Tully and then if you're still bad you go to Mrs Wright". "Then you get your name put in the School Book and Mrs Wright sends a letter home". "But no one has actually had that". "You get house points for rewards and get stickers in your own book – you can chose the colours – and when you've got enough stickers, you get a certificate. Everyone in the school has got their own book."

Tom Bellward, Dean Flight and Calvin Wright. One boy lives in Leigh, one in Charcott and one in Tonbridge.

"My best subjects are PE and Maths – I go up to the staff room to do things like decimals and we're doing long division. My worst subject is history – it goes on for ever. We're doing Britain since 1930 – all the war and things. It gets a bit boring". "I don't like Maths – it's hard and I don't like English – I don't like writing. But PE and Art are good. We do rounders and we're studying different artists – Lichtenstein and the person who does the Coke cans – he's called Andy Warhol. Then we try to copy the style". "Yes, English is boring. PE's good. We do rounders unless it's wet. Then we play benchball in the Iron Room. You put a bench at both ends, then it's like basketball except you have to get the ball on to the top of the bench".

"School uniforms aren't a good idea. You all look the same. It's pointless. You can't be yourself." "I think the uniforms are a good idea. If you go on a big outing, you can see everyone from the School in red". "But we don't go on that many outings and anyway there are other schools with red uniforms." "When I'm at home, I like designer clothes. I spend all my birthday money on them". All three agree and given lots of names – Adidas, Nike and so on.

Pocket money varies from family to family and sometimes varies with current circumstances. "I get eleven pounds a month". "I don't get regular pocket money". "All of us – there's four of us – used to get five pounds a week but it's stopped just now because our car went through the hedge".

"At home, we all play games on the computer – racing games – things like that – but, in the summer, we're usually outside. My Mum keeps my room tidy".

"I spend some of my money on tennis – I have coaching lessons at the Tennis Club. And we all go out on our bikes". "Sometimes we play tennis on the Green". "I go fishing with my step-dad. We've got loads of gear. And I'm going sea fishing with my grandfather when I go on holiday. I've got crabbing nets and things".

"We all think it's a good village to live in but there aren't as many shops as there used to be. There used to be the Post Office and shop on the Green by the phone box". "And a butcher". "Yes: and it was only 25p for a can of drink in the old Post Office".

Emma Child, Lydia Wright and Laura Warwick. *Emma and Lydia come from Leigh. Laura lives at Powder Mills. All three families have moved into the area, although the village feels like home to all the girls.*

They all particularly like the once a week Literacy Hour which has been introduced this year. " We work in groups – we listen to stories on tapes – we write stories on computers, describing islands and things – desert island – describe your imagination".

There is also a daily Numeracy Hour "from ten past nine to ten past ten

– it's excellent; I love it". "It's absolutely horrible". "I quite like it" "We have a CD called 'Maths Workshop' and there's ones called 'I Love Science' and 'I Love Spelling'. "If you finish your main work, you can get on to the computer and do a bit more. Then you save it and go back to it when you can".

All three have their own computers at home, although one is getting a new version this week. "The one we've got now has only got Windows 91 – it's very old". They do homework on their computers. "If we haven't got a printer or things, we go round to the others."

Boys and girls do separate things – the girls like 'It' or 'Hopscotch'. "The boys just come up to annoy". "The boys play football". "We mix a bit with the boys – some of us".

The village is really liked. "It's lovely". "It's got the Green". "It's peaceful". "There's lots of places to go". "Everyone's really nice, apart from X and he's awful". "I really like the village".

What kind of thing might you want to do when you grow up? "I definitely don't know what I'm going to do". "I think I might like to be an air hostess" says one. "Trolley Dolly" answers another. "I might want to be a secretary or work with animals but not a vet – you have to spend so much time on it. The really interesting things, you have to take such a long time". "I'd like to be a Handy Andy and work with tools and things". "I'd quite like to be a judge – you go bang, bang and ask for silence in court".

End of Century

Chris Rowley

This book is about the village during the Twentieth Century; the people who live and have lived in it; and the changes that there have been in the hundred years. Anna, my wife, and I have lived here for over thirty five years. We bought Oak Cottage in the winter of 1964 by mistake when my mother-in-law's estate agent friend put in a bid for it on our behalf at an auction we did not attend. My wife had liked the arched window. I was very doubtful. Although the fearsome butcher – as he appeared at the time – Mr Wells, told us the Green looked lovely in the summer with all the trees, Oak Cottage looked bleak on a wet November day.

We were befriended by many people but one statement sticks in our minds. Sid and Nell Haste lived at 1 Barden Cottages. Nell gave us cups of tea and warmth as we struggled to completely gut and redo our house. She seemed totally part of the village and yet, when I asked her about it, she said: "No: we're outsiders: we've only been here thirty five years". And when Sid retired, they moved back to Norfolk which they felt was home – even though their daughter Joyce (Mrs Goad) still lives in Hildenborough Road.

There is a difference between those who have lived in the village all their lives and newcomers like the Hastes or ourselves or, even, Bill Crocker or Ben Fagg. It does not mean that either 'side' resents the other or do not become friends with the other, but there are spoken and unspoken memories shared from school days onwards between people who were born in the village.

Over the century, the social mix has not so much disappeared as become less pronounced. The class divisions which were so clear, not just in 1900 but up to the Second World War, have much changed. Even in the 1960's, I would not have called Mr Coates in the Harrods of a village shop 'Spenser' or Mr Wells in the butcher 'Stan'. Now, few would think of the owners of the village store as Mr Johnson and Mrs Johnson. In 1900, the village largely belonged to the Hall Place Estate: now the houses are largely owned by individuals or to a lesser extent by the Kent Housing Trust and

PARTICULARS AND CONDITIONS OF SALE

of

THE FREEHOLD PROPERTY

known as

OAK COTTAGE

THE GREEN, LEIGH, Nr. TONBRIDGE, KENT

IDEAL FOR MODERNISATION

FOUR BEDROOMS. TWO LIVING ROOMS. KITCHEN.
WALK-IN LARDER. GARAGE SPACE.

TO BE OFFERED FOR SALE BY AUCTION

(unless previously sold)

at the

ROSE & CROWN HOTEL, TONBRIDGE

on

FRIDAY, 8th JANUARY, 1965

at 2.30 p.m.

VACANT POSSESSION ON COMPLETION

Solicitors:
Messrs. Biddle, Thorne, Welsford & Barnes,
1 Gresham Street,
London, E.C.2.
Tel.: Monarch 9741.

Auctioneers:
Messrs. Graham Walker & Co.,
161 High Street, Tonbridge, Kent.
Tel.: 4433 (2 lines).
(24 hour answering service.)

the change has altered the social relationships. If there is a social divide today, it is based more on whether the children go to Leigh School. It is not spoken about but is consciously or unconsciously a division. Most of the people who have lived in the village since the 1920s or earlier have remarked how strong the class divisions were when they were younger (and usually added that the present situation is much more pleasant).

The changes over the hundred years have in many ways been rapid and dramatic. In other ways, which are perhaps less obvious, things have stayed very similar. The virtual universal access to electricity, water, sewage have dramatically changed everyday life. (Lavatories and privies provoked more amazement than any aspect of life when I talked with the nine year olds at the School about life in 1920 for a nine year old). Whereas at the start of the century, one in six children in England died in their first year and a child was considered poor if he or she did not have shoes, it is now the lack of up-to-date computer equipment which is more likely to be an embarrassment for the child concerned and their friends; and infant mortality is, thankfully, a very rare occurrence.

The advent of the car has not just meant more travelling on a daily basis both for work and for holidays and entertainment but an increased speed of life – the number of things fitted in by most people. There is undoubtedly less of what Dick Wood called 'Gate Leaning'. The almost universal car ownership and the few jobs inside the village, combined with a larger number of houses and smaller families, are inclined to mean that not so many people know "nearly everyone in the village". A hundred years ago, everyone would have known everyone: and even thirty or forty years ago, most people – except the commuting men – knew most other people in the village, at least by sight.

The extra cars may have helped change things but the majority of the villagers who responded to the Village Design Statement questionnaire were very worried by the flow and speed of traffic through the village. Interestingly, the school children were not concerned – they thought it natural – just part of the life of the village. However, a different, if associated traffic problem which looks as if it will increasingly intrude into village life, is parking. Thirty years ago, one particular group of four cottages had no cars and no garages: it now has one garage, one off-road parking space and eight cars. Soon the Green, the High Street, Lower Green and other parts of the parish – both inside and outside the village, will be lined with cars, as houses and cottages are taken over by a younger generation with more vehicles.

Lawrence Biddle felt that the two major changes in the village in the last fifty years had, first, been the decline in the number of farms and the consequent decline in agricultural employment; and, secondly, the rise of the commuter. Certainly the development of transport and the changes in the type and place of employment have been great. The opportunities for jobs for boys, but more particularly for girls, have grown dramatically. For Dorothy and Kath Fautly and their contemporaries, virtually the only job was in service. Now girls in the School talk of being an air stewardess or a judge.

The number of people who stay – who are able to stay – in the village, particularly the children who are born in the village, is often mentioned as being something which has sadly passed. Certainly a hundred or even fifty years ago, a good number of the families had lived in the village for several generations: but just as many families had arrived from other villages or even from different parts of the country. And while it is said to be difficult for young people brought up in the village to get a house when they marry today, it was never that easy.

What has dramatically changed is not the number of people in the village. That has stayed relatively stable in the century. There were 1,480 people in the parish at the time of the 1891 census (1,245 in 1841). By the 1991 census there were 1,518, although this has increased with the building of Well Close and some minor infilling. The dramatic change has been the number of houses, which has virtually doubled, and the consequent reduction in the number of people per house from nearly five per house in 1891 to around three per house now. Most of the houses are larger too – a fair proportion of homes have been extended – as well as bigger new houses. Each person today probably has, on average, three times the square footage of housing when compared with villagers a hundred years ago.

The village is proud of its social mix, if the answers to the Village Design Statement questionnaire are accepted. Since the Thirties, the village has had a steady increase in what was called Council Housing – Barnetts Road, Penshurst Road, The Forstall, Crandalls and Meadowbank: but over the century there has also been an equally large increase in privately built houses, both individually and in groups, first Garden Cottages; then Lealands Avenue/Green View Avenue and the Penshurst Road's two stages of expansion; then Wyndham Avenue/Close; then in Lower Green; and most recently, at Well Close. On virtually every occasion, the villagers of the time objected to the new development proposals. On most occasions, no notice was taken of the objections by the planning authorities – or, at least that is how people feel. But, perhaps, it would also be fair to add that ten or twenty years later those houses are accepted and, more importantly, the people in them have, mostly, become part of the village. (The only residual annoyance being the usually poor or inappropriate design of the majority of the houses – both private and public).

Several changes or aspects or happenings in the village over the last half century were not mentioned very much or purposely avoided. For reasons known to everyone, our one murder was passed over – too sad for many reasons. The scale of the resistance to Well Close has been avoided, as has the outcry (mistaken as the expert forecast) about the building of the flood barrier. One other change aroused nervousness because people felt that, if mentioned, it might sound critical of others in the village. Up until the 1950s, the Church of England in the village seemed to have an internal unity, in spite of the normal tensions within any type of church or village organization. (Earlier there had been the chapel for those with a lower church or more independent or more fervent approach). Over the last twenty years, however, St Marys has grown into two fairly separate types of congregation. While many people would see this development as offering a wider choice within the village and welcome it, there are undoubtedly concerns about it. What cannot be denied is that the diversity exists – and that probably more people are now attending the church in total than were doing so twenty or forty years ago.

Oak Cottage – after it was extended to the left in 1969.

In the first half of the century middle class people were more likely to buy a home in the village, live there for some time and then retire elsewhere. In the second half of the century there has been a slight change. The list of those who moved here when they were fairly newly married and who have not only stayed for twenty, thirty or forty years but seem likely to stay for good is long; and there are many other families of the slightly younger generation who look like staying. A different type of change is that when children born in Leigh grow up – whether they went to the village school or not – virtually all have left or will leave. It is not that they did not like the village – seemingly they loved their first fifteen or twenty years in Leigh – but the kind of jobs and the life-style they lead at the end of the century (even more than the cost of houses in Leigh) make it very likely that they will move on.

At the end of Queen Victoria's reign and to a large extent until 1945, it was usually the middle class people who were on the village clubs' committees. Nowadays, it is more mixed, with the School Governors having parent members and the Parish Council containing a mix of born-in-the-village and 'newcomers' of most social classes – although the description 'social class' is probably at odds with how people in the village like to think of themselves or others. A hundred years ago and fifty years ago, the cry used to be that there were no younger people in the village to replace the general ageing committee members. The cry is still heard today and yet new people do come forward, whether it is for the Cricket Club or the Parish Council, the Legion or the Historical Society.

If there is one sub-theme that I had not quite expected, it is the reactions of fathers and grandfathers to the First World War – their general unwillingness (or inability) to explain the awfulness of what they went through in serving their country. Each village owes a debt to such men who have fought over the century and the Leigh War Memorial – like so many others around the country – is to their memory and the memory of those who came back with stories they could not tell.

The village is said to 'Have Had Everything' by the inhabitants who remember the first half of the century. Yet in 2000, according to the replies to the Village Design Statement questionnaire, the people in the village today still seem to find it a satisfactory place to live – for its friendliness and its liveliness as much as for its buildings and surrounding countryside. There are all its many clubs and societies – probably more than ever before. And if there are fewer hedgerows, virtually no hop gardens, and the banks of the Medway are less verdant, we all know that we live in a particularly beautiful part of the world, with a huge variety of footpaths and a wonderful variety of natural life around us. Perhaps we can look back and think of the time when Leigh was more self-sufficient (or more isolated), yet accept that in a somewhat different way the village does still have everything – well, almost everything.

The oak tree at sunset.

APPENDICES

APPENDIX ONE

Why and How the Book was Written

Five or six years ago, I became increasingly sad that a number of old people with interesting memories of the village had died without their stories being recorded. I talked to Dorothy and Kath Fautly and was fascinated by what they told me. I therefore decided to compile a short book.

The original intention was to concentrate on the period from 1900 (where Lawrence Biddle's book ended) up until the start of the Second World War (when Morgen Witzel's book began). However, the more people talked to me, the more I found that they wanted to compare the 1920s with the 1940s or the 1930s with the 1970s. I therefore included what they told me. Over the last year or so, I have purposely interviewed people who have talked more about the post war period and recently I talked with a few people who I asked to mention some of the main activities in the village over the last thirty years. Finally, as so many people had talked about their school days, I asked permission from Mrs Terri Wright, the current headmistress, to talk with the older children in the school.

I have always been well aware that there were at least two dangers with the book – repetition and over-rosy memories. I have left in some types of repetition because, if one story or idea has seemed important to several people, it helps to show the village's preoccupations. Often, too, the different versions of the incident helped to give a more rounded view. However, I tried to avoid too much repetition by asking a good number of people to concentrate on one particular aspect of the village only.

With regard to the mechanics, I did not use a tape recorder. There were several reasons. Having spent many years looking at the verbatim record of filmed interviews for television current affairs and documentary programmes, I am aware of how unstructured most people are when they are chatting: perhaps surprisingly, transcripts are usually time-consuming and not particularly useful. The other aspect is that, on the whole, people do not like tape recorders. I, therefore, took a huge number of notes – obtaining as near as possible the verbatim clauses and phrases. Often, whilst I scribbled, my wife, Anna, would continue to ask questions, although, on the whole, there were few pauses in what I was being told. I then wrote out the notes, rearranging the order and amalgamating repetitions where necessary and gave a first version to the person or couple concerned.

I had guaranteed to everyone that they would have the right to alter or expand anything they had said or that I had misunderstood. The possibility of rosy coloured memories of a (possibly mythical) bygone era when the sun always shone, could have occurred – and, perhaps, on occasions, has occurred. The reader will have to judge. However, I felt that it was not for me to tell people, who I had come to like, that they weren't 'being accurate'; and, in any case, there were usually enough recollections of the less cheering aspects of life in the past or acknowledgements that the village was still a good place to live to avoid an over-simplistic view of a glorious past.

The lengths of my talks with people varied. On several occasions, it must have been a total of twenty or thirty hours over a good number of months. On one occasion, I was also given three hundred pages of documents to 'read properly to get the full picture'. With most people I talked twice and then met again to chat through the corrections. In two instances, I only talked over the phone – and am still sad that I have not or cannot meet face to face.

The reception of the first draft varied from those who thought everything was acceptable – 'put what you like' – to those who were worried about my (their) grammar. Normally there were three to five versions. In only two cases – as well as Dick Wood – the contributions were written out wholly by the contributor. In one case, an absolutely marvellous description of one aspect of Leigh came back as a detailed technical dissertation without any of the comments about the village: we compromised – after six versions ....

I started with a short book in mind. I have allowed myself to be talked into a long book. I hope people will think it worth it.

Thanks, Apologies and Acknowledgements

THANKS

My thanks go to two types of people – the talkers and the toilers.

I have talked with over ninety people, all of whom feature briefly or at length in the book. I have enormously enjoyed every single talk – often with people who I had only previously known in a nodding, good-morning sort of way but in a good number of cases who knew nothing about me. I found everyone willing to confide in me and – although I have no idea how they think of me – I think of them with the very greatest fondness and respect. My thanks.

The toilers have included Anna, my wife – not just for quite often asking questions, but for listening to so many different versions of so many chapters – and laughing in the right places; and to Patrick Wood – and Diana – for proof reading and sage advice (and suggesting correct clerical nomenclatures, almost none of which I have put into the mouth of people who did not use them!). Ro Love and Mike Rice helped with early typing but the bulk of the typing – probably 2,000–3,000 printed pages – has been done by two totally unflappable, patient and interested ladies – Sally Overton for two years and Joyce Field for the last hectic year. Very many thanks indeed.

APOLOGIES

I have a list of at least thirty people with whom I wanted to talk but, to my great regret, I have not had the space to do so. Please accept my most sincere apologies.

ACKNOWLEDGEMENTS FOR PHOTOGRAPHS

Contributors to the book have been trusting in lending me their precious personal photographs. Two other sources of photographs were invaluable. Roy and Betty Fuller have amassed a large collection of post cards – and larger pictures – which they have lent me, together with explanations and funny stories; and David Hallett has also very kindly allowed me to choose from his collection.

As I went through the two or three hundred photos that I was offered, I noted the publishers (where they were given). I have tried to contact all these firms to ask their permission but some no longer seem to exist. The following have very kindly given their permission for me to use their material and I am most grateful.

1. *The Kent & Sussex Courier and Sevenoaks Chronicle – Martin Oxley, Editor*
   Bell Ringing – New Year 1969
   Stoolball Team June 1960
   Special Constables
   A Houghton/B Bastable – Cups at Produce Association Show
   Village Green Stompers May 1978
   Bert Hunt – ballmaker – Making The Quilt
   1951 Festival of Britain, Leigh Lunch Party

2. *J L Allwork Photos Ltd, 177 High Street, Tonbridge – Judy and Colin Beer*
   Lower Green, Leigh (including Belton Bakery
   Old Forge, Leigh ?1925/1930
   Parade in Leigh, Coronation Day (1911)
   Leigh Green
   Mr Fautly reading
   Geoffrey, 3rd Lord Hollenden with Alfie Houghton c. 1955
   Ballmaking – Blocking Out mid-1970
   Ballmaking – Holing the quarters

3. *The Times*
   Leigh Cricket Club v. S. Nutfield 1929

4. *J Salmon Ltd, 100 London Road, Sevenoaks – H.F. Salmon, Managing Director*
   "Leigh Church"
   "Church Lane, Leigh"
   Church and South View
   Pauls Farm Oast "A Kentish Farm"

5. *Bill Love of Tonbridge*
   Traction Engine outside the Post Office

6. *Fotek Ltd, Bramble Road, Swindon, Wilts*
   1999 School photo

Other publishers:

H H Camburn, Tunbridge Wells
   Lightfoots c 1908
   Post Office (in the Square) ?1910
   The Brickmakers Arms ?1920
   The Brickmakers and The Fleur de Lis 1918

Lower Green ?1920
Village Shop, Leigh ?1920
Barden Road ?1929
Green View Avenue ?1928/30
Green View Avenue ?1928/30
War Memorial and Church ?1920s?

Bryan Horner Ltd 177 High Street, Tonbridge (became part of J.L. Allwork Ltd)
Group photo outside Hall Place ?1920/?1925

Daniel Bros Ltd, Lewisham
West Gate ?1910

B C Flemons, 191 High Street, Tonbridge
VAD Nurses outside Leigh Village Hall c 1916
Football Team 1920
Leigh Scout Troup at Tonbridge Castle 1926
Inside Village Hall as VAD Hospital c 1916
Kath and Dorothy Fautly as children c 1916
Leigh Fire Brigade in Forge Square 1926
Car in the River at Ensfield Bridge ?1930

Durrent, St James Park, Tunbridge Wells
Leigh Fire Brigade practising with manual ?mid 1920

E A Sweetman & Son (Sunshine Series) Tunbridge Wells
The Old Forge, Leigh 1920s
Hall Place ?1920

Special Press, 13 Johnson's Court, Fleet Street, London EC4
Blacksmith and small boys

W T Munns, 8-9 Windmill Street, Gravesend
Scouts ?1930

R A P Co Ltd, London EC4 (Printer)
Old Barn Tea Room ?1930 published by A W Tomlinson

Mockford, Tonbridge
Leigh (Green and Powdermill Lane) 1906
Brickmakers (with celebration at end of war ?1918?

Index

Index

Additions and Reviews

Additional information: The Leigh Historical Society has a large amount of extra material to add to the picture of the people, places and events mentioned in this book, both on its website (www.leighhistorical.org.uk) and in its archive. However, there are certain specific corrections and additions which are worth recording.

Dr E.A. (Ernest) Barclay: throughout the First Edition his name is misspelt. It was, in fact, Dr Rockingham Berkeley. He did not actually "die of cancer" (p.30). After army service during the Second World War, he moved to a practice in Wales and died in his seventies after a stroke.

The Walder family – misspelt on some occasions, as Warder.

Sir Malcolm Sargent: p. 28 – misspelt in First Edition.

The War Memorial: p. 59. There were a number of mistakes in the First Edition. In the First World War Section:

Royal West Kent Regiment	UPTON H (not Upton W)
Kings Liverpool Regiment	BRAMLETT W
Middlesex Regiment	HORSEY H (not Hornsey H)
Kings Royal Rifle Corp (not KPR)	POCOCK S
27th Light Cavalry	RUSSELL L (Russell R)
Machine Gun Corp (not MGL)	BATCHELOR S TAYLOR J

In the Second World War Section:

Hampshire Regiment	HORAN S J L (not Horans)

Bill Simmonds: pp. 60/61. Anne Warboys has pointed out that neither she nor her husband, Wal, were actually Australians. She also says that the name of their house on the deeds was "No 1 & 2 Park Cottages" but the locals said it was always known as "The White House" when she arrived.

Dick Wood: p. 78 on – his actual name was Henry Victor Wood, but he was known to his family as "Harry" and to everyone else as "Dick".

Forge Square photograph: p.159. After the Second World War, the Estate found it difficult to afford to replace the original thatched roof; and the tiles in the photo were used.

Great Barnett's Oast: p. 177. In the photo, the current name of the Oast should have read "Moat Farm", in the First Edition, not "Oast Farm".

Longhurst: p. 234 – misspelt as Longchurch in the School Log.

Leigh Special Constables: p. 269. Fuller details of those in the photo have been offered by Jack Lucas who thinks the date was probably 1944/5, not late 1930s. Back row from left to right: A J "Joey" Walder (who built Lealands Ave); H "Bob" Jones (Hall Place Gardener); Ernest Lidlow (worked at Paul's Farm); the two Skinner brothers; W. Taylor; J. Anderson (lived at Charcott). Middle Row: Bill Baldwin (lived at Blue Anchor pub) although others claim it is W. Sturt; George Thomson (Estate Clerk); Spenser "Spen" Coates (grocer); Alfred Houghton (Estate Agent); Jack Lucas senior also known as Jack Draper; Dave Fuller (the insurance man from Garden Cottages); Fred Grant (from Charcott); A C "Bert" Humphrey (from Waterworks Lane); and, probably, J. Fuller. Front Row: Frank Hawkins (local historian); J H Barnett (from Elizabeth Cottage); Donald E Whitehead (Chief Special Constable and High St. butcher); George Parrett (Sergeant Special Constable and shop-keeper next to Bat & Ball); George Chandler (Lightfoots); Peter Ferguson (Head Gardener, Hall Place); and George Cornelius (Village Constable).

Joan Sargeant: p. 363 & 366 – misspelt in First Edition

"... It is one of the most comprehensive, intimate and beautifully fashioned books on village life that I have ever read – I heartily recommend a village book that has everything." *Bob Ogley from* The Sevenoaks Chronicle *(Author of* Kent Chronicles of The Century*)*

" 'We Had Everything ...' has sold really well – almost like a best-selling novel. People are buying it as a present for friends or relatives who remember what life was like in the old days. It's beautifully produced and people like that." *Kathy Allen of John Adams Bookshop, Tonbridge*

"Chris Rowley says that he started with a short book in mind and has allowed himself to be talked into a long book. He hopes people will think it worth it. Without a doubt they will ... The book will give immense pleasure." *Frank Chapman, local history expert in the Kent & Sussex Courier*

"I am sure the book will become a blue print of life in an English village: and I am certain that no other village life in the world is like the close-knit English village life – at least I have never seen it in any of the villages I have been to in various parts of the world, especially in the US where 'villages' can extend to a twenty mile radius ... " *from a writer and local historian*

"We have been reading the book to our old people and they love it. It brings back so many memories of the days before and after the War – happy and sad things – in a wonderful way. There are some marvellous characters in it too." *Joan Driscoll, Head of Woodgate Centre*

"First of all congratulations. It is a very handsome book – just up my street." *Melvyn Bragg – TV & Radio Producer/ Presenter and author of* 'Speak for England', *an oral history book on Wigton*